The Process of Statistical Analysis in Psychology

Sara Miller McCune founded SAGE Publishing in 1965 to support the dissemination of usable knowledge and educate a global community. SAGE publishes more than 1000 journals and over 800 new books each year, spanning a wide range of subject areas. Our growing selection of library products includes archives, data, case studies and video. SAGE remains majority owned by our founder and after her lifetime will become owned by a charitable trust that secures the company's continued independence.

Los Angeles | London | New Delhi | Singapore | Washington DC | Melbourne

The Process of Statistical Analysis in Psychology

Dawn M. McBride

Illinois State University

Los Angeles | London | New Delhi
Singapore | Washington DC | Melbourne

FOR INFORMATION:

SAGE Publications, Inc.
2455 Teller Road
Thousand Oaks, California 91320
E-mail: order@sagepub.com

SAGE Publications Ltd.
1 Oliver's Yard
55 City Road
London EC1Y 1SP
United Kingdom

SAGE Publications India Pvt. Ltd.
B 1/I 1 Mohan Cooperative Industrial Area
Mathura Road, New Delhi 110 044
India

SAGE Publications Asia-Pacific Pte. Ltd.
3 Church Street
#10-04 Samsung Hub
Singapore 049483

Acquisitions Editor: Abbie Rickard
Content Development Editor: Morgan Shannon
Editorial Assistant: Jennifer Cline
Production Editor: Olivia Weber-Stenis
Copy Editor: Erin Livingston
Typesetter: C&M Digitals (P) Ltd.
Proofreader: Jeff Bryant
Indexer: Rick Hurd
Cover Designer: Scott Van Atta
Marketing Manager: Jenna Retana

Printed in Canada

ISBN 978-1-5063-2522-4

This book is printed on acid-free paper.

19 20 21 10 9 8 7 6 5 4 3

Brief Contents

Detailed Contents

3 Probability and Sampling   55

PART II: DESCRIPTIVE STATISTICS   73

4 Central Tendency   75

10 Related/Paired Samples *t* Test 197

11 Independent Samples *t* Test 213

16 Chi-Square Tests 319

Preface

My goal in writing this text was to provide an introduction to statistics in the behavioral sciences as a tool for understanding data collected in research studies in this field. The same examples and similar format and definitions are included here as in *The Process of Research in Psychology* methods text to aid instructors who teach both courses or a sequence of courses that blend methods and statistics together. However, this text is also written to stand alone as an introductory statistics text for instructors teaching this course on its own.

Instead of compartmentalizing each concept within a single chapter, in this text, concepts are discussed, where appropriate, in multiple chapters to show how concepts are related. For example, the concepts of average scores and variability in a set of scores are introduced in Chapter 1 in reference to data from research studies but are also described in Chapters 4 and 5, where these concepts are more fully explored and calculations are shown. In addition, research designs are discussed in Chapter 1 but are also illustrated in examples in each of the chapters in the text and in the Thinking About Research sections at the end of each chapter. Research studies are well illustrated throughout the text, both from the perspective of a student conducting his own research study and from the perspective of someone encountering research and statistics in her daily life (e.g., in media sources) that might impact her decision making.

My hope is that students will gain a foundation for using statistics in psychological research as well as enough statistics knowledge to make them better consumers of the research and statistics used in daily life decision making.

Acknowledgments

I'd like to acknowledge a number of important people who helped in many ways in the writing of this text and helped improve it from its initial drafts. First is Jeff Wagman, who provided support and helpful discussion during the writing of this text as well as doing additional household chores and chauffeuring Connor, giving me extra time when needed. In addition, my family, friends, and colleagues provided support and helpful feedback during the writing process. In particular, I thank J. Cooper Cutting for helpful feedback on chapter drafts and for being a most excellent colleague and collaborator on text writing and teaching. I also thank Corinne Zimmerman and Marla Reese-Weber for weekly lunches and social support. Several reviewers also provided valuable suggestions that greatly improved the quality of the text, especially my graduate student, Rachel Workman. At SAGE, I'd like to thank Reid Hester for his valuable assistance in getting this project started and Abbie Rickard, who enabled its completion. I also thank the students at Illinois State University who have taken my PSY 138 and PSY 231 courses and have influenced my teaching of this material and the Provost and College of Arts and Sciences at Illinois State University for granting me a sabbatical to begin the writing of the text. All the individuals named here contributed in important ways to the production of this text and have my sincere thanks and gratitude.

The author and SAGE gratefully acknowledge the contributions of the following reviewers:

Johnathan Forbey, Ball State University

Paul Foster, Middle Tennessee State University

Courtney McManus, Colby–Sawyer College

Michael Ray, The College at Brockport

Jeannette Stein, University of Michigan–Flint

Matthew Zagumny, Tennessee Tech University

About the Author

Dawn M. McBride is a professor of psychology at Illinois State University, where she has taught research methods and statistics courses since 1998. Her research interests include automatic forms of memory, false memory, prospective memory, and forgetting. She also teaches courses in introductory psychology, cognition and learning, and human memory. She is a recipient of the Illinois State University Teaching Initiative Award and the ISU SPA/Psi Chi Jim Johnson Award for commitment to undergraduate mentorship, involvement, and achievement. Her nonacademic interests include spending time with her family, traveling, watching Philadelphia sports teams (her place of birth), and reading British murder mysteries. She earned her PhD in cognitive psychology from the University of California, Irvine, and her BA from the University of California, Los Angeles.

PART I

Why Do We
Use Statistics?

Chapter 1

Why Statistics?

As you read the chapter, consider the following questions:

1.1 Why do we use statistics to analyze data?

1.2 How do descriptive and inferential statistics differ?

1.3 Why are there so many different kinds of statistical tests?

1.4 What are the methods we use to collect data?

1.5 How do the methods used to collect data affect the statistics we use?

WHAT CAN STATISTICS DO FOR ME?

Imagine that you have just purchased a new bookshelf from IKEA or Target. You get the box home, open it up, and find 38 pieces with instructions on how to assemble the bookshelf, including pieces of wood, screws, nails, nuts, and bolts. The instructions also say that you will need some tools to help you assemble your bookshelf: a hammer, a flat head screwdriver, a Phillips head screwdriver, and an Allen wrench. Sound familiar? Most of us have been faced with this type of situation before, and if you have not, you probably know someone who has assembled furniture they have bought. Is this usually an easy task? Sometimes it is, if all the pieces are in the box, you have all of the right tools and know how to use them, and have a good set of instructions to follow. However, there are times when you are asked to use a tool you do not have or know how to use or are given instructions that are difficult to follow.

Statistics as a Tool

The situation described here (and shown in Photo 1.1) is very similar to the process of using statistics to understand data from a research study. The pieces you are given in the box are similar to the data you have collected. You collected the appropriate data to help you answer a

©iStock/monkeybusinessimages

research question ("How often do college students feel anxious?" or "What is the effect of anxiety on test performance?"). The tools (hammer, screwdrivers) are the statistics you can use to organize and analyze the data you collected. This is like assembling the pieces of the book-shelf using the tools: You can use different types of statistics to assemble the data into something you can more easily understand and interpret. Finally, you have instructions. This text and the instruction you are receiving in the course you are taking are the instructions for how to assemble your data into something that is easier to interpret. That is what this text is all about—provid-ing instructions on how to use statistics as tools to better understand and interpret the data you have. But the starting place is always the collection of data. Thus, in this chapter and throughout the text, we will also discuss some of the issues relevant to data collection, such as measurement and research design types, to help you see the connection between the collection of data and the statistics we choose as tools for understanding those data.

The process of using statistics can be frustrating at times for a beginner, but statistics are essential for understanding your data. Knowing something about statistics can help you bet-ter understand arguments made with statistics or how data can be used to solve problems in society or an organization. Imagine that you had a set of data (e.g., a set of numbers from customers representing satisfaction with the products made by the company you work for) but no tools for assembling those data into something you can interpret. How would you answer your research question about how satisfied your customers are? This would be like trying to assemble the pieces of your bookshelf without your hammer and screwdrivers—a task that would be extremely difficult or impossible. The statistics you will read about in this text provide the tools you need to better understand your data. Statistics can help you summarize the scores (e.g., "On average, how satisfied are your customers?"), examine how different the scores are from participant to participant (e.g., "What is the range of scores in the data set?"), display the average scores in organized graphs and tables, and test predictions you have about average scores in different groups of participants or from the same participants at different times. You can even use statistics to examine relationships between different sets of data (e.g., "Are customers with more information about your company more satisfied with your company's products?"). In this text, we will consider statistical tools for accomplishing each of these different tasks.

Statistics in the Media

Statistics are everywhere. Think about how often you encounter statistics in your daily life. You will see that statistics are all around you. Because they are useful tools for organizing and understanding data, you will see that statistics are used quite often in many different sources of information you encounter in your daily life. When you applied to your college or university, you probably encountered some basic statistics about the students at that institution. At Illinois State University (see Photo 1.2) where I teach, for example, a quick glance at the admissions web page states that 55% of the students are women, the average ACT score for incoming freshmen in Fall 2012 was 24.0, and 68% of classes have 29 or fewer students in them. Why does the admissions page include these statistics? To provide information about the students who attend the

Photo 1.2   Many colleges and universities provide statistics about their students to help prospective students decide if they want to apply for admission.

university and what the university is like to prospective students who might want to apply. This information can help a student decide if Illinois State University is a place to which they might be offered admission and if it is a place they would like to be for college.

Where else might you encounter statistics? Most media sources will use statistics to present information about something they are reporting on or to try to argue a particular point of view. For example, a recent article in the *New York Times* online stated that from 2003 to 2013, heart attack rates have dropped by 38% (Kolata, 2015). Let's consider what this means. Does this mean that you, as an individual, now have a 38% lower chance of having a heart attack than you did in 2003? No, that is not the right conclusion to make from this statistic. The main reason this is incorrect is that this statistic is based on the rates of heart attacks across a large number of individuals and individual differences can influence these values. This is one of the reasons that research studies typically involve the measurement of behaviors of a large group of individuals instead of one person to answer the research question. We will discuss this issue further later in the chapter.

Let's consider another set of statistics also presented by the *New York Times*: An article presented information about a study that looked at the relationship between teen smoking rates and the legal age of cigarette sales in a city in Massachusetts (Bakalar, 2015). The city raised the age limit to 21 for cigarette sales. Other nearby cities did not change their age limit, which remained at 18 years of age (see Figure 1.1 for an illustration of this study). The researchers compared self-reported smoking behaviors for individuals under the age of 18 in the city with the 21-year age limit and individuals in a nearby city with an 18-year age limit. They found that cigarette purchases by individuals under 18 years of age dropped by 6.8% in the city with the

Figure 1.1   Description of a Study Comparing Self-Reported Cigarette Purchases by People Under Age 18 in Cities With Different Age Limits for Cigarette Purchases

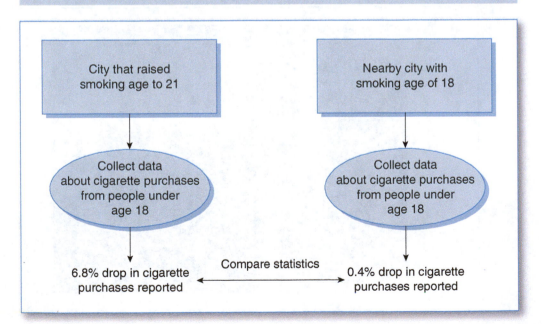

21-year age limit. In the cities with a lower age limit (18-year), cigarette purchases by individuals under 18 years old only dropped by 0.4%. Consider what these statistics could mean for proposing a nationwide increase in the age to legally buy cigarettes.

Let's consider one more example that might be something more related to your own daily life: cell phone use while driving. The Centers for Disease Control (CDC, 2015) reported that 17% of crashes in the United States in 2011 involved distracted driving, which includes behaviors such as texting and eating while driving. The graph in Figure 1.2 shows data from a research study reported by the CDC comparing rates of cell phone use in the United States and three other European countries. What can we learn from the statistics presented in Figure 1.2? Well, one thing is clear: People in the United States seem to use their cell phones more often while driving than people in these European countries. But what is the effect of cell phone use on driving performance? These statistics do not really give us the answer to this question. Instead, we must look at the statistics reported in published research studies to better answer this question.

One thing to be aware of is that statistics can be presented in many different ways. Knowing how statistics can be used can help you identify cases in which they are being presented in a biased way to make an argument. For example, suppose you hear on the news that a study found that people who use cell phones more than six hours a day have a higher rate of brain cancer than people who use their cell phones for less time per day. Should you reduce your use of your cell phone based on this report? Your answer should depend on knowing more details about the study. For example, how large was the increase in cancer rates? It could be very small

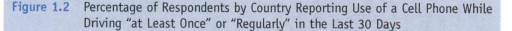

Figure 1.2 Percentage of Respondents by Country Reporting Use of a Cell Phone While Driving "at Least Once" or "Regularly" in the Last 30 Days

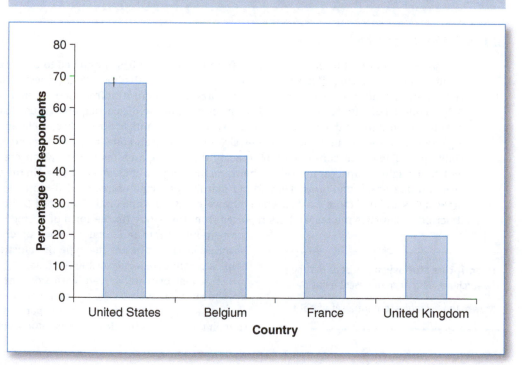

❧

Statistically significant: a statistical outcome indicating that the data from the individuals measured show that an effect or relationship exists

(e.g., less than 1%) or rather large (e.g., 36%). You should also consider how the study was conducted—were there other differences across these groups of people that could cause a difference in cancer rates besides the amount of time they use their cell phones (e.g., anxiety levels)? Finally, even if the difference in cancer rates seems large, is this difference between groups statistically significant (i.e., considering the data from the individuals measured in the study, is the difference between groups large enough to generalize to all people who use cell phones)? Your knowledge of statistics can help you identify what you need to know about the statistics others report so that you can use the information to consider your own behavior.

Stop and Think

1.1   Consider some statistics you have encountered recently in your daily life. In what way(s) have these statistics influenced your thinking about an issue?

1.2   Review the statistics presented from the *New York Times* on the decrease of heart attack rates. What additional information do you think you would need to apply this rate reduction statistic to an individual's current heart attack probability?

1.3   Review the description of the study about teen smoking rates. Based on the statistics presented, would you recommend a national increase in the age to buy cigarettes to 21 years? Why or why not?

Statistics in Research

The statistics reported in the media come from research studies conducted to better understand behavior and what affects it. Consider a research study that looks at the question of how cell phone use affects driving performance. Drews, Hazdani, Godfrey, Cooper, and Strayer (2009) conducted a study to compare driving performance while participants focused all their attention on driving and while driving and texting. Participants in the study completed a driving task in a simulator under both single-task (only driving) and dual-task (driving and texting) conditions. They then compared how quickly the participants responded when presented with brake lights from a car in front of them and the number of crashes they had in the single-task and dual-task conditions. They found that the participants responded more slowly to brake lights and had more crashes when they were driving while texting. Figure 1.3 shows the descriptive statistics the researchers reported from this study (in the form of average scores for response time and total number of crashes). Descriptive statistics are the type of statistics that help us summarize (or describe) the data.

Let's consider what we can learn from the statistics shown in Figure 1.3. The top graph shows us the mean or average response time for the participants to step on the brake in the driving simulator when they

❧

Descriptive statistics: statistics that help researchers summarize or describe data

Mean: the average score for a set of data

Figure 1.3 Mean Response Time and Number of Crashes for Only Driving (Single-Task) and Driving While Texting (Dual-Task) Conditions in the Drews et al. (2009) Study

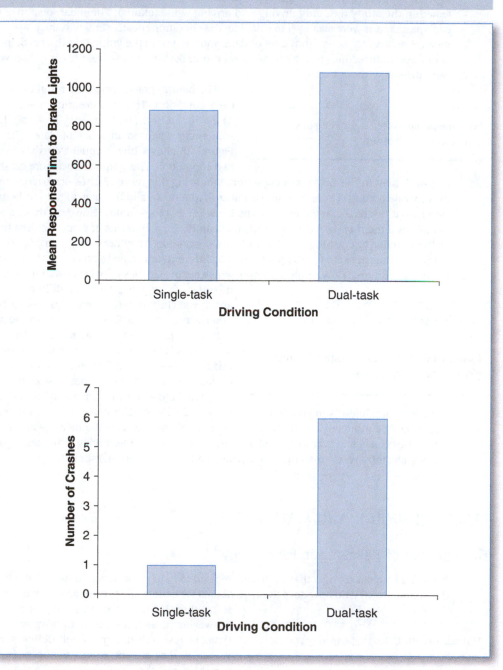

saw brake lights on the car in front of them. To find these values, the researchers took all the response times for braking responses when the brake lights appeared (this happened 42 times per participant) and calculated an average response time for each participant. Then, they averaged all the participants' average response times to get the mean for each situation or condition tested in the study (i.e., only driving and driving while texting). The mean response times for each participant were averaged to calculate the condition means shown in the graph. Thus, the mean is an average score from a set of data. You can see in the graph that the participants were about 200 milliseconds (0.2 seconds) slower to brake when they were texting than when they were driving without texting.

❧

Frequency: how often a response or score occurs within a data set

The bottom graph shows the number of crashes in each condition. This is a descriptive statistic known as the frequency. The frequency is simply how often something occurred in a set of data. The graph in Figure 1.3 shows how frequent crashes were in the two conditions. This graph shows more crashes in the dual-task than in the single-task condition, indicating that more crashes occurred when people drove while texting. These descriptive statistics (the mean and frequency) help us better understand what the data can tell us from the Drews et al. (2009) study. However, these statistics do not tell us if the dual-task condition is significantly worse in terms of response time for braking or the number of crashes than the single-task condition. Why not? Well, imagine we redid the study with another set of participants and got different descriptive statistics that were similar for the two conditions. How would we know which set of statistics to believe? And in fact, we could

❧

Variability: the spread of scores in a distribution

Inferential statistics: statistics that help researchers test hypotheses

do this study over and over with different participants and get slightly different mean values each time. In other words, there will be variability in the scores not only from person to person but also from study to study. This is where inferential statistics and hypothesis testing come in. Inferential statistics are the type of statistics that help researchers test their hypotheses. They will help answer the question for drivers overall: Does driving while texting really result in worse driving performance? In fact, the researchers in this study conducted two different inferential statistics tests for the mean response time and number of crashes data and concluded from these tests that the driving while texting condition was significantly worse than the just driving condition for both measures.

RESEARCH DESIGN AND STATISTICS

The Purpose of Research in Psychology

It should be clear by now that statistics are used to help us understand data. But where do the data come from? And how does the type of data we collect affect the statistics we use to understand them? The rest of this chapter will focus on answering these questions. As I discuss the different types of research designs, I will define some of the variables that are important to these designs. The variables are the attributes that can differ across

❧

Variables: attributes that can vary across individuals

individuals, which can be measured from individuals but can also be controlled by the researcher.

New knowledge in scientific fields of study (such as psychology) relies on research studies. This is the primary means of learning new things about the world in a scientific way: Go out and observe them. For example, if we want to know whether punishment will change behavior less effectively than a reward, the best way to answer this question is to observe and compare individuals' behavior after they have been rewarded for a behavior and after they have been punished for failure to perform the behavior. This comparison will show us whether behavior is affected in a different way for reward versus punishment. This kind of study will give us the clearest answer to our question. In another case, we might want to know how anxiety in college students relates to their scores on their final exams (see Photo 1.3). To answer this question, we might ask students to answer some items on a questionnaire about anxiety just before finals to measure their level of anxiety. We might then also measure their scores on their final exams (or obtain the scores from their records with their permission) to determine if the two measures are related (i.e., change together across the group of students in our study).

In both of these cases, we are observing the behaviors to learn about them. In the first example, we are directly observing a behavior in two situations (rewards and punishments), and in the second example, we are observing self-reported thoughts and behaviors on a questionnaire and scores on exams. When we make observations, we produce data that we need to understand. But how we make those observations is just as important as how we analyze the data. In addition, the way we make the observations will affect how we use statistics to understand them. Therefore, it's important to know something about research methods before

Photo 1.3   Research question: How anxious are college students before final exams?

©iStock/Wavebreakmedia

Figure 1.4   Steps in the Research Process

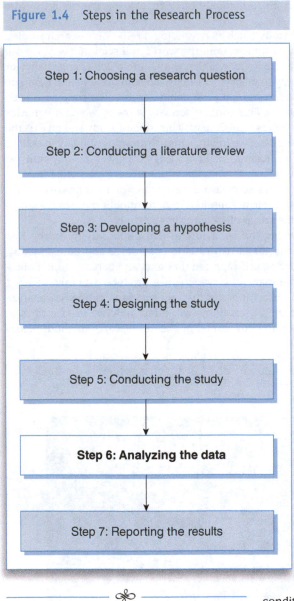

Step 1: Choosing a research question

Step 2: Conducting a literature review

Step 3: Developing a hypothesis

Step 4: Designing the study

Step 5: Conducting the study

Step 6: Analyzing the data

Step 7: Reporting the results

Experiment: a type of research design that involves the comparison of behavior observed in different situations

Correlational study: a type of research design that examines the relationships between different measures of behavior

we can understand how we use statistics to understand the data that come from these methods. To get a better sense of where statistics fits into the process of research, take a look at Figure 1.4. It shows the steps in conducting research and where statistics fit into this process (Step 6: Analyzing the Data). In the next section of this chapter, I will briefly describe a couple of common methods that are used to observe behavior to help you see how this process works. The choice of method is based on the type of question a researcher wants to answer.

Different Research Designs

The two examples I already described (comparing behavior after rewards and punishments and relating anxiety measured from responses on a questionnaire to final exam scores) each represent two of the most common methods of observing behavior: an experiment and a correlational study. Experiments will help us determine if something causes a behavior, but correlational studies can only help us determine if there is some kind of relationship (which might *not* be a causal relationship) between two measures. When we compare behavior in two situations or conditions (parts of an independent variable), we are typically using an experimental design, either a true experiment if individuals in our study are randomly assigned to the situations we want to compare or a quasi-experiment if the individuals are in those situations already in some way. In our rewards and punishments example, the feedback is the independent variable (which is the causal factor we are interested in) and the conditions that are compared with this independent variable are the rewards and punishments. In the next section, I will discuss these concepts further and describe some additional examples of experiments.

Experiments

The goal of an experiment is to examine how a situation of interest (e.g., the outcome of a behavior; a reward or punishment) changes a behavior. The situation of interest is called the *independent variable*. Researchers use experiments when they want to gain information about the causes of behavior. Let's consider an example of an experiment: What are the effects on your behavior of the stories you were read as a child? Lee, Talwar, McCarthy, Ross, Evans, and Arruda (2014) examined this question in an experiment that looked at the effects of stories on lying in children. They played a toy identification game with children 3 to 7 years old. A sound was played from the toy that was located

Independent variable: a variable in an experiment that changes across or within subjects to allow comparison of behavior in those different situations

Quasi-experiment: a type of research design that involves the comparison of behavior observed in different situations, but where subjects are not randomly assigned to the different situations

behind them, and they were asked to try to identify the toy without looking at it. Before the last toy was identified, the researcher left the room to retrieve the story. Children were videotaped to determine if they peeked at the toy or not. The researcher then returned and read a randomly assigned story to the child (see Figure 1.5 for the stories read). After reading the story, which had a lying theme with a positive outcome (classic George Washington story), no lying theme (the tortoise and the hare), or a lying theme with a negative outcome (the rest of the stories in Figure 1.5), the children were asked if they had peeked at the toy while the researcher was out of the room. From the video observations, it was determined if the children told the truth or not. Figure 1.5 presents the percentage of children who heard each story who told the truth about peeking at the toy. The asterisk shows where there was a statistically significant difference between stories: Only the positive-outcome story increased the percentage of children who told the truth over the other types of stories. Thus, stories with a lying theme and a positive outcome have a positive effect on honest behavior in children, but stories with a lying theme and a negative outcome do not seem to change honest behavior as compared with a story that was not about lying.

The conditions being compared in the Lee et al. (2014) experiment were the different stories—the story the children heard was the independent variable. The experiment was designed specifically to determine if the story they heard caused a difference in the children's honesty. Thus, honesty was the behavior they were interested in measuring. This is known as the dependent variable. Every research study has at least one dependent variable because there is at least one behavior that is being measured in every study.

Dependent variable: the behavior of interest that is observed in a research study

This is true regardless of the type of research design being used. However, independent variables are specific to experiments and quasi-experiments.

Here is another example that further illustrates the difference between true experiments and quasi-experiments: You're trying to decide whether you should bring your laptop to class to take notes on or if you should just leave it home (it's heavy, after all) and take notes in a notebook by hand (see Photo 1.4). An experiment can help you decide if the laptop is worth lugging to class. Researchers Mueller and Oppenheimer (2014) conducted an experiment to figure out if taking notes on a laptop is better or worse for learning of lecture material than taking notes with pen and paper. They had college students come to the lab and take notes with either a laptop or with pen and paper, whichever way they normally took notes in their classes. They took notes on a TED Talk video presented to them. Later, they answered questions about

Figure 1.5   Results From the Lee et al. (2014) Study Showing the Effects of Different Stories on the Percentage of Children Who Peeked and Then Told the Truth

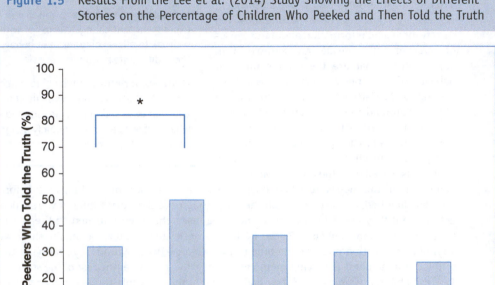

SOURCE: Lee, Talwar, McCarthy, Ross, Evans, & Arruda (2014). Can classic moral stories promote honesty in children? Psychological Science, 25, 1630–1636.

the material presented in the TED Talk and their responses were scored for accuracy. Across three different studies, students performed better overall on the questions after taking notes by hand than after taking notes on a laptop. Thus, these results suggest that it may not be worth it to carry your laptop to class. However, because the students were allowed to choose the method they typically used to take notes, Mueller and Oppenheimer's studies do not qualify as true experiments. Instead, they are quasi-experiments because there may be something that changed across subjects other than note-taking method that could explain the results. Perhaps, for example, students who learn more easily already use the by-hand method for taking notes and thus this group contained better learners because the students were not randomly assigned to the two note-taking methods. A true experiment with the note-taking method randomly assigned to the students would help rule out other explanations of the results.

As we discuss statistics in more detail in the coming chapters, you will see that experiments and quasi-experiments typically employ the same types of statistics to analyze data. This is because both of these designs focus on comparing behavior across conditions. One the main differences between them is that the conditions being compared can occur within subjects in experiments, but not in quasi-experiments (where they can only occur between

Photo 1.4 The research question asked by Mueller and Oppenheimer (2014) in their study was this: Which is better for learning in a lecture, taking notes by hand or typing them using a laptop?

©iStock/diego_cervo, ©iStock/michal-rojek

❧

Between-subjects variable: changing situations across different groups of subjects in a research study

Within-subjects variable: changing situations within a single group of subjects in a research study such that each subject experiences of all the different situations being compared

subjects). The difference is that in a between-subjects variable, different groups of people experience the different conditions being compared. This was the case for both the children's stories and note-taking studies presented above. However, in an experiment, a researcher may choose to compare situations as a within-subjects variable. This allows one to compare behavior in different conditions for the same person. This type of variable can be useful when the behavior of interest varies a lot across subjects. Using a within-subjects variable can help rule out differences in behavior seen in the study that could occur between subjects. The choice between independent variables that are manipulated between subjects and within subjects will affect the kinds of statistics tests that are used to understand the data, as you will see in later chapters of this text.

Stop and Think

1.4   For each of the following studies, identify the independent and dependent variables:

a.   You want to know if having a cell phone out while you study is a distraction, so you conduct a short study to figure this out. You observe your friends while they study for their coursework. You record whether each one has a cell phone out while they study and place them in either the "cell phone" group or "no cell phone" group, based on what you observe. Then you record how many minutes out of an hour of studying they appear to be on task. You compare the two groups of people to see if they differ in time on task.

b.   Your statistics instructor has recruited students to be in a study in his lab. You sign up for the study, and when you participate, this is what you are asked to do: You are asked to complete two blocks of trials where you have to decide if a string of letters that appears on the screen is a real word or not as quickly as you can. During one block of trials, you focus entirely on this task. In the other block of trials, you are asked to also hold a short list of words in memory until the end of the block, when you have to recall them. You are told that the purpose of the study is to examine the effect of the memory task on your ability to decide if the strings of letters are words.

1.5   For each of the studies listed above, identify whether it is an experiment or a quasi-experiment.

1.6   For each of the studies in 1.4, identify whether the independent variable was manipulated between subjects or within subjects.

Correlational Studies

Another common research design used in psychological studies is the correlational study. As described earlier, a correlational study examines relationships between measured dependent variables. In other words, correlational studies help researchers determine if two behaviors are related in some way. The relationship could be *causal*, such that one behavior causes the other, or it could be *indirect*, such that both behaviors are caused by a third factor. The correlational study cannot tell you which type of relationship exists with the level of certainty that an experiment can, but it can tell you if the behaviors you're observing change together in some way.

If behaviors are related, this means that as one changes, the other also changes. This change could be one in which both behaviors increase or decrease together or the change could be one in which as one behavior increases, the other decreases. This is the difference between a positive relationship and a negative relationship between measures. Figures 1.6 and 1.7 illustrate two results from correlational studies. In Figure 1.6, two outcomes are shown in the graphs between the percentage of dream reports with

Positive relationship: a relationship between variables characterized by an increase in one variable that occurs with an increase in the other variable

Negative relationship: a relationship between measures characterized by an increase in one measure that occurs with a decrease in the other measure

Figure 1.6   Data From a Study by Propper et al. (2007) Showing No Relationship Between Television Exposure and Dreams With Attack-Related or Threat-Related Content Before the September 11, 2001 Terrorist Attacks in the United States and a Positive Relationship Between These Measures After the Attacks

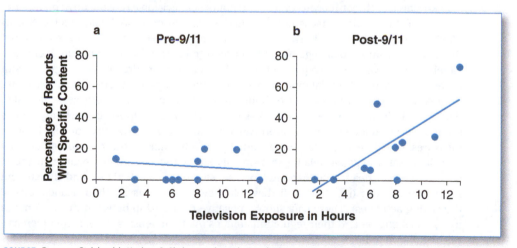

SOURCE: Propper, Strickgold, Keeley, & Christman (2007). Is television traumatic? Dreams, stress, and media exposure in the aftermath of September 11, 2011. *Psychological Science, 18,* 334–340

Figure 1.7   Data From a Study by Inzlicht et al. (2006) Showing That Stigma Sensitivity and Self-Regulation Are Negatively Related

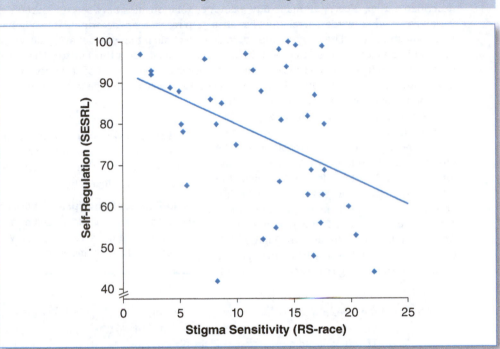

SOURCE: Inzlicht, McKay, & Aronson (2006). Stigma as ego depletion; How being the target of prejudice affects self-control. Psychological Science, 17, 262-269.

attack-related or threat-related content and hours of television exposure on September 11, 2001, the day of the terrorist attacks in the United States (Propper, Srickgold, Keeley, & Christman, 2007). In the graph shown in Panel A, no relationship is seen between these measures before the attacks because no change occurred in reported dreams as TV exposure increased, but in Panel B, a positive relationship is seen after the attacks; more dreams were reported along with more TV exposure. No relationship exists in Panel A because there is no consistent change in dream reports as the number of hours of television exposure increases—the data show a flat line that does not increase or decrease. However, dream reports consistently increase with the increase in television exposure in Panel B, showing a positive relationship between these measures. In Figure 1.7, data from a study by Inzlicht, McKay, and Aronson (2006) are shown that illustrate a negative relationship. In this study, the researchers examined the relationship between African American students' sensitivity to racial stigma and the students' self-regulation abilities (i.e., how well they felt they could focus on their academic work amid distracting activities). These data show a negative relationship between the students' sensitivity to racial stigma and their regulation abilities: As their sensitivity to stigma increased, their self-regulation abilities decreased.

Figures 1.6 and 1.7 illustrate the three types of relationships that can be found in a correlational study. A finding of *no relationship* indicates that the two dependent variables do not consistently change together. A finding of a *positive relationship* indicates that the two dependent variables consistently change together in the same direction (both go up together and both go down together). A finding of a *negative relationship* indicates that the two dependent variables consistently change together, but in different directions (as one goes up, the other goes down). However, the most important thing to remember about correlational studies is that they do not provide direct causal information about the relationship. In other words, just because a relationship is found between the two variables does not mean that a change in one variable *causes* a change in the other variable. Thus, whenever you hear a report about a relationship between two variables, think to yourself, "Correlation does not imply causation," and consider other things that could be causal factors to explain the relationship. Unless an experiment has been conducted, you must consider the possibility that the relationship is not a causal one.

The way you measure your dependent variables in a correlational study affects the statistics you use to look for relationships. The next chapter will examine the different ways that behaviors can be observed and measured. But before we look at the process of data collection in more detail, there are a couple of issues to consider in research: validity and reliability.

Stop and Think

1.7   Consider the differences between experiments and correlational studies as you read the research questions below. For each question, which type of study (experimental or correlational) would be better for answering the question? Explain your answers.

a.   Do energy drinks help you focus more while studying?

b.   Do anxious people tend to sleep less?

c.   Does eating red meat give you cancer?

d.   Who earns a higher starting salary in their first job, people with higher college grade point averages (GPAs) or people with higher aptitude test scores (ACT, SAT, etc.)?

1.8   Consider the description of the Inzlicht et al. (2006) study presented in this section. How could these researchers have examined a causal relationship between stigma and self-regulation? Why do you think they chose to conduct a correlational study instead?

Issues in Research: Validity and Reliability

Validity

One of the biggest differences between experiments and correlational studies involves *validity*. Validity is how well the study tests what you want it to test. There are a few different types of validity to consider in a research study. One type is internal validity, the degree

Internal validity: the degree to which a research study provides causal information about behavior

to which a study provides causal information about behavior. Experiments tend to have higher internal validity than correlational studies because they provide better tests of causal relationships. However, experiments can also differ in how much internal validity they have. An experiment that is designed to focus exclusively on the independent variable as the cause of a change in the dependent variable will have higher internal validity because it controls other factors to rule out other possible explanations of a change in the dependent variable across the conditions.

External validity: the degree to which the results of a study apply to individuals and realistic behaviors outside the study

---

Another type of validity to consider is external validity, the degree to which a study provides information about behavior that exists outside of the study. A study with higher external validity will examine behaviors that exist in the everyday lives of the individuals being studied. The more artificial the situation set up in a research study, the lower the external validity because the behaviors observed might also be artificial. This means that the more a researcher controls for additional factors that can cause the observed behaviors to change (i.e., increases the internal validity), the more artificial the behaviors may be due to the control of those other factors. Thus, internal and external validity can affect one another as a researcher designs a study. In some cases, correlational studies that have lower internal validity may have higher external validity.

Construct validity: the degree to which a measure is an accurate measure of the behavior of interest

---

Other types of validity, such as construct validity, relate to whether or not you have chosen a good way to measure the behavior. Construct validity is typically considered for surveys and questionnaires that are designed to measure a behavior through self-reports. If the items on the survey do a good job measuring the behavior you are interested in, then the survey has good construct validity. These types of measures can be used in experiments or correlational studies, but they are more common in correlational studies, making construct validity an important issue when surveys and questionnaires are used as measures.

Reliability

Reliability refers to the consistency of a measure of behavior. If the measure of behavior provides the same values each time it is measured under the same or similar circumstances, then it is a reliable measure. Issues of reliability can arise when multiple researchers are measuring or observing behaviors. If individuals are being observed for specific behaviors by different researchers, it is possible that each researcher is recording or measuring the behaviors in a different way. This is an issue of inter-rater reliability. If

---

Inter-rater reliability: a measure of the degree to which different observers measure behaviors in similar ways

Test–retest reliability: indicates that the scores on a survey will be similar when participants complete the survey more than once under similar circumstances

---

each researcher measures the behavior in different ways, the measures will be inconsistent and will not accurately reflect the behavior of interest. Thus, with multiple observers, it is important to check the inter-rater reliability of the measurements to ensure that they are consistent. Reliability can also be about the consistency of measurements over time or across items of survey or questionnaire. If the circumstances are the same, then a measure with good test–retest reliability will provide a similar score each time it is used to measure a behavior from the same individual. A survey with good internal consistency will yield consistent scores across items that address the same behavior of interest. In other words, there should be a relationship between the different items about the

Internal consistency: a form of reliability that tests relationships between scores on different items of a survey

same behavior. Thus, having a reliable measure of a behavior can increase the validity of your study, making it an important issue to consider when choosing a measure of behavior.

Statistics can help a researcher determine how reliable a measure is. For example, internal consistency and consistency across different observers/raters of behavior can be determined using statistics that examine the relationships between scores on different items or from different raters. Although the details of these statistics will not be specifically addressed in the chapters of this text, you may come across these reliability measures as you read about research that reported using surveys, questionnaires, or independent raters of behavior.

Stop and Think

1.9 Suppose you come across each of the surveys described below. Which issue seems to be the bigger problem, validity or reliability?

a. You see a survey in a magazine about the quality of your relationship with your significant other. The items on the survey ask questions about your favorite color, favorite food, and favorite type of music.

b. You complete a survey as part of a research study on eating behaviors of college students. The items ask how much you like to eat different types of foods. You complete the survey once while you are hungry and then again one year later after you have eaten a large meal. Overall, your ratings are lower the second time you take the survey.

1.10 Explain how an unreliable measure of behavior can lower the internal validity of a research study.

CHAPTER SUMMARY

1.1 Why do we use statistics to analyze data?

Statistics help us summarize a set of data and test hypotheses about behavior. They are important tools in understanding data from research studies in which we learn new knowledge about behavior.

1.2 How do descriptive and inferential statistics differ?

Descriptive statistics help us summarize a set of data. They include graphs and tables of the data, calculated values that represent typical scores, and values that represent the difference between the scores.

Inferential statistics help us test hypotheses made about the data. They use the descriptive statistics to determine the likelihood of obtaining our data when a hypothesis about the data is true.

1.3 Why are there so many different kinds of statistical tests?

There are many different ways to observe behavior, so many statistics have been developed to help researchers understand the observations that they have used. In addition, different statistics are helpful for the types of research designs described in this chapter. For example, experiments and correlational studies rely on different types of inferential statistics to answer the research questions asked in each of these designs.

1.4 What are the methods we use to collect data?

A brief description of some of the methods used in collecting data was provided in this chapter with an emphasis on the differences between experiments that provide causal information and correlational studies that provide information about relationships between different types of measures. The statistics we use to test our predictions about the data will depend on the methods used to collect those data and the scale of those measures.

1.5 How do the methods used to collect data affect the statistics we use?

As already mentioned, experiments and correlational studies use different inferential statistics because data are collected to answer different kinds of research questions in these designs. In addition, the observation techniques can vary across these designs, which require different types of statistics to better understand them. For example, in survey studies, there are statistics to help us examine the validity and reliability of the survey. The rest of this text will discuss this question in much more detail.

THINKING ABOUT RESEARCH

A summary of a research study in psychology is given below. As you read the summary, think about the following questions:

1. Was this study an experiment or a correlational study? Remember that an experiment will contain an independent variable, but a correlational study will not.

2. Identify the dependent variables. Explain how these variables were measured in the study.

3. Consider the validity of this study. Which types of validity discussed in this chapter are relevant for this study?

4. In what way(s) is reliability important in this study?

5. Examine the graph presented in Figure 1.8. Why are there two lines in this graph? What do the two lines represent in the study? Does this graph help you understand the data from the study? Why or why not?

6. How were inferential statistics used in this study?

   Duffy, K. A., & Chartrand, T. L. (2015). The extravert advantage: How and when extraverts build rapport with other people. *Psychological Science, 26,* 1795–1802.

   Note: Study 1 of this article is described below.

Purpose of the Study. Extraverts are known to have more social interactions than introverts, but how do they do it? What behaviors do extraverts exhibit that give them a social edge? Researchers Duffy and Chartrand (2015) designed a study to answer this question. They hypothesized that one important aspect of extraverts' behavior was mimicking other people they wanted to get along with. Their study compared the relationship between mimicry and extraversion under two conditions: one in which subjects were given some motivation to get along with someone else during a task (goal-present condition) and one in which subjects were not given this motivation (goal-absent condition).

Method of the Study. This study included 84 female undergraduate students as participants. Half of the participants were randomly assigned to the goal-present condition and the other half were assigned to the goal-absent condition. In the goal-present condition, the subjects were told that the task worked better when people got along with each other. In the goal-absent condition, this instruction was not given to the subjects. The participants were asked to complete a task in which they took turns with another subject (who was actually a trained researcher) describing presented photographs. During this task, the researcher performed easily mimicked behaviors (e.g., touching her hair or face, tapping her foot). During the task, the subject was filmed to examine the amount of time they spent mimicking the behaviors. Two researchers later coded the films to measure the time. At the end of the task, the subjects completed a questionnaire measuring their level of extraversion.

Results of the Study. The relationship between extraversion score and time spent mimicking was examined separately for the two goal groups. Figure 1.8 presents the relationship for each condition. Using inferential statistics, the researchers confirmed that there was a positive relationship between extraversion score and mimicry in the goal-present condition, but there was no relationship between these variables in the goal-absent condition.

Figure 1.8   Data From the Duffy and Chartrand (2015) Study

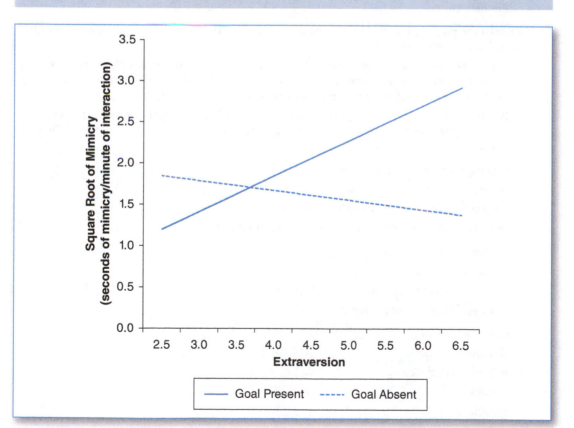

SOURCE: Duffy & Chartrand (2015). The extravert advantage: How and when extraverts build rapport with other people. *Psychological Science, 26*, 1795-1802.

Conclusions of the Study. From the results of this study, the researchers concluded that extraverts mimic others they wish to get along with as a way to effectively socially interact with them. However, they only seem to exhibit the mimicry behaviors when they have the goal of getting along with another person. Thus, mimicry seems to be one behavior that extraverts use to get along well with others.

TEST YOURSELF

1. Imagine you've heard an ad that states something like "Four out of five dentists recommend using Product *X*."

   a. Which of the following statistics is this statement most likely based on?

      - When they asked five dentists if they recommend Product *X*, the first four said "yes" and the last one said "no."
      - When they asked a sample of dentists if they recommend Product *X*, 80% of the sample said "yes."
      - When they surveyed a sample of dentists, 80% of them said they would use Product *X*.

   b. What other information might you want to know before you decide if you want to use Product *X*?

2. Consider the graphs presented in this chapter. Notice how they are constructed. Answer the questions about the graphs below.

   a. For the graphs presented in Figure 1.3, what is presented on the *x*-axis (the horizontal axis)? What is presented on the *y*-axis (the vertical axis)? Which of these is the independent variable in the Drews et al. (2009) study and which is the dependent variable?

   b. For the graphs presented in Figure 1.6, what do each of the dots in the graphs represent? How do these graphs differ in structure from the graph presented in Figure 1.5? Note the differences you see between these graphs.

3. A quasi-experiment is an experiment in which _____.

   a. three or more groups of subjects are compared

   b. subjects are not randomly assigned to groups

   c. the relationship between two measured variables is tested

4. Inferential statistics help us _____.

   a. summarize the data

   b. rule out alternative explanations of the results

   c. test hypotheses about the results

5. A graph is a form of _____.

   a. descriptive statistic

   b. inferential statistic

   c. validity

   d. reliability

Read the following scenario to answer questions 6-9. Imagine that a research team is investigating the role of participant mood on memory for a film clip. They randomly assign participants to one of two mood-induction conditions (happy versus sad) and ask them to complete a multiple-choice test on the film clip content and a demographic questionnaire (class year, age, gender). They find that, on average, participants in the sad mood condition answered 80% of the questions correctly, and the happy mood condition answered 75% correctly.

6. The researchers want to know how much of their sample is comprised of freshman, sophomores, juniors, and seniors. What type of statistic can they use to gather this information?
   a. Descriptive statistics
   b. Valid statistics
   c. Inferential statistics
   d. Experimental statistics

7. Imagine that the researchers hypothesized that a sad mood results in better memory than a happy mood. What type of statistic can they use to gather this information?
   a. Descriptive statistic
   b. Valid statistic
   c. Inferential statistic
   d. Experimental statistic

8. What is the independent variable?
   a. The memory test for the film clips
   b. The mood condition
   c. The class year of the participants
   d. None of the above

9. What is the dependent variable?
   a. The memory test for the film clips
   b. The mood condition
   c. The class year of the participants
   d. None of the above

Read the following scenario to answer questions 10-14. A researcher has conducted a study on the effect of text color on student retention of class material. His experiment procedure used an old, slightly stained overhead projector, and his colleagues warn him that his results may not generalize to other real-world settings, since most projectors do not have the same stain patterns.

10. His colleagues are questioning the _____ validity of the study.
    a. internal
    b. external
    c. construct
    d. face

11. A researcher has developed a survey designed to assess students' fears about research methods and related coursework. Her data suggest that students get roughly the same scores when they take the assessment more than once. This is one indicator that her assessment has high _____ reliability.

    a. consistent

    b. inter-rater

    c. test–retest

    d. internal

12. Every study has an independent variable.

    a. True

    b. False

13. Every study has a dependent variable.

    a. True

    b. False

14. The methods used by an experimenter are crucial to the _____ validity of a study.

    a. internal

    b. external

    c. construct

    d. both (a) and (b)

Chapter 2

The Starting Place: Data and Distributions

As you read the chapter, consider the following questions:

2.1 What is the difference between a population and a sample?

2.2 What kinds of data are collected in psychological studies?

2.3 What is a distribution and how does its shape affect our analysis of the data?

2.4 How can computer programs help us examine distributions of data?

POPULATIONS AND SAMPLES

Have you ever wondered about the opinion polls presented by media news sources and how accurate they are? Consider a poll done on global warming by ABC News/*Washington Post* taken in November 2015 (http://www.pollingreport.com/enviro.htm). People were asked if they considered global warming a serious problem facing the country (Photo 2.1). From those polled, 63 % said yes, it was a serious problem. We can compare this with a poll conducted in May and June of 2015 by the Pew Research Center (http://www.pollingreport.com/enviro.htm). In this poll, people were asked if global warming was a serious problem and only 46 % said it was very serious. Why is there such a large difference between the reported percentages? Did many people suddenly decide that global warming was a big problem between June and November? This is one possible explanation, but it is not very likely. Another possible explanation could be that different people answered the question in the two polls. One way to determine this is to look at the information provided about the polls. The ABC New/*Washington Post* poll describes that it was from 1,004 adults nationwide (in the United States) with a margin of error of plus or minus 3.5. The Pew Research poll describes that it was from 5,122 adults nationwide with a margin of error of plus or minus 1.6. Is this information important? What does it tell us about the validity of the polls?

In fact, the information provided about the polls can be important in deciding whether the information from the poll is accurate (i.e., valid). The Pew Research poll surveyed more people, which allowed for a smaller margin of error. This means we can be more certain

Photo 2.1   How many people believe that global warming is a serious problem? Polls can provide some information about this, but it is important to consider the sample and population for the poll to determine its validity.

©iStock/pum_eva

❧

Population: a group of individuals a researcher seeks to learn about from a research study

Sample: the group of individuals chosen from the population to represent it in a research study

Sampling error: the difference between the observations in a population and the sample representing that population in a study

that the percentage of all adults in the United States who would report global warming as a very serious problem is close to 46%. What we're looking at here is the difference between a population and a sample, and the information provided helps us determine how well the sample represents the whole population (see Figure 2.1). The *population* in this case is all adults in the United States. This is the group of individuals we are trying to learn about with the poll. The *sample* is the set of people who answered the question in the poll. They were selected from the population in an attempt to represent the opinions of the whole population without having to ask the whole population (which would be impossible, given the population's size). How well the sample represents the population of interest is a function of the sample size, the way in which the sample was chosen, how many people chosen actually responded or chose to participate, and a few other factors that researchers must consider when conducting any type of research study. Differences between the sample and the population contribute to sampling error. Sampling error exists

Figure 2.1   The Sample Is Chosen to Represent the Population in a Study

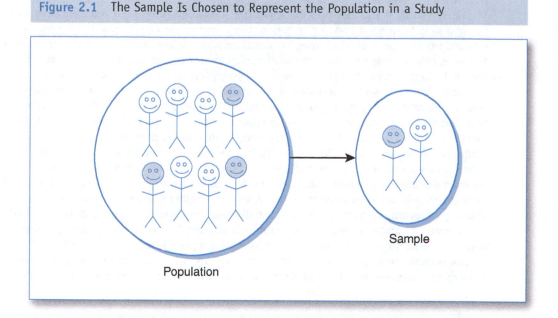

Sample

Population

any time we collect data from a sample of the population because we will never be able to get the exact population data from a sample of the population. Each sample is a different subset of the population and will provide different scores, resulting in different means across samples. We're trying to estimate the population mean using the sample mean, so with each sample, we will be at least a little bit wrong about the population mean. This difference between the sample mean and the population mean is the sampling error.

One way to think about this is someone trying to figure out what picture is on a puzzle with only a small part of the puzzle put together. We're not likely to understand the whole picture from just one part of the puzzle; however, the more of the puzzle we have together (i.e., the larger the sample size), the better we'll be at guessing the picture. But putting the whole puzzle together would be difficult and time-consuming if there were thousands or millions of pieces. So instead, we make our best guess from the part of the puzzle we can put together in our study (the sample). With only a small part of the puzzle put together, though, we're not going to get the whole picture exactly right. Thus, there is some error in our guess from our sample (sampling error). The margin of error reported for polls (such as those described here) provides an estimate of the sampling error. This is an estimate of how far off the reported percentage in our data is likely to be from the population percentage. Thus, knowing the sample size and margin of error for opinion polls can help you decide if the poll is useful in telling you how people really think about an issue.

It is very rare that a researcher will observe the entire population in a research study, so samples are almost always used in order to represent the population in the study by collecting data from a realistic number of individuals. This is due to the size of most populations—they tend to be very large because researchers want to be able to learn about the behavior of large groups of individuals, not just a small set of people, as in our survey examples where we wanted to know about how Americans felt about global warming. Thus, a smaller sample was chosen to collect data from in the study. If you have ever participated in a research study, then you have been a member of a sample selected from a population. Many research studies in psychology use samples selected from the population of college students because it is a sample that is fairly easy to obtain. However, *college students* is too narrow a population for some studies because college students tend to be fairly educated, higher income, and young, giving us a biased sample for these characteristics from the whole population of adults. Because of this possible bias, researchers have begun to sample from larger populations of individuals using online technologies to deliver surveys and experimental tasks to a larger population. For example, a fairly recent study by Brown-Iannuzzi, Lundberg, Kay, and Payne (2015) sampled their participants from a large population of adults using the Amazon site MechanicalTurk. This site rewards people with small amounts of money in their account for completing research studies. Brown-Iannuzzi et al. sampled individuals from this site to learn how one's sense of one's own wealth, relative to others' wealth, influences one's political ideas about the redistribution of wealth in society (their research suggested that relative wealth does affect one's political ideas on this issue; see Figure 2.2). MechanicalTurk is becoming a popular method for selecting a large sample from the very large population of adults in the world. We will consider more issues of sample selection in Chapter 3.

The population and sample of a research study are important for choosing the statistical tools researchers use to better understand data. As you will see in Chapter 3, the way that you

Figure 2.2 Results From Brown-Iannuzzi et al.'s (2015) Study Comparing Support for Redistribution of Wealth Based on Experimental Conditions of Relative Wealth Compared With Others' Wealth; Greater Support for Redistribution Was Found for Low-Status Participants Than for High-Status Participants

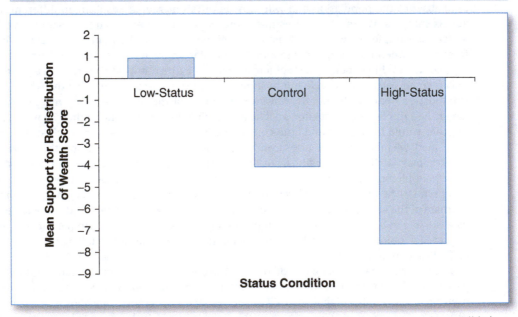

SOURCE: Brown-Iannuzzi, J. L., Lundberg, K. B., Kay, A. C., & Payne, B. K. (2015). Subjects status shapes political preferences. *Psychological Science, 26*, 15–26.

choose a sample from a population can affect the validity of your study. Discussions in the chapters in Part III of this text will show you how hypotheses are made about populations before a sample is chosen. Finally, the type of data collected from the sample will influence the statistics we choose to summarize the data (i.e., descriptive statistics) and to test our hypotheses about the population (i.e., inferential statistics).

TYPES OF DATA

There are many different types of data that can be collected in psychological research studies. A researcher attempts to choose the best measure for the behavior they want to observe. This choice is important because it can affect the internal validity of the study—a poor choice can mean that the data do not actually measure the behavior of interest. In other words, researchers try to determine a good operational definition of the behavior they are interested in. An operational definition is the way a behavior is measured in a particular study. It provides a way for a researcher to measure a behavior that is not directly observable. Operational definitions are a necessary part of the

---
Operational definition: the way a behavior is defined in a research study to allow for its measurement
---

Photo 2.2   There are many ways to measure depression; a researcher operationally defines the behavior to allow its measurement.

©iStock/AntonioGuillem

research process because many behaviors can be defined in multiple ways, and the researcher needs to know what to measure from the individuals in the sample when they collect their data. For example, what behaviors should be measured to learn about one's level of depression (see Photo 2.2)? There are many ways we could operationally define depression: how often someone smiles in an hour (fewer smiles = more depression), observers' ratings of how lethargic someone seems (lower ratings of energy level = more depression), or a score on a questionnaire of self-reported thoughts and behaviors that we think are present in someone who is depressed (sleeping more often, loss of appetite, feelings of sadness, etc.). Thus, a researcher has many choices when they want to measure depression, and they try to come up with the most valid measure (within the practical limitations of the research study) for the behavior they want to learn about.

Scales of Measurement

One choice that is made by the researcher in operationally defining a behavior for a research study is the scale of measurement they use. The scale of measurement will be important in determining which statistics are used to describe the data and test hypotheses about the data. Table 2.1 presents an overview of the different scales of measurement and an example of each type.

Nominal Scales

Many measurements use categories to describe the behavior that is observed or reported by the participants. For example, if you want to ask someone to indicate their current mood, you might give them response choices such as happy, sad, excited, anxious, and so on. This type of measurement is called a nominal scale because it involves non-ordered categories that are nonnumerical in nature. You cannot order these moods from highest to lowest—they are simply different. Some types of demographic information collected in research studies are measured on a nominal scale. Questions about someone's gender or major in college are good examples of these types of nominal scales.

Nominal scale: a scale of data measurement that involves non-ordered categorical responses

---

Ordinal Scales

Any time you rank order your preferences for different things, you are using an ordinal scale. Rankings in a competition (1st, 2nd, 3rd, etc.) also measure individuals on an ordinal scale.

Table 2.1 Scales of Measurement

Scale	Definition	Example
Nominal	Unordered categories	University where degree was earned
Ordinal	Categorical, ordered categories	Letter grades earned in a course (A, B, C, D, F)
Interval	Numerical categories without a true zero point	Ratings on personality surveys with values from 1 to 5
Ratio	Numerical categories with a true zero point	Age measured in days since birth

Ordinal scales are measures that involve categories that can be ordered from highest to lowest. However, the ordered categories are not necessarily equally spaced on an ordinal scale. Imagine you are asked to report your level of anxiety today on a scale that includes response choices of *not at all anxious, a little anxious, fairly anxious*, and *very anxious*. On this scale, the difference between *a little anxious* and *fairly anxious* may be smaller than the difference between *fairly anxious* and *very anxious*. Thus, this is considered an ordinal scale because the categories can be ordered from highest to lowest level of anxiety, but the categories are not always equally spaced across the scale.

> **Ordinal scale:** a scale of data measurement that involves ordered categorical responses

Interval Scales

If the ordered categories on a scale are equally spaced, then the scale is known as an interval scale. Interval scales are used when the researcher wants to know that the difference between any two values on the scale is the same across all values of the scale. Typically, this involves numerical responses. Many rating scales on questionnaires are interval scales because they ask participants to rate their agreement with statements or their likelihood of performing specific behaviors on a numerical rating scale. An example of such a scale might be to rate how much you agree with the statement "Global warming is a serious issue facing society today" on a scale of 1 to 10, where a higher number indicates higher agreement. Such scales do not have a true zero point, because the values cannot be considered ratios of one another. For example, because there is a minimum and maximum score on a 1 to 10 scale, there is no way to determine the ratio function between scores—a score of 4 is not twice that of a score of 2 (2 is only one value higher than the minimum, whereas 4 is three values higher than the minimum). The scores on the scale are not distributed in this way.

> **Interval scale:** a scale of data measurement that involves numerical responses that are equally spaced, but the scores are not ratios of each other

Ratio Scales

A numerical scale with a true zero point allows for values that are ratios of one another. This is known as a ratio scale. On ratio scales, you can determine what score would be twice as high as another score. Some examples of ratio scales are accuracy on a task, speed to complete a task, and age. A score of 50 % accuracy is twice as high as a score of 25 % accuracy. Ratio scales are often used in systematic and controlled measures of behavior, a topic we will discuss later in this chapter. Note that interval and ratio scales are often grouped together because data from these scales are typically analyzed in the same way and there are cases where it is difficult to determine if a scale is truly an interval scale. The important difference to note for the scales of measurement and how they are analyzed is whether they involve numbers or categories as responses on the scale.

> **Ratio scale:** a scale of data measurement that involves numerical responses in which scores are ratios of each other

---

Stop and Think

2.1 For each study description below, identify the population and the sample.

 a. A researcher recruits students from a fifth-grade class at an elementary school to examine math abilities on a standardized test in children who are 9–10 years old.

 b. A researcher recruits college students from the university subject pool to test the effect of time pressure on accuracy in completing a task.

 c. Older adults are recruited from a retirement center to examine sources of anxiety in retirees. Anxiety is measured using survey items in which the participants rate their level of anxiety on a 1 to 7 scale for different issues that might be anxiety inducing (e.g., financial security, failing health, etc.).

 d. Patients who have suffered a traumatic brain injury (TBI) are included (with their consent) in a study of how one's diet after the injury affects recovery time (measured in number of days they stay in the hospital after their injury) from a local hospital.

2.2 For each study described in 2.1, identify the most likely scale of measurement used in the study.

Survey Data

We have already discussed some issues with sampling from populations to collect survey data in this chapter. Using surveys to measure behavior can also limit the types of measures that a researcher can use to observe those behaviors. Although any of the scales of measurement described in this chapter can be used in surveys, the measures are limited to an individual's report of their thoughts and behaviors. In other words, surveys indirectly measure the behavior of interest in a study. They rely on responses to items that together provide information about the behavior. The survey score is an operational definition of that behavior. However, the way survey responses are presented can greatly affect the results. Consider the surveys on global warming described at the beginning of this chapter. Do you notice any differences in the responses used in the polls? In fact, the difference in survey response options is likely the reason for the differences in the percentage of people who agreed with the survey statement. In the first survey, people stated that they *strongly agreed* that global warming was a serious problem. In the second survey, the percentage reported was for people who *very strongly agreed* with this statement. It may be that a fair percentage of people in the second survey chose a response of *strongly agree* instead of *very strongly agree*. In the first survey, there was no *very strongly agree* option, so some of the people who chose the *strongly agree* response may in fact have felt very strongly about their agreement. Because the response choices are different in the two surveys, it can appear as if they obtained different results.

In addition, there are some issues related to the self-report nature of survey data that can influence the validity of the data. Because surveys rely on reports of the behavior from the

Photo 2.3   Survey responses can be prone to social desirability bias, in which participants try to respond in a way that makes them look more positive.

©iStock/mediaphotos

participants themselves, the validity of the measurement may not be as high as when the researcher directly observes those behaviors. Participants may not have an accurate perception of their own behaviors, making the reports subjective. Further, participants may wish to portray their behaviors more positively than they actually are, an issue known as social desirability bias. If participants respond to survey items in a way that makes them appear more positive, they are reducing the validity of the behavioral measure (see Photo 2.3).

Social desirability bias: bias created in survey responses from respondents' desire to be viewed more favorably by others

Because survey data have some issues that can affect their validity, researchers are careful in checking the construct validity of surveys and questionnaires when they are first used to make sure that they accurately measure the behaviors of interest. Reliability of surveys and questionnaires is also examined before they are used as measures of a behavior to ensure that they will produce consistent results when they are used in research studies.

Systematic/Controlled Measures

Another type of data collected in many research studies is more systematic and controlled in nature. In experimental studies, where internal validity is increased through control of the measurement of the behaviors and the situations in which they are observed, researchers often employ more systematic and controlled measures (see Photo 2.4). These measures are more direct observations of behavior than the self-reports collected on surveys (e.g., accuracy or speed in performing a task), which can provide more internally valid measures of behavior, but they can also have lower external validity than the behaviors measured in surveys because the control imposed during the observations can influence the behaviors observed. When someone knows they are participating in a research study, they may try harder in completing a task (or may perform worse due to lack of motivation because they know they will get research credit regardless of their performance), changing their accuracy and speed in performing the task compared with a more naturalistic setting.

Consider the experiment conducted by Metcalfe, Casal-Roscum, Radin, and Friedman (2015) to compare older and younger adults' memories for facts. Both young and older adults were

Photo 2.4   Systematic measures of behavior sometimes involve collecting responses on a computer to allow for direct measures of behavior in terms of speed or accuracy in completing a task.

©iStock/LuckyBusiness

asked to answer a series of general knowledge questions (e.g., "In what ancient city were the Hanging Gardens located?" Correct answer: Babylon). For each answer, they provided a rating of their confidence for their response on a 1 to 7 scale. Feedback was then given for their answer (correct or incorrect with the correct answer given as feedback). After a short delay, they were then tested on 20 of the questions for which they made high-confidence errors (i.e., they answered incorrectly but were highly confident in their incorrect response) and 20 questions where they made low-confidence errors (i.e., they answered incorrectly but were not very confident in their incorrect response) to determine final test accuracy on these questions. The mean accuracy for each group and type of question is shown in Figure 2.3. Older adults showed better memory on the final test—an atypical finding—especially when they had low confidence in their original response. The researchers measured memory accuracy as a controlled measure: They carefully chose the items presented to the participants and tested their memory in a lab, where they could control other factors that contribute to memory other than the age group and the participant's confidence in their responses. This control increased the internal validity of the study in providing a good test of the comparison of younger and older adults. However, this control of the measure and the situation may have reduced the realism of the memory being tested. For example, because the participants knew that the researchers were interested in their memory performance, they may have tried harder on the task (especially the older participants, for whom research participation may be a less-common experience) and raised their memory levels compared with how they would perform in a less controlled setting. This shows how controlled observations of behavior can have high internal validity but may also have lower external validity.

Figure 2.3   Memory Accuracy Data From Metcalf et al.'s (2015) Study

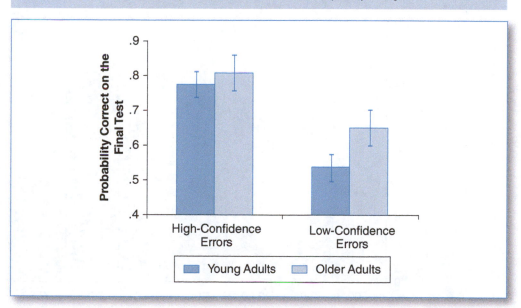

SOURCE: Metcalf, Casal-Roscum, Radin, & Friedman (2015). On teaching old dogs new tricks. *Psychological Science, 26*, 1833–1842.

FREQUENCY DISTRIBUTIONS

Let's now consider what the data we collect in different situations might look like. When we collect a set of data, we have a distribution of scores to consider. This distribution might range over the entire scale of measurement (e.g., participants have used all of the values on a 1 to 7 rating scale in their responses) or it might be restricted to just a small range of scores (e.g., participants have only used the values between 3 and 6 on the 1 to 7 rating scale). In addition, the scores might cluster close to one value on the scale with very few values at the high and low ends of the scale. Or the scores could be equally spaced along the values of the scale. Thus, different distributions can have different characteristics depending on the variability seen in the scores. A good way to examine the distribution and see what it looks like is to create a frequency distribution table or graph. The frequency distribution will indicate how often each value in the scale was used by the participants in their responses or in measurements of their behavior.

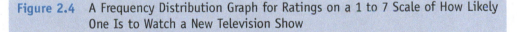

Distribution: a set of scores

Frequency distribution: a graph or table of a distribution showing the frequency of each score in the distribution

To create a frequency distribution graph by hand, you place the scores on the *x*-axis of the graph and then indicate the number of times each of those scores appears in a set of data with the bar height along the *y*-axis. Figure 2.4 shows a frequency distribution graph for responses

Figure 2.4   A Frequency Distribution Graph for Ratings on a 1 to 7 Scale of How Likely One Is to Watch a New Television Show

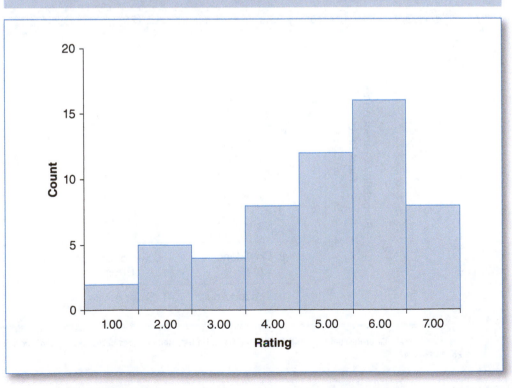

Table 2.2   A Frequency Distribution Table for Ratings on a 1 to 7 Scale of How Likely One Is to Watch a New Television Show

Score	Frequency	Percentage	Cumulative Percentage
1	2	3.6	3.6
2	5	9.1	12.7
3	4	7.3	20.0
4	8	14.5	34.5
5	12	21.8	56.4
6	16	29.1	85.5
7	8	14.5	100.0

on a 1 to 7 scale that might be present from a survey question asking how likely someone is to watch a new show on television after watching an ad for that show. The graph shows that the respondents used all the scores on the scale, but most of the scores were clustered around the values of 5 and 6 (these were the most frequent scores in the distribution). Table 2.2 shows a frequency distribution table of the same set of scores. To create the table, the scores are listed in one column and the frequency count of each of the scores in the distribution is listed in the second column. For example, 16 respondents rated their likelihood of watching the new show at a 6 on the 1 to 7 scale. The other columns in the table show the percentage of all the scores in the distribution at that value and the cumulative percentage from lowest to highest that adds in all previous percentages as you move from one score to the next.

Shape of a Distribution

One thing we can see more easily using a frequency distribution is the shape of the distribution. The shape of the distribution can affect the choices a researcher makes in analyzing the data with inferential statistics. Look at the frequency distribution in Figure 2.4—what do you notice about its shape? Is the distribution symmetrical, with each half of the distribution above the most frequent score (a score of 6) the mirror image of each other? Or are the scores clustered more toward one end of the distribution than the other? If the distribution shows a mirror image across the most frequent score, then it is a symmetrical distribution. Symmetrical distributions occur naturally in some types of data. For example, standardized test scores typically show symmetrical distributions with an average score in the center and each half of the distribution around the average showing fewer scores at each end of the scale in a similar pattern. Figure 2.5 shows a fairly symmetrical distribution of data in a frequency distribution graph. These data repre-

Symmetrical distribution: a distribution of scores where the shape of the distribution shows a mirror image on either side of the middle score

sent the distribution of letter grades in a college course where the instructor has "curved" the grade the distribution around an average grade of C (i.e., made it symmetrical around the C grade).

Many distributions, however, show clustering of scores toward the top or bottom end of the scale. In fact, without curving, grade distributions in many college courses show a clustering of grades toward the high end of the grade scale, often because there are more people in a course who do well than who do very poorly. When scores are clustered at one end of the scale or the other in a distribution, it is known as a skewed distribution. Skew in a distribution can affect the comparison of different measures of what is considered a typical score (as you will see in Chapter 4). Speed in completing a task often shows a skewed distribution, especially if the research participants complete multiple trials of the task. For example, a task speed distribution is shown in Figure 2.6. You can see in this distribution that most of the scores cluster toward the low end of the scale because the partici-pants are trying to complete the task quickly, based on the instructions. However, there are a few scores higher up on the scale where a participant was especially slow in completing the task. This could be due to a short lapse in attention or a particularly difficult trial that affected their speed. However, there will not be the same pattern of very fast trials at the low end of the scale because the lowest the scores can go is 0 on the scale, keeping the fast scores from spreading out at the low end.

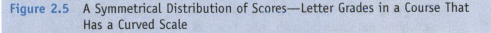

Skewed distribution: a distribution of scores where the shape of the distribution shows a clustering of scores at the low or high end of the scale

Figure 2.5   A Symmetrical Distribution of Scores—Letter Grades in a Course That Has a Curved Scale

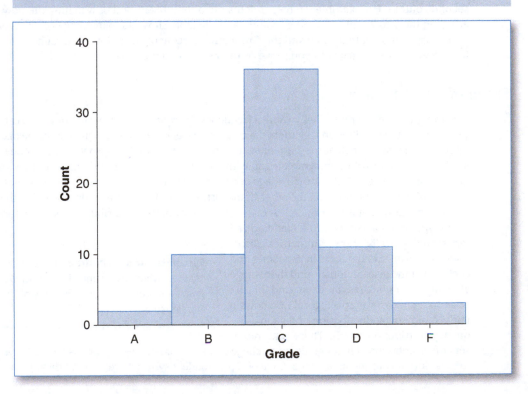

Figure 2.6   A Skewed Distribution of Scores—Speed of Task Completion

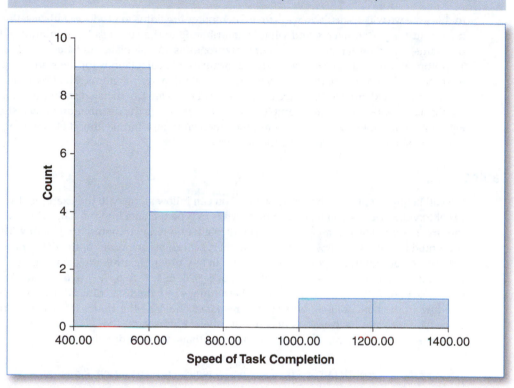

Stop and Think

2.3   Frequency distribution tables and graphs are types of statistics—are these tables and graphs descriptive or inferential statistics? Explain your answer.

2.4   Explain how internal validity is increased in a study using systematic/controlled measures of behavior.

2.5   Create a frequency distribution table or graph for the following set of data using ranges of scores by 10 (i.e., frequency for 51–60, 61–70, etc.):

77, 75, 78, 56, 90, 68, 65, 63, 73, 77, 74, 78, 72, 79, 82, 85, 88, 52, 96, 71

Does this distribution appear to be symmetrical or skewed in shape? Explain your answer.

This is why most distributions of data that measure task speed are skewed. This distribution represents a *positive skew*, where the tail of infrequent scores is at the high end of the scale. A *negative skew* shows the opposite pattern—the tail of the distribution is on the low end of the scale.

FREQUENCY DISTRIBUTIONS IN EXCEL®

In this text, we will discuss two ways to use computer programs to produce statistics. While it is important for you to understand what is contributing to the statistics being produced by the programs, most researchers use computer programs to calculate statistics for their data. Therefore, in this text you will see both the formulas and calculations for the statistics and the instructions for producing those statistics using the computer programs. The first program we will consider is Microsoft Excel. Excel can be used to create frequency distribution tables and graphs. Let's work through an example of how it works using the distribution of data shown in Figure 2.4 and Table 2.2. These data are hypothetical ratings for likelihood of watching a new television show after viewing an ad for the show.

Tables

We will begin by entering the rating scores. You can follow along with the example if you have Excel to work with as you read. The first step is to type the data into the data window. This is the first column shown in Figure 2.7. The data are entered with one score per row. They are presented in order from lowest scores to highest scores, but the order of the data entry in this column is not important; you can enter them in any order. Here are the data to enter: 1, 1, 2, 2, 2, 2, 2, 3, 3, 3, 3, 4, 4, 4, 4, 4, 4, 4, 4, 5, 5, 5, 5, 5, 5, 5, 5, 5, 5, 5, 5, 5, 6, 6, 6, 6, 6, 6, 6, 6, 6, 6, 6, 6, 6, 6, 6, 6, 7, 7, 7, 7, 7, 7, 7, 7. Type these ratings into the first column in your Excel data window. In the next column, enter in the response choices—the values from 1 to 7. In some cases, you may not have exact scores to enter here, but because these data are from a survey with a rating scale, we can enter the exact scores that are in the distribution.

Figure 2.7   Excel Data Window Showing a Frequency Distribution Table

	A	B	C	D	E
1	DATA	SCORES	COUNTS	PERCENTAGE	CUMULATIVE PERCENTAGE
2	1	1	2	3.636363636	3.636363636
3	1	2	5	9.090909091	12.72727273
4	2	3	4	7.272727273	20
5	2	4	8	14.54545455	34.54545455
6	2	5	12	21.81818182	56.36363636
7	2	6	16	29.09090909	85.45454545
8	2	7	8	14.54545455	100
9	3				
10	3				
11	3				
12	3				
13	4				
14	4				

Note: Excel is a registered trademark of Microsoft Corporation.

The third column will include our counts for each score. You could count these by hand from the list of data above, but for large data sets, this would be time-consuming and you might make a mistake. Instead, we can use the formulas in Excel to calculate the counts. We will use the COUNTIF command here. To use a command in Excel, type = and then the command; so in the COUNTS column's first cell, you can type =COUNTIF. The COUNTIF command will include the range of scores you want to count (all the scores in the DATA column) and the specific score you want to count. Your COUNTIF command will be =COUNTIF(range,score). To calculate the counts, type a (, then highlight all of the scores in the DATA column to enter the range (by dragging the cursor over the whole column), and then type ,"="& (comma, quotation mark, equal sign, quotation mark, ampersand). Then highlight the score in the SCORES column you want to count (or you can just type in the score you want). This will then add the score you are looking at. If you want a range of scores here, you can use COUNTIFS (instead of COUNTIF) include sets of < or > before the & and score to indicate a range. Close the) and then hit enter. If you included labels at the top of the columns as in Figure 2.7, your first cell should look like this before you hit return (you can see the formula by clicking on a cell to show it in the bar at the top):

=COUNTIF(A2:A56,"="&1) or =COUNTIF(A2:A56,"="&B3)

You should see a count of 2 in the COUNTS column for a score of 1 (see Figure 2.7). Repeat this formula for each score to calculate counts in your COUNTS column.

The next column in our frequency distribution table is the percentage of the total that each count represents in the data set. To calculate this value, type =, highlight the value in the COUNTS column, then /COUNT(. Then highlight the scores in the DATA column and type). Then type *100 and hit enter. Your first cell should look like this (again, if you have a column header):

=C2/COUNT(A2:A56)*100

You should see the percentage of scores that had a value of 1 in the data set in the PERCENTAGE column (see Figure 2.7).

The last column in our table is the cumulative percentage of values for each score. This will tell us what percentage of the scores is at a certain value or lower. To calculate this value, again begin by typing = to indicate a formula, then highlight the next value in the PERCENTAGE column, type +, and then highlight the previous value on the CUMULATIVE PERCENTAGE column (if there is one) before hitting enter. For the first score, the cumulative percentage will simply be the percentage value. Your completed table should look similar to the one shown in Figure 2.7.

Summary of Steps

- Type the data into a data window in Excel (1st column).
- Type in response choices (2nd column).
- Type in **=COUNTIF(range, scores)** command (3rd column).
- Repeat COUNTIF command for each score or range of scores to complete third column.
- Calculate percentages for each score using **=score cell/COUNT(range)*100** (4th column).
- Calculate cumulative percentages by successively adding up the percentages for each score (5th column).

Figure 2.8   Excel Chart Showing a Frequency Distribution Graph

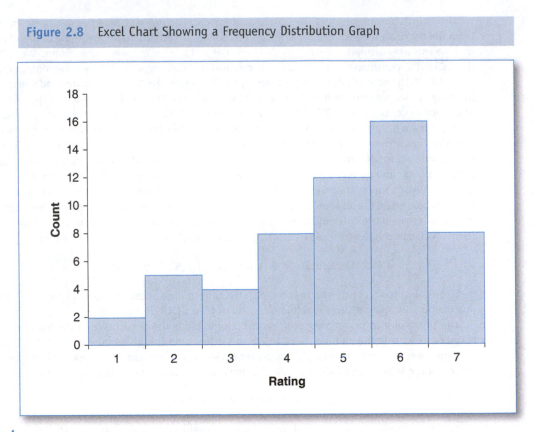

Graphs

Excel can also create a frequency distribution graph of these data for us. To create the graph, highlight the SCORES and COUNTS columns of values. Then click the Charts function window. Excel's default is typically a bar graph for these types of data, but your settings may be different, so you may need to choose the Column Graph option. To show the distribution shape, choose the option under Chart Layouts that shows the bars adjacent in the graph. You should then have a graph that looks like the one in Figure 2.8. You can type in axis labels and change the fill color of the bars to format as you like.

FREQUENCY DISTRIBUTIONS IN SPSS®

The second computer program I will describe in this text is SPSS. SPSS is a common program used by researchers for descriptive and inferential statistics in psychology. You may be asked to use this program in some of your psychology courses to analyze data from research studies. In many cases, it will produce the statistics you want more easily than

Note: SPSS is a registered trademark of International Business Machines Corporation.

Excel. However, this program is not as commonly available as Excel, which is why there is instruction for both programs provided in this text.

Tables

As with Excel, the first step in using SPSS is to enter the data you wish to examine. The data window in SPSS has a similar set up to the one in Excel. However, you will define the variable names and details in a separate tab of the window. An example of the data window in SPSS is shown in Figure 2.9. As in Excel, each row contains data from a different participant and each column indicates a different variable. Thus, the first column contains the ratings for desire to watch the television show for each participant from our earlier example as in the Excel window. However, to label this variable, we need to choose the Variable View tab at the bottom of the window. This view will allow you to name the variable (as I have done here with the label *Rating*). See Figure 2.10 for the Variable View in SPSS.

Once our data are entered and labeled, we are ready to create our frequency distribution table. To create a table, we will choose the Frequencies function in the Descriptive Statistics menu under the Analyze menu at the top. Different versions of SPSS look a bit different for these menus, so first find the Analyze menu (or tab) at the top of the window; then choose Descriptive Statistics and then Frequencies. You should see a small window pop up that looks like Figure 2.11. To create the table for the ratings, make sure the Rating variable is highlighted (if not, click on it), and then click the arrow to move it into the Variable(s) box. Be sure to keep the Display frequency tables box checked. The OK button should then be available. When you click OK or hit enter, a new Output window will appear. Your table will be displayed as shown in Figure 2.12. The Valid column shows the scores in the distribution, the Frequency column shows the counts for each score (including a total count), the Percent and Valid Percent columns show the percentage of

Figure 2.9   Data Window for SPSS

	Rating	var	var	var
1	1.00			
2	1.00			
3	2.00			
4	2.00			
5	2.00			
6	2.00			
7	2.00			
8	3.00			
9	3.00			
10	3.00			
11	3.00			
12	4.00			
13	4.00			
14	4.00			
15	4.00			
16	4.00			
17	4.00			
18	4.00			
19	4.00			
20	5.00			
21	5.00			
22	5.00			
23	5.00			
24	5.00			
25	5.00			
26	5.00			
27	5.00			
28	5.00			
29	5.00			
30	5.00			
31	5.00			
32	6.00			
33	6.00			
34	6.00			

Figure 2.10   Variable View Window for SPSS

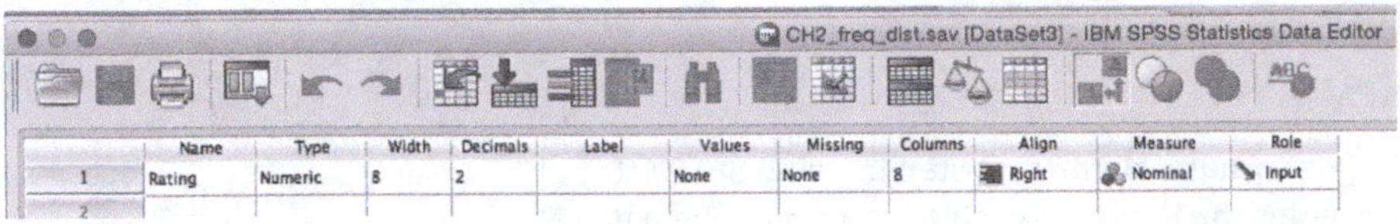

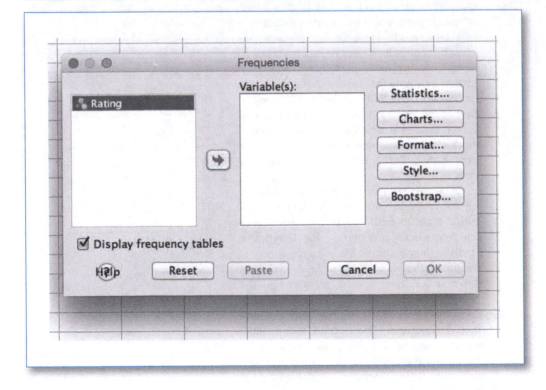

Figure 2.11   Frequencies Window in SPSS

scores in the distribution that are at that score, and the Cumulative Percent column shows the cumulative percentage for each score. You can compare this table with those shown in Table 2.2 and Figure 2.7 to see the similarities across the different program versions of the same table.

Figure 2.12   Frequency Distribution Table in SPSS, Seen in the Output Window

Rating

		Frequency	Percent	Valid Percent	Cumulative Percent
Valid	1.00	2	3.6	3.6	3.6
	2.00	5	9.1	9.1	12.7
	3.00	4	7.3	7.3	20.0
	4.00	8	14.5	14.5	34.5
	5.00	12	21.8	21.8	56.4
	6.00	16	29.1	29.1	85.5
	7.00	8	14.5	14.5	100.0
	Total	55	100.0	100.0	

Summary of Steps

- Type the data into a data window.
- Label the variable in Variable View tab.
- Choose Descriptive Statistics in the Analyze menu at the top.
- Choose Frequencies from the Descriptive Statistics choices.
- In the Frequencies window, choose the variable(s) you are interested in by highlighting the variable(s) and using the arrow in the center of the window.
- Make sure the Display Frequency Tables box is checked.
- Click OK; your table will be shown in the Output window.

Graphs

A frequency distribution graph can also be created using the Frequencies function. If you click on the Charts option in the Frequencies window (see Figure 2.11), a new window will open with chart options. Choose the Histograms option and click Continue. Then when you click OK, both your Table and your Graph will appear in the output window. The graph will look like

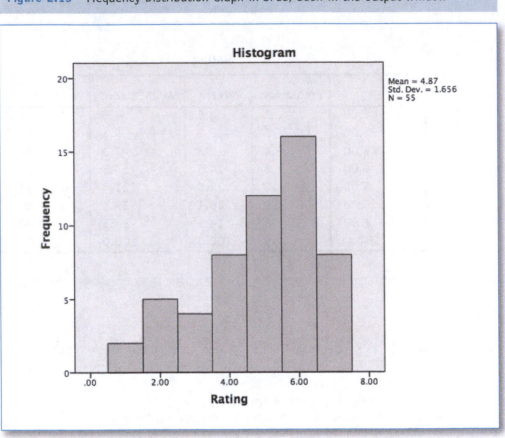

Figure 2.13. Notice that some additional descriptive statistics are also provided alongside the graph. We will discuss these statistics in the upcoming chapters.

SUMMARY OF FREQUENCY DISTRIBUTIONS

Frequency distribution tables and graphs are useful in helping summarize a distribution of scores. They allow us to see the shape of the distribution and clustering of scores in a particular part of the distribution. They can be created by hand, but Excel and SPSS can create them more easily for us, reducing the chance of error if our data have been entered into the program correctly. As we continue to discuss additional descriptive statistics in the next few chapters, you will see that these programs are quite useful in calculating our statistics.

Stop and Think

Create a frequency distribution graph in both Excel and SPSS for the following final exam scores according to letter grade groupings with 90%–100% = A, 80%–89% = B, 70%–79% = C, 60%–69% = D, below 60% = F:

83, 92, 100, 90, 74, 58, 84, 78, 85, 78, 72, 60, 67, 92, 92, 88, 88,
66, 60, 80, 88, 58, 92, 84, 84, 59, 80, 68, 78, 86, 76, 80, 64,
84, 68, 58, 72, 88, 89, 72, 88, 65, 80, 84, 68, 73, 92

2.6   Does this distribution appear to be symmetrical or skewed? If the shape is skewed, describe the skew (i.e., positive or negative skew).

2.7   About how many students received an *A* on the final? How many received a *D* or *F*?

CHAPTER SUMMARY

2.1   What is the difference between a population and a sample?

A population is the group of individuals a researcher wants to learn about. The sample is the portion of the population that participates in the research study. This is the group of individuals observed by the researcher.

2.2   What kinds of data are collected in psychological studies?

Many different kinds of data are collected in research studies. Survey responses and systematic/controlled responses on a task are two common examples of the types of data researchers collect. Four measurement scales define the type of measurements used in the data collected: nominal, ordinal, interval, and ratio scales.

2.3   What is a distribution and how does its shape affect our analysis of the data?

A distribution is a set of scores collected as data. The shape of a distribution can take many forms, but two common shapes are symmetrical and skewed shapes. These shapes will affect our choice of both descriptive and inferential statistics, as we will see in the coming chapters.

2.4   How can computer programs help us examine distributions of data?

Many computer programs can help us create or calculate the statistics we want to use to examine our data. Two common programs discussed in this text are Excel and SPSS. These programs can make the creation/calculation of statistics easier and reduce the chance for errors in calculation. However, we will still need to understand what is being calculated in each type of statistic in order to accurately interpret our results.

THINKING ABOUT RESEARCH

A summary of a research study in psychology is given below. As you read the summary, think about the following questions:

1. One of the primary differences between experimental and correlational studies is the comparing of different conditions in experiments and testing of relationships between measured variables in correlational studies. Which does this study appear to be: experimental or correlational?

2. Identify the dependent variables (DVs) measured in the study. For each DV, which scale of measurement do you think was used?

3. Consider the validity of this study. Does this study seem to have higher internal or external validity? Explain your answer.

4. If you were to construct a frequency distribution of the scores for inclusion of background in the participants' speech, what do you think you would include as the scores?

5. Examine the graph presented in Figure 2.14. In what way do these results address one of the researchers' hypotheses?

   Stephens, N. M., Townsend, S. S. M., Hamedani, M. G., Destin, M., & Manzo, V. (2015). A difference-education intervention equips first-generation college students to thrive in the face of stressful college situations. *Psychological Science, 26,* 1556–1566.

Purpose of the Study. In this study, the researchers tested the long-term positive effects of an intervention on first-generation college students. Two years before the study, some of these students had participated in a difference-education event where the advantages of differences in social backgrounds of students in adjusting to college were discussed. Other students had participated in a control event on adjusting to college that did not emphasize social differences. In the study, both groups of students were asked to complete some tasks that generated stress for them. One of these tasks was to give a speech, as if to incoming students, describing how their backgrounds influenced their adjustment to college. The researchers predicted that (1) students who participated in the difference-education event would mention their social backgrounds in the speech more than the students who attended the control event and (2) students who participated in the difference-education event would show greater physiological coping responses (as measured a balance in hormone levels) than the students who attended the control event.

Method of the Study. Participants in the study included 56 first-generation college students (i.e., neither parent attended college) at the end of their second year of college who had attended either the social differences event or the control event in their first few weeks of college. Participants were asked to present a five-minute speech that could help the researchers develop materials for incoming students. The participants had two minutes to prepare the speech and were asked to speak about how their

Figure 2.14   Hormone Results From the Stephens et al. (2015) Study

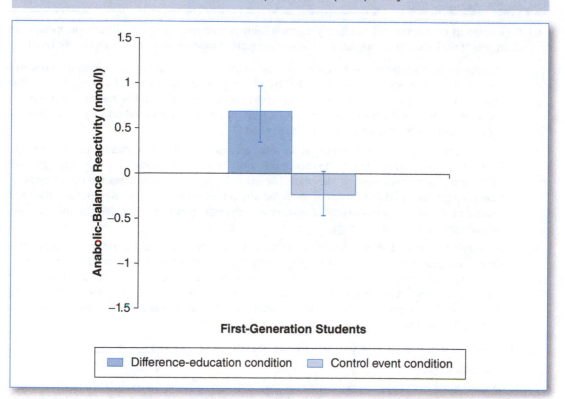

SOURCE: Stephens, Townsend, Hamedani, Destin, & Manzo (2015), A difference-education intervention equips first-generation college students to thrive in the face of stressful college situations. *Psychological Science, 26,* 1556–1566.

background had influenced their transition to college. Speeches were recorded to allow for content analysis. After completing the speech, the participants were asked to complete a word search puzzle and some math and verbal problems from the GRE test. Hormone levels were measured in saliva at several points during the study to examine stress reactions.

Results of the Study. Analyses showed that students who had attended the difference-education event mentioned the influence of their family and friends from home more often in their speech than the students who attended the control event. In addition, students who attended the difference-education event showed a better balance of reactive hormones during stress than did the students who attended the control event (see Figure 2.14).

Conclusions of the Study. The researchers concluded that both of their hypotheses were supported: Attending the difference-education event when they entered college increased the likelihood they would mention their backgrounds as influential in their adjustment to college and increased their hormone balance. These results suggest that a difference-education intervention has a long-term effect on adjustment to college for first-generation students.

TEST YOURSELF

1. For each study description below, identify the most likely population of interest, identify the operational definition of the behavior of interest, and identify the scale of measurement of the dependent variable.

   a. College student participants are asked to play a virtual ball-tossing game during which some participants are systematically excluded from the game a short time after they begin. The study tested the effects of social exclusion on the participants' mood. The researchers then ask the students to complete a mood survey in which they rated their mood on a 1 to 7 scale, with higher numbers indicating a more positive mood.

   b. To examine the effect of diet on cognitive abilities, researchers taught rats to navigate a maze to reach a food reward. Half of the rats in the study were fed a special diet high in sugar; the other group of rats was fed the standard rat chow. The rats were then tested in the maze after being fed the assigned diet for two weeks. The amount of time it took the rats to reach the food reward in the maze was measured. Rats on the high-sugar diet took longer to run the maze on average than the normal diet rats.

   c. A study was conducted to examine the effects of violence on social behaviors in young children. Five-year-olds were asked to play a superhero video game with mild violence (e.g., punching, throwing, etc.). Two researchers who were not aware of the purpose of the study observed the children's behavior at recess. The number of social behaviors seen (e.g., helping another child, playing cooperatively with another child, etc.) was recorded on a school day both before and after they played the video game.

2. Providing responses on a survey to make yourself look better is called _____.

   a. symmetrical bias

   b. skewed bias

   c. social desirability bias

   d. ratio bias

3. In a research study on navigation, participants were asked to judge the distance of a landmark in the environment from their current location. This dependent variable was measured on a(n) _____ measurement scale.

   a. nominal

   b. ordinal

   c. interval

   d. ratio

4. In a research study, you are asked to indicate your college major on a survey. This dependent variable was measured on a(n) _____ measurement scale.

   a. nominal

   b. ordinal

   c. interval

   d. ratio

5. You are conducting a study that uses IQ tests. On these tests, the participants score an average of 100. All other scores are evenly distributed above and below this average. What type of distribution is this?

    a. Skewed distribution

    b. Symmetrical distribution

    c. Hypothetical distribution

    d. Faulty distribution

6. _____ scales typically involve numerical scores, whereas _____ do not.

    a. Interval, ratio

    b. Ratio, nominal

    c. Nominal, ordinal

    d. Ordinal, nominal

7. Survey data are always accurate.

    a. True

    b. False

8. A frequency distribution graph can show you the shape of a distribution.

    a. True

    b. False

9. Systematic and controlled measures are more direct observations of behavior than the self-reports collected on surveys.

    a. True

    b. False

10. Of the following choices, which are good operational definitions of anxiety?

    a. Scores on an anxiety scale

    b. Score on an exam

    c. A general feeling of helplessness

    d. Both (a) and (c)

Chapter 3

Probability and Sampling

As you read the chapter, consider the following questions:

3.1 What role does probability play in selecting a sample and the results obtained from the sample?

3.2 What are the different ways we can sample from a population?

3.3 What is the distribution of sample means?

3.4 How accurately can we estimate the population values from a sample?

CONCEPTS OF PROBABILITY

What are the odds of winning the lottery (Photo 3.1)? What do they depend on? Most people do not have a very accurate sense of their chance of winning the lottery—if they did, there might be fewer people playing the lottery. How about something easier to imagine—what are the odds of tossing a coin and getting three heads in a row? You may be able to estimate the chance of three heads in a row more easily than the odds of winning the lottery (see Figure 3.1). Okay, how about something more practical—what is the chance it's going to rain today? Although this value is much harder to determine than the odds of winning the lottery or getting three heads in a row, it is typically much more valuable in our everyday lives.

Probability comes into play in many situations in our lives. Collecting data is no exception—we use concepts of probability whenever we collect data from a sample to learn about a population. We also use probability in testing hypotheses using the data we collect. Therefore, it is important to understand how probability works and how we can use that knowledge to conduct research on behavior and understand the statistics we use to analyze our data.

Sample Outcomes

Let's consider again our example of tossing a coin and getting three heads in a row (see Figure 3.1). Each time we toss the coin, we are, in fact, sampling the coin with possible

outcomes of heads or tails. Our result of three heads in a row is a combination of the outcomes of each of those tosses. If we consider all the possible outcomes of three coin tosses, we can determine the probability of getting three heads in a row. In Figure 3.1, all possible outcomes are shown. How many possible outcomes are there in total? If we consider all possible ways that three coin tosses could play out, we have eight possible outcomes. Only one of these eight outcomes contains three heads (the first one listed in Figure 3.1). We can calculate this proportion out of the total possible outcomes for our result of three heads in a row to determine its probability. From the figure, you can see that each outcome is 0.125 of all of the outcomes of three coin tosses, which is the same a 12.5% chance of getting this result. This is how we can determine the probability of any result in our data: by considering the total number of possible outcomes and calculating the proportion of those outcomes that correspond with our result of interest. You could calculate the odds of winning the lottery this same way, but there are many more possible outcomes of the number sequence for the lottery than of three coin tosses, so this would be a much more complicated process. But you can imagine that the proportion of those outcomes for just one number sequence (i.e., the winning number) would be very, very small.

This process using probability can also be used to consider the likelihood of obtaining a specific sample mean for a specific population. In fact, this is how we will test hypotheses for our research studies: by considering the likelihood of obtaining the sample mean we got for our sample, given what we know about the population we want to learn about.

| Figure 3.1 | Probability of Getting Three Heads in Three Coin Tosses |

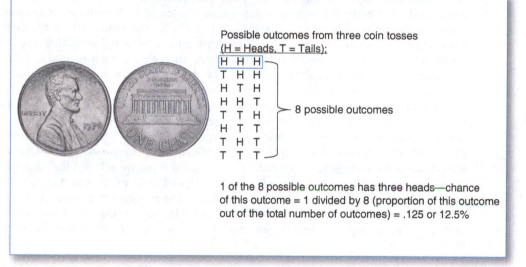

Possible outcomes from three coin tosses
(H = Heads, T = Tails):

H H H
T H H
H T H
H H T
T T H
H T T
T H T
T T T

8 possible outcomes

1 of the 8 possible outcomes has three heads—chance
of this outcome = 1 divided by 8 (proportion of this outcome
out of the total number of outcomes) = .125 or 12.5%

Sampling From a Population

When we collect data from a sample in a research study, we are doing something quite similar to tossing a coin. When we choose an individual from the population to observe their behavior, we are choosing them (and their data) from the population with a certain probability, just as we obtain the outcome of the coin toss. The behavior we observe from that individual is the outcome of the toss, but there are typically more than two possible outcomes. In fact, the outcomes are partly determined by the scale of measurement we use (you can review scales of measurement in Chapter 2). If we choose a nominal or ordinal scale, then the response choices on those scales will determine the possible measurement outcomes from an individual. A similar constraint occurs with some interval scales—rating scales typically restrict the responses to whole numbers between two values, making the possible outcomes one of those values. Ratio scale values are constrained by a range at the bottom end but can be broken down into smaller and smaller increments (e.g., hours, minutes, seconds, milliseconds, etc.), constraining the number of possible outcomes according to the unit of measure. But with ratio scales, there are often a large number of possible outcomes (e.g., any value from zero and up).

Probability will also help us determine how likely our sample data are for the population we want to learn about. In fact, probability is a very important part of the hypothesis testing procedure. We will consider how likely it is that we obtained our sample mean from all the possible sample means that could be obtained from samples from our population of interest. This is similar to how we determined the chance of obtaining all heads in three coin tosses using the probability for this outcome relative to all the possible outcomes for three coin tosses. These concepts will be further discussed later in this chapter in the section on the distribution of sample means.

Another way to think about sampling from a population is using a dartboard analogy. You can consider the entire dartboard the population of interest, with each location representing a score from someone in that population (see Figure 3.2). The individuals in the sample are the darts. We select an individual (and their score on our measure) by hitting a spot on the dartboard with a dart. A collection of darts is our sample. We are not measuring all the scores in the population. As we've already discussed in Chapter 2, for most populations, this would be too difficult, given their large size. Instead, we choose individuals from the population to measure their behavior (in our analogy, the darts on the board). Then we attempt to estimate the actual population's average score from the average score in our sample. If we assume that the actual population's average score is at the center of the dartboard, you can imagine from the placement of the darts on the board that with different samples, our accuracy in determining the population's average score may differ with each sample we select. This results in a different sample mean for each sample. This is the sampling error we discussed in Chapter 2: the difference between the average population score and the average score in our study's sample. Our goal is to reduce sampling error as much as possible. But how can we do that in our study? One way is to use a good sampling technique to choose the individuals from the population for our sample.

Figure 3.2   Dartboard Analogy for Sampling From a Population. The Board Represents the Whole Population of Scores; the Darts Represent Scores From Individuals in the Sample.

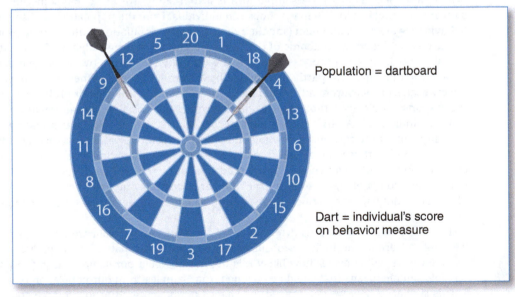

Population = dartboard

Dart = individual's score on behavior measure

©iStock/JPLDesigns, ©iStock/Fredex8

Stop and Think

Try sampling on your own using a pair of dice.

3.1   How many different outcomes are there for a roll of a pair of dice? If you add together the values on each die, what is the most common value outcome from a roll of the two dice? What is the probability of obtaining the most common value on a roll?

3.2   Roll the dice 20 times and record the total score on each roll. Was the most common outcome your most frequent outcome? Why do you think this result occurred?

3.3   Make a frequency distribution graph of your roll outcomes using any of the procedures discussed in Chapter 2. Does the distribution of scores appear to be symmetrical or skewed? Explain your answer.

SAMPLING TECHNIQUES

Sampling from a population is a two-step process: (1) select individuals from the population for the sample and (2) observe the behaviors you are interested in (i.e., collect the data) from the individuals in the sample. We will look here at the first step: the different ways we can select the individuals for our sample (see Figure 3.3). This can be an important decision in the research process, because the way a researcher samples from a population for their study can influence the amount of sampling error present in their data. The closer the sample data come to the data that exist in the whole population, the less sampling error you will have. However, making sure that the sample is chosen so that the population is represented well in the sample (e.g., has similar demographics) can be difficult with large samples. Thus, researchers often attempt to balance the desire to reduce sampling error and select a representative sample with the practical limits of selecting individuals from very large populations. This balance plays out in the choice between a probability sample and a convenience sample. With both types of sampling techniques, though, the goal is to select a representative sample from the population that will minimize any bias that will cause your sample data to differ from the data that the entire population would provide.

> **Probability sample:** a sample chosen such that individuals are chosen with a specific probability

Probability samples are chosen such that everyone in the population has a specific, predetermined chance of being selected at random for the sample. In other words, probability determines how likely any one individual is to be chosen for the sample. A convenience sample (also called a purposive sample), on the contrary, does not allow individuals to be chosen with a known probability from the population. Instead, individuals are chosen

> **Convenience/Purposive sample:** a sample chosen such that the probability of an individual being chosen cannot be determined

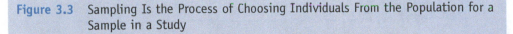

Figure 3.3   Sampling Is the Process of Choosing Individuals From the Population for a Sample in a Study

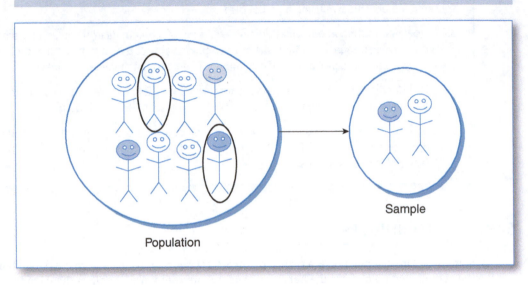

Sample

Population

from the population based on convenience of their availability for the sample. Thus, probability samples are more likely to be representative of the population, but convenience samples are much easier to select and are often used in cases where researchers want to learn about a very large population (e.g., all adults, all children of ages 5 and 6, etc.). This means that sampling error will typically be smaller with probability samples. However, for some behaviors of interest that may not differ much across individuals (e.g., some types of biological or cognitive behaviors), sampling error can be small with either type of sample, meaning that convenience samples can be used without too much concern that the sample is not representative. We will discuss these issues as we look at some different kinds of samples of each type. Table 3.1 provides an overview of the different sampling techniques discussed in the next sections.

Probability Samples

There are a few different kinds of probability samples that can be used to provide a good representation of the population. In all these samples, the researcher determines the probability of selecting an individual from the population for the sample. However, this can be done in a few different ways. In a simple random sample, all individuals in the population have an equal chance of being selected for the sample. Thus, the chance of any one person being selected is one divided by the total number of people in the sample (see Figure 3.4). This works the same way as the probability of getting three heads in a row tossing a coin, the example described earlier in this chapter. The probability of the outcome is the proportion of the

Simple random sample: sample chosen randomly from the population such that all individuals have an equal chance of being selected

Table 3.1 Overview of Sampling Techniques

Technique	Characteristics	Example	Advantages	Disadvantages
Simple random	Each member of the population has an equal probability of being selected using random sampling.	Students are chosen randomly from a list of all students at a university.	Reduces sampling error by choosing from all members of the population to best represent the population	Difficult to ensure that each member of a large population can be chosen in a sample
Cluster	Clusters of individuals are identified and then a subset of clusters is randomly chosen to sample from.	Doctors who work at hospitals are chosen for a sample by identifying all hospitals in different areas of the United States and then randomly choosing 10 hospitals in each area of the United States to sample from.	Makes it easier to choose members randomly from smaller clusters to better represent the population	Can ignore segments of the population that are not in the clusters chosen for the sample
Stratified random	Members of a population are selected such that the proportion of a group in the sample is equal to the proportion of that group in the population using random sampling.	Registered voters are randomly selected from lists of Democrats and Republicans to equal the proportion of registered Democrats and Republicans in the United States.	Reduces bias due to an identified characteristic of the population by equating proportions in the sample and the population for that characteristic to better represent the population	Similar to simple random sampling—can be difficult to ensure equal probability of being chosen from a large population
Convenience	Members of population are chosen based on convenience and on who volunteers.	Sample is chosen from students who volunteer to complete an extra credit assignment in their psychology course.	Easier to obtain than probability samples	May not represent the population properly due to selection bias because random sampling is not used

outcomes of interest divided by the total number of outcomes. In the case of a simple random sample, the outcome of interest is that a specific individual is selected and the total number of outcomes is the total number of individuals in the population. Simple random samples use the random selection process to create a representative sample, but this requires that a researcher first identify all the individuals in the population in order to randomly select some of them. This may be a difficult process for some very large populations. Opinion surveys, such as the one on global warming described at the beginning of Chapter 2, typically identify individuals in the population through their phone numbers and select them by randomly dialing a phone number to call the individuals selected. This allows everyone with a phone in the population an equal

Figure 3.4 Simple Random Sample

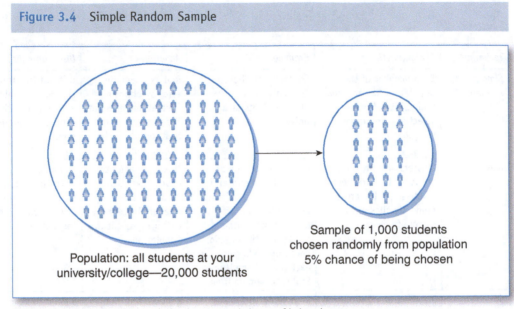

Population: all students at your
university/college—20,000 students

Sample of 1,000 students
chosen randomly from population
5% chance of being chosen

NOTE: Each individual in the population has an equal chance of being chosen.

Cluster sample: sample chosen randomly
from clusters identified in the population

---

chance of being selected. However, this process might still provide a sample that is biased in some way with more individuals from a certain geographic area, racial or ethnic group, gender, or income bracket. Thus, there are other types of probability samples that can be used to attempt to reduce these sources of bias in the sample.

Another type of probability sample is a cluster sample. Cluster samples help reduce bias due to oversampling from a group or cluster within the population. These clusters can exist based on geographic location, being a member of a club or an institution (such as a college or university), or being a student in a class. For example, imagine you wanted to survey the opinions of college students on the current cost of tuition at their university from a population of all students in your country. Depending on the selection process you choose, a simple random sample might accidentally overselect students at cheaper or more costly schools and bias your sample. A simple random sample might also be difficult to use because you would need to identify all students at all colleges and universities in order to use an unbiased process for selecting your sample. Instead, a cluster sample can allow you to select a sample with a better balance of the cost of tuition at different schools by first identifying a small cluster of schools within each price range you have predetermined and then randomly selecting students from each cluster to ensure that you get students from each tuition cost range in your sample (see Figure 3.5). This will reduce the bias in your sample from the different tuition costs across schools and give you a more representative sample from your population. This cluster sample also allows you to more easily identify the individuals you will sample from the population because you can more easily obtain a list of students from a small set of schools than from all the schools in your country.

Figure 3.5 Cluster Sample: Clusters Randomly Chosen From a Population

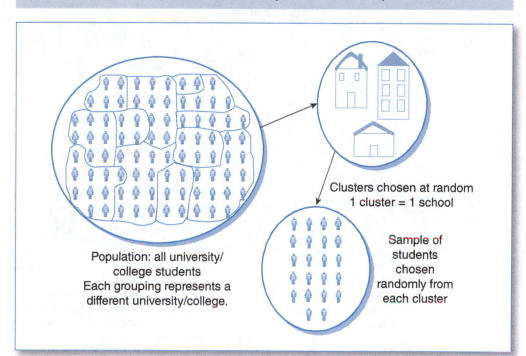

Population: all university/
college students
Each grouping represents a
different university/college.

Clusters chosen at random
1 cluster = 1 school

Sample of
students
chosen
randomly from
each cluster

Another method of reducing bias in a sample is to use a stratified random sample. Stratified random samples allow researchers to control the percentage of their sample that falls into a specific category. For example, if the population of interest is unequal in gender and men and women differ on the behavior of interest, a researcher might wish to match the percentage of men and women in their sample to the percentage of men and women in the population to make sure that gender is represented the same way as in the population. This type of stratified sample could be used to select students at your university or college for a study. Suppose you wanted to survey students at your university or college on their use of social media to connect with their friends. If you do not want differences across gender to influence the study results, you could use a stratified random sample to select the same percentage of men and women for your sample as exists in your student population (e.g., 40% men, 60% women). Figure 3.6 illustrates how the selection of this sample might work. Stratified random samples help reduce bias by keeping the representation of different population characteristics equal across the sample and the population. You just need to identify these characteristics ahead of time and select participants in a way that retains the breakdown of those characteristics in your sample. This will ensure that your sample represents the population on these characteristics (e.g., gender, location of residence, income level, etc.).

Stratified random sample: a sample chosen from the population such that the proportion of individuals with a particular characteristic is equivalent in the population and sample

Figure 3.6   Stratified Random Sample

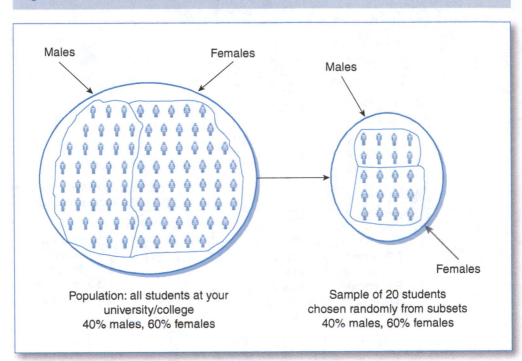

Population: all students at your
university/college
40% males, 60% females

Sample of 20 students
chosen randomly from subsets
40% males, 60% females

Convenience Samples

In many cases, the issue of identifying all the individuals in a large population to allow for random sampling is too difficult to overcome. For these situations, researchers often use convenience samples to select a sample from the population. Instead of randomly sampling individuals from the population, convenience samples rely on samples that are convenient to obtain, such as from a university subject pool or from users of the website, MechanicalTurk. Convenience samples can take the form of a volunteer sample, in which volunteers from a group of individuals make up the sample (see Figure 3.7), or of a quota sample, in which the sample is selected from available individuals with equivalent proportions to the population on some characteristic (similar to a stratified random sample, but without the random selection).

Convenience samples are much easier to obtain than probability samples but can sacrifice some internal validity of the study due to an increase in sampling error. The more biased the sample (i.e., different from the overall population), the more sampling error there is. The more sampling error there is, the harder it is for a researcher to test their hypothesis. This process will become clearer as we go deeper into our discussion of how hypothesis

Volunteer sample: a sample chosen from the population such that available individuals are chosen based on who volunteers to participate

Quota sample: a sample chosen from the population such that available individuals are chosen with equivalent proportions of individuals for a specific characteristic in the population and sample

Figure 3.7   Convenience Sample

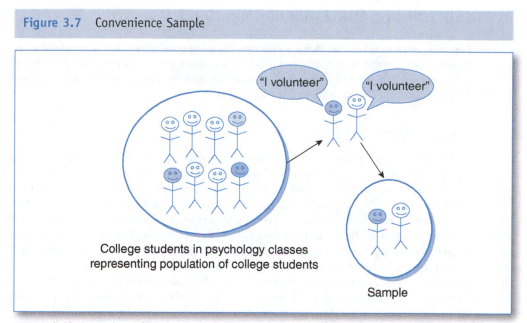

College students in psychology classes
representing population of college students

Sample

NOTE: Individuals are chosen from the population based on whom the researcher has easy access to and who volunteers from this group.

testing and inferential statistics work in later chapters. However, you should be aware that a study conducted with a convenience sample might reduce the researchers' ability to generalize their results to the population of interest due to the possibility of a nonrepresentative sample.

Stop and Think

3.4   For each study description below, identify both the population of interest and the sampling technique used:

a. University administrators want to determine the frequency of underage drinking at their school. They randomly select students from the registration records to send an anonymous survey to, with the percentages of men and women in the sample equal to the percentage of men and women at that university.

b. A researcher is interested in mimicking behaviors that affect cooperation in a task. Psychology students from the participant pool are recruited to answer questions in the presence of a confederate (a researcher pretending to be a participant) who mimics the participants' body postures during the questioning. Then the participants are asked to work with the confederate to complete a task that requires that they work together. The amount of time taken to complete the task is measured.

3.5   Imagine you are designing a study to test whether people with more money are happier than people with less money. Identify the population of interest for your study and describe how you would select a sample from this population.

DISTRIBUTION OF SAMPLE MEANS INTRODUCTION

The previous section of this chapter described how we conduct the first step of sampling—how to select our sample from the population. This section will focus more on the second step—collecting the data from the individuals in a sample and discovering how probability plays a role in connecting our sample data to our population.

Connecting Samples to Populations

Each time we select a sample from a population (regardless of the sampling technique we use), we are likely to have some amount of sampling error because we are not testing the entire population in our study. One goal we have in sampling is to minimize the sampling error as much as possible. One way to do that is to use a large sample. Think about how the sample size can influence sampling error. If we have the largest sample possible, we would be testing the entire population. In that case, there would be no sampling error. But the largest sample possible is typically too large to include in our study. Therefore, we reduce the size of the sample to make it more reasonable to conduct our study. But the more we reduce the sample size, the fewer people we have from the whole population to collect our data from, which will increase our chance of collecting data that differ from the entire population. Each time we reduce our sample size, we increase the risk that our sample data differ from the entire population because we are removing people that are in the population from our sample. If we decrease the sample size all the way down to one person, we would maximize our sampling error (not what we want) because we are basing our data on just one individual, who is most likely to differ from the mean of the population.

Look back at Figure 3.2. Testing just one individual from the population (a sample size of one) is like estimating the population mean from just one dart throw. But if we make more and more dart throws, we're more likely to average those dart throws to a value closer to the center of the dartboard, where the population average is. Thus, we want to choose a sample size that is big enough to reduce sampling error but small enough that we will be able to test that sample in our study. A large enough sample will reduce the error in the data and give us a better estimate of the actual population average. In other words, it will be a more valid (i.e., accurate) measure of the population data. When we estimate sampling error to calculate inferential statistics for our data, we will use the sample size in our measure of the validity of our estimate.

How much the scores differ from each other in the sample is also an important factor in connecting our sample to the population. The more variability there is in the sample data, the less reliable it is as an estimate of the population data. If you consider the dartboard again, you can imagine how the darts would look for two players, one with good aim and one with poor aim (see Figure 3.8). Both samples (sets of darts) are centered around the population average at the center of the dartboard, but the top sample is clustered closer to that average and the bottom sample is clustered farther from that average. The top sample (with good aim) has lower variability in where the darts landed, so we can trust that sample as more likely to be closer to the population data than the highly variable sample at the bottom. If the same people threw those darts again (or we collected new samples in the same way from the population), we are likely to get a similar set of data from the player in the top panel than from the player in the bottom panel, making the "good aim" samples more reliable in their measure of the population

Figure 3.8 Samples of Darts on a Dartboard, One With Low Variability (Panel A) and One With High Variability (Panel B)

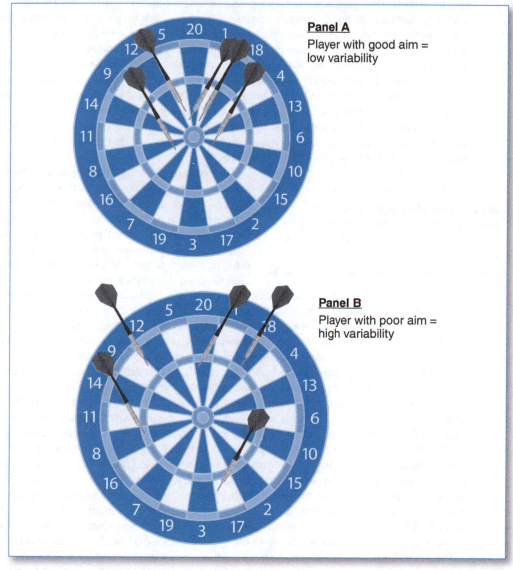

Panel A

Player with good aim = low variability

Panel B

Player with poor aim = high variability

©iStock/JPLDesigns, ©iStock/Fredex8

average that we want to learn about. When we estimate sampling error to calculate inferential statistics for our data, we will use the variability in our data in our measure of the reliability of our estimate of the population data. Thus, both the sample size and the sample variability will be used in our estimate of the sampling error in our data.

The Distribution of Sample Means

Something else that is important when we want to learn about a behavior of interest for a population is to conduct multiple studies to test different samples from the population. Why is this important? Well, just as the scores within a sample can differ from one another, the average scores we get from different samples can also differ from each other. This means that with just one sample, we can be very close to the population average or very far from the population average. That is why we do not assume that we have *proven* something about a behavior from a single study. A single study (with a single sample) provides support for knowledge about behavior but does not provide definitive knowledge about behavior. With just one sample, we might not have measured the population data accurately. Often, researchers will conduct multiple studies (sometimes published together in one article, sometimes in separate articles) to investigate a behavior so that they can be sure the results they have are both valid and reliable. They want to be able to make accurate conclusions from the data and that often means showing the same (or similar) results with different samples.

❦

Distribution of sample means: the distribution of all possible sample means for all possible samples of a particular size from a population

Let's consider how the mean scores from different samples might look relative to the actual population average. Figure 3.9 shows a distribution of possible sample means (i.e., the distribution of sample means) for samples pulled from a population with a mean score of 100 on some measure of interest. The mean score from each sample for a large number of samples selected from this population is plotted on the graph, with the mean scores from the samples shown on the x-axis and the number of samples showing that mean on the y-axis (you can review frequency distribution graphs in Chapter 2 if you do not remember how this works). You can see that most of the sample means cluster around the population mean of 100, but there are sample means as high as 115 and as low as 85 for the different samples. If we choose just one sample from this distribution (as we would by selecting one sample from the population and collecting data from this sample), the sample mean might be close to the population mean or it could be far from the population mean. It's more likely (than not) that we will get a sample mean near the population mean, but we could still by chance select a sample with a mean that is very different from the population mean. Thus, probability plays a role in how well we estimate the data for the population with the data from our sample.

The differences you see in the sample means in Figure 3.9 provide one explanation for the flip-flopping of research findings we sometimes see reported in the media. You may have seen reports stating that "red wine drinkers had better levels of HDL cholesterol" (Oaklander, 2015) along with statements in other reports saying, "It turns out that there's no information to suggest that red wine is better than any other form of alcohol for your heart" (Kane, 2012). Which one should you believe? The problem is that each of these reports may be based on just one study that contains a single sample from the population. One of these samples might be closer to the actual population mean for the measure than the other. But we do not know where in the distribution of sample means we are in these studies without the inferential statistics. In fact, inferential statistics rely on the distribution of sample means to provide some probability that our hypothesis about the population is supported by our data. We will discuss how this works further in Chapters 7 and 8 when we talk about hypothesis testing. For now, keep in mind that data from one sample will not tell us everything we need to know about the research questions we are asking with our study, because by chance, we may not have collected data from our sample that does a good job of representing the population data.

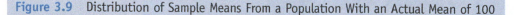

Figure 3.9 Distribution of Sample Means From a Population With an Actual Mean of 100

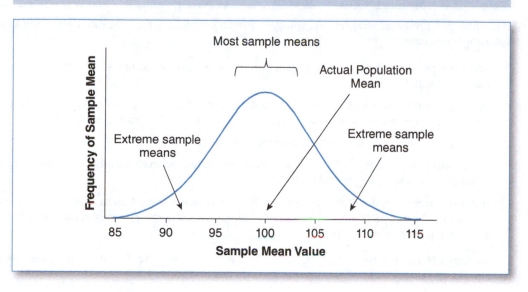

CHAPTER SUMMARY

3.1 What role does probability play in selecting a sample and the results obtained from the sample?

Probability plays an important role in both selecting a sample and how well the sample data estimate the population data and also in obtaining samples that provide the best representative sample. In probability samples, the chance of any individual being selected for the sample is known and can be determined ahead of time. The sample mean also has a particular probability of estimating the population mean that may not be known while collecting the sample.

3.2 What are the different ways we can sample from a population?

Probability samples can be created with a particular chance for each member of the population to be selected. Convenience samples do not select individuals based on chance but instead select a sample based on an individual's availability for the study.

3.3 What is the distribution of sample means?

The distribution of sample means is a frequency distribution containing the sample means from all possible samples selected from a population. It is a useful distribution (as we will see in later chapters) in determining the probability that a hypothesis is true.

3.4 How accurately can we estimate the population values from a sample?

The accuracy of our estimate of the population data depends on several factors, including the sample size and the variability of the scores in the sample. However, for any sample, with a set probability that we choose, we can calculate a range of values that the population means likely falls within.

THINKING ABOUT RESEARCH

A summary of a research study in psychology is given below. As you read the summary, think about the following questions:

1. What was the dependent variable (DV) in these experiments? What measurement scale was the DV measured with?

2. Why do you think the researchers conducted two experiments instead of one? In what way does a second experiment strengthen the conclusions they made in the first experiment?

3. What was the population of individuals they sampled from?

4. Which sampling technique do you think was most likely used in this study? What are some disadvantages of this sampling technique?

5. If the researchers had replicated Experiment 1 with the same method in a new experiment with a new sample, do you think they would have found the same mean scores in each condition as in Experiment 1? Why or why not?

Roediger, H. L., III, & Karpicke, J. D. (2006). Test-enhanced learning: Taking memory tests improves long-term retention. *Psychological Science, 17,* 249–255.

Purpose of the Study. These researchers were interested in the best study technique for remembering educationally relevant information for later testing. In two experiments, they compared two study techniques: rereading the passage to be remembered and recalling the passage to be remembered. They predicted that recalling the passage would result in better memory performance on a later test than rereading the passage.

Method of the Study. College students participated in the two experiments: 100 students in Experiment 1 and 180 students in Experiment 2. In Experiment 1, participants first read a passage about the sun or about sea otters for seven minutes. They were then asked to seven minutes either rereading the passage or recalling the information in the passage. After a two-minute break, they then were asked to read the other passage (whichever they had not read in the first portion of the study) for seven minutes. Then they were asked to either reread the passage or recall the passage (again, whichever task they had not done for the first passage). Thus, all participants received both types of study techniques. Finally, all participants were asked to recall the passages after five min, two days, or one week. Experiment 2 used the same procedure, except that participants only read one passage and reread the passage three times (SSSS), reread the passage twice and recalled it once (SSST), or recalled it three times before the final test (STTT). There was also no two-day final test group in Experiment 2.

Results of the Study. Results from Experiments 1 and 2 are shown in Figures 3.11 and 3.12. In Experiment 1, the only group that performed better on the final test after rereading instead of recalling was the five-minute delay group. For the two-day and one-week delay groups, recalling the passage resulted in better scores on the final test than rereading the passage. Experiment 2 showed similar results to Experiment 1. With a five-minute delay, the group that reread the passage three times scored the highest on the final test, but with a one-week delay, the group that recalled the passage three times scored the highest on the final test.

Conclusions of the Study. These results suggest that for delays longer than five minutes, the best study technique for remembering information is to recall that information. The more frequently the

Figure 3.11 Results From Experiment 1 of Roediger and Karpicke's (2006) Study

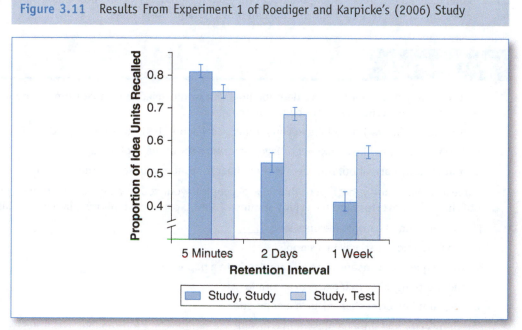

SOURCE: Roediger & Karpicke (2006). Test enhanced learning: Taking memory tests improves long-term retention. *Psychological Science, 17,* 249–255.

Figure 3.12 Results From Experiment 2 of Roediger and Karpicke's (2006) Study

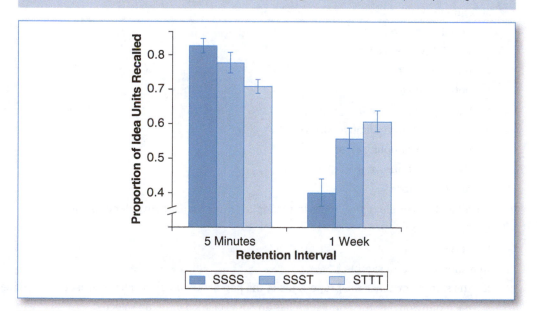

SOURCE: Roediger & Karpicke (2006). Test enhanced learning: Taking memory tests improves long-term retention. *Psychological Science, 17,* 249–255.

participants recalled the information, the better they did on a test one week after initial study. These results also suggest that recalling information can protect against forgetting.

TEST YOURSELF

1. For each study description below, describe how you would select a sample from the population using one of the techniques described in this chapter:

    a. You want to know how adults in your country feel about the issue of immigration.

    b. You want to know how anxious college seniors are about their job prospects.

    c. You want to learn about how people remember information based on their mood.

2. You read about a survey that reports that 86% of people in your country are happy with their present job. The margin of error reported is plus or minus 2.5%. Explain what this margin of error tells you.

3. The distribution of sample means shows _____.

    a. the frequency of scores in a sample

    b. the frequency of means from all samples from a population

    c. the sampling error that exists in a sample

    d. the sampling error that exists in a population

4. Sampling error will only be present in convenience samples, not in probability samples.

    a. True

    b. False

5. Our measure of sampling error is affected by _____.

    a. sample size

    b. population size

    c. variability in the data

    d. both (a) and (b)

    e. both (a) and (c)

6. Probability plays a role in _____.

    a. selecting a representative sample

    b. estimating sampling error

    c. the mean of our sample

    d. all of the above

7. A probability sample typically has less sampling error than a convenience sample.

    a. True

    b. False

8. In a simple random sample, _____.

    a. the sample matches the proportions in the population on some characteristic (e.g., gender)

    b. each individual in the population has an equal chance of being selected

    c. individuals are selected at random from preexisting groups in the population

Chapter 4

Central Tendency

As you read the chapter, consider the following questions:

4.1 What can we learn about a distribution from measures of central tendency?

4.2 How are the mean, median, and mode used as measures of central tendency?

4.3 How do the mean, median, and mode compare for different distributions?

4.4 Which measure of central tendency should I use when describing a distribution?

CENTRAL TENDENCY IN DISTRIBUTIONS

Imagine that you are a member of the student government board at your college or university. The board is trying to decide whether they should lobby the school's administration for new choices at the food court in your student center (Photo 4.1). Knowing that you have learned some things about research and statistics, the board has tasked you with the job of determining how much the students at your school like the current food court choices. To determine this, you are conducting a research study to survey the students at your school. You have selected a sample of 150 students who eat at the food court and asked them to complete your survey to rate how much they like the current food court choices on a scale of 1 to 7. Now you have to figure out how to turn all these survey responses into a score that you can report to the student board. How can you do this?

In this chapter, we will begin to consider some descriptive statistics that will help you summarize your set of data to better understand your scores (see Figure 4.1 for an overview of using descriptive statistics). The three main types of descriptive statistics are central tendency, variability, and visual representations (i.e., tables and graphs) of the data. Each of these types of descriptive statistics will help us better understand the distributions of data we are looking at. Figure 4.1 shows you how you can decide which measures are best for reporting your data set. This chapter focuses on measures of central tendency, which are

---

Central tendency: representation of a typical score in a distribution

---

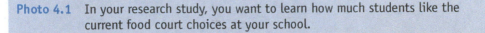

Photo 4.1   In your research study, you want to learn how much students like the current food court choices at your school.

©iStock/PeopleImages

❦

Median: the middle score in a distribution, such that half of the scores are above and half are below that value

Mode: the most common score in a distribution

measures of a *typical* score in a distribution. These measures summarize data as single values to help researchers better understand what the data look like overall. You can think of central tendency as a value that represents the entire distribution that will fall somewhere in the middle of most distributions.

There are three main measures of central tendency: mean, median, and mode. We have already discussed the mean as the average score in a distribution, and it is the measure you are probably most familiar with. It is also the measure most often reported for distributions of data. However, the median and mode are useful when distributions are skewed or bimodal in shape (i.e., there are two common scores that may not fall in the middle of the distribution) or are in some way affected by extreme scores that will influence the mean to a greater degree than the median and mode. Thus, it is important to understand all these measures and in which situations you should use each one (Photo 4.2). For each of these measures, we will consider how to calculate it by hand, using Excel, and using SPSS. This model will be followed for most of the statistics we will discuss in the rest of the chapters of the text.

MEAN

As I mentioned, the mean is the most commonly reported measure of central tendency and it is a good one to start with because it is fairly intuitive as the average score. You have likely

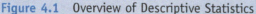

Figure 4.1 Overview of Descriptive Statistics

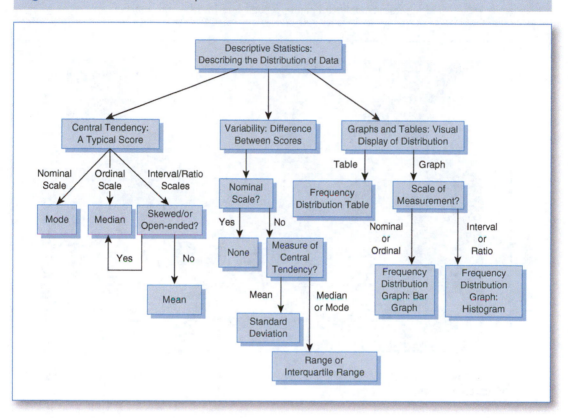

calculated a mean before for a set of scores, but we will cover how to calculate the mean by hand while introducing the symbols we will use for later calculations of other statistics to help you become familiar with these symbols. We will then look at how to calculate the mean using Excel and SPSS software.

Calculating the Mean by Hand

Because the mean is simply the average of the scores, to calculate the mean, you simply need to add up all the scores and then divide by the number of scores. Let's represent this calculation for our sample of data as a simple formula:

$$\text{Mean} = \bar{X} = \frac{\Sigma X}{n}$$

This is a commonly used formula for calculating a sample mean. The $\bar{X}$ is a symbol that stands for the sample mean. The Σ symbol (called a *sigma*) indicates that you should add up whatever comes after this symbol. In this case, you are adding the Xs, which means you should add up all the scores in the set of data. The n stands for the number of scores in the sample. Let's

Photo 4.2   It is important to understand how the measures of central tendency compare and how to calculate each one in different ways.

©iStock/eternalcreative

look at how we would do this to calculate the mean of our food court survey scores. To calculate the mean for those data, we add up all the 1 to 7 ratings that the students in the sample provided on the survey. Then we divide this number by the number of scores in the sample ($n = 150$). That would give us an average rating on the 1 to 7 that we could report back to the student board.

The formula presented above is the one used to calculate a sample mean. In some cases, we will be looking at a known population mean. This is possible for some kinds of data. For example, many standardized tests have a known population mean, because all the students in the population (e.g., all students taking the test that year) take the test and their scores can be used to calculate the mean for the population of students who took the test. This is how you know where your score on a test such at the SAT or ACT falls relative to all other students who took the test: It can be compared with the population mean for the test. The population mean is calculated in the same way—you add up all the scores in the population and divide by the number of scores—but we use different symbols to represent population values in our statistics. Using different symbols (and therefore, different formulas) helps us keep track of which type of mean we are looking at: one for the sample or one from the whole population. The formula for the population mean is:

$$\text{Population mean} = \mu = \frac{\Sigma X}{N}$$

In this formula, the population mean is represented by a μ symbol and the total number of scores by a N, but the calculation is the same in that you are adding up (i.e., Σ) the scores (the Xs) and then dividing by the number of scores. You will encounter this formula for the population mean again in later chapters.

One way to think of the mean of a distribution is as the balancing point of the distribution. The mean score is the tipping point in the center. Figure 4.2 illustrates how this works. Suppose you have a balancing scale where blocks represent each score in the sample. The size of the block represents the frequency of a score. For the top scale in Figure 4.2, the blocks add up to three on each side, because there are three standard blocks on the right and one standard block and one double block (two of that score in the data set) on the left. The mean is in the middle of the distribution for this set of scores. This is what will happen when we have a symmetrical distribution—the mean will be the middle score.

However, what would happen if we added another standard block to the left side (see the bottom two scales in Figure 4.2)? The added block/score would tip the scale to the left requiring an adjustment to the mean. Now, the mean is no longer at the center of the scale—it is

Figure 4.2   The Mean Is the Balancing Point of a Scale—for Symmetrical Distributions, It Will Be in the Middle, but for Skewed Distributions, It Will Be Adjusted Toward the High or Low Scores

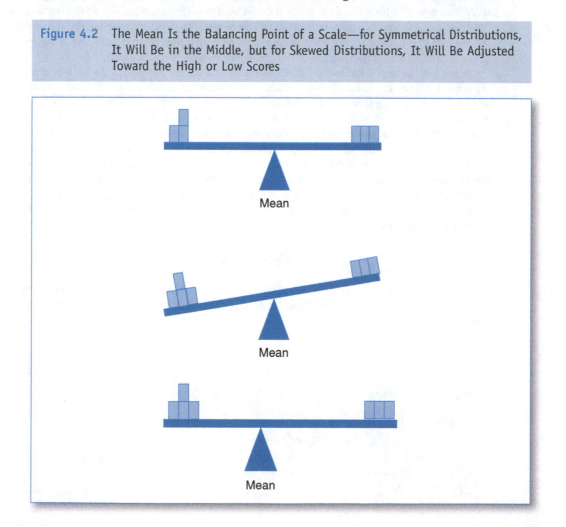

—— ✂ ——

Outlier: an extreme high or low score in a distribution

pushed toward the left to account for the new score. This is like adding a low score to our data set—it will adjust the mean to a lower value. This is also what happens when an extreme score, called an outlier, is present in our data set. Outliers bias the mean toward the high or low end of the scale, depending on whether they are extremely high or extremely low. These distributions are then positively skewed (toward high scores) or negatively skewed (toward low scores). The smaller our sample size and the more extreme the outlier score is, the more these extreme scores will affect the mean in a skewed distribution. We will consider the effects of extreme scores in skewed distributions again as we discuss the median of a distribution.

Calculating the Mean With Excel

Excel is a useful software program for calculating measures of central tendency, especially for large data sets in which hand calculation could be time-consuming and lead to errors. As with the creation of frequency distribution tables and charts, the first step in using Excel to calculate the mean is to enter the scores into the data window. It is important to double check the entering of the scores, as this step is where errors could occur in the calculations.

To see how to use Excel to calculate the mean of a distribution, let's go back to our example from Chapter 2: ratings of how much people want to watch a new TV show on a 1 to 7 scale. The ratings for this distribution were: 1, 1, 2, 2, 2, 2, 2, 3, 3, 3, 3, 4, 4, 4, 4, 4, 4, 4, 4, 5, 5, 5, 5, 5, 5, 5, 5, 5, 5, 5, 5, 6, 6, 6, 6, 6, 6, 6, 6, 6, 6, 6, 6, 6, 6, 6, 7, 7, 7, 7, 7, 7, 7, 7. We can enter these ratings into the Excel data window, as in Figure 2.7. To calculate the mean of these scores, we will use the AVERAGE function in Excel. In a blank cell in the window, type =AVERAGE(. You can then click on the first cell for the scores and drag your mouse down the last cell for the scores. This should automatically fill in the first and last cells you want to include in the calculation with a colon between them and an end). You could also simply type in the cells if you wish, then close the function with an end). Your finished formula should look like this:

=AVERAGE(A2:A56)

When you hit enter, the mean of the scores (4.87) should appear in the cell containing your formula. This is the mean rating of the food court choices at your school from your sample on the 7-point scale.

Summary of Steps

- Enter the data into a column in the data window.
- In an empty cell, type **=AVERAGE(**.
- Highlight the scores you want to include or type in the cell letter/numbers.
- Close with an end parenthesis and hit enter.

Calculating the Mean With SPSS

SPSS can also be used for calculating measures of central tendency. Using our same ratings scores from above, we can begin with these data entered into our data window as in Figure 2.9. To calculate the mean for these scores, we will use the Descriptives function under Descriptive Statistics in the Analyze menu at the top. A Descriptives window will appear as shown in Figure 4.3. Click on your ratings variable in the left box and then the arrow to move it into the Variable(s) box on the right. Then choose Options and ensure that the Mean box is checked. Then click Continue and then OK to open an Output window. The Output box containing your mean will appear in the Output window as shown in Figure 4.4. This box also contains the number of scores in the data set, the highest (maximum) and lowest (minimum) scores in the data set, and the standard deviation—a measure of variability that we will discuss in Chapter 5.

Summary of Steps

- Enter the data into a column in the data window.
- Label the data in the Variable View tab.
- Find Descriptive Statistics in the Analyze menu at the top.
- Choose the Descriptives function in the Descriptive Statistics options.
- Move the data column into the Variable box by highlighting it and clicking on the arrow (Figure 4.3).
- Under Options, make sure the Mean box is clicked.
- Click Continue and OK; your mean will appear in the Output window (Figure 4.4).

Figure 4.3   The Descriptives Window in SPSS

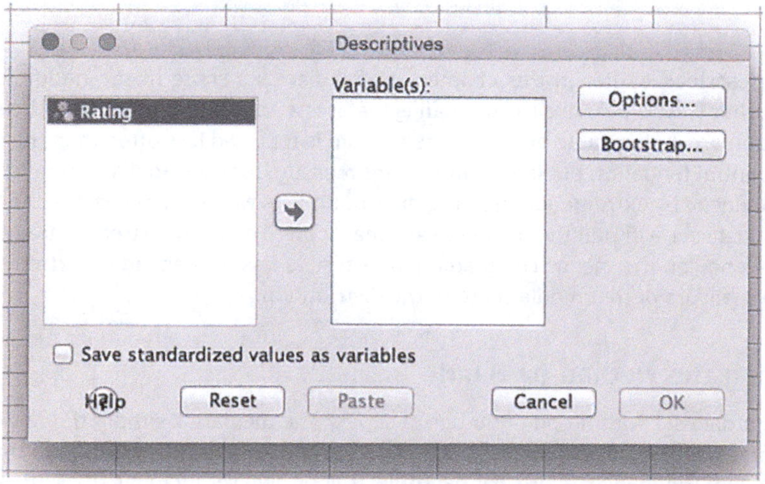

Figure 4.4   The Output Box in SPSS Showing the Calculated Mean for the Ratings Data

→ **Descriptives**

[DataSet1] /Stats Text/CH2_freq_dist.sav

Descriptive Statistics

	N	Minimum	Maximum	Mean	Std. Deviation
Rating	55	1.00	7.00	4.8727	1.65613
Valid N (listwise)	55				

Stop and Think

4.1   For which type of distribution (e.g., symmetrical, skewed) will the mean be a score in the middle of the distribution?

4.2   For each set of scores below, calculate the mean by hand or with Excel or SPSS. How does the mean compare for these two sets of scores? Why do you think the mean is different for the two distributions?

- 50, 58, 63, 55, 52, 60, 54, 53, 61, 50
- 50, 58, 63, 55, 52, 60, 54, 53, 61, 96

MEDIAN

As described earlier in this chapter, the median is a score in the middle of the distribution. Another way to describe the median is that it is a value at which 50% of the scores in the distribution are at that value or lower. The median is reported less often than the mean as a measure of central tendency, but it is an important measure for skewed distributions, where the mean is influenced by extreme scores in the distribution. As we saw in the last section, an extreme score in a data set will pull the mean toward that score. The more extreme the score, the stronger its influence on the mean. The median, however, is less influenced by extreme scores, because it is a measure of the middle score in the distribution.

Calculating the Median by Hand

For a data set with an odd number of scores, the median is simply the middle score when the scores are listed from lowest to highest. Counting into the distribution to the middle score will give you the median score. For example, if your data set includes the scores 50, 52, 53, 54, 55,

58, 60, 61, 63, the median score is 55, because it is the 5th score out of nine total scores. Compare this with the mean of 56.22 and you will see that the mean is pulled more toward the larger scores in the top end of the distribution, as the scores cover a range of eight values on the scale, whereas the lower scores only cover a range of five values on the scale. For a set of data with an even number of scores, the median is the average of the two middle scores. For this data set—50, 50, 52, 53, 54, 55, 58, 60, 61, 63—the median is the average of 54 and 55, or 54.5. Notice that the scores are ordered from lowest to highest. That is important in finding the middle score. If they are not ordered in this way, you will not easily find the median.

Calculating the Median Using Excel

Excel can also be used to calculate the median of a distribution. Let's look again at our ratings for desire to watch the new TV show that we considered for Excel and SPSS in the previous section. To calculate the median for these scores, we will use the MEDIAN function. It works in a similar way to the AVERAGE function we used to calculate the mean for these data. To calculate the median, in an empty cell type =MEDIAN(. Then drag the cursor over the data in the column or type in the cells (A1:A56) with a colon separating the cell markers. End the function with a) if it is not automatically filled in. Your completed function statement should look like this:

=MEDIAN(A1:A56)

Then hit enter. The median of 5 (on our 7-point rating scale) will appear in the cell.

> **Summary of Steps**
>
> - Enter the data into a column in the data window.
> - In an empty cell, type **=MEDIAN(**.
> - Highlight the scores you want to include or type in the cell letter/numbers.
> - Close with an end parenthesis and hit enter.

Calculating the Median Using SPSS

Calculating the median using SPSS is similar to the method used to calculate the mean with this software. However, to calculate the median, we must use the Frequencies function under Descriptive Statistics in the Analyze menu, as the median is not listed as a choice in the Options for the Statistics function. Figure 2.11 in Chapter 2 shows the Frequencies window we used to create the frequency distribution table for these data. Once again, you will need to click on the ratings in the left window and then the arrow to move it into the Variable(s) window. Then click on the Statistics button to choose the Median box. Figure 4.5 shows this box with the Median chosen. You may also notice that there is a box for the Mean and one for the Mode (we will discuss the mode in the next section). Thus, using the Frequencies function, you can calculate any of the measures of central tendency discussed in this chapter using SPSS. Once you click Continue in the Statistics window, it will take you back to the Frequencies window, where you can then choose OK to calculate the Median. The output will contain the median in the top box with the frequency distribution table we created in Chapter 2 for these data (see Figure 4.6). The same median given in Excel (a score of 5) is shown in the figure.

Summary of Steps

- Enter the data into a column in the data window.
- Label the data in the Variable View tab.
- Find Descriptive Statistics in the Analyze menu at the top.
- Choose the Frequencies function in the Descriptive Statistics options.
- Move the data column into the Variable box by highlighting it and clicking on the arrow.
- Under Statistics, click the Median box (Figure 4.5).
- Click Continue and OK; your median will appear in the Output window (Figure 4.6).

Figure 4.5   The Frequencies: Statistics Window in SPSS

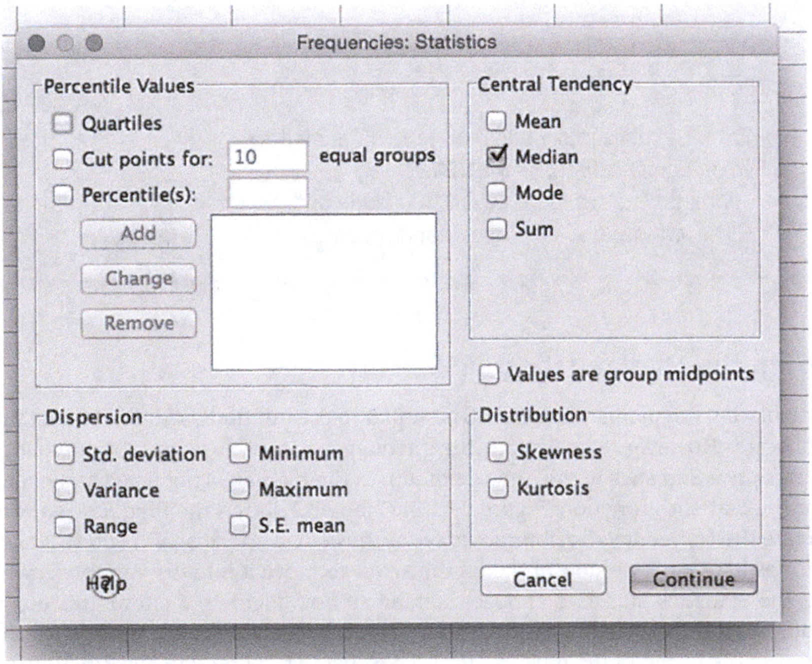

Figure 4.6   The Output in SPSS Showing the Calculated Median for the Ratings Data

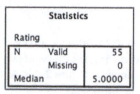

➡ **Frequencies**

[DataSet1] /Stats Text/CH2_freq_dist.sav

Statistics		
Rating		
N	Valid	55
	Missing	0
Median		5.0000

MODE

Our third measure of central tendency is the mode. The mode is simply the most common score in the distribution. In fact, we can easily determine the mode from a frequency distribution table of a data set by looking at the score that occurs most often in the frequency column. The mode is useful to report when it differs from the mean and median. For example, if you have a data set that contains many scores at the top and bottom of the scale (e.g., a data set with 1 to 5 ratings with many *1*s and *5*s), the mode will give you a better measure of a typical score than the mean or median, which will fall between these values. Another use of the mode is for data from a nominal scale (look back at Figure 4.1 and the choice for the nominal measurement scale), where there are no numbers that can be used to calculate the mean or median. For example, if you have asked students to report their major on a demographic scale, you would likely report the frequencies of different majors listed with the mode as the most common major for the people in your sample. Although the mode is the simplest of the measures of central tendency to calculate, we will still discuss how to obtain the mode using the different methods we have covered for the other measures. Excel and SPSS can be especially useful for obtaining the mode when your data set is large so that you do not need to count the scores in your distribution.

Calculating the Mode by Hand

As described in the previous paragraph, the mode is the most common score in a distribution. Thus, if your data set contains the values: 1, 2, 3, 5, 5, 1, 5, 5, 3, 5, 5, 2, 5, 4, 3, 5, 5, 2, 1, 5, the mode is fairly easy to determine. There are ten scores of value 5 in this data set, which is easily seen as the most frequent score in the data set. There are far fewer than ten of each of the other scores on the 1 to 5 rating scale here (the next most frequent are the scores of 1, 2, and 3, all with three scores at each of these values).

Calculating the Mode Using Excel

The MODE function in Excel will determine the mode of the distribution for you. This is useful with large data sets, such as our television show ratings distribution. To calculate the mode for this data set, type =MODE(into an empty cell in the data window. Then highlight the ratings or type in the A1:A56 range for these data and end with a). Thus, your function to calculating the mode will look like this:

=MODE(A2:A56)

When you hit enter, the mode of 6 will be shown, as this is the most frequent rating used by the individuals in this data set. You can compare this value with the most frequent score shown in the frequency distribution table shown in Figure 2.7 in Chapter 2; there were 16 scores of 6 in this data set, which is about 29% of the scores.

Summary of Steps

- Enter the data into a column in the data window.
- In an empty cell, type **=MODE(**.
- Highlight the scores you want to include or type in the cell letter/numbers.
- Close with an end parenthesis and hit enter.

Calculating the Mode Using SPSS

As described in the previous section on calculating the median, to calculate the mode in SPSS, we will also use the Frequencies function under the Descriptive Statistics menu in the Analyze menu. In the Frequencies: Statistics window shown in Figure 4.5, check the box for Mode. The output box will then include the mode as shown in Figure 4.7. I have included the mean, median, and mode in the output of Figure 4.7 so that you can see how they compare for this distribution. The mean is the lowest value (4.87), followed by the median (5.00), and then the mode (6.00). This ordering shows how the mean is pulled toward the lower scores in this distribution, which are far less frequent than the higher scores of 4, 5, 6, and 7. Thus, the median and mode do a better job than the mean of capturing the typical scores in this distribution because the mean is more greatly influenced by the fewer low scores in the distribution. We will discuss how these values compare a bit more in the next section.

Summary of Steps

- Enter the data into a column in the data window.
- Label the data in the Variable View tab.
- Find Descriptive Statistics in the Analyze menu at the top.
- Choose the Frequencies function in the Descriptive Statistics options.

- Move the data column into the Variable box by highlighting it and clicking on the arrow.
- Under Statistics, click the Mode box (Figure 4.5).
- Click Continue and OK; your mode will appear in the Output window (Figure 4.7).

Figure 4.7   The Output in SPSS Showing the Calculated Mean, Median, and Mode for the Ratings Data

➡ **Frequencies**

[DataSet1] /Stats Text/CH2_freq_dist.sav

Statistics

Rating

N	Valid	55
	Missing	0
Mean		4.8727
Median		5.0000
Mode		6.00

Stop and Think

4.3   For each data set below, calculate the median and mode. (Hint: Don't forget to put the scores in order from lowest to highest before you calculate the median.) How do these values compare for each data set—which one seems to be more representative of the scores in the data set? Explain your answer.

- 1 to 5 Ratings on Satisfaction with Courses in One's Chosen Major: 4, 2, 4, 3, 4, 4, 5, 4, 1, 4, 3, 3, 4, 5, 4, 5, 1
- Accuracy on a Categorization Task (Percentage Correct): 78, 87, 90, 91, 75, 76, 88, 87, 77, 75, 92, 95, 78, 92, 87

4.4   In your own words, explain why the median is a better measure of central tendency than the mean for distributions that contain extreme scores.

WHICH MEASURE OF CENTRAL TENDENCY SHOULD I USE?

Throughout this chapter, we have discussed some differences across the mean, median, and mode as measures of central tendency of a distribution. But how do we choose which measure of central tendency to report for a specific distribution? The answer will depend on different aspects of the distribution, some of which we have already discussed.

Shape of the Distribution

As I already mentioned, the mean is the most commonly reported measure of central tendency. It is also the measure that people are most familiar with. It provides a good representative value that uses all the scores in the distribution in its calculation. In addition, as you will see in our discussion of variability in Chapter 5, the mean is involved in the calculation of the standard deviation and variance measures of variability. It will also provide a value near the middle of the distribution when the distribution is symmetrical (or close to it) in shape. However, the disadvantage of the mean as a measure of central tendency is that by using all the scores in the distribution for its calculation, it is influenced more by extreme scores than the median or mode.

Skewed distributions with extreme scores at the high or low end of the distribution are often better represented by the median. The median will give you the middle score (or average of the two middle scores) in a distribution, resulting in a fairly representative value for distributions that are skewed. Consider the distribution shown in Figure 4.8. This frequency distribution

Figure 4.8   Distribution of Exam Scores Comparing Mean and Median

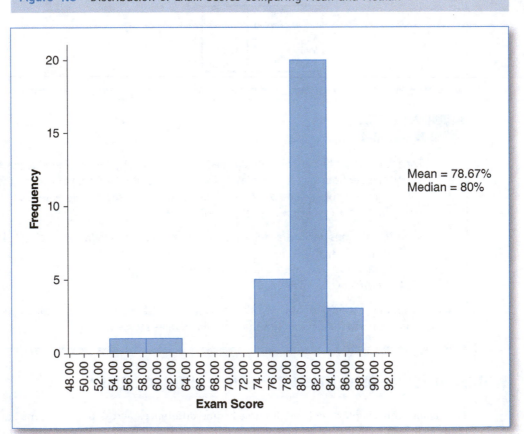

graph shows the scores from a final exam. What do you notice about the scores? Most of the scores are clustered between the values of 80% and 82%, but there are two very low scores down at 56% and 59%, likely from students who did not study well for the exam. If we calculate the mean for these scores, we get a value of 78.67%, which is lower than where most of the scores are. However, the median is 80%, which is a more representative value for these exam scores, because it is closer to where most of the scores actually are. The mean is being pulled toward the two extremely low scores in the distribution.

Another common distribution that is positively skewed is reaction times in a task. This type of distribution was described in Chapter 2—there are some scores in this distribution that are much higher than where the rest of the scores are, giving the distribution a tail on the high end of the scale. These much higher reaction times pull the mean toward the high end, making the mean response time seem much higher than it would be without these outliers. The median provides a better measure for this type of distribution because it gives us the middle score for reaction times that better represents the speed on the task for an individual.

Type of Data

Another good use of the median as a measure of central tendency is for ordinal data. When data are measured using an ordinal scale, the mean does not provide a good representation of the scores, because the values on the scale are categories rather than values with equal distance between them. On such scales, there isn't a clear balance point for the scale (which is what the mean provides), but there is often a middle value. Thus, the median can provide a representative score on the scale. Consider a data set that contains responses regarding class rank: freshman, sophomore, junior, or senior. These are ordinal data because they can be ordered from lowest to highest, but how would you calculate a mean for these data? It would be difficult to do—our formula to add up the scores and divide by the total number of scores would not work. However, there would be a middle value on this scale if all the responses were ordered from highest to lowest. For example, if our sample contained 10 freshmen, 25 sophomores, eight juniors, and two seniors, the median would be the sophomore level, because half of the people in the sample are at the sophomore level or lower. However, reporting a mode for these data would also be appropriate, as the mode would indicate the class rank for the majority of students in the sample.

Another example where the median would be a better measure of central tendency because the mean is difficult to calculate is an open-ended response category in our data set. For example, suppose you were responding to a survey that asked how many hours a week you study for your statistics course. The responses you are given are 2 hours, 3 hours, 4 hours, 5 hours, and 6 or more hours. The last category of 6 or more hours is open-ended; it does not define the highest value in the category. Thus, our mean formula would not work here either. But our median calculation for the middle score (e.g., 5 hours) would work because we could find the score where 50% of the responses are at that score or lower.

Nominal scales, where categories cannot even be ordered from highest to lowest, create another problem for central tendency calculations. For nominal data, we cannot apply our formula for calculating the mean (there aren't any numbered scores to add up) and we cannot find the middle scores because we cannot order our scores from highest to lowest. Thus, for nominal data, the mode is our only option for reporting central tendency. For example, if your food court survey asked students to list their favorite food court option, the most commonly listed response would be the only measure of central tendency you could report.

Another case where the mode is a good measure to use is when the response scale only has two possible values. This type of distribution is a *bimodal* distribution. You may be able to order the values in terms of which one is higher (e.g., 0 or 1), but calculating the mean and median will not provide a good representation of this distribution. Both the mean and median will come out somewhere between the two values, which does not represent the scores very well. Thus, the mode is a better measure (e.g., most values were at a 1) than the mean or median.

Figure 4.9 presents a flow chart to help you decide which measure of central tendency to use in a specific situation. If you look back at Figure 4.1, you will see that it is an enlargement of the central tendency portion of that flowchart. To use the flowchart in Figure 4.9, answer each question as you go through the chart and follow the links for your answers to determine which measure is best for your distribution of data.

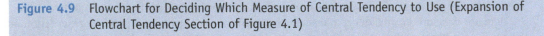

Figure 4.9 Flowchart for Deciding Which Measure of Central Tendency to Use (Expansion of Central Tendency Section of Figure 4.1)

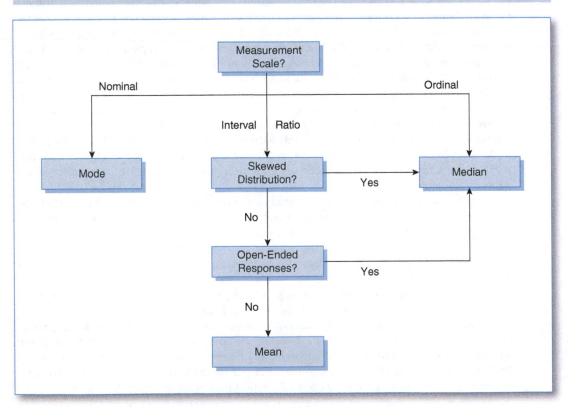

4.5 For each measure described below, indicate which measure of central tendency you would choose and why. Figure 4.9 may help you decide by answering the questions in the chart that you are able to determine from the description of the measure.

- speed to complete a Sudoku puzzle, measured in seconds
- responses indicating which time of day (morning or afternoon) someone prefers to study for an exam
- rating on a 1 to 5 scale indicating how pleasant someone found a social experience he or she is asked to participate in during a study

4.6 You have designed a survey for a research study you are conducting as part of a course. You are interested in how many children people are interested in having in the future to see if this is related to how many siblings one grew up with. For each item, you ask people to respond with one of the following choices: 0 children/siblings, 1 child/sibling, 2 children/siblings, 3 children/siblings, and 4 or more children/siblings. Explain why the median or mode would be a better measure of central tendency for these data than the mean.

Calculation Summary

<u>Mean</u>: Add up the scores in the data set and divide by the total number of scores.

<u>Median</u>: For data sets with an odd number of scores, put the scores in order from lowest to highest and then find the middle score. For data sets with an even number of scores, put the scores in order from lowest to highest and then average the two middle scores.

<u>Mode</u>: Count the frequencies (i.e., how often each score appears) of the scores—the mode is the score(s) with the highest frequency in the data set.

CHAPTER SUMMARY

4.1 What can we learn about a distribution from measures of central tendency?

Central tendency measures provide a description of the typical score in a distribution.

4.2 How are the mean, median, and mode used as measures of central tendency?

The mean is the average, the median is the middle score, and the mode is the most common score. Each of these measures gives us summary value for the scores in a distribution, but in different ways.

4.3 How do the mean, median, and mode compare for different distributions?

Because the mean is the average of the scores, it will be more influenced by extreme scores than the other measures. Thus, for a skewed distribution, the mean will be closest to the extreme scores, followed by the median and the mode, which will be closer to the middle of the distribution. For symmetrical distributions, however, the three measures will provide the same value that is in the middle of the distribution.

4.4 Which measure of central tendency should I use when describing a distribution?

The mean is the most commonly used measure of central tendency; thus, it is often reported for comparison with other data sets. However, with skewed distributions, it is best to provide the median in addition to or instead of the mean. The mode is useful when describing data sets with many scores at the high and low ends of the scale or when reporting data on a nominal scale.

THINKING ABOUT RESEARCH

A summary of a research study in psychology is given below. As you read the summary, think about the following questions:

1. Was this study an experiment or a correlational study?

2. Identify the dependent variables. Describe how these variables were measured in the study.

3. For the mental speed and friends' ratings variables, what scale of measurement do you think was used?

4. For mental speed, which measure of central tendency do you think would be best to report? Why?

5. For social skills and charisma ratings, which measure of central tendency do you think would be best to report? Why?

> von Hippel, W., Ronay, R., Baker, E., Kjelsaas, K., & Murphy, S. C. (2016). Quick thinkers are smooth talkers: Mental speed facilitates charisma. *Psychological Science, 27,* 119–122.

Purpose of the Study. In this study, the researchers explored possible cognitive abilities that are related to social skills and one's charisma. Specifically, they examined whether one's mental speed could predict social skills related to social comfort, conflict, and interpreting others' feelings. They also tested whether one's mental speed could predict how charismatic, funny, and quick-witted one was.

Method of the Study. Two studies were conducted. Each study included 200 participants that included groups of friends. In Study 1, participants completed an intelligence test (control measure), a five-factor personality survey (control measure), and 30 general knowledge questions (e.g., "Name a precious gem."). General knowledge questions provided the measure of mental speed, as participants were asked to answer the questions aloud as quickly as possible and their time to answer was measured on each question. Participants also completed three-item surveys for both social skills and charisma, rating each person in their friend group on a 1 to 7 scale. In Study 2, the participants completed the same general knowledge questions, social skills and charisma ratings, and personality survey as in Study 1. In addition, participants in Study 2 also completed speeded left–right dot detection and pattern-matching tasks as measures of mental speed and surveys for self-control, self-efficacy (i.e., self-esteem), narcissism, social values, and self-confidence as control measures.

Results of the Study. Analyses of the data tested whether participants' mental speed (time to complete cognitive tasks) predicted their friends' ratings of their social skills and charisma with control measure (e.g., intelligence, personality, etc.) removed. For both studies, faster mental speed predicted higher charisma ratings from friends but did not predict social skills ratings from friends.

Conclusions of the Study. This study supported the researchers' prediction that mental speed is predictive of charisma but did not support their hypothesis that mental speed is predictive of social skills. They suggest that future research should examine how mental speed is involved in charismatic social functioning.

TEST YOURSELF

1. For each of the data sets below, calculate the mean, median, and mode.
   a. 1, 3, 4, 4, 4, 5, 7
   b. 1, 1, 1, 1, 1, 2, 2, 7
   c. 1, 2, 3, 2, 2, 5, 7, 7, 7, 2, 7, 2, 7, 7, 2

2. For each data set in the question above, which measure of central tendency would you choose as the most representative of the data set? Explain why you chose that measure.

3. How do the mean, median, and mode compare for symmetrical and skewed distributions (i.e., which is highest and lowest in value)?

4. Which measure of central tendency is most commonly reported?
   a. Mean
   b. Median
   c. Mode
   d. None of the above

5. Which measure of central tendency is most affected by extreme scores?
   a. Mean
   b. Median
   c. Mode
   d. None of the above

6. Which measure of central tendency is most appropriate to report for skewed distributions?
   a. Mean
   b. Median
   c. Mode
   d. None of the above

7. Which measure of central tendency is most appropriate for nominal data?

   a. Mean

   b. Median

   c. Mode

   d. None of the above

8. Which measure of central tendency will provide the middle score in a symmetrical distribution?

   a. Mean

   b. Median

   c. Mode

   d. All of the above

9. The purpose of reporting a measure of central tendency is to indicate the spread of the scores in the distribution.

   a. True

   b. False

10. The mean of a distribution is a descriptive statistic.

    a. True

    b. False

11. In a positively skewed distribution, the mean will be lower than the median.

    a. True

    b. False

12. The mean is the best measure of central tendency to report when there are open-ended responses on the measurement scale.

    a. True

    b. False

Chapter 5

Variability

As you read the chapter, consider the following questions:

5.1 What can we learn about a distribution from measures of variability?

5.2 How are the range and standard deviation used as measures of variability?

5.3 How do the range and standard deviation compare for different distributions?

5.4 Why does the standard deviation calculation differ for samples and populations?

VARIABILITY IN DISTRIBUTIONS

Let's once again consider our example from the beginning of Chapter 4: You are conducting a survey for the student government board at your school to examine the students' satisfaction with the current food court options at the student union. You've conducted your survey asking people to rate how much they like the current food court choices on a scale of 1 to 7. You have survey responses from 150 students. Let's assume you've calculated the mean rating from the sample and found that mean rating is 5. You are getting ready to report back to the student board that, overall, people are fairly satisfied with the food choices. However, you start to wonder just how often the ratings were close to a rating of 5. In other words, did most students choose a rating close to 5 (i.e., between 4 and 6) or did the ratings cover the entire scale, with some students very dissatisfied (i.e., ratings of 1 or 2) and more students fairly satisfied (i.e., with ratings of 5, 6 and 7)? One way to answer this question is to consider the variability of the scores in the sample.

Variability is simply a description of how different the scores are from one another in the distribution. If something varies, it means that it differs from other things in some way (see Photo 5.1) such that high variability in a distribution means that the scores are widely spread out across the scale. Low variability means the opposite—that the scores are very similar and clustered around a middle value. If the students in our sample used the entire 1 to 7 scale (i.e., there were scores in the data set for all values from 1 to 7), then the variability in our sample data would be higher than if the ratings all had values of 4, 5 and 6 on the scale. However, both of these situations could yield a mean of 5, as in our survey data.

Figure 5.1 shows the difference between these two possible distributions. In the high variability graph, the scores are spread out across the whole 1 to 7 rating scale, but in the low variability graph, the scores are clustered between the values of 4 to 6. In both cases, the mean is 5, showing that variability can be high or low, regardless of what the mean of a distribution is. Although extreme scores affect the mean, the extreme scores in the high variability graph are at both the high and low end of the scale, so this data set gives you the same mean of 5 that you get from the distribution in the low variability graph, where there are no extreme scores.

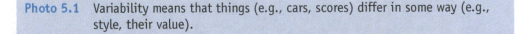

Photo 5.1   Variability means that things (e.g., cars, scores) differ in some way (e.g., style, their value).

©iStock/Kolopach

Figure 5.1 High and Low Variability Distributions of Satisfaction Ratings

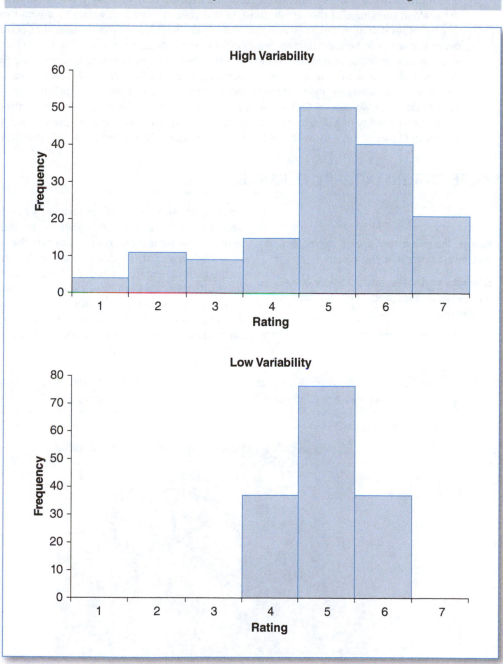

You may also notice in these graphs that the high variability distribution has a negative skew (i.e., more extreme scores in the low end of the distribution, showing a tail at the low end of the scale in the shape of the distribution). In this case, the median would be a better measure of central tendency to report (see Figure 4.9 for an overview of the measures of central tendency), as it would better reflect the majority of the ratings that are on the high end of the scale. However, the median in this distribution is also 5 because the two middle scores are 5s in the distribution. This is the same as the median in the low variability graph (also 5), so the variability is not affecting the mean or the median for these distributions (although in some skewed distributions, as we saw in Chapter 4, the median will be a different value from the mean). Thus, the variability of a distribution can be seen in frequency distribution graphs such as those shown in Figure 5.1. Let's now consider ways to measure the variability of a distribution.

RANGE AND INTERQUARTILE RANGE

Range: the difference between the highest and lowest scores in a distribution

Discrete variables: measures with whole number scores that cannot be subdivided into smaller units

One way to easily measure the variability in a distribution is with the range. The range is the difference between the highest and lowest scores in the distribution. The range for the distribution in the high variability graph in Figure 5.1 is 6 (7 − 1 = 6), but the range for the distribution in the low variability graph is only 2 (6 − 4 = 2). The range is a useful measure of variability for discrete variables, where the values are whole numbers that cannot be further divided (e.g., the number of children one has; see Photo 5.2).

Photo 5.2 Discrete variables are measures that cannot be divided into smaller units, such as how many children one has.

©iStock/andresr

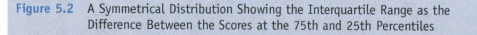

Figure 5.2   A Symmetrical Distribution Showing the Interquartile Range as the Difference Between the Scores at the 75th and 25th Percentiles

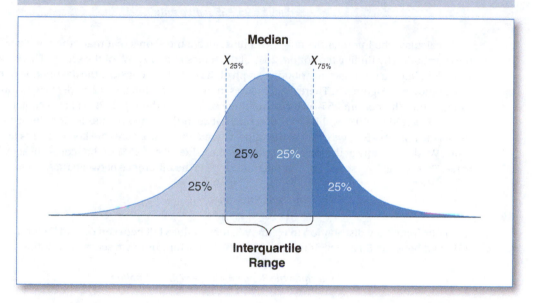

One problem with the range as a measure of variability is that it is greatly affected by extreme scores. Even one extreme score on the high or low end of the scale will expand the range to that value. The interquartile range can be used instead for distributions with extreme scores. The interquartile range is the range of the scores in the middle part of the distribution. In other words, it is the range of values in the middle of the distribution between which 50% of the scores lie. The interquartile range is determined from the difference between the values where 25% of the scores are above and below the median. Thus, it is the range of the middle 50% of the scores. Figure 5.2 shows the interquartile range for a hypothetical symmetrical distribution. I will describe this calculation further below.

Interquartile range: the difference between the scores that mark the middle 50% of a distribution

Calculating the Range and Interquartile Range by Hand

The processes described above for determining the range and interquartile range can be expressed as formulas for hand calculations. For the range, it is the difference between the highest and lowest scores, which can be represented by the following formula:

$$Range = X_{maximum} - X_{minimum}$$

The difference between the maximum and minimum scores (Xs) is the range. Suppose we had a distribution containing exam scores from a class where the highest score is 95 points (out of 100 points) and the lowest score is 55 points (see Figure 5.3). In this distribution, our range is

$$Range = 95 - 55 = 40 \, points$$

To calculate the interquartile range, you must locate the scores that mark the middle 50% of the distribution by finding the bottom 25% of the scores and top 25% of the scores. This is easiest when looking at a frequency distribution graph of the data. Let's consider the distribution of exam scores shown in Figure 5.3. There are 12 scores in this distribution (i.e., 12 students who took the exam). Thus, the bottom 25% will contain three scores and the top 25% will also contain three scores. The middle 50% will be the six scores between these two points. To find the score that marks the bottom 25%, we count to the value where 25% of the scores are below. This is our $X_{25\%}$ score. We do the same at the top end to count to the value where 25% of the scores are above that value. This is our $X_{75\%}$ score. The interquartile range is the difference between these values:

$$Interquartile \, Range = X_{75\%} - X_{25\%}$$

In our frequency distribution in Figure 5.3, these values fall between 65 and 70 for the lower 25% and between 80 and 85 for the upper 25%. Thus, for our exam score distribution we have

$$Interquartile \, Range = 82.5 - 67.5 = 15 \, points$$

Figure 5.3   A Distribution of Exam Scores—$X_{25\%}$ = 67.5 Points and $X_{75\%}$ = 82.5 Points

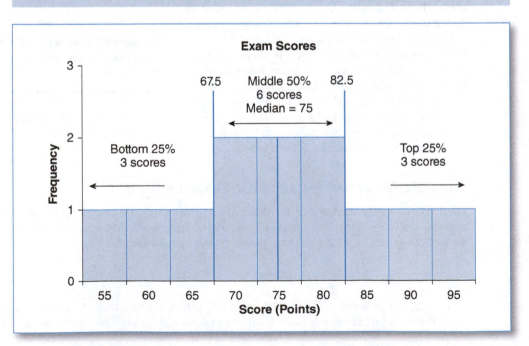

This means that 50% of the exam scores cover a range of 15 points. Notice that the median (the score that marks the 50% point in the distribution) falls in the middle of the interquartile range at a score of 75 points.

Calculating the Range and Interquartile Range Using Excel

Now, let's consider how our software tools can help us calculate the range and interquartile range for a distribution. To determine the range in Excel, we can use the MIN and MAX functions to find the lowest and highest scores in a distribution. Figure 5.4 shows a screenshot of the Excel data window containing the scores in our exam scores distribution. We can use the following formula to calculate the range:

=MAX(A1:A12)–MIN(A1:A12)

Figure 5.4 Data Window for Excel Showing the Example Exam Scores Data

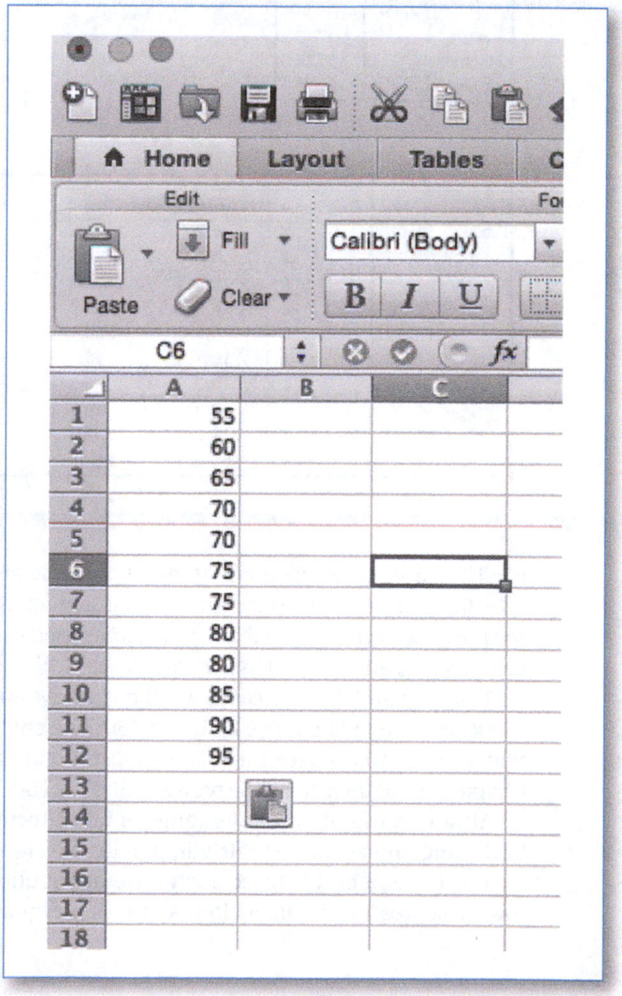

This formula will calculate our range of 40 points if we type it into an empty cell in our data window. These scores can also easily be placed in order from the lowest to highest scores using the SORT function in the DATA menu at the top of the window. You could also use the Sort & Filter function in the Home tab. Using this SORT (or Sort & Filter) function, we can see that the lowest score is 55 and the highest score is 95. The range is the difference between these scores (i.e., range = 95 − 55 = 40 points).

The interquartile range calculation in Excel is a bit more complex. We need to determine the point at which 25% of the scores are below that value and the point at which 75% of the scores are below that value. The easiest way to do this is to create the frequency distribution graph shown in Figure 5.3 and then count the scores to get to these points in the distribution. The procedure for creating frequency distribution graphs in Excel is discussed in Chapter 2.

Figure 5.5 Output Window From SPSS Showing the Range, Minimum and Maximum Scores, and the Frequency Distribution Table Containing the 25th and 75th Percentiles for the Interquartile Range Calculation

➡ **Frequencies**

[DataSet0] /Users/dmmcbri/Desktop/5_4.sav

Statistics

Exam Scores

N	Valid	12
	Missing	0
Range		40.00
Minimum		55.00
Maximum		95.00

Exam Scores

		Frequency	Percent	Valid Percent	Cumulative Percent
Valid	55.00	1	8.3	8.3	8.3
	60.00	1	8.3	8.3	16.7
	65.00	1	8.3	8.3	25.0
	70.00	2	16.7	16.7	41.7
	75.00	2	16.7	16.7	58.3
	80.00	2	16.7	16.7	75.0
	85.00	1	8.3	8.3	83.3
	90.00	1	8.3	8.3	91.7
	95.00	1	8.3	8.3	100.0
	Total	12	100.0	100.0	

Calculating the Range and Interquartile Using SPSS

In SPSS, the range and interquartile range can be calculated using the following menu structure: Analyze => Descriptive Statistics => Frequencies that we used to calculate the median and mode in Chapter 4. The range is one of the Statistics options in the Frequencies window (see Figure 4.5). We can also choose the options for the Minimum and Maximum scores to use the same procedure as in Excel when we sorted the scores from lowest to highest.

Figure 5.5 shows the Output window from SPSS for the range and minimum and maximum scores of our exam score distribution. The frequency distribution table will also be provided in the output window for SPSS. In that table, you can see where the 25th and 75th percentiles fall. Using the table, we see that the 25th percentile is listed at a score

65. The 75th percentile is also given in the table at a score of 80. Thus, the interquartile range is 80 − 65 = 15. Note that this provides the same interquartile range value as our hand calculation in the previous section, even though the scores used to calculate it are slightly different. Either method gives us the same interquartile range.

The 25th and 75th percentiles will not always automatically fall at a score in the frequency distribution table in SPSS. The 25th and 75th percentiles may fall between scores in a distribution. If that occurs, you can create a frequency distribution graph using SPSS (the procedure is described in Chapter 2) and then count the scores to find the 25th and 75th percentiles as we did using Figure 5.3.

Although the interquartile range is not affected by extreme scores as much as the range, both range measures are fairly imprecise measures of variability, because the range measures do not include all of the scores in the distribution. The range only includes the highest and lowest scores in its calculation, and the interquartile range only includes the scores that fall at the 25% point (i.e., the 25th percentile) and the 75% point (i.e., the 75th percentile) in the distribution. However, the standard deviation includes all the scores in the distribution in its calculation. Thus, the standard deviation is a better measure of variability than the range. We will discuss the standard deviation in the next section.

Stop and Think

5.1 Consider the two possible sets of data below, both containing 1 to 7 ratings on satisfaction with the food court options at your school. Just by looking at the data themselves, which distribution do you think has higher variability? Why do you think that?

- 5, 4, 5, 3, 4, 5, 4, 4, 3, 2, 4, 5, 4, 4, 5, 3, 5, 4, 5
- 2, 4, 1, 3, 5, 6, 7, 3, 4, 5, 6, 4, 5, 6, 1, 2, 7, 3, 4

5.2 Calculate the range for each of these distributions. Was your guess in 5.1 about which has higher variability correct?

STANDARD DEVIATION

As described in the previous section, the range and interquartile range are fairly imprecise measures of variability in a distribution because they only include a subset of the scores in their calculations. A more precise measure of variability that includes all the scores in the distribution is the standard deviation. Simply put, you can think of the standard deviation as representing the average distance between the scores and the mean (see Figure 5.6). However, you will shortly see that we can't simply calculate the average distance because in all distributions that value would be zero. The positive and negative differences between the scores and the mean will balance out and give us a value of zero, because the mean is the balance point of the distribution. Instead, we will have to remove the direction of the differences from the mean by squaring the differences between the scores and the mean in our calculation and taking the average of the sum of those squared differences. This will give us a measure known as the variance, which in itself is a measure of variability that we will use in some calculations of inferential statistics in later chapters. But when we take the square root of the variance to reverse our squaring transformation, we get the standard deviation.

Standard deviation: a measure representing the average difference between the scores and the mean of a distribution

Variance: the squared standard deviation of a distribution

The standard deviation is a common measure of variability for a set of scores, and you will see it reported more often in research than the range or interquartile range. It is used as an

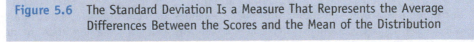

Figure 5.6   The Standard Deviation Is a Measure That Represents the Average Differences Between the Scores and the Mean of the Distribution

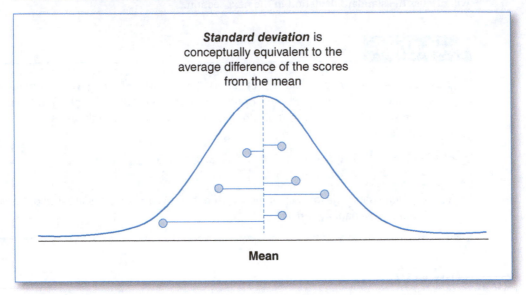

estimate of sampling error (the difference between our sample statistics and those that we would get from the whole population) for our data when we calculate inferential statistics comparing the means for two samples/conditions or comparing a sample mean with a known population mean. We will discuss these inferential statistics, known as *t* tests, in Chapters 9, 10, and 11. But for now, let's just consider how we calculate the standard deviation and what it tells us about our distribution of scores.

Calculating the Standard Deviation by Hand

Because the standard deviation is the average difference between the scores and the mean, we'll need to know the mean of our distribution before we begin our calculation. Let's use our example exam score distribution from the previous section. The mean of the distribution is 75 points. You can verify this by calculating the mean for the scores shown in Figure 5.4. We'll use this mean to calculate the differences between the scores and the mean. That's our first step: Calculate the difference between each score and the mean. For our exam scores, we'll have

$$55 - 75 = -20$$

$$60 - 75 = -15$$

$$65 - 75 = -10$$

$$70 - 75 = -5$$

$$70 - 75 = -5$$

$$75 - 75 = 0$$

$$75 - 75 = 0$$

$$80 - 75 = 5$$

$$80 - 75 = 5$$

$$85 - 75 = 10$$

$$90 - 75 = 15$$

$$95 - 75 = 20$$

These are our differences, also called *deviations*, from the mean. Because we are calculating the average, the next step would be to add the deviations up and divide by the number of scores. But what happens when you add these up? You get zero. This will happen every time we add up the deviations because the mean is the balancing point of the distribution. The deviations for scores above the mean balance with the deviations for scores below the mean to give us zero when we add them up. To get around this issue, we need to add an important part to Step 1: Square the deviations. If we transform the deviations by squaring them, we take away the sign (positive or negative) and we will no longer get zero when we add them up.

<u>Step 1</u>: Calculate the difference between each score and the mean and square the differences.

If we square the deviations we just calculated, we get

$$(-20)^2 = 400$$

$$(-15)^2 = 225$$

$$(-10)^2 = 100$$

$$(-5)^2 = 25$$

$$(-5)^2 = 25$$

$$(0)^2 = 0$$

$$(0)^2 = 0$$

$$(5)^2 = 25$$

$$(5)^2 = 25$$

$$(10)^2 = 100$$

$$(15)^2 = 225$$

$$(20)^2 = 400$$

Now, we're ready for Step 2: adding up the squared deviations. Adding up these squared deviations will give us a value known as the *sum of squared deviations* or just *sum of squares*. This is often abbreviated with *SS* in equations (as you will see shortly).

Step 2: Add up the squared deviations to get the sum of squares (*SS*).

Adding these up will give us

$$400 + 225 + 100 + 25 + 25 + 0 + 0 + 25 + 25 + 100 + 225 + 400 = 1550$$

Now, for Step 3, we need to take the average of the squared deviations by dividing by the total number of scores. Our distribution includes all the students in the class, so it is actually a population distribution instead of a sample (you will see why this is important in the next section). For Step 3, then, we can just divide by the total number of scores to get the average sum of squares. This is a value known as the *variance* and it is indicated by the symbol σ^2 for a population and s^2 for a sample.

Step 3: Divide by *N* for a population to get the variance (σ^2).

For Step 3, we will divide the sum of squares (1550) by the number of scores (12) to get the following:

$$Population\ variance = \frac{1550}{12} = 129.17$$

This is the variance of our exam score distribution. We just have one step left now: to reverse the squaring transformation we did earlier for the deviations. Step 4 is to take the square root of the variance:

Step 4: Take the square root of the variance.

$$Population\ standard\ deviation = \sqrt{129.16667} = 11.37$$

This means that the average difference between the exam scores and the mean of 75 is 11.37 points. This value represents the average difference between the scores and the mean in the distribution. A large standard deviation indicates that the scores in the distribution are spread out across the measurement scale. A small standard deviation indicates that the score in the distribution are packed close to the mean.

Now, let's put all these steps together into formulas for the population standard deviation:

$$\sigma = \sqrt{\frac{\Sigma\left(X - \bar{X}\right)^2}{N}} \ \ or \ \ \sigma = \sqrt{\frac{SS}{N}}$$

Thus, our formulas contain our four steps:

Step 1: Calculate the difference between each score and the mean and then square the difference: $\left(X - \bar{X}\right)^2$

Step 2: Add up the squared deviations to get the sum of squares: $(SS) - \Sigma(X - \bar{X})^2$

Step 3: Divide by N for a population to get the variance: $(\sigma^2) - \dfrac{\Sigma(X-\bar{X})^2}{N}$

Step 4: Find the square root of the variance: $\sqrt{\dfrac{\Sigma(X-\bar{X})^2}{N}}$ or $\sqrt{\dfrac{SS}{N}}$

Populations Versus Samples

The calculation described above is how we would determine the standard deviation for a population distribution of scores (i.e., if the entire population was tested). However, with a sample, we have fewer scores contributing to our variability. This means that the variability of a sample will be lower than the variability of the population the sample represents. Because of this difference, we have to correct for the fact that there are fewer scores in our sample using a term known as the degrees of freedom. The degrees of freedom are the number of scores that can vary in a set of scores with a known mean (which we have already calculated to determine the deviations). Once we know the mean, all the scores, except one, can be any value (i.e., they are "free to vary"). Thus, degrees of freedom for a sample are one less than the number of scores. We'll use this term ($n - 1$) instead of N to calculate the average of the sum of squares for a sample.

> ❧
>
> **Degrees of freedom:** the number of scores that can vary in the calculation of a statistic

To show you how this calculation is different, let's assume that instead of 12 people in the course, there are 100, but we only have a sample of exam scores from 12 of the students in the class. Now our data set in Figure 5.4 is from a sample instead of from the population. This will change our calculation of the standard deviation a bit as described above to include the degrees of freedom. Our formula for the sample standard deviation is

$$s = \sqrt{\frac{\Sigma(X-\bar{X})^2}{n-1}} \text{ or } s = \sqrt{\frac{SS}{n-1}}$$

Using this formula, the standard deviation for the sample of exam scores is

$$s = \sqrt{\frac{1550}{12-1}} = \sqrt{140.91} = 11.87$$

The standard deviation for this sample is higher for a sample than for all 12 scores as a population, because this sample is meant to represent the population of scores from all 100 students, which should be higher because it contains more scores. Whenever we calculate the standard deviation, we will need to first determine if we are working with a sample or a population so that we can choose the correct formula.

Calculating the Standard Deviation Using Excel

In many cases, we will have a lot of scores in our distribution, making it time-consuming to calculate the standard deviation by hand. Excel can be used to calculate the standard deviation of a set of scores for us to save time and reduce the chance of a calculation error. However, it is still important that you understand the hand calculations of the statistics you are using so that you know what the values mean when they are calculated with a software program.

Excel contains formulas for the standard deviation. The STDEV function is for samples and will use the formula with the degrees of freedom ($n - 1$) in its calculation. You can verify this by typing in the formula below into an empty cell of the data window shown in Figure 5.4:

$$=STDEV(A1:A12)$$

This formula will give you a standard deviation of 11.87 (when rounded to two significant digits) that matches our hand calculation for the sample standarddeviation (s). To calculate the standard deviation for a population, you need to use the STDEVP function (P for population). Thus, for the same scores as a population, your standard deviation function would be:

$$=STDEVP(A1:A12)$$

This formula will give you a standard deviation of 11.37 (when rounded to two significant digits) that matches our hand calculation for the population standard deviation (σ) we calculated in the previous section.

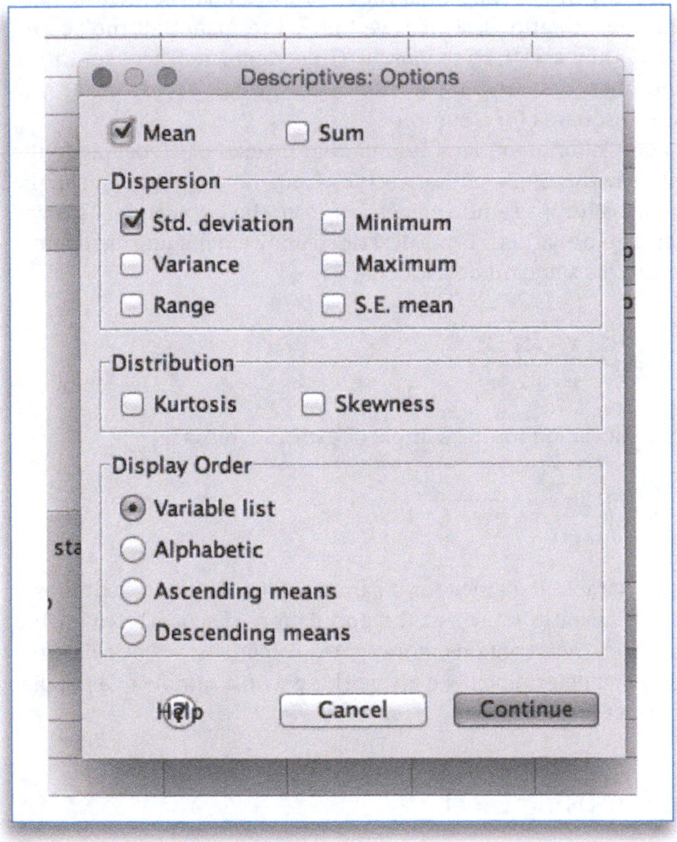

Calculating the Standard Deviation Using SPSS

SPSS will also easily calculate the standard deviation of a set of scores. In the Analyze menu, under Descriptives, you can choose the Standard deviation box under Options in this window (Analyze → Descriptive Statistics → Descriptives → Options; see Figure 5.7 for the Descriptives:Option window view). However, if you run this function in SPSS, you will see that it is for a sample standard deviation (see Figure 5.8 for the Output for the exam scores

Figure 5.7 Descriptives Options Window in SPSS

Figure 5.8 SPSS Output Window Showing the Sample Standard Deviation (*s*) for the Exam Scores Distribution

➡ **Descriptives**

[DataSet1] /Stats Text/SPSS_Excel_files/5_5.sav

Descriptive Statistics

	N	Mean	Std. Deviation
Exam Scores	12	75.0000	11.87051
Valid N (listwise)	12		

distribution). For a population of scores, the value provided by SPSS for the standard deviation would need to be transformed by multiplying it by the square root of $\sqrt{\frac{(n-1)}{n}}$. For most software packages, including Excel and SPSS, the default calculation for the standard deviation is for a sample rather than a population, because the entire population is rarely tested in research studies.

WHICH MEASURE OF VARIABILITY SHOULD I USE?

The choice between the range, interquartile range, and standard deviation measures of variability primarily depends on the scale of measurement used to collect the data. If you are using a nominal data scale, variability cannot be quantitatively measured for your distribution, so none of these measures is appropriate. If you are using an ordinal, interval, or ratio scale, then you must next consider which of the measures of central tendency is most appropriate for your distribution. If you calculated the mean, then you can use the standard deviation to measure variability. If you calculated either the median or mode, then you can choose either the range or the interquartile range to measure variability. Remember that the interquartile range will be less affected by extreme scores, so that is a better measure to use if you have extreme outliers in your distribution. Figure 5.9 provides a flowchart of this decision process that focuses on the variability section of Figure 4.1 on descriptive statistics.

Figure 5.9   Flowchart for Deciding Which Measure of Variability to Use (Expansion of Variability Section of Figure 4.1)

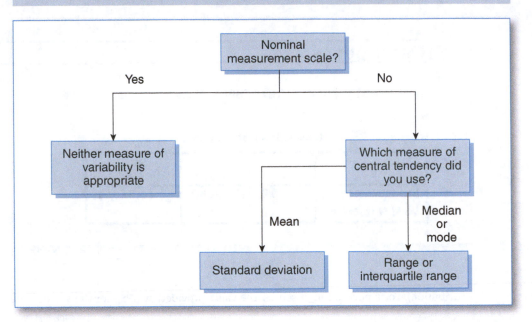

Stop and Think

5.3   In your own words, explain why the standard deviation provides a more precise measure of variability for a distribution. In what situation is it the most appropriate measure to use?

5.4   Calculate the standard deviation for the two sets of data (from populations) below. In what way are the data sets related? How does this relationship influence the standard deviation for the data?

- 1, 3, 2, 5, 1, 3, 4, 5, 1
- 2, 6, 4, 10, 2, 6, 8, 10, 2

5.5   For the sets of data above, now assume they are data from samples (instead of from populations). How will the standard deviations of the distributions change from those in 5.4?

Calculations Summary

Range: the highest score minus the lowest score

Interquartile range: the score at the 75th percentile minus the score at the 25th percentile

Standard deviation: You will need to have the mean calculated already in order to calculate the standard deviation.

Step 1: Calculate the deviation between each score and the mean and square the difference.

Step 2: Add up the squared deviations to get the sum of squares (SS).

Step 3: Divide by N for a population (σ^2) or $n-1$ for a sample (s^2) to get the variance.

Step 4: Take the square root of the variance to get the standard deviation (σ for a population and s for a sample).

CHAPTER SUMMARY

5.1   **What can we learn about a distribution from measures of variability?**

Measures of variability provide some information about how much the scores in a distribution differ from one another.

5.2   **How are the range and standard deviation used as measures of variability?**

The range measures the difference between the highest and lowest scores in a distribution to provide you with a sense of how much of the measurement scale the scores cover. The standard deviation conceptually measures the average distance between the scores and the mean of the distribution. This measure provides you with a sense of how much the scores differ from the center of the distribution.

5.3   **How do the range and standard deviation compare for different distributions?**

The range only uses the two most extreme scores in the distribution, so it is a fairly imprecise measure of variability. It does not provide any information about the scores between these two extremes. The standard deviation uses all the scores in its calculation, so you are getting a more precise measure of variability from the standard deviation.

5.4   **Why does the standard deviation calculation differ for samples and populations?**

The standard deviation is the average of the differences between the scores and the mean. For a population, this value is calculated using N to determine the average. However, the sample, as a representative of the population, will have lower variability than the whole population because you are not obtaining scores from every member, only a subset of the population. Thus, we adjust the standard deviation calculation for a sample to account for its lower variability and still provide a good estimate of the variability in the population the sample represents. We do this using $n-1$ (which are the degrees of freedom) in our calculation of the average of the deviations between the scores and the mean.

THINKING ABOUT RESEARCH

A summary of a research study in psychology is given below. As you read the summary, think about the following questions:

1. Identify the dependent variable in this study. What type of measurement scale was used for this dependent variable?

2. Given the measure of central tendency reported in the graph in Figure 5.10, which measure of variability would be best for these researchers to report? (You can use Figure 5.9 to help you determine this.)

3. Figure 5.10 shows the standard deviations for the data from the experiment as lines extending from the bars in the graph. Explain why there are two separate measures for standard deviation shown in this graph.

4. Do the standard deviations appear to be about the same or do they indicate larger variability in looking times for one type of photo than the other? Why might you expect the variability for the two types of stimuli to be similar?

Macchi Cassia, V., Turati, C., & Simion, F. (2004). Can a nonspecific bias toward top-heavy patterns explain newborns' face preference? *Psychological Science, 15,* 379–383.

Note: Only Experiment 1 of this study is described below.

Purpose of the Study. The researchers were interested in examining the causes of previous findings showing that newborns prefer faces compared with other stimuli. Many of the previous studies

Figure 5.10 Data and Face Stimuli From the Study by Macchi Cassia et al. (2004) Showing Longer Looking Times at the Upright Faces

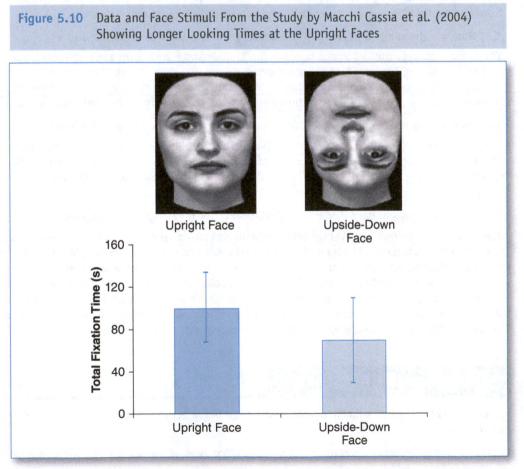

SOURCE: Macchi Cassia, Turati, & Simion (2004). Can a nonspecific bias toward top-heavy patterns explain newborns' face preference? *Psychological Science, 15,* 379–383.

showing this result used drawings of faces to show to the infants rather than real faces, so these researchers first tested whether the face preference would occur for photographs of actual faces shown to the infants.

Method of the Study. The participants in the study were 20 newborn infants, between 25 and 73 hours old. Photos of a woman's face were shown to the infants in upright and upside-down versions (see Figure 5.10). The two versions were shown side-by-side on the screen, once on the left side and once on the right side for each version. For these two trials, the researchers measured the amount of time the infants looked at each version of the face (upright and upside-down) during the trial by viewing videos of the infants taken during the trials.

Results of the Study. Figure 5.10 shows the mean looking time for each of the faces (height of the bars) and the standard deviations (lines extending from the bars) for these data. Using inferential statistics, the researchers determined that the infants looked longer at the upright face than the upside-down face.

Conclusions of the Study. This showed that newborns' face preference can be shown using photos of actual faces. This was shown by the longer mean looking times at the upright (normal orientation) faces compared with the upside-down (scrambled features) faces.

TEST YOURSELF

1. For each of the data sets below, which appears to have the highest variability? Explain your answer.
   a. 3, 3, 4, 4, 4, 2, 3
   b. 1, 1, 1, 1, 1, 2, 2, 7
   c. 4, 2, 3, 2, 3, 5, 7, 7, 7, 4, 7, 2, 7, 7, 3

2. For each data set above, calculate the range and standard deviation.

3. Compare the standard deviations you calculated in the previous question. Do these values match your guess in Question 1?

4. Which measure of variability is most commonly reported?
   a. Range
   b. Interquartile range
   c. Standard deviation
   d. Variance

5. Which measure of variability is most appropriate for a distribution in which the best measure of central tendency is the mean?
   a. Range
   b. Interquartile range
   c. Standard deviation
   d. None of the above

6. Which measure of variability is most appropriate for a distribution in which the scores are measured on a nominal scale?

   a. Range

   b. Interquartile range

   c. Standard deviation

   d. None of the above

7. Which measure of variability is most appropriate for a distribution in which the best measure of central tendency is the median?

   a. Range

   b. Interquartile range

   c. Standard deviation

   d. Either (a) or (b)

8. Degrees of freedom are used in calculating the standard deviation for a population.

   a. True

   b. False

9. The variability of scores for a sample will be lower than the variability in the population it represents.

   a. True

   b. False

10. The range measures consider all of the scores in a distribution in their calculations.

    a. True

    b. False

11. Explain why we need to square the deviations from the mean in our calculation of the standard deviation.

Chapter 6

Presenting Descriptive Statistics

As you read the chapter, consider the following questions:

6.1 What are the different ways I can present data from a study?

6.2 How do I choose the best way to present my data?

6.3 What are the differences between pie charts, bar graphs, and line graphs?

6.4 How can I create graphs using software?

6.5 What is APA style and why is it important?

Let's continue discussing our food court survey study from the previous two chapters. Suppose you have collected your data and calculated descriptive statistics from your student survey of the choices at your school's food court. Now you need to decide how to present them to the student board. Should you graph the data or present them in a table? If you choose a graph, what type of graph should you use? If you present the data in a table, how should you organize it? Suppose you want to present your data by class rank (i.e., freshman, sophomore, etc.) to see if there are differences for students who will be on campus longer. Will this change your choice of presentation method? This chapter will focus on answering these questions along with presenting graphs and tables in the appropriate style for writing in the behavioral sciences: American Psychological Association (APA) style.

One of the choices you will need to make in presenting your data to others is whether to present the data in a graph or a table (see Photo 6.1). A graph can show aspects of the data, such as the shape the distribution or comparison of variable conditions, more visually and clearly than a table does. However, a table will present more precise values (i.e., the actual numbers) that a graph typically will not. Thus, your goals in presenting your data should be considered when you make this choice. In Chapter 2, we discussed frequency distribution tables and graphs. These graphs/tables are used to present frequency data from the whole distribution and will help show the shape of a data distribution. In this chapter, we will focus more on graphs and tables that illustrate descriptive statistics (e.g., central tendency, variability) and show comparisons across groups and conditions in a study.

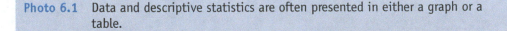

Photo 6.1 Data and descriptive statistics are often presented in either a graph or a table.

©iStock/andresr

DESCRIPTIVE STATISTICS IN GRAPHS

Graphs can present a visual display of the descriptive statistics you have calculated for a set of data. However, the type of graph you choose to present your data will partially depend on the type of data you have collected. Generally, data for categorical variables (i.e., categories as in nominal and ordinal scales of measurement or whole numbers that cannot be divided into smaller units as in rating scales) are presented in pie charts and bar graphs, whereas data for continuous variables (i.e., numerical scores that can be subdivided into smaller units) are presented in line graphs. You will also need to consider which variables you will include in your graph because you may have a categorical independent variable for your x-axis and a continuous variable as your dependent variable for your y-axis. In this case, you must consider what type of variable is being placed on the x-axis of the graph to determine which type of graph you will use.

⚜

Categorical variables: measures with responses as categories that cannot be divided into smaller units

Pie charts: graphs of categorical variables where proportions are represented as a portion of the pie

Bar graphs: graphs of data for categorical variables where the bar height represents the size of the value (e.g., mean)

Pie Charts

Although pie charts are not used as often as bar graphs and line graphs in reporting data from behavioral studies, you may see them used on occasion, as they are useful in presenting percentage response data for simple surveys from different categories of responses or respondents. For example, we might wish to display a pie chart of our food court survey respondents by class rank to show the distribution of class rank within our sample. A pie chart will show the proportion of our respondents at each class rank to help us determine whether our sample is representative of the students we wished to survey. Figure 6.1 shows a pie chart for the class rank variable in the survey data set. From this chart, you can see that class rank is not equally distributed in your sample. Although the proportions of freshmen and sophomores are similar, there are many more seniors and juniors than there are freshmen and sophomores. This means that if you're more interested in the opinions of students who will be at the school in the coming years, you have not represented those students very well in your sample. There are several possible reasons for this distribution: Upperclassmen may be more likely to hang out in the places in which you conducted your survey, upperclassmen may be more motivated to complete your survey, and so on. But this information is good to know when you are interpreting your data and deciding what recommendation you will make about the food court choices to the student board.

Continuous variables: measures with number scores that can be divided into smaller units

Line graphs: graphs of data for continuous variables in which each value is graphed as a point and the points are connected to show differences between scores (e.g., means)

Figure 6.1   Pie Chart of Class Rank in the Survey Data Sample

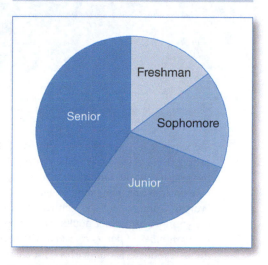

Figure 6.2 presents another example of a pie chart for exam scores in a course. In this case, the percentage of correct scores from the data shown in Figure 4.8 have been translated to letter grades (an ordinal scale) to show the distribution of grades on the exam. However, you should note that if we want to graph the scores shown in Figure 4.8 as the percentage of correct scores, a pie chart would be inappropriate because pie charts are meant for categorical variables and the percentage of correct scores is a continuous variable. In this pie chart, you can see that most students received a *C* on the exam, similar proportions of students received *B*s and *D*s, and the fewest number of students received *A*s and *F*s. Thus, while it was difficult to earn an *A* on this exam, it was also not likely that a student earned an *F*.

Bar Graphs

Categorical variables can also be represented in bar graphs. Bar graphs show the value of a variable with the height of a bar for each category of the variable. Figure 6.3 shows a bar graph of the exam grade distribution to compare with the pie chart in Figure 6.2. The bar graph displays

Figure 6.2   Pie Chart of Grades on a Class Exam

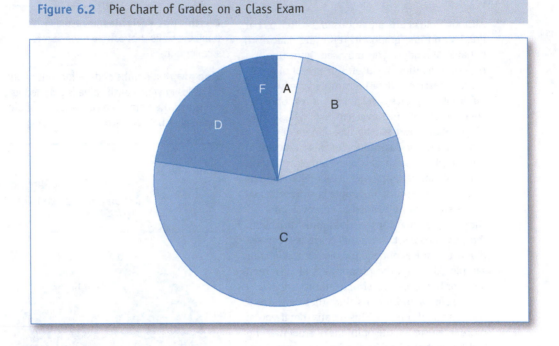

the same information as the pie chart, but in a different format. The bar heights indicate the proportions of students in the course that earned each letter grade on the exam. It is clear from the graph that the largest proportion of students in the course earned a grade of *C* on the exam.

Consider another example: Figure 6.4 shows data from a decision-making study conducted by Worthy, Gorlick, Pacheco, Schnyer, and Maddox (2011) comparing performance on a strategy task for younger and older adults. The categorical variable of *age group* is shown on the *x*-axis with *mean number of points earned* as the continuous performance measure on the *y*-axis. Bar height indicates the performance level for each age group and shows the higher number of points earned by the younger adults than the older adults in the task. Also notice the lines extending from the bars. These are the 95% confidence intervals (i.e., the range of the estimated population means with a specific level of probability). You will typically see these lines presented in bar graphs that show measures of central tendency (most often the mean) by group or categorical condition in research studies. The lines will show the confidence intervals for the means or another measure of variability, such as the standard deviations or the standard errors (discussed further in Chapter 9) to illustrate some of the information that is important for testing for differences between the means in inferential statistics. We will discuss the logic of hypothesis testing in Part III of this text.

One thing to note about the *y*-axis for the graph in Figure 6.4 is the range of values shown on this axis. Although the points earned scale likely extends down to a low point of 0 for this measure, the researchers chose to present the values as extending from 480 to 530 total points in this graph. Different factors might have contributed to this choice. For example, the researchers might have chosen the lowest value of 480 on this axis based on the lowest score earned by any one participant in their study; this might then show the actual range of points values relevant for their study. However, imagine that they had used 0 as the lowest value on the *y*-axis—how would the group difference appear in this graph? Because of the large range in values on the

Figure 6.3 Bar Graph of Grades on a Class Exam

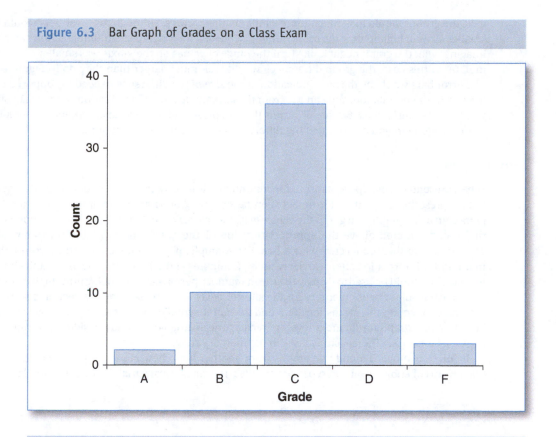

Figure 6.4 Data From the Worthy et al. (2011) Study Shown in a Bar Graph

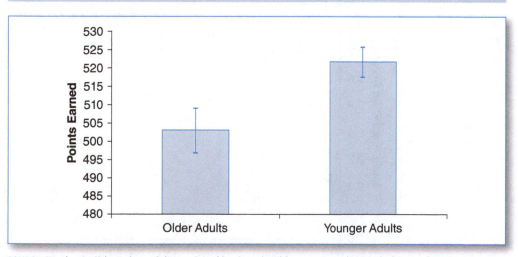

SOURCE: Worthy, Gorlick, Pacheco, Schnyer, & Maddox (2011). With age comes wisdom: decision making in younger and older adults. *Psychological Science, 22*, 1375–1380.

axis, the groups would look much more similar in their scores, although the error bars would be smaller as well, highlighting the score difference needed for a significant difference. You can also imagine what the graph might look like if the range of values on the *y*-axis was smaller (e.g., 490 to 530). In this case, the group differences would look much larger than they do in Figure 6.4. The error bars would be the only indication of the size of the difference needed to support a difference in the population. You can see from these examples that manipulation of the scale on a graph can be misleading. Beware of graphs that are presented to make an argument and look for error bars to help you determine if the differences shown are important or not.

Line Graphs

When presenting descriptive statistics for continuous variables such as an amount (e.g., dosage of a drug prescribed, amount of time between tasks), line graphs are more appropriate than bar graphs. In a line graph, you graph the values (e.g., means) for each group or condition as points on the *y*-axis centered above the appropriate value of the continuous variable on the *x*-axis. The points are then connected with a line. For example, if you conducted a study comparing memory for information after two delay times, 5 minutes and 20 minutes, the line graph shown in Figure 6.5 could be used to display the mean memory performance by delay time. In this graph, the typical result of better memory for the shorter delay is clearly seen by the declining slope of the line connecting the means for the 5 and 20 minute conditions. There may also be separate lines in a line graph for different levels of a categorical variable for study designs with multiple causal factors (e.g., different study tasks in the memory study).

Figure 6.6 shows bar and line graphs from another hypothetical memory study comparing two groups of subjects on two types of variables: the categorical variable of age group (Panel A)

Figure 6.5 Memory Data for Two Delay Times in a Line Graph

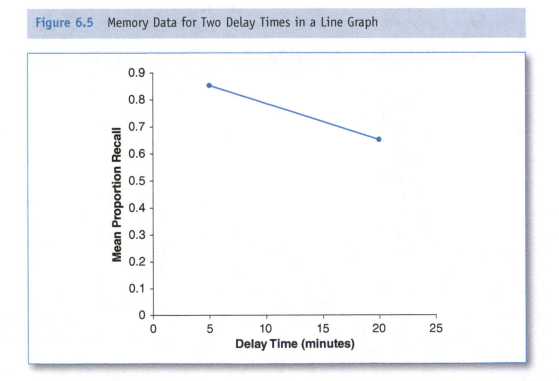

Figure 6.6   (a) Bar Graph Showing the Comparison of Mean Memory Scores for Children and Adults

(b) Line Graph Showing the Comparison of Mean Memory Scores Based on Years of Education

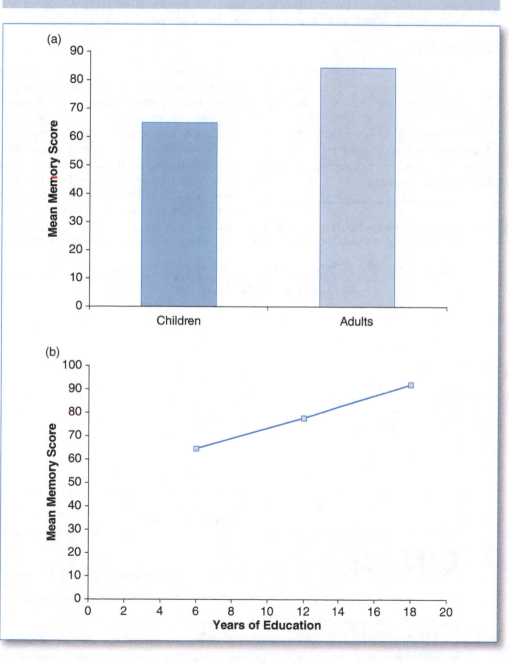

and the continuous variable of years of education (Panel B). These graphs show the difference between the construction of bar and line graphs and their uses. Both graphs show the difference in memory performance across the groups, but this difference is shown as a discrete mean difference for the groups in the bar graph and as the continuous difference based on the number of years of education for the subjects in the line graph. This figure shows the difference in the kinds of variables that these two graph types are used for in displaying descriptive statistics (e.g., mean performance on a task) from data distributions.

Scatterplots

A scatterplot is another type of graph you might see in a published paper or need to create for a correlational study. Unlike the graphs described in the previous sections, scatterplots display a data point for each individual in the data set with one measured variable on the *x*-axis and another measured variable on the *y*-axis. Scatterplots are typically used to show the relationship in scores between two continuous variables measured from a sample. They are useful in illustrating the strength and type (positive or negative) of relationship between the variables. Figure 6.7 shows a scatterplot for a hypothetical data set showing the negative relationship between hours of television watched per week and grade point average (GPA). These graphs will be discussed further in Chapter 15, where correlation statistics are described.

❧

Scatterplot: a graph showing the relationship between two dependent variables for a group of individuals

---

Figure 6.7   Scatterplot Showing the Negative Relationship Between Hours of Television Watched per Week and GPA

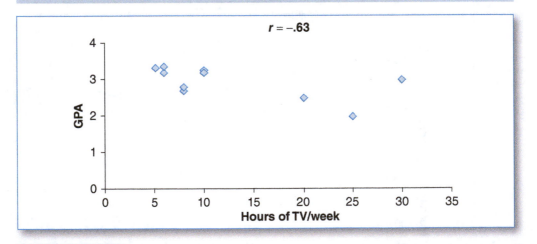

- number of males and females in your sample
- grade level of the students in your sample

6.2 For each set of data described below, indicate which type of graph (pie chart, bar graph, or line graph) you would choose to illustrate the data and why you would choose that type of graph:

- number of students in each major at your university/college
- amount of time it took to solve different kinds of puzzles
- mean performance on a task by age in years

Creating Graphs in Excel

In Chapter 2, we covered the procedure for creating frequency distribution graphs in Excel. As you saw there, we cannot easily create graphs from raw data in Excel. The data must first be transformed into descriptive statistics (e.g., frequency counts, means, etc.). This will also be the case for creating pie charts, bar graphs, and line graphs in Excel. Let's go through the process for creating the graphs in Figures 6.2, 6.3, and 6.5 in Excel.

Figure 6.8   Excel Data Window Showing Proportion of Students Earning Each Grade

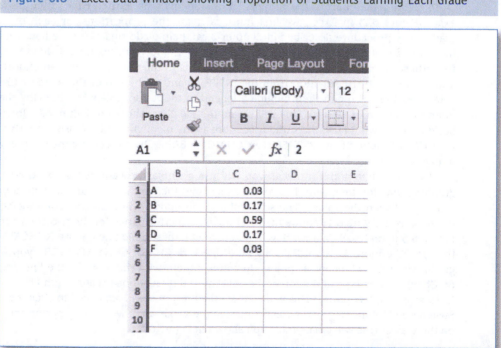

Figure 6.9 Pie Chart From Excel for Letter Grades Earned on a Class Exam

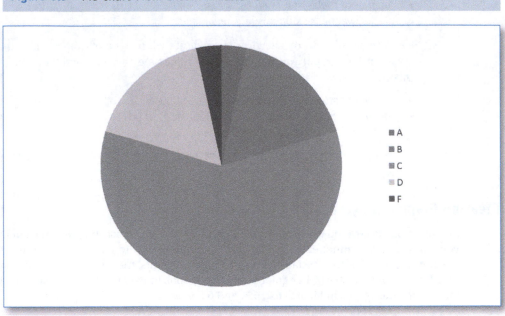

To create a pie chart of the proportion of students who earned each letter grade on the exam (Figure 6.2) in Excel, we first must calculate the proportions for each of the letter grades. The procedure described in Chapter 2 can help us do this. Once we have the proportions, our Excel data window will include the values shown in Figure 6.8. To create a graph from these frequencies, you can highlight the cells in the window and then choose the PIE option in the CHART function from the INSERT menu at the top of the window (INSERT ➜ CHART ➜ PIE). You can then include a legend of the letter grades by choosing the legend option under Chart Design. This will create the pie chart shown in Figure 6.9. To create the bar graph, we would use the same procedure as the pie chart, but choose the BAR option in the CHART function instead (INSERT ➜ CHART ➜ BAR). This will create the bar graph shown in Figure 6.10.

To create a line graph in Excel, you will use a similar procedure, but use the scatterplot graphing function to ensure that your x-axis shows the continuous variable with appropriate spacing between the values. The scatterplot graph option will place the continuous variable on the x-axis. Figure 6.11 shows the mean memory performance for the two delay times from Figure 6.5 in an Excel data window. If you highlight these cells and choose XY SCATTER from the CHART options in the INSERT menu (INSERT ➜ CHART ➜ XY SCATTER), you will see a graph with the two means as points. To connect them with the lines for the line graph, click on Change Chart Type at the top of the window and then choose Scatter with Lines under the XY Scatter graphs options. This will connect the lines. You will also need to click the button to Switch Row/Column to put the Delay times on the x-axis and the memory performance means on the y-axis. This will create the graph shown in Figure 6.5.

Figure 6.10   Bar Graph From Excel for Letter Grades Earned on a Class Exam

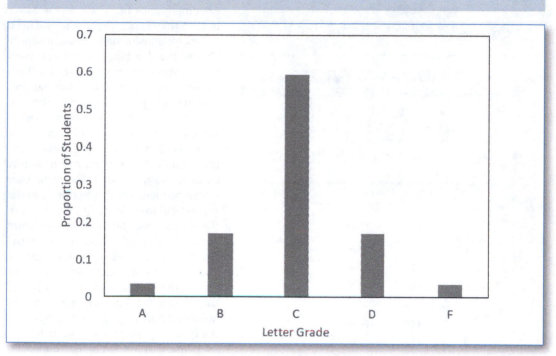

Figure 6.11   Data Window From Excel Showing Mean Memory Performance Data by Delay Condition

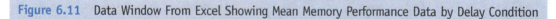

Figure 6.12   SPSS Data Window Showing Data From the Likelihood to Watch a New TV Show Described in Chapter 2

	ting	AgeGroup	var	var
1	1.00	18–24		
2	1.00	25–35		
3	2.00	36–50		
4	2.00	Over 50		
5	2.00	18–24		
6	2.00	25–35		
7	2.00	36–50		
8	3.00	Over 50		
9	3.00	Over 50		
10	3.00	Over 50		
11	3.00	Over 50		
12	4.00	Over 50		
13	4.00	36–50		
14	4.00	36–50		
15	4.00	36–50		
16	4.00	Over 50		
17	4.00	Over 50		
18	4.00	25–35		
19	4.00	18–24		
20	5.00	Over 50		
21	5.00	36–50		
22	5.00	Over 50		

Print

Creating Graphs in SPSS

Creating graphs from raw data is easier in SPSS than Excel. The data do not need to first be transformed—you can simply choose the graphing options you want for the variables in your data set. Let's consider once again the example presented in Chapter 2 concerning the likelihood of watching a new television show after viewing an ad for the show. Figure 6.12 shows the data window for these data with survey ratings in the first column and age group of the participant (a new variable for this example) in the second column. To create graphs with these variables, choose the Graphboard Template Chooser function from the Graphs menu at the top of the window. You will see the variables you have named in the data set on the left side of the window that opens. Choose the variables you want to graph and then choose the type of graph you wish to make.

To make a pie chart of the frequencies for the age group variable, click on that variable on the left side and then choose the Pie of Counts option that appears on the right. Then click OK. This will create the pie chart you see in Figure 6.13. If you choose the Bar of Counts graph option instead of the Pie of Counts option, you can create a bar graph of the number of participants in each Age Group as shown in Figure 6.14. As described earlier, both of these graphs are appropriate for categorical variables (such as age group) and can be used to display these data. Both graphs show that the largest age group in the sample was the 50 and over group.

You could also choose to display the mean ratings given by each age group in a bar graph. To create this graph, choose the Legacy Dialogs function under the Graph menu at the top of the window and then the Bar option for the bar graph. A small window will appear with graph options. With only one categorical

Figure 6.13 Pie Chart Showing the Breakdown of Age Groups in the Sample

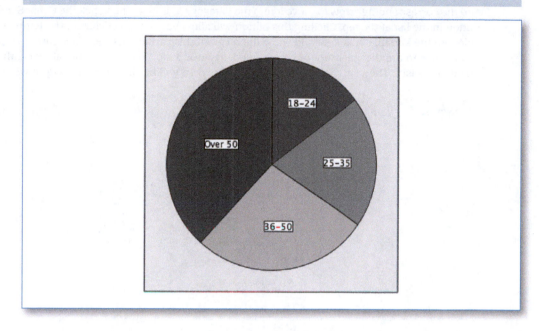

Figure 6.14 Bar Graph Showing the Breakdown of Age Groups in the Sample

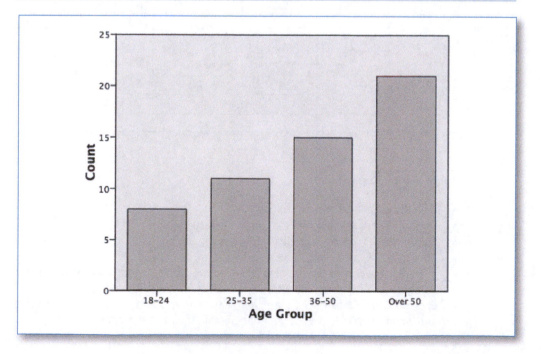

variable to place on the *x*-axis, you can choose the Simple option and then click on Define in this window. In the next window that appears (see Figure 6.15), click on the Age Group variable and the corresponding arrow to move it into the Category Axis box. Then click the Other Statistic option in the list at the top. Clicking this button will allow you to then click over the Rating variable into the Variable box. It should show the mean of this variable, as seen in Figure 6.15 (you can change to another measure of central tendency using the Change Statistic tab beneath the box if you wish). Then click OK. The graph in Figure 6.16 will be shown in the Output window.

Figure 6.15 Variable Definition Window for the Legacy Dialogs Graphs Function in SPSS

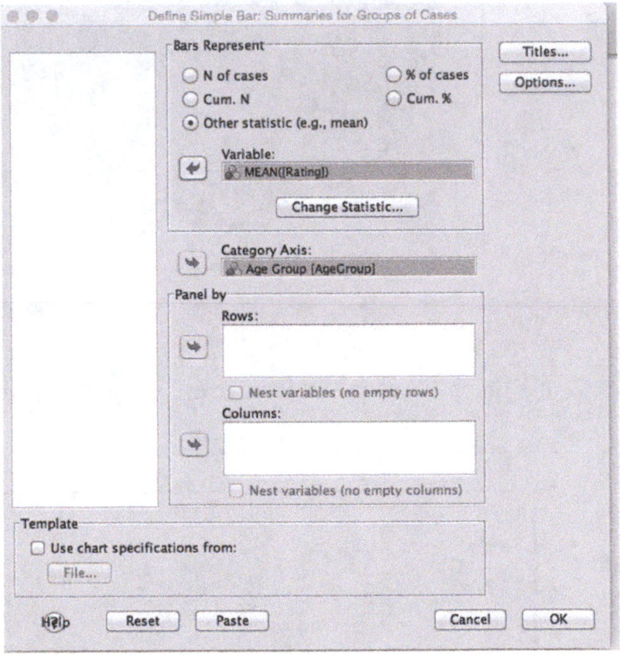

Summary of Steps

- Type the data into the data window.
- From the Graph menu at the top, choose Legacy Dialogs.
- Choose the Bar option from this list.
- Choose Simple and click Define.
- In the Define Simple Bar window (see Figure 6.15), click your *x*-axis variable into the Category Axis box using the arrow.
- Click on Other Statistic and place your *y*-axis variable into the Variable box using the arrow and click OK to display your bar graph in the Output window.

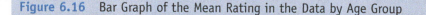

Figure 6.16   Bar Graph of the Mean Rating in the Data by Age Group

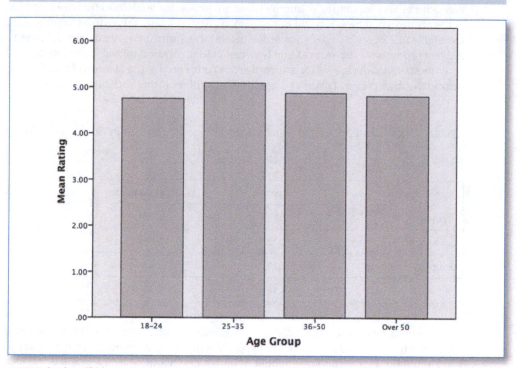

SOURCE: Sanders, Shirk, Burgin, & Martin (2012). The gargle effect: Rinsing the mouth with glucose enhances self-control, *Psychological Science, 23*, 1470–1472.

Line graphs in SPSS follow a similar procedure to that used to create Figure 6.16. However, instead of the Bar option in the Legacy Dialogs, you would choose the Line option. The variables are defined in the same way. Remember that line graphs should be used only when the variable you want to graph on the *x*-axis is a continuous variable.

DESCRIPTIVE STATISTICS IN TABLES

As an alternative to graphs to display data distributions or descriptive statistics, tables can be used. In Chapter 2, I discussed the procedure for creating frequency distribution tables to illustrate a data distribution and the columns that are typically displayed in these tables. However, in the presentation of research studies, you are more likely to see tables that present descriptive statistics from data sets, so we will focus on that type of table in this section.

A common table used in research articles and presentations is a table of central tendency statistics (most often the means) by level of the variables present in the design of a study. For example, we might choose to display the mean ratings by year in school in a table for our food court survey example. Table 6.1 illustrates how such a table might look. In this table, mean ratings are presented by year in school along with the number of participants in each level of year in school and a measure of the variability (standard deviation) for the survey ratings.

This is a common format for tables that present descriptive statistics for a data set, such as the one used in this example. Note that this table is not pasted from SPSS Output and does not contain vertical bars separating columns. These are important guidelines for adhering to APA style in the creation of tables. You will not be able to copy and paste tables from Excel or SPSS to create a table in APA style, and if you use the Insert Table function in Word, you will have to format the table to remove the vertical line between columns. You might also see tables in APA style with the standard deviations (or standard errors) presented in the Means column in parentheses next to the mean value. This is a common method of reporting variability in tables in APA style.

Table 6.1   Mean Ratings and Standard Deviations for Food Court Survey Data by Year in School

Year in School	Mean	Standard Deviation	n
Freshmen	3.63	1.77	8
Sophomores	4.22	1.92	9
Juniors	5.19	1.47	16
Seniors	5.36	1.40	22

Another thing to note is that descriptive statistics should be presented in the format (graph or table) that best displays the test of the hypothesis or conclusions made from the data. However, you should not repeat this presentation as both a graph and table. If a graph is the best way to display the data set or descriptive statistics, then only present these in a graph and do not also include a table showing the same information. The table or graph is meant to help the audience or reader better understand a summary of the data and the conclusions that can be drawn from the data. Inferential statistics are then presented in the text to provide the hypothesis tests. How to present the inferential statistics by type of test will be discussed in later chapters. Here I have focused on the presentation of descriptive statistics and data distributions.

APA STYLE FOR GRAPHS AND TABLES

One thing you may notice as you begin to read empirical research articles (i.e., published reports of a study that collected data) is that there is a fairly common structure to these articles with the sections in the same order in each article. Depending on the length of the article and the design or topic of the study, some sections may be omitted, renamed, or combined with other sections, but the general structure and purpose of each section are consistent from article to article. This structure comes from the style rules of the American Psychological Association (APA, 2009), also known as APA style. The main sections of an APA style research report/article are Abstract, Introduction, Method, Results, and Discussion. The Abstract provides a paragraph summary of the study. The Introduction provides a description of the topic of the study, relevant background research, purpose of the study, and hypotheses for the results. The Method section provides the details of the participants, design, materials/stimuli/apparatus, and procedure for the study.

The Results section provides descriptive and inferential statistics and a description of the analyses performed on the data. Finally, the Discussion section provides a review of the results with reference to the hypotheses stated in the Introduction section and relevant past findings, along with possible future directions and general conclusions from the study.

The graphs and tables described in this chapter are typically referred to in the Results section of a research report. However, when an author types up the manuscript (i.e., before it is published), these graphs and tables are placed on their own pages at the end of the manuscript in accordance with APA style rules. Graphs are referred to as *figures* in APA style. Each figure and table is given a title (see Table 6.1 for an example) that describes what is presented in the figure or table and typically includes the relevant variables. However, a description of the figure or table is also provided in the Results section, where the author refers the reader to the figure/ table as they describe the data. Although these rules may, in some cases, seem arbitrary and difficult to follow, they provide a consistent organization to help readers follow the report of the study and know where to look in a research report for specific information about a study. You will likely encounter APA style structure many times as you learn the process of conducting research and using statistics to understand data. The Thinking About Research sections at the end of each chapter in this text are organized by the major sections of an APA style article to help you get used to this structure.

Stop and Think

6.3 For the data set below, create a graph in Excel or SPSS that is appropriate for the variables described:

Mean percentage accuracy on a category judgment task by task instruction condition (complete the tasks as quickly as possible versus complete the task as accurately as possible)

Speed instruction: 76, 52, 89, 75, 70, 61, 90, 88, 75, 81

Accuracy instruction: 90, 85, 87, 66, 82, 77, 95, 90, 99, 79

6.4 Which of the following is consistent with APA style for figures and tables?

a. Embed the figure/table within the Results section.

b. Embed the figure/table within the Method section.

c. Do not duplicate data in both a figure and table.

d. Provide a single title that describes all figures/tables at once.

6.5 In which section of an APA style report should you refer to the figures/tables of descriptive statistics?

a. Abstract

b. Introduction

c. Method

d. Results

CHAPTER SUMMARY

6.1   What are the different ways I can present data from a study?

Frequencies from a data set can be presented in frequency distribution tables and graphs. You can also present the descriptive statistics from a data set in tables and graphs to illustrate the differences (or similarities) across groups or conditions. Categorical variables should be displayed in pie charts or bar graphs, and continuous variables should be displayed in line graphs.

6.2   How do I choose the best way to present my data?

First, you should consider whether a graph or table is the best way to present data. This choice will depend on what aspects of the data you wish to highlight to your audience. If you choose a graph, then consider the types of variables you have in your study design to choose between the graph types.

6.3   What are the differences between pie charts, bar graphs, and line graphs?

Pie charts show values as portions of a circle ("pie slices"). Bar graphs show the values for levels of a variable or response categories as the height the bars in the graph. Line graphs show the relationship between values on a continuous scale. Bar and line graphs often include a measure of the variability in the data if the x-axis contains an independent or grouping variable.

6.4   How can I create graphs using software?

Both Excel and SPSS can be used to create the graphs described in this chapter. The details are described by graph type. In Excel, however, you often must calculate some descriptive statistics before you can graph the data.

6.5   What is APA style and why is it important?

APA style is a set of rules for writing research reports. It provides a consistent structure for research reports to help readers easily understand the report of the study and quickly find information they are looking for.

THINKING ABOUT RESEARCH

A summary of a research study in psychology is given below. As you read the summary, think about the following questions:

1. Identify the independent and dependent variables in this study. For each variable, indicate if it is a categorical or continuous variable.

2. Based on your description of the design for the previous question and the hypothesis the authors made, what data would you want to display for this study? Does Figure 6.17 display these data well? Why or why not?

3. Identify the type of graph used in Figure 6.17.

4. Other than the graph type used in Figure 6.17, what other options could the authors have used to display their data that are appropriate for their design?

5. Do the data shown in Figure 6.17 allow the authors to test their hypothesis? Why or why not?

Sanders, M. A., Shirk, S. D., Burgin, C. J., & Martin, L. L. (2012). The gargle effect: Rinsing the mouth with glucose enhances self-control. *Psychological Science, 23,* 1470–1472.

Purpose of the Study. The researchers examined possible causes of the impairment of self-control. Previous studies have shown that there is a limited amount of self-control that one can engage in; if one task requires self-control, performance on a second task that requires self-control will be impaired. This study tested the idea that self-control energy is influenced by the presence of glucose. Two groups of subjects were compared on their performance for a task that required self-control: One was given glucose and one was not. The researchers predicted that the group given glucose would show better performance on the self-control task than the group not given glucose.

Method of the Study. Students completed the study to fulfill a course requirement. They first completed a task that required self-control: crossing out *E*s in a page of text based on a complex rule (i.e., cross out some *E*s, but not others). Then all subjects completed a second task requiring self-control while swishing lemonade around in their mouths. They did not swallow the drink. For half of the subjects, the lemonade was sweetened with glucose and for the other half, the lemonade was sweetened with Splenda (no glucose). The task they completed was a Stroop task, where words were presented in colored font. Subjects were asked to name the font color as quickly as possible. On some trials, the word was a color word that was different from the font color (e.g., the word *blue* printed in red font). These trials require self-control because it is hard not to read the word that interferes with the font color. Reaction time to name the font color was recorded on the Stroop trials. Subjects then rated the sweetness and pleasantness of the lemonade.

Results of the Study. Figure 6.17 presents the mean reaction time results on the Stroop task for each group of subjects. The statistical test run on these data showed that the glucose group has a significantly lower mean reaction time than the no glucose group.

Figure 6.17 Mean Reaction Time Results for the Two Groups

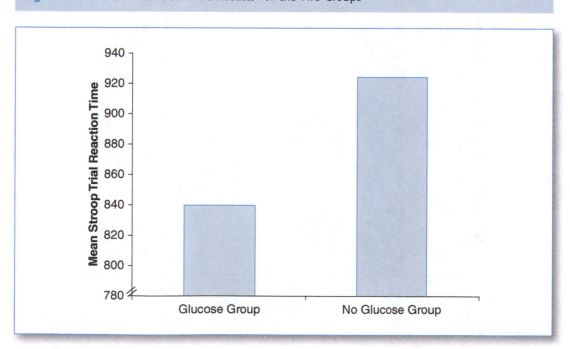

SOURCE: Sanders et al. (2012) study

Conclusions of the Study. The results of the study support the idea that the presence of glucose can provide more energy for self-control in tasks that require it.

TEST YOURSELF

1. For each of the data sets described below, indicate which type of graph you would choose to display the data and why you would choose that graph.

   a. Scores from 0 to 100 on an anxiety scale by gender of participant

   b. Number of psychology majors versus other majors in your statistics course

   c. Mean speed (in seconds) to complete a set of puzzles—participants worked on either math puzzles or spatial navigation puzzles

2. For each data set in the question above, list the variables present in the description and indicate if each variable is categorical or continuous.

3. Provide a written description of the data presented in the graph in Figure 6.18. What type of graph is this?

Figure 6.18   Test Yourself #3

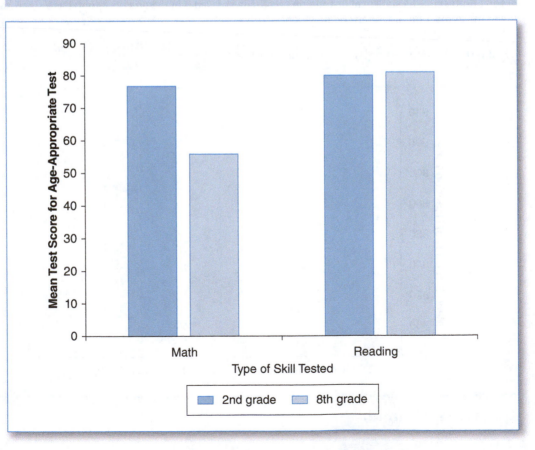

4. Where should you place tables and figures of data in an APA style research report?

    a. Embedded within the Results section

    b. On a separate page at the beginning of the paper

    c. On a separate page at the end of the paper

    d. Embedded within the Introduction

5. Which graph is most appropriate for data with categorical variables?

    a. Pie chart

    b. Bar graph

    c. Line graph

    d. Both (a) and (b)

    e. Both (b) and (c)

6. Which graph is most appropriate for data with continuous variables?

    a. Pie chart

    b. Bar graph

    c. Line graph

    d. Both (a) and (b)

    e. Both (b) and (c)

7. Whenever you present data in a graph, you should always also include the exact values from the graph in a table.

    a. True

    b. False

8. Creating graphs in SPSS usually requires calculation of descriptive statistics before you begin.

    a. True

    b. False

9. Inferential statistics are typically presented in graphs in a research report.

    a. True

    b. False

10. What is the purpose of including a graph or table of data in a report of a study?

PART III

Basics of Hypothesis Testing

Chapter 7

The Normal Distribution and z Scores

As you read the chapter, consider the following questions:

7.1 What is a standardized score?

7.2 How are standardized scores useful?

7.3 What is the normal distribution?

7.4 How can the normal distribution be used to test hypotheses about populations?

So far, I have discussed how we summarize data to better understand the data distributions and what the data can tell us. In Part III of this text, I will discuss how we use data to test hypotheses and answer our research questions. The basic logic will rely on some of the concepts we have already covered: central tendency (Chapter 4), variability (Chapter 5), the distribution of sample means (Chapter 3), and probability (Chapter 3).

To help you understand the goals of hypothesis testing, consider this example: You want to know if taking the online quizzes your instructor has assigned this semester helps students in your course prepare for exams (see Photo 7.1). To answer this research question, you conduct a study to compare the mean final exam score in your course for students who took the online quizzes this semester with the mean final exam score for all the previous semesters, when online quizzes were not available for students to take. In other words, you want to compare the current exam mean with the exam mean for the population of all classes who have taken the final exam in the past without the aid of online quizzes. Your instructor tells you that the mean score for all past classes is 75 (she has taught this course many times in her career). She also tells you that the mean for the students who took the online quizzes this semester is 82. Is 82 significantly higher than the population mean of 75, showing that the online quizzes helped raise exam scores, or is 82 just a slightly higher value by chance because the current sample of students happened to score a bit higher than the population mean? Figure 7.1 shows the comparison of these values in the population distribution of exam scores. How can you determine

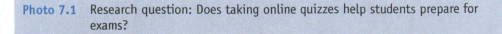

Photo 7.1   Research question: Does taking online quizzes help students prepare for exams?

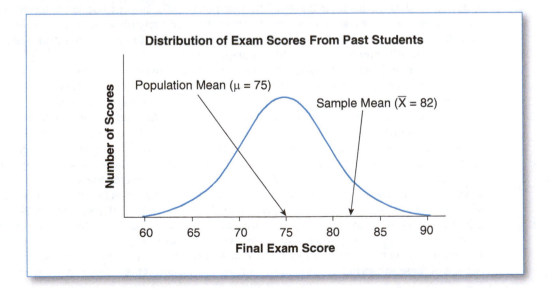

©iStock/Geber86

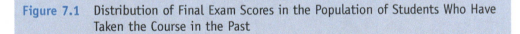

Figure 7.1   Distribution of Final Exam Scores in the Population of Students Who Have Taken the Course in the Past

whether 82 is significantly higher than 75 or
not in terms of a comparison to the population of all past classes? The answer is to use a
standardized score known as a *z score*!

❧

z-score: A standardized score that indicates the
location of a score within a population distribution

THE *z* SCORE TRANSFORMATION

Transforming data to *z* scores provides a way of locating a score in a standardized distribution. This
transformation can be useful in cases where we want to compare two scores that come from two
different populations. Here's a classic example: Do you weigh more than your dog? Unless you have
a very large dog, in absolute measurement of weight, you probably weigh more. But if we consider
how heavy your dog is compared to other dogs and how heavy you are compared to other humans
(male or female), then the comparison would be more informative in terms of your relative weights.
We can do this by transforming your weight and your dog's weight into *z* scores. Figure 7.2 shows
these weight distributions in the relevant populations. The top graph shows the distribution of dog
weights for the population of all dogs, the bottom left graph shows the distribution of human male
weights for the population of adult males at all ages, and the bottom right graph shows the distribution
of human female weights for the population of adult females at all ages. Notice that both the mean
and standard deviation (SD) for each distribution are given and the SDs are marked on the distributions
and that the means and standard deviations are different across the distributions. With *z* scores, we
can compare scores that come from very different distributions on the same measurement scale.

**Figure 7.2   Distribution of Weights (in Pounds) for Dog, Human Male, and Human
Female Populations**

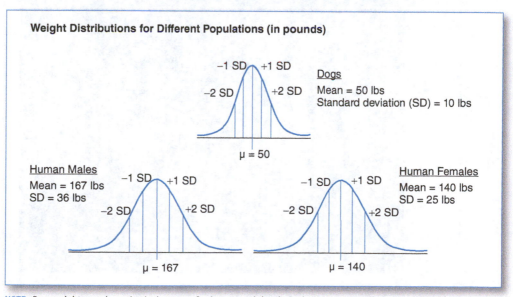

NOTE: Dog weights are hypothetical; source for human weights is Ogden, Fryar, Carroll, & Flegal (2004).

Locate your weight on the male or female distribution graph. Are you above or below the mean? How many standard deviations are you away from the mean (e.g., less than 1 SD, more than 1 SD, more than 2 SDs, etc.)? Now, locate your dog's weight on the dog distribution graph (if you do not have a dog, you can borrow my dog, Daphne, who is 53 pounds; see Photo 7.2). Is your dog within 1 SD of the mean? (If you're using Daphne, she's less than 1 SD above the mean.) Next, compare the location of your weight in the appropriate weight distribution (human male or female) and your dog's weight in the dog distribution. How do these locations compare relative to the means of the distributions? This will help you answer the question of whether or not you are heavier than your dog. If, for example, you are 1 SD below the mean in your weight distribution, but your dog (or Daphne) is less than 1 SD above the mean in the dog weight distribution, then your dog (or Daphne) is heavier than you are in terms of relative weights. That's how we use z scores to compare scores from different distributions.

A z score transformation for an entire distribution of scores works the same way as the dog/human weight example I just described. Using a z score transformation standardizes the scores according to the population they come from to allow us to compare the scores by giving us the location of the scores in their distribution. Thus, a z score is a value that represents the distance of a score from the population mean in terms of how many standard deviations the distance represents in that distribution. A score can be 1 SD above the mean, 1.5 SDs below the mean,

Photo 7.2 My dog, Daphne; she is 53 pounds.

Figure 7.3   An Example *z* Score Distribution

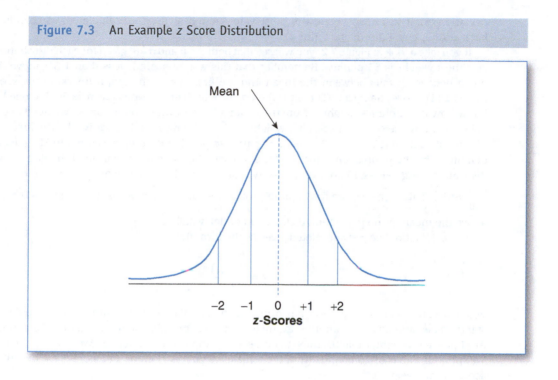

3 SDs above the mean, and so on. The *z* score will tell us the distance from the mean in SD units. And the sign of the score (positive or negative) tells us whether the score is above or below the population mean.

For any distribution, we can transform all the scores in the distribution to create a *z* score distribution for the original distribution. Figure 7.3 shows an example *z* score distribution. In other words, we could standardize all the scores in a distribution to create a *z* score distribution for those scores. In all cases, the mean of the *z* score distribution will be zero, because the *z* scores represent the distance from the mean, so the mean distance in a *z* score distribution should be zero (i.e., the mean minus the mean equals zero). The standard deviation will always be 1.0, because the transformed scores will be in SD units once we've converted the scores to values that represent how many standard deviations there are from the mean of zero in our new distribution. The shape of the standardized (i.e., *z* score) distribution, however, will be the same as the original distribution. If the original distribution is symmetrical, the *z* score transformed distribution will be symmetrical.

Calculating a *z* Score by Hand

Now, let's look at how we transform our data scores to *z* scores. I will begin with how to calculate *z* scores by hand and the formula notations for *z* scores using Daphne's weight. As described in the previous section, a *z* score represents a score's distance from the mean in SD units. Therefore, we need to know the mean for the population (μ) and the population standard deviation (σ). If you need a review of these values and how they are calculated, you can look back at Chapters 4 (for μ) and 5 (for σ).

If you take a look at Figure 7.2, you will see that both the μ and σ are given for each distribution. Daphne's weight is 53 pounds. Remember that this weight score is less than 1 SD above the mean because it falls between the mean and the first line in the graph (marking the score that is 1 SD above the mean). The μ for the dog weight distribution is given as 50. We need to know how far Daphne's weight is from the mean (μ) and in which direction, so we need to calculate a difference score between her weight (53) and the mean (50). That will be the first part of our calculation (53 − 50 = +3). The next part is to put that difference score into SD units by dividing it by the population standard deviation (σ). The standard deviation of the dog weight distribution is given as 10 pounds, so we will divide the difference score (+3) by the σ of 10 $\left(\frac{+3}{10}=+.3\right)$. This is the z score for Daphne's weight: +0.3. In other words, her weight is 0.3 SDs above the mean in the population distribution of dog weights.

The calculation we just completed gives us the formula:

$$z = \frac{(X - \mu)}{\sigma}$$

where X is the score we want to transform, μ is the population mean, and σ is the population standard deviation. Let's try another example using this formula and my weight of 150 pounds. Am I heavier or lighter than Daphne? The z score comparison will tell us. We will use the μ of 140 pounds and σ of 25 pounds from the female weight distribution in Figure 7.2. Thus, the z score for my weight is

$$z = \frac{(150 - 140)}{25} = \frac{+10}{25} = +.4$$

Stop and Think

7.1   Let's try another example: Compare the weight of my husband, Jeff (135 pounds) with another dog I know named Rafiki (7.5 pounds; see Photo 7.3). First calculate the z scores for Jeff's weight and Rafiki's weight using the correct means and standard deviations presented in Figure 7.2 (Jeff is male). Compare the two z scores. Who is heavier: Jeff or Rafiki?

7.2   Now try the z score transformation for your own weight using the distributions presented in Figure 7.2. If you have a dog (and know its weight), you can also calculate the z score for your dog's weight. Compare the two z scores (or use Daphne's z score; see the text in this section showing the calculation). Are you heavier or lighter than your dog (or Daphne)? How about compared to Rafiki?

7.3   What does a z score of −1.5 tell you about the location of that score in the distribution?

If we compare my weight z score of +0.4 and Daphne's weight z score of +0.3, we see that I am, in fact, heavier than Daphne for our relative weight distributions (but not by much!).

Calculating a z Score Using Excel

Calculating a z score using Excel is simply a matter of typing in the z score formula into a cell in the data window. If you have your score (X) typed into a single cell, you can use that cell in the formula. Or you can simply put the score into the formula itself. The formula to type into a cell in Excel for calculating Daphne's weight is

$$= (53 - 50)/10$$

Using this formula, you will see the same value we calculated earlier (0.3) appear in that cell in the spreadsheet. If you have all the population scores entered into Excel before your z score calculation, you can calculate the population mean (μ) and standard deviation (σ) using the AVERAGE formula to determine these values ahead of time if you do not already have them.

Photo 7.3   This is Rafiki the dog; he is 7.5 pounds.

SOURCE: Photo by Diana M. Steakley–Freeman

Calculating a z Score Using SPSS

The procedure for calculating z scores in SPSS is also fairly simple. You first need to have the score(s) you want to use in the calculation in a column in the data window. Once you have the scores entered, you can choose the Compute Variable function from the Transform menu at the top. This will open the window shown in Figure 7.4. In the Target Variable box, you will need to name the new variable that contains the z score(s) (e.g., z score). Then in the Numeric Expression box, you can create the z score equation using the column containing your score(s) and the known population μ and σ. Figure 7.4 shows how this equation might look for Daphne's weight as a z score. When you click on OK, the z score(s) will appear in a new column in the data window with the label you have given to the new variable that contains the z scores.

Summary of Steps

- Type the data into a column in the data window.
- Choose Computer Variable from the Transform menu at the top.
- In the Computer Variable window (see Figure 7.4), name your new z score variable in the Target Variable box.
- Type in the formula for the z score (see Figure 7.4). You can click your data variable into the Numeric Expression box by highlighting it and clicking on the arrow.
- When you click OK, the calculated z scores will appear in a new column in the data window.

Figure 7.4   Compute Variable Window in SPSS Showing the Equation for Calculating a z Score for Scores in the First Column of the Data Window

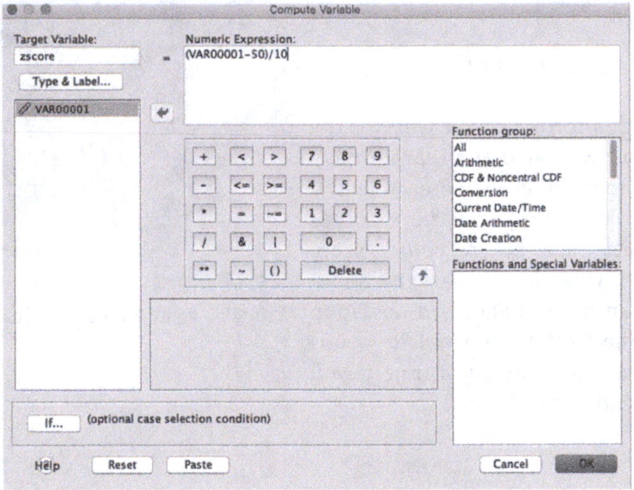

THE NORMAL DISTRIBUTION

Now that you know how to calculate a z score and what it tells you about a score's location in a distribution, let's look at how this information can be useful in testing hypotheses. Knowing the location of a score in the population can help us do this. Let's go back to the example we started the chapter with: You want to determine if the online quizzes in your course help students prepare for the final exam. You know the score you want to compare with the distribution (the current class mean of 82) and the population mean for the distribution ($\mu = 75$) from your instructor. What else do you need in order to calculate the z score for the current class mean? (If you need a hint, look back at the formula for the z score to see what is missing). What's missing is the population standard deviation (σ). Let's suppose your instructor gives you that—it's the standard deviation from the set of all past final exam mean scores for the course without online quizzes: σ = 3. Now you have all the information needed to find the location of the current class's mean score in the population distribution of all past mean exam scores without online quizzes. We can calculate the *z* score using the following formula:

$$z = \frac{(82-75)}{3} = \frac{7}{3} = +2.33$$

This *z* score tells us that the current class mean with online quizzes is 2.33 SDs above the population mean of exam scores without online quizzes. Does this tell us whether the online quizzes increased the score? It will help us with this, but we need more information before we know whether the quizzes increased the mean score or not.

What we need to know now is the shape of the population distribution of mean scores without online quizzes. Suppose that this distribution looks similar to the one shown in Figure 7.5. You can see from the graph that the distribution is symmetrical. But it is also a special type of symmetrical distribution known as the normal distribution. You've probably heard about normal distributions before, but you may not have known what makes them different from other distributions. Not only are normal distributions symmetrical, but the proportion of scores in each part of the distribution is already known. In other words, a specific portion of the scores in the distribution falls between

Normal distribution: a symmetrical distribution in which the percentage of scores in each portion of the distribution is known

Figure 7.5   The Population Distribution of Exam Scores Without Online Quizzes—a Normal Distribution

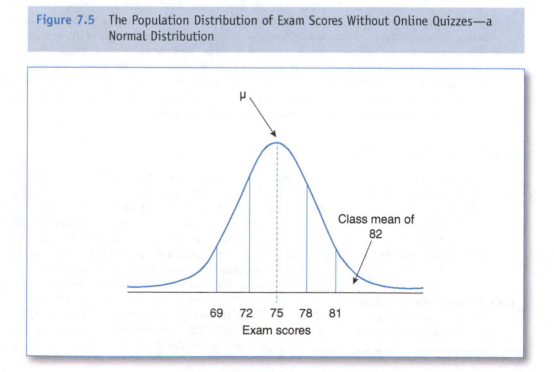

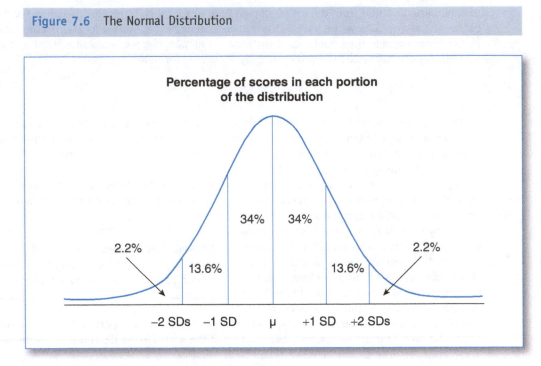

Figure 7.6   The Normal Distribution

the mean and one standard deviation in the distribution, both above and below the mean (i.e., 68%). You can see this portion in the normal distribution shown in Figure 7.6 (34% above the mean and 34% below the mean). In fact, the percentage of scores that falls in each part of the distribution for the segments marked by the standard deviation units is already known. Thus, we know how likely it is that a score will fall into different parts of the normal distribution. For example, we know that 68% of the scores fall within 1 SD of the mean and that 95% of the scores will fall within 2 SDs of the mean (you can verify this by adding up the percentages for the portions above and below the mean within 2 SDs in Figure 7.6).

Locating a *z* Score in the Normal Distribution

Knowing the percentage of scores in different portions of the normal distribution is useful because it can help us determine the likelihood of getting a specific range of scores (e.g., the *z* score we calculated for Daphne's weight [+0.3] or a score higher or lower than that score) in the distribution. In other, words, it can tell us how common a score is for that distribution. The percentage values shown in Figure 7.6 are useful for determining the likelihood of obtaining a *z* score that falls within 1 or 2 SDs from the mean, but how do we determine the likelihood of obtaining a score that is in between these values, such as Daphne's weight *z* score of +0.3? The answer is to use the Unit Normal Table that contains the proportion of scores for different sections of the normal distribution for many *z* score values. Appendix B of this text contains a Unit

Unit Normal Table: a table of the proportion of scores in a normal distribution for many different *z* score values

Table 7.1 A Section of the Unit Normal Table

Column A z Score	Column B Proportion in Body	Column C Proportion in Tail
.25	.5987	.4013
.26	.6026	.3974
.27	.6064	.3936
.28	.6103	.3897
.29	.6141	.3859
.30	.6179	.3821
.31	.6217	.3783
.32	.6255	.3745
.33	.6293	.3707
.34	.6331	.3669
.35	.6368	.3632
.36	.6406	.3594
.37	.6443	.3557
.38	.6480	.3520
.39	.6517	.3483
.40	.6554	.3446

NOTE: The entire table is shown in Appendix B.

Normal Table that you can use to find the proportion value for the z score you are looking for. Let's look at the columns of this table: Column A contains the z scores and Columns B and C contain the proportion in body and proportion in tail for the normal distribution. Columns B and C are related such that Column C contains the part of distribution that is not in Column B (i.e., Column C = 1 – Column B). Table 7.1 shows a small part of the Unit Normal Table where the z score of 0.30 is located (one of the rows marked in blue).

If you read across the table to Columns B and C for a z score of 0.30, it shows a proportion of 0.6179 for the proportion in body and 0.3821 for the proportion in tail. This means that 61.79% of the scores in the normal distribution are at a z score of +0.30 or lower and 38.21% of the scores in the distribution are at a z score of +0.30 or higher. This also tells us that Daphne's weight score is a fairly common score in the dog weight distribution because, although it's not right at the 50/50 point in the middle where the mean is (and where the most common scores are), it's still pretty close to the mean with many scores both above and below this value. Thus, the Unit Normal Table can help us determine the likelihood of a range of scores in the normal distribution when we want to know how likely it is that we would obtain a z score at or above or below a specific value. We're not at the point where we can test a hypothesis yet, but as you'll see in the next section, knowing the likelihood of obtaining specific z score values is the first step.

But before we look further at how we can use the Unit Normal Table to test our hypothesis, let's practice using this table a bit more. Let's go back to my weight z score of +0.40 and see if we can determine what the likelihood of getting this score or lower is using the table in Appendix B. Look again at Table 7.1. The row with the z score of 0.4 is marked in blue as well. If you read across the table to Columns B and C, you will see that the chance of getting a z score of +0.40 or lower is 65.54% (Column B) and +0.40 or higher is 34.46%. If we compare these percentages with the ones given for a z score of +0.30, we see that the score of +0.40 is a little less common because there is a lower percentage of scores at that value or higher in the distribution.

Let's now consider how the table works for negative z scores: Suppose we want to know the likelihood of obtaining a z score of -0.40 and lower. In this case, the percentages are the same, but now Column C contains the chance of getting this score or *lower* in the distribution. This is because Column C is the percentage of scores in the tail of the distribution, which is the portion that does not contain the mean of the distribution. Because negative z scores are below the mean, the tail part is now the part that is *lower* than that score. Column B, the body of the distribution, shows the percentage for the portion of the distribution that does contain the mean. For negative z scores, Column B will be the percentage of scores *higher* than that score. Thus, you will need to pay attention to the sign (+ or −) of the z score when you decide which column of the table to use in determining the correct percentage for scores you are looking for.

Using the Normal Distribution to Determine the Probability of a Sample Mean

Now we can use the Unit Normal Table to figure out the likelihood of a range of scores. Let's consider how this information is useful in determining whether online quizzes increased the final exam mean in your course compared with final exam means from past courses when the online quizzes were not available (the example we started the chapter with). To answer this question, we need to go back to a concept we discussed in Chapter 3: the distribution of sample means. Remember from that chapter that the distribution of sample means is the distribution of means from all possible samples of a specific size from the population. In other words, if we are looking at a sample size of 30 students (the number who take your course each semester) and the entire population of students were to take that course (without online quizzes) at some point in their college career, the distribution of sample of means would contain the final exam means for all of those classes. We can then use the mean from the distribution of sample means along with its standard deviation to determine the current class's mean exam score using the z score we calculated earlier. The mean and standard deviation from your instructor were $\mu = 75$, $\sigma = 3$, and the z score we calculated for your class mean of 82 was +2.33 (see Figure 7.7).

Figure 7.7   Distribution of Sample Means for Course Final Exam Mean *z* Scores

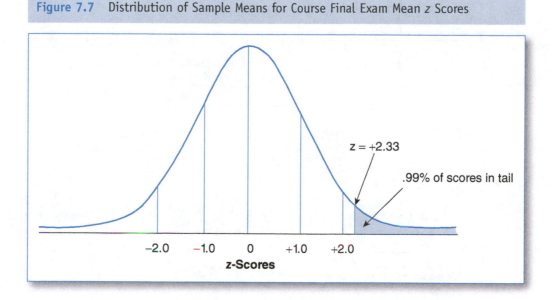

z = +2.33

.99% of scores in tail

−2.0   −1.0   0   +1.0   +2.0

z-Scores

If we also know that the population for the class final exam mean scores is a normal distribution, we can use the Unit Normal Table to determine how likely it is that we would get a mean score of 82 or higher in the population of means for courses without online quizzes. If you look at Appendix B at the end of the text using the method we followed in the previous section, you'll find that the percentage of scores in the distribution with *z* score +2.33 or higher is 0.99% (i.e., less than 1%). Figure 7.7 shows the location of the *z* score and the percentage of scores in the tail of the distribution of sample means. This value is listed in Column C of the Unit Normal Table (we are looking at a positive *z* score so we need the value from the proportion in tail from the table). This is a pretty unlikely score from the set of all exam means for this course. This tells us there's a very low chance that our mean score of 82 came from this population because it is a very uncommon score for this distribution. However, in order to determine if the class mean of 82 is really higher than the overall mean of 75 (i.e., if the online quizzes really helped), we need to compare our class mean of 82 with scores in the distribution of sample means. We will consider how to do this in the next chapter, but our goal will be to determine the location of our class mean in the distribution of sample means using a *z* score calculation. This is how *z* scores can help us test our hypotheses, but we would need to know the population mean and standard deviation to calculate the *z* score and that the population is a normal distribution to use this method. Otherwise, the proportion values in the Unit Normal Table are not accurate. In the next chapter, we will also consider how we decide if a mean score is unlikely enough to decide it probably does not come from the distribution of sample means.

Used in this way, the *z* score can be used in a one-sample *z* test as an inferential statistic that can help us test hypotheses. Figure 7.8 shows the full flowchart for choosing an inferential statistic for your study. In the next chapter, we will discuss the process of hypothesis testing in more detail.

Figure 7.8   Statistical Test Decision Flowchart

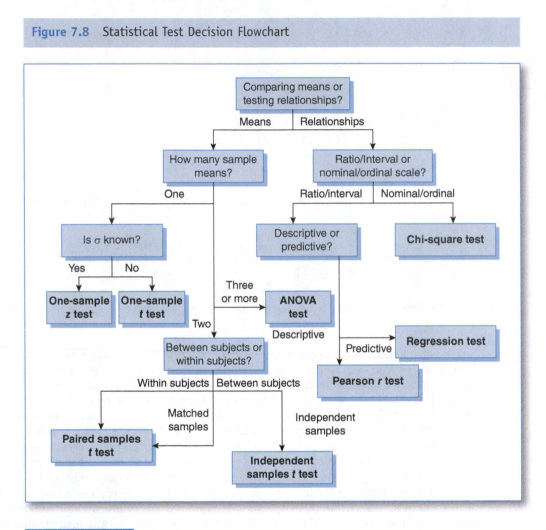

7.4   Using the Unit Normal Table, find the proportion of scores in the normal distribution that are at the value or above in the distribution:

a.   +1.25

b.   −0.08

c.   −2.17

7.5   Explain what is meant by the column descriptions of proportion in *Body* and proportion in *Tail* from the Unit Normal Table.

7.6   Suppose you wanted to know whether caffeine reduces sleep. You conduct a simple study on yourself in which you record the number of hours you slept on nights when you've had caffeine after 7 p.m. and calculate a mean number of sleep hours of 7.25. Suppose that you also know that for all nights when you haven't had caffeine, you sleep an average of 8.5 hours with a standard deviation of 0.5 hours and that your number of hours slept distribution is a normal distribution. Use the *z* score transformation and Unit Normal Table procedures discussed in this chapter to determine how likely it is that your mean sleep time with caffeine is a score (based on the proportion in the tail) in your population distribution of mean sleep times without caffeine.

CHAPTER SUMMARY

7.1   What is a standardized score?

A standardized score is a score that has been transformed based on its location from the population mean and put in to standard deviation (SD) units. It is also called a *z* score and can be used to compare the location of scores in their different distributions.

7.2   How are standardized scores useful?

Standardized scores (or *z* scores) allow us to easily determine the location of the score in its population distribution, compare the locations of scores across different population distributions, and convert an entire distribution into *z* scores without changing its shape.

7.3   What is the normal distribution?

A normal distribution is a special type of symmetrical distribution where the percentage of scores in different portions of the distribution is known and can looked up in the Unit Normal Table.

7.4   How can the normal distribution be used to test hypotheses about populations?

If we know that a population of scores is normally distributed, we can use *z* scores and the Unit Normal Table to determine how likely it is that a sample mean came from that population using its distribution of sample means. If it is a very uncommon score, then it probably did not come from that distribution (or population) and can help us determine if something we want to compare is different in some way. The next chapter will discuss this process and the steps for testing hypotheses in more detail.

THINKING ABOUT RESEARCH

A summary of a research study in psychology is given below. As you read the summary, think about the following questions:

1.   Identify the independent and dependent variables in this study. Does this study appear to be an experiment or not? How do you know?

2. The Results section describes the transformation of body mass index (BMI) scores to zBMI scores. Explain what the researchers can learn about a child's BMI score from its corresponding zBMI score. Why didn't the researchers simply use the untransformed BMI scores in their analyses?

3. Suppose that for the distribution of BMI scores for a 4-year-old female child of has a $\mu = 15$, $\sigma = 1$. If a female 4-year-old in this study has a BMI score of 13.5, what would their zBMI score be?

4. For the z score you calculated in the question above, what is the likelihood of having a score at that value or lower in the BMI distribution?

5. If the authors wished to compare the Learning about Activity and Understand Nutrition for Child Health (LAUNCH) program participant mean BMI score with the mean BMI score for the control group who only received pediatrician care, how could they use the Unit Normal Table to accomplish this?

> Van Allen J., Kuhl, E. S., Filigno, S. S., Clifford, L. M., Connor, J. M., & Stark, L. J. (2014). Changes in parent motivation predicts changes in body mass index z-score (zBMI) and dietary intake among preschools enrolled in a family-based obesity intervention. *Journal of Pediatric Psychology, 39,* 1028–1037.

Purpose of the Study. These researchers were interested in the effectiveness of an obesity intervention program on preschoolers with high body mass index (BMI). More specifically, they investigated the effects of parent motivation and changes in motivation over the course of the intervention program on its effectiveness in reducing BMI score in the children. The Learning about Activity and Understand Nutrition for Child Health (LAUNCH) program was compared with enhanced standard pediatrician visits in their influence on BMI score, consumption of different types of food, and physical activity during the program period.

Method of the Study. Sixty children were recruited from pediatric practices who were between 2 and 5 years old, had a BMI at or above the 95th percentile for their age and gender, and had at least one parent with a BMI score at or above 25. Half of these children were assigned to the LAUNCH program and half continued to see their pediatrician at their normal time. Outcome measures (physical activity, number of servings of different types of food, and BMI) were collected before the start of the program, after the six-month program period, and after another six months for a follow-up measure. Parent motivation for the program was also measured using the Parent Motivation Inventory (PMI) both before and after the program.

Results of the Study. The analyses focused on the children who participated in the LAUNCH program to examine effects of parent motivation (as measured by PMI score) on the outcome measures. Because children were at different ages and of different gender, their BMI scores were transformed from z scores to standardized BMI scores (zBMI) in analyses. Analyses indicated that increased PMI scores from pretest to posttest were associated with decreased zBMI scores at the six-month follow-up measurement. Increases in PMI were also related to decreases in servings of sugary foods. However, PMI scores were not associated with changes in activity level.

Conclusions of the Study. The results of the study suggest that parent motivation is an important factor in the effectiveness of childhood obesity programs.

TEST YOURSELF

1. A standardized score is _____.

    a. a z score

    b. a score that has been transformed to allow comparisons across distributions

    c. a new score that represents the original score's distance from the distribution mean in standard deviation units

    d. all of the above

2. A z score of −1.45 indicates that _____.

    a. the original score is between 1 and 2 standard deviations above the mean

    b. the original score is between 1 and 2 standard deviations below the mean

    c. the original score is not in the population distribution because it is negative

    d. the original score cannot be transformed into a standardized score

3. The Unit Normal Table can tell us _____.

    a. the z score for a score in a distribution

    b. the z scores for all the scores in a distribution

    c. the percentage of scores at a specific z score or higher in the normal distribution

    d. the percentage of scores at a specific z score or higher in a skewed distribution

4. For a population with $\mu = 100$ and $\sigma = 10$, what is the z score for a score of 90?

    a. +10

    b. − 10

    c. +1.0

    d. − 1.0

5. For the population described above, what is the z score for a score of 120?

    a. +20

    b. − 20

    c. +2.0

    d. − 2.0

6. Calculating a z score can help us test a hypothesis about a population.

    a. True

    b. False

7. A z score will tell us the distance from the mean of a score in a distribution but not the direction of that location from the mean.

    a. True

    b. False

8. The Unit Normal Table will tell us the exact probability of a z score in any distribution.

    a. True

    b. False

9. You are taking two psychology courses: Cognition and Research Methods. On the same day, you take an exam in both courses. In Cognition, you score a 78 on the exam ($\mu = 75$ and the $\sigma = 3$). In Research Methods, you score an 82 ($\mu = 78$ and the $\sigma = 5$). In which class did you actually do better on the exam?

10. Some intelligence tests have a $\mu = 100$ and $\sigma = 10$. If you score a 110 on an intelligence test with this distribution, what is the z score for your score?

11. Explain why a z score is called a standardized score.

12. For each z score below, find the percentage of scores at that value or higher in the normal distribution:

    a. +1.67

    b. -2.02

    c. -0.80

    d. +0.08

13. Your score on a course exam was 95 and your z score on this exam was +2.0. The distribution of exam scores had a $\sigma = 5$. What was the mean on the exam?

14. A standardized math test for 5th graders has a $\mu = 50$. A student scores 60 on this exam and their z score is +1.50. What is the σ for the standardized test?

Chapter 8

Hypothesis-Testing Logic

As you read the chapter, consider the following questions:

8.1 What is the standard error?

8.2 How can we use a population mean and the standard error to test a hypothesis?

8.3 What are the steps in hypothesis testing?

8.4 What is statistical significance and what does it tell us about our hypothesis?

8.5 What types of errors exist in our hypothesis-testing procedure?

8.6 How can I reduce the chance of an error in testing hypotheses?

In the last chapter, we began to discuss how we use z scores to test hypotheses about data using the Unit Normal Table. In this chapter, we will continue this discussion and further define the steps and logic of hypothesis testing using inferential statistics. To better understand our goals in hypothesis testing, let's review the example we used in Chapter 7: You are taking a course in which the instructor has introduced online quizzes to help you study for exams. She has taught this course many times, but this is the first time she has used the online quizzes in the course. You want to know whether the online quizzes are helping the students perform better on the exams (see Photo 8.1). To answer this question, you decide to compare the mean on the final exam for your class to the final exam mean for all previous classes. Your instructor tells you that the mean for the final exams from all previous students is 75 (i.e., $\mu = 75$) with a standard deviation of 3 (i.e., $\sigma = 3$). She also tells you that your class mean on the final exam was 82 (i.e., $X = 82$). In the last chapter, we used this information to calculate the location of your class mean in the population of final exam scores with $\mu = 75$ and $\sigma = 3$. We also used the Unit Normal Table to determine that a score of 82 is quite unlikely in this distribution (i.e., there is only a 0.99 % chance of getting a score of 82 or higher in this distribution). However, this only tells us the location of the mean score in the population of all final exam scores. In order to figure out if the mean exam score for your class is significantly higher than the mean scores

©iStock/LuckyBusiness

for the previous classes, we will need to look at the location of this mean in the distribution of sample means based on the class (i.e., sample) size. That is the general process for testing hypotheses using any of our inferential statistics tests: to find the location of the sample mean in the distribution of sample means for that population and decide if it is an extreme (i.e., unlikely) score in that distribution. We will start with the hypothesis test using z scores and this research question (see Photo 8.1) because you are already familiar with z scores from the previous chapter.

USING THE NORMAL DISTRIBUTION TO TEST HYPOTHESES

Recall from Chapter 7 that in the online quiz example, we are looking at a normal population of final exam scores to compare with your class mean of 82. Although we were able to find the location of this score in the population of final exam scores, this did not quite tell us what we want to know—whether this is a likely mean from the distribution of sample means for the class size of 30. What we really want to know is whether the mean of 82 is an unlikely mean score for classes that did not have online quizzes available. This will tell us (with a certain probability) that the online quiz class mean is different from the mean scores without the online quizzes. Thus, we need to figure out how likely a mean this is in the distribution of sample means. In order to find out how likely this mean is in the distribution of sample means, we will need to look more closely at that distribution.

The Distribution of Sample Means Revisited

As I have described in previous chapters, the distribution of sample means is a special distribution that contains all the sample means we would get if we were to draw all the possible samples of a specific size from the population and determine each sample's mean score. In other words, the distribution of sample means' scores are the sample means from all possible samples of specific size drawn at random from the population. Recall from Chapter 7 that a z score is calculated based on the distance of the score from the mean divided by the standard deviation of the distribution (i.e., $z = \dfrac{(X-\mu)}{\sigma}$). Thus, if we want to calculate a z score for a sample mean to determine how likely it is that it came from the distribution of sample means for that population, we will need to know the mean and standard deviation for this distribution. If we were to calculate the mean of all the sample means from samples drawn from the population, we would end up with the population mean μ; thus, the mean of the distribution of samples is equal to the population mean μ. So, if we know the population mean, we will also know the mean of the distribution of sample means.

Things get a bit trickier in determining the standard deviation for the distribution of sample means. Recall from the discussion of sampling that the larger our sample is, the closer we will get to the actual population values in our sample. Thus, sample size will influence the spread of the scores in our distribution of sample means. The larger the sample size (n), the lower the variability in the distribution of sample means because we're getting a better estimate of the population mean with each sample. Thus, the standard deviation for the distribution of sample means is based on σ and n. If we know these values, we can calculate the standard deviation of the distribution of sample means, known as the standard error. The standard error represents the sampling error present in our samples (i.e., how much we expect the sample to differ from the population). We can calculate the standard error using the following formula:

> **Standard error:** the estimate of sampling error that is determined from the standard deviation of the distribution of sample means

$$\sigma_{\bar{X}} = \frac{\sigma}{\sqrt{n}}$$

where $\sigma_{\bar{X}}$ is the standard error, σ is the population standard deviation, and n is the sample size for the sample we are looking at. In other words, $\sigma_{\bar{X}}$ is the standard deviation of the distribution of sample means we want to locate our sample mean in.

Finally, we need to consider the shape of the distribution of sample means. If the population is normal, then the distribution of sample means is also normal. This means we can use the Unit Normal Table to find the proportion of scores in different parts of the distribution of sample means, as we did for the distributions in Chapter 7. However, even if the population distribution's shape is unknown (or known to be something other than normal), we can still determine the shape of the distribution of sample means using the central limit theorem. The central

> **Central limit theorem:** a mathematical description of the shape of the distribution of sample means that states that for a population with mean μ and standard deviation σ, the distribution of sample means for sample size n will have a mean equal to μ, standard deviation equal to the standard error, and a shape approaching a normal distribution as n becomes very large

limit theorem is a mathematical description of the shape of the distribution of sample means that will allow us to determine if the distribution of sample means is normal in shape. This turns out to be very important in inferential statistics because, in many cases, we do not know the shape of the population. The central limit theorem states that for a population with mean μ and standard deviation σ, the distribution of sample means for sample size n will have a mean equal to μ, standard deviation equal to the standard error, and a shape approaching a normal distribution as n becomes very large (i.e., approaches infinity). In practical terms, the shape of the distribution of sample means is almost exactly normal any time n is greater than 30. Thus, we can use the Unit Normal Table to determine the proportion of scores in different sections of the distribution of sample means whenever our sample size is greater than 30.

Conducting a One-Sample z Test

Based on the description of the distribution of sample means in the previous section, you should be able to see how we can use a known population μ and σ to calculate a z score for a sample mean to determine its location in the distribution of sample means. We will need to adjust our z score formula a bit to fit the distribution of sample means:

$$z_{\bar{X}} = \frac{(\bar{X} - \mu)}{\frac{\sigma}{\sqrt{n}}}$$

The new z score ($z_{\bar{X}}$) for the distribution of sample means will tell us the location of our sample mean within this distribution. If our population is a normal distribution or our sample size is greater than 30, we can then use the Unit Normal Table to determine how extreme a score this is in the distribution of sample means. For our example with $\mu = 75$, $\sigma = 3$, and $\bar{X} = 82$, we can calculate $z_{\bar{X}}$:

$$z_{\bar{X}} = \frac{(82 - 75)}{\frac{3}{\sqrt{30}}} = \frac{7}{\frac{3}{5.48}} = \frac{7}{.55} = +12.73$$

This is a different value than the z score of $+2.33$ that we calculated in Chapter 7 for the location of the score in the population of final exam scores. That is because we have calculated the location of the sample mean in the distribution of sample means here that has a smaller standard deviation than the population of scores.

If you look in a Unit Normal Table, you will see that a z score of 12.73 is very large—in fact, the table given in Appendix B only goes up to a z score $+4.00$, where only 0.003% of the scores in the distribution are at this z score or higher. Thus, there will be less than 0.003% of the scores in the distribution of sample means at $+12.73$ or higher. This tells us that our class mean of 82 is a very rare sample mean in the distribution of sample means for final exam means in classes without online quizzes. But how rare does it have to be before we can decide that it probably doesn't belong in this distribution of means? The standard we use in the behavioral sciences for determining this is 5% (i.e., a proportion of 0.05 in the distribution), meaning there's only a 5% chance (or less) that our sample mean came from this distribution. If the percentage of scores for a sample mean z score is at 5% or less for that score or higher (or lower for negative z scores), then we can conclude that it is rare enough for us to decide that it is different from the means in this distribution. In other words, our class mean of 82 is higher (with less than 0.003% probability) than what is expected for the final exam mean from a class that did not have online quizzes. Therefore, we can conclude that the online quizzes did help students score higher on the final exam. This is the general process we use in inferential statistics. In the next section, we will consider this process as a series of steps to follow to test our hypothesis.

Stop and Think

8.1   Using the standard cutoff probability of 0.05 or lower, find the z score in the Unit Normal Table that corresponds to this probability value (Hint: Look for the closest value to 0.05 without going over in the proportion in *Tail* column). Using the z score you found as a comparison, if your sample mean had a z score of +4.50 for the distribution of sample means, what would this tell you about your hypothesis?

8.2   The Graduate Record Exam (GRE) Verbal test is reported to have a mean score of about 150 and a standard deviation of about 8 (Educational Testing Service, 2016). The GRE prep course you are thinking of taking advertises that it can improve scores on this test. They report that the mean score for this year's class of 100 students scored a mean of 160 on the test. Based on these values, is it worth it to take the class?

LOGIC OF HYPOTHESIS TESTING

As you saw in the example in the previous section, the starting place for our hypothesis-testing procedure is a research question we want to answer. For the example I have been using in this chapter, the question was whether or not online quizzes helped students achieve a higher score on the course's final exam. The one-sample z test we conducted helped us determine an answer to this question. Now let's consider another research question: Does memory ability change as one ages? A reasonable hypothesis is that memory ability does change with age. How can we test this hypothesis? We can conduct a study comparing memory for older and young adults and compare their memory scores. A hypothesis-testing procedure using inferential statistics can help us.

The hypothesis-testing procedure can be summarized in five steps:

Step 1: State your research question and make hypotheses about the answer.

Step 2: Set a decision criterion for making a decision about the hypotheses.

Step 3: Collect your sample data.

Step 4: Calculate statistics.

Step 5: Make a decision about the hypotheses.

Table 8.1 provides an overview of these steps that you can refer to as I discuss them further in this chapter. In the next few sections, we will go through each step for our memory and aging research question.

Table 8.1   Overview of the Hypothesis-Testing Steps

Step 1: State Hypotheses	State research question and develop null and alternative hypotheses using literature in the research area.
Step 2: Set Decision Criterion	Set the decision criterion alpha (α) as a probability that the sample mean is a score in the distribution of sample means; consider how your alpha level will influence the chance of Type I and Type II errors in your test.
Step 3: Collect Sample Data	Design your study to test your hypotheses, recruit sample participants/subjects, and collect data on the dependent variables of interest.
Step 4: Calculate Statistics	Summarize data with descriptive statistics; choose an appropriate inferential statistics test and calculate the inferential statistic and corresponding probability (p) value for that statistic.
Step 5: Make a Decision	Compare the statistic p value with α; make a decision to either reject or retain the null hypothesis based on this comparison and then decide if you can accept the alternative hypothesis.

Step 1: State Hypotheses

For this example, we have already stated our research question: Does memory ability change with age? We have also stated our hypothesis about the answer to this question: Memory does change with age. Thus, part of this step is already complete. One thing to note is that the hypothesis we are making is about the population of people, not about our sample. It is the population we want to learn about when we conduct our study. We are only using the sample to represent this population because we cannot test the entire population. Thus, the hypotheses we make are always about a population we want to learn about. We could state our hypothesis as "In the population of people, memory changes with age."

Scientific/Alternative hypothesis: the hypothesis that an effect or relationship exists (or exists in a specific direction) in the population

Null hypothesis: the hypothesis that an effect or relationship does not exist (or exists in the opposite direction of the alternative hypothesis) in the population

In the hypothesis-testing procedure, the hypothesis made by the researcher is usually the scientific/ alternative hypothesis (it is the alternative hypothesis to an important hypothesis that you will read about next). The scientific or alternative hypothesis is the hypothesis either that an effect of the independent or subject variable exists (for an experiment or quasi-experiment) or a relationship between the variables exists (for a correlational study). For our example, the hypothesis that memory changes with age in the population of people is the scientific/alternative hypothesis that is consistent with predicting that aging causes a change in memory ability for individuals in the population. However, we also must consider a second hypothesis in our test: the null hypothesis. The null hypothesis is the opposite hypothesis to the scientific/alternative hypothesis: that an effect or relationship does not exist in the population. The null hypothesis is also important to state in Step 1 of our procedure because, as you will see later in this chapter, it is the null hypothesis we are directly learning about when we calculate our inferential statistics in Step 4 and make a decision about in Step 5.

For our example, then, we will have two hypotheses to state to complete Step 1: the scientific/alternative hypothesis (denoted by H_1 or sometimes as H_a for *alternative*) and the null hypothesis (denoted by H_0). We can state these hypotheses as

H_0: *In the general population, memory abilities do not change with age* or *In the general population, different age groups have the same mean memory scores.*

The null hypothesis makes the opposite prediction from the alternative hypothesis: *Memory abilities do not change with age.*

H_1: *In the general population, memory abilities change with age* or *In the general population, different age groups have different mean memory scores.*

What we have considered above is called a two-tailed hypothesis because we are considering both possible directions of the difference between means in the hypothesis. In other words, our alternative hypothesis does not predict whether younger or older individuals will have higher memory scores; it simply states that the mean scores for younger and older individuals in the population will be *different*. It does not include a prediction about which population will have higher scores. However, for this study, you might find previous studies that indicate that as people age their memory abilities decline. Thus, you could make a directional or one-tailed hypothesis. As a one-tailed hypothesis, our alternative hypothesis could be stated as

Two-tailed hypothesis: both directions of an effect or relationship are considered in the alternative hypothesis of the tes

One-tailed hypothesis: only one direction of an effect or relationship is predicted in the alternative hypothesis of the test

H_1: *In the general population, older individuals have lower memory scores than younger individuals.*

We could also make the opposite prediction (e.g., H_1: *In the general population, older individuals have higher memory scores than younger individuals*), but the first hypothesis stated above is more likely to be consistent with the results of previous studies. For this alternative hypothesis, our null hypothesis must include any other possible outcomes, so our null hypothesis is

H_0: *In the general population, older individuals have higher memory scores than younger individuals or the memory scores of the two age groups are the same.*

For a one-tailed hypothesis, the null hypothesis contains the predictions of no effect or relationship *and* the effect or relationship in the direction opposite to that predicted in the alternative hypothesis. See the top portion of the flowchart in Figure 8.1 for a comparison of one-tailed and two-tailed hypotheses for this study.

Figure 8.1 Flowchart of the Steps in Hypothesis Testing for Memory and Aging Example

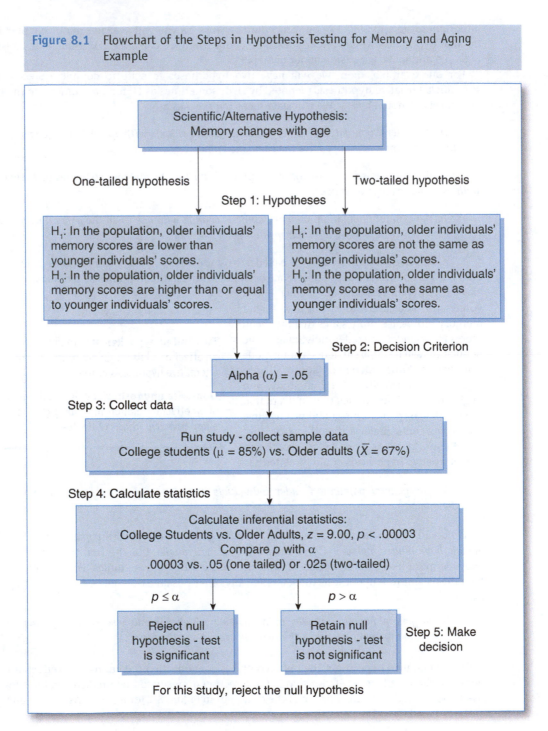

One-tailed hypotheses are typically made only when a researcher has a logical reason to believe that one particular direction of the effect will occur. Thus, one-tailed hypotheses are often made when the other direction of the effect logically should not occur or does not answer the research question. They may also be made when the literature review of an area indicates that one direction of the effect has been shown consistently over a number of research studies.

> ### Stop and Think
>
> 8.3 For each of the following statements, indicate if a one- or two-tailed test is most appropriate:
>
> - Taking aspirin reduces the chance of a heart attack.
> - Quizzing yourself before a test will increase your test score compared with simply rereading your notes.
> - Completing a puzzle under a time constraint will affect your accuracy.
> - Sleep affects depression.
>
> 8.4 For each statement above, state the alternative and null hypotheses.

Step 2: Set Decision Criterion

Now that we have completed Step 1 and have stated our alternative and null hypotheses, we can move on to Step 2 and set our decision criterion. Let's consider what we are doing when we set this value.

In inferential statistics tests, we are calculating a value that tells us the location of the sample mean in a distribution, just as we did with z scores in the last chapter. But the values we have from the sample are descriptive statistics in the form of a mean score (or, in some cases, a value indicating the strength of a relationship—more will be described about this type of test in Chapter 15). Thus, we are looking at the location of a sample mean in the distribution of sample means as we did earlier in this chapter. The decision criterion value marks off a portion of this distribution that represents the most extreme scores. It is also called the alpha level, because the criterion probability is denoted by the Greek letter α. As described earlier, the criterion is typically set at 0.05 (i.e., 5% of the most extreme scores) in research in the behavioral sciences. This means that we want to look at the proportion in tail from the Unit Normal Table that sets off this part of the distribution (and its corresponding z score—see Stop and Think 8.1 earlier in this chapter). Figure 8.2 illustrates this portion of the distribution of sample means. The shaded areas are the portion of the distribution that are considered the most extreme scores equal to the decision criterion. If we have a two-tailed hypothesis, we

Alpha level: the probability level used by researchers to indicate the cutoff probability level (highest value) that allows them to reject the null hypothesis

Figure 8.2 Distribution of Sample Means When the Null Hypothesis Is True

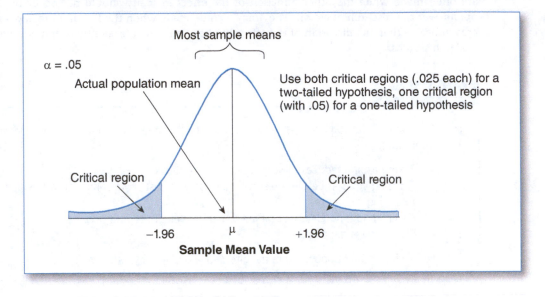

must consider both shaded tails of the distribution so the criterion proportion is split in two (i.e., 0.025 in the upper tail and 0.025 in the lower tail). If we have made a one-tailed hypothesis, then we only need to consider one shaded tail that contains the entire proportion—which tail depends on the direction we have predicted: The upper tail if we predict the mean will be higher and the lower tail if we predict that the mean will be lower. The shaded portion is known as the critical region of the distribution because it is the part we are looking at to see if we can reject the null hypothesis (one of our possible decisions in Step 5).

Critical region: the most extreme portion of a distribution of statistical values for the null hypothesis determined by the decision criterion (i.e., alpha level—typically 5%)

Notice in Figure 8.2 that the distribution of sample means corresponds to the sample means when the null hypothesis is true. This is the distribution we will consider in our hypothesis test. We will locate our test statistic in this distribution (is it in the shaded portion(s) or not?) and make a decision about the null hypothesis depending on whether our sample mean is extreme for this distribution or not. This is because the evidence provided by the inferential test is the likelihood of obtaining the data in the study if we assume the null hypothesis is, in fact, true. That is what the inferential test focuses on: What is the chance of obtaining the data in this study when the null hypothesis is true? If the chance is fairly high, then there is no evidence to reject the null hypothesis. If the chance is very low, then the researcher takes that as evidence against the null hypothesis, rejects it, and supports the alternative hypothesis that there is an effect or relationship. It is important to set your decision criterion before you begin the study so that you have a clear basis for making a decision when you get to Step 5. If we wait to choose our alpha level, we might be tempted to make the wrong decision because our probability value seems low enough. This could result in an error in our hypothesis-testing procedure. I will discuss these errors and how we use our decision criterion to make a decision further as we consider Step 5: Making a decision.

Step 3: Collect Sample Data

In Step 3, we are ready to design our study to test our hypothesis, recruit a sample, and collect our data. This process was discussed in more detail in Chapters 1 and 2, where we considered where data come from. This might be a good time to review the summaries of those chapters.

For our example (looking at whether memory changes with age), we might design a study looking at memory abilities for college students and older adults. For example, suppose we know the population mean and standard deviation of a standardized memory test for college students because many of them have taken it as they participated in research studies. We might then design a study where we recruit a sample of older adults to complete the memory test to see how their mean score on the test compares. Our sample of older adults represents the population of all older adults (e.g., over the age of 60). We can then consider where our sample mean falls in the distribution of sample means for college students to see if the older adults' mean score is an extreme score in this distribution based on our decision criterion. If it is, we can decide to reject the null hypothesis (H_0: Memory does not change with age) and conclude that the older adults' memory scores appear to be part of a different distribution with a lower (or higher) mean. See Figure 8.1 for an overview of our study.

Step 4: Calculate Statistics

As Figure 8.1 shows, the known population mean μ for the standardized memory test in our study is 85% and our sample mean $\bar{X}$ is 67%. What we want to know from our hypothesis test is whether 67% is different enough from 85% to conclude that older adults show different memory abilities from the young adults. To determine this, we will need to calculate an inferential statistic. If we know the standard deviation for the memory test for the population of college students, we can use our one-sample z test. Figure 8.3 shows the relevant portion of the inferential statistics flowchart for a one-sample z test. Suppose we know that the standard deviation is $\sigma = 20$ and that the population of memory scores is a normal distribution. With this information, we're ready to calculate the $z_{\bar{X}}$. For this example, the calculation is

$$z_{\bar{X}} = \frac{(85-67)}{\frac{20}{\sqrt{100}}} = \frac{18}{20/10} = \frac{18}{2} = +9.00$$

We can use the Unit Normal Table in Appendix B to find the probability value (also known as a *p value*) associated with this z score. We have already seen earlier in this chapter that the highest value in the table is 4.00 with a *p* value of 0.00003. So we know that the *p* value for 9.00 will be

p **value:** probability value associated with an inferential test that indicates the likelihood of obtaining the data in a study when the null hypothesis is true

Figure 8.3   Portion of the Statistical Test Decision Flowchart for a One-Sample *z* Test

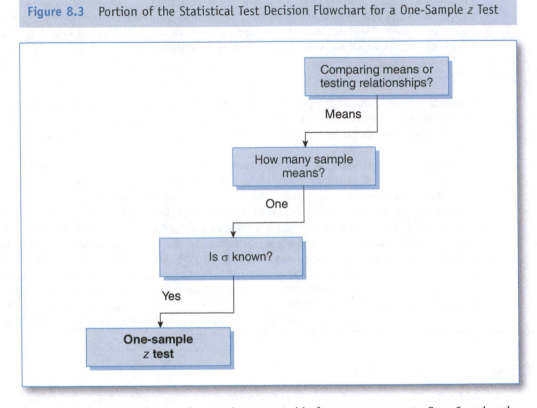

lower than 0.00003. This *p* value is what we need before we move on to Step 5 and make a decision.

However, before we move on to our last step, let's consider what would happen if we did not know the population standard deviation value, as is often the case in a research study. Without the σ value, we cannot calculate the standard error as we have done for our one-sample *z* test. Instead, our standard error will need to be calculated from an estimate of the population σ. The best guess we can make for this value is the standard deviation in our sample, because the sample values are meant to represent the ones we would find in the population. Thus, our standard error formula would be

$$s_{\bar{X}} = \frac{s}{\sqrt{n}}$$

This calculation of the standard error changes the test statistic calculation and becomes a new statistic known as *t* (instead of *z*). We could then conduct a one-sample *t* test instead of a *z* test to test our hypothesis. We will discuss this test in Chapter 9.

Things get even more complicated if we don't know the population μ either. In this case, we would have to represent both age groups' populations in our study with separate samples: a sample of college students and a sample of older adults. We can still calculate a *t* statistic, but it will be a new inferential test called an independent samples *t* test. This test is discussed in Chapter 11. Later chapters in this text will also consider cases where there are more than two samples in a study with an inferential test known as analysis of variance (ANOVA). However, in each inferential test, we are using the same hypothesis-testing procedure with the five steps described in this chapter.

All the inferential statistics described in this text use a calculation that relies on differences or relationships seen in the data with an estimate of sampling error divided out of these differences or relationships. Thus, the test statistic is a value representing the differences or relationships seen in the sample data corrected for chance differences or relationships that could be seen due to relying on samples (instead of whole populations). If the test statistic is a low value, then the differences/relationships seen in the sample are likely due to chance sampling factors. If the test statistic is a high value, then the differences/relationships seen in the sample are likely due to actual differences/relationships that exist in the population. These outcomes correspond to the decisions we can make in the test.

Step 5: Make a Decision

In our last step, we need to make a decision about the null hypothesis based on how unlikely our sample mean is in the distribution of sample means that would exist when the null hypothesis is true. We will either find evidence against the null hypothesis and reject it or fail to find this evidence and retain it. How unlikely does a sample mean have to be before we decide it did not come from this distribution of sample means and reject the null hypothesis? This is where our alpha level comes into play. It is the proportion of our distribution of sample means that falls into the critical regions. Figure 8.2 shows these regions for $\alpha = 0.05$, our standard alpha level (bounded by the z scores of ± 1.96). It is the highest probability that a sample mean came from this distribution of sample means that we will accept as evidence against the null hypothesis. It is set by the researcher at a low value (such as 0.05) to allow rejection of the null hypothesis only when it is very unlikely that the sample mean came from the distribution of sample means for the null hypothesis. *In other words, the decision to reject or not reject the null hypothesis is based on the probability of obtaining the data in the sample when the null hypothesis is true.* A low alpha level helps us avoid an error in our hypothesis-testing procedure.

The probability of a sample mean appearing in the distribution of sample means is compared with the alpha level in an inferential test. Remember that most sample means occur near the actual population mean, so if the probability is high that the sample mean came from this distribution, then it is more likely that the null hypothesis is true, given the data we collected. If the p value is equal to or lower than the alpha level, then we can reject the null hypothesis as unlikely to be true. If the p value is higher than the alpha level, we cannot reject the null hypothesis, as it might be true (however, the test does *not* provide evidence *for* the null hypothesis, only against it).

Now, consider our example once again. Figure 8.1 shows the z and p values we determined in the previous section for our sample data. In Step 5, we compare the p value with our α level. For this example, we compare 0.0003 versus half of 0.05, which is 0.025 (we have two critical regions with a two-tailed test, so we divide α in half here). If our p value is lower than α, as it is here, we can reject the null hypothesis that memory does not change with age. If we reject this hypothesis, then we will have supported the alternative hypothesis that it does change with age. Looking back at the means, the older adults showed a lower mean score than the population of college students. Thus, we can conclude for this study that memory declines with age.

Stop and Think

8.5 Suppose the *z* score we had calculated for our example in this chapter was +2.30. In this case, what would our *p* value be? With an $\alpha = 0.05$, what decision would you make for this example?

8.6 Consider another example: An anxiety questionnaire is known to have $\mu = 50$ and $\sigma = 5$ in the general population. A sample of 50 college students is given the questionnaire after being asked to prepare a 5-minute speech on a topic of their choosing to see if this task elevates their anxiety level from what is expected based on the population mean score on the questionnaire. The sample mean is $\bar{X} = 58$.

- State the alternative and null hypotheses for this study. Is the alternative hypothesis one-tailed or two-tailed?
- Calculate the one-sample *z* score for this sample. What is the probability of obtaining this *z* score when the null hypothesis is true?
- For an alpha level of 0.05, what decision would you make for this study? What can you conclude about the speech preparation task and its effect on anxiety level?

TYPES OF HYPOTHESIS-TESTING ERRORS

One thing that is important to keep in mind is that we are using probability to make our decision in the hypothesis-testing procedure. The test statistic's *p* value tells us the chance of obtaining that statistical value (using the sample data to calculate it) when the null hypothesis is true. Even if we reject the null hypothesis as our decision in the test, there is still a small chance that it is, in fact, true. Likewise, if we retain the null hypothesis as our decision, it is still possible that it is false. These are the kinds of errors that can be made in our hypothesis test, and they are always possible because we are relying on a probability (not a certainty) to make a decision.

Table 8.2 illustrates the different possible outcomes of a hypothesis test. The columns represent the reality for the population being studied: Either the null hypothesis is true and there is no effect/relationship (e.g., older adults do not have different memory scores and their mean memory score is the same as the population mean for the younger adults), or the null hypothesis is false and there is an effect/relationship (e.g., older adults do have different memory scores and their mean memory score is not the same as the population mean for the younger adults). When a hypothesis test is conducted, the researcher does not know whether the null hypothesis is true or false. However, as described in the previous section, the inferential test is conducted to look for evidence that the null hypothesis is not true. If that evidence is found, the researcher decides that the null hypothesis is false and rejects it. This is the outcome represented in the first row of Table 8.2. If, in fact, the null hypothesis is false, the researcher has made a correct decision in the test, because the decision matches the reality about the null hypothesis. However, it is possible to make the wrong decision. Thus, the outcome to reject the null hypothesis in the first row under the column where the null hypothesis is actually true is an error. The researcher's decision does not match the reality for the null hypothesis. This is called a Type I error and indicates that the researcher has rejected the null hypothesis when it is really true (e.g., we find in our study that older adults have a different memory score mean from the young adults, but in the

> **Type I error:** an error made in a hypothesis test when the researcher rejects the null hypothesis when it is actually true

population of older adults, they do not have a different mean score). The chance of making a Type I error is determined ahead of time by the researcher when an alpha level is chosen. Thus, in tests with $\alpha = 0.05$, there is a 5% chance of making a Type I error.

Table 8.2 Possible Outcomes of a Statistical Test

Decisions	Null Hypothesis Is Actually False	Null Hypothesis Is Actually True
Reject the null hypothesis	Correct decision!	Type I error
Fail to reject the null hypothesis	Type II error	Correct decision!

The second row in Table 8.2 illustrates test outcomes for the other decision that can be made in the significance test: retaining or failing to reject the null hypothesis, which occurs when evidence against it is not found in the test. A correct decision is made in the test when the decision is to fail to reject the null hypothesis and this hypothesis is really false (bottom right box). However, another type of error, called a Type II error, can be made when the null hypothesis is not rejected but is actually false (e.g., we find in our study that older adults do not have a different mean memory scores than young adults, but in the population, older adults do

> **Type II error:** an error made in a hypothesis test when the researcher fails to reject the null hypothesis when it is actually false

have a different mean score from the younger adults). This means that an effect or relationship exists in the population but was not detected in the data for the sample. The chance of a Type II error is more difficult to determine. There are several factors that can influence the probability of a Type II error, including the alpha level chosen, the size of the effect or relationship, and the sample size in the study. The researcher can lower the chance of a Type II error by using an optimal sample size and making sure that the study is designed to maximize the effect or relationship being studied. By keeping the Type II error rate low, you are increasing the power of your hypothesis test to detect an effect or relationship that actually exists. Thus, it is important to keep Type II errors in mind as you design your study to conduct a powerful test of the hypothesis.

> **Power:** the ability of a hypothesis test to detect an effect or relationship when one exists (equal to 1 minus the probability of a Type II error)

Predicting the Null Hypothesis

As mentioned above, in many cases, the alternative hypothesis is also the researcher's hypothesis. The researcher predicts that an effect or relationship exists in the population. However, in some cases, the researcher may wish to predict that an effect or relationship does not exist in the population. Is this an appropriate thing for a researcher to do when using inferential statistics? Many would argue that it is not appropriate for a researcher to predict the null hypothesis because significance tests do not provide evidence for the null hypothesis. In fact, most papers that are published in psychological journals describe studies that showed significant results (Francis, 2013), because it can be difficult to draw strong conclusions from studies that do not show significant results. However, power analyses can be used to estimate the chance of a Type II error occurring and the null hypothesis being falsely retained. While any single study with nonsignificant results is not sufficient to provide support for the null hypothesis, a series of studies that have a reasonable level of power to detect effects (80% or higher is the generally accepted level; Cohen, 1988) that all show the same nonsignificant results may provide some support for the null hypothesis. Thus, if researchers want to predict the null hypothesis, they must be prepared to conduct several studies in order to obtain some support for their hypothesis. Many researchers (e.g., Francis, 2013; Greenwald, 1975) also argued that a bias against the null hypothesis can result in researchers ignoring studies that do not find significant effects (which can be caused by the bias against publishing them). In addition, because it is important that theories of behavior can be falsified, it is sometimes necessary to predict the null hypothesis in order to truly test a theory. Finally, in order to get around this issue, several researchers (e.g., Cohen, 1990, 1994; Loftus, 1993) have suggested alternatives to the hypothesis-testing procedure described in this chapter as a means of interpreting data.

STATISTICAL SIGNIFICANCE

One concept not yet discussed in this chapter is what it means for a hypothesis test to be a *significant test*. If the p value for the test statistic is less than or equal to the alpha level, the test is said to be significant. In other words, a significant inferential test means that the null hypothesis can be rejected, the alternative hypothesis has been supported, and the researcher can conclude that there is an effect or relationship for the data in the current study. This means that hypothesis tests where the decision is to reject the null hypothesis are reported as *significant* tests.

❧

Significant test: the *p* value is less than or equal to the alpha level in an inferential test, and the null hypothesis can be rejected

---

Note that this term does not mean *important* in the way this term is typically used outside of statistics. A hypothesis test can be significant in the statistical sense without being very important at all. In fact, with a large enough sample size, it is often easy to obtain a significant difference between groups that is based on subject differences unrelated to the study or a significant statistical relationship between factors that are not related in any meaningful or causal way (e.g., amount of rainfall in a month and number of people buying soda in that month). So be aware that statistical significance may not mean that a result tells us something important about behavior.

Stop and Think

8.7   For each description below, indicate the situation: correct decision, Type I error, or Type II error.

- An effect of amount of sleep on mood exists, but the results of the study were not significant.
- A relationship between early reading and later academic achievement exists, and the results of the study were significant.
- An effect of caffeine on work productivity does not exist, but the results of the study were significant.

Calculation Summary

<u>Standard error</u>: Population standard deviation divided by the square root of the sample size

<u>One-sample z test</u>: Sample mean minus the population mean, divided by the standard error

CHAPTER SUMMARY

8.1   What is the standard error?

Standard error is a measure of variability in the distribution of sample means that takes sample size into account. It provides an estimate of sampling error for our hypothesis test.

8.2   How can we use a population mean and the standard error to test a hypothesis?

The one-sample z test and t test both consider the difference between a measured sample mean and a known population mean with our estimate of sampling error in the form of the standard error removed in the calculation of the test statistic. This statistical value is then used to determine the probability (p) value of getting our sample mean in the distribution of sample means for the population. A low p value indicates an extreme score for the distribution, making it possible to reject the null hypothesis that the sample mean is from this distribution.

8.3   What are the steps in hypothesis testing?

The five steps of hypothesis testing take us through the procedure described (see Table 8.1 for an overview of the procedures by step):

Step 1: State hypotheses.

Step 2: Set decision criterion.

Step 3: Collect sample data.

Step 4: Calculate statistics.

Step 5: Make a decision.

8.4   What is statistical significance and what does it tell us about our hypothesis?

A statistically significant hypothesis test is one where we have decided to reject the null hypothesis based on the evidence found in the sample data against it. If we reject the null hypothesis, we can accept the alternative hypothesis, which is typically the hypothesis we have made as researchers.

8.5   What types of errors exist in our hypothesis-testing procedure?

Hypothesis-testing procedures can result in either Type I or Type II errors, depending on the decision we make in Step 5. If we reject the null hypothesis in error (i.e., the null hypothesis is actually true), then we are making a Type I error. If we retain the null hypothesis in error (i.e., the null hypothesis is actually false), then we are making a Type II error.

8.6   How can I reduce the chance of an error in testing hypotheses?

Setting our decision criterion alpha to a low value will reduce the chance of a Type I error. Increasing our sample size and/or effect size will increase power, which is the same as reducing the chance of a Type II error.

THINKING ABOUT RESEARCH

A summary of a research study in psychology is given below. As you read the summary, think about the following questions:

1. Identify the five steps of hypothesis testing in this article description. Indicate what was determined at each step. State what you think are the null and alternative hypotheses for this study.

2. Why do you think the participants were blindfolded in this this study? What source of possible bias does this control for?

3. What is the likely reason the authors used a one-sample *t* test instead of a *z* test to analyze their results?

4. Based on the description of this study, what population mean μ do you think the authors compared their sample mean with?

5. Based on the information in this chapter, what formula do you think they used to calculate standard error in their inferential test?

> Wagman, J. B., Zimmerman, C., & Sorric, C. (2007). "Which feels heavier—a pound of lead or a pound of feathers?" A potential perceptual basis of a cognitive riddle. *Perception, 36,* 1709–1711.

Purpose of the Study. Wagman et al. investigated the perceptual causes of why people answer the riddle about the respective heaviness of equal masses of lead and feathers as if one feels heavier. In their study, participants were asked to hold a box of lead bearings and a box of feathers of equal weight and indicate which box felt heavier. Based on the size/weight illusion (where larger objects are expected to be heavier regardless of actual mass) as applied to mass distribution of objects, the researchers predicted that participants would select the box of lead at a different rate than chance due to the different mass distributions of lead and feathers within the boxes.

Method of the Study. Participants included 23 blindfolded students. Each participant completed 20 trials, in which they held one box in their palm and then a second box in the same palm. One box held lead pellets and one box held feathers. The objects were secured within the box to keep them from creating any sound stimuli that could be used to make judgments. They were then asked to indicate which box felt heavier, the first box or the second box. Lead and feather boxes were presented in a random order on each trial. If participants could not determine a difference in heaviness between the boxes, chance performance (10 responses for the 1st box and 10 responses for the 2nd box) was expected.

Results of the Study. To test their hypothesis that the boxes did not feel equally heavy to the participants, the researchers conducted a one-sample t test on the number of trials (out of 20) that each participant reported the box of lead felt heavier. The mean number of times participants reported the box of lead felt heavier was 11.12 times out of the 20 trials. They found that this sample differed significantly from chance with a calculated t value of 2.64 with a p value of 0.015. APA style for reporting the statistic is $t(22) = 2.64, p = 0.015$.

Conclusions of the Study. The results of the study suggest that objects with equal mass can be perceived at different heaviness due to the difference in mass distribution within a held box of lead and feathers.

TEST YOURSELF

1. The standard error is _____.
   a. determined from the population standard deviation and the sample size
   b. is an estimate of the sampling error
   c. the variability of the distribution of sample means
   d. all of the above

2. The alpha level is the _____.
   a. chance that the null hypothesis is true
   b. the chance that the null hypothesis is false
   c. the decision criterion for rejecting the null hypothesis set by the researcher

3. The researcher's hypothesis is typically the opposite of the _____ hypothesis.
   a. alternative
   b. null
   c. population

4. The hypothesis-testing procedure can provide evidence against the _____.
   a. null hypothesis
   b. alternative hypothesis
   c. distribution of sample means standard error

5. The possible decision(s) in Step 5 of the hypothesis-testing procedure are to _____.

   a. reject the null hypothesis

   b. accept the null hypothesis

   c. retain the null hypothesis

   d. only (a) and (b)

   e. only (a) and (c)

6. The hypothesis-testing procedure will tell us the probability that the null hypothesis is true.

   a. True

   b. False

7. The best estimates of the population mean and standard deviation when these values are not known are the mean and standard deviation values in the sample.

   a. True

   b. False

8. The inferential test statistic represents the difference between means with sampling error removed.

   a. True

   b. False

9. Explain why errors are always possible during hypothesis testing.

10. You pulled several all-nighters last semester to study for your final exams. You want to know if staying up all night hurt your exam performance so you will know if it is worth it to stay up all night to study. You calculate the mean score for all of the finals you have ever taken in college (your exam population μ) and find that $\mu = 87\%$ with $\sigma = 5\%$. Assume you know that this population of scores has a normal distribution. You use as your sample the mean score on all five of the final exams you took last semester, $X = 83\%$.

    a. What are the null and alternative hypotheses for this example? Is this a one- or two-tailed test?

    b. Use a one-sample z test to determine if your all-nighters hurt your performance.

    c. Suppose that in reality, all-nighters do hurt your performance on exams. In this case, what type of decision has occurred in your test: correct decision, Type I error, or Type II error?

11. What is the easiest way to reduce Type II errors? What problem does this method of reducing Type II errors create? (Hint: Consider statistical significance vs. practical significance.)

PART IV

The Nuts and Bolts of Statistical Tests

Chapter 9

The *t* Distribution

As you read the chapter, consider the following questions:

9.1 How does the distribution of *t* scores differ from the distribution of *z* scores?

9.2 How can we use the *t* Table to make a hypothesis-testing decision?

9.3 How do standard error and estimated standard error differ?

9.4 How can we conduct a one-sample *t* test using statistical software?

Imagine this scenario: You do not believe in extrasensory perception (ESP), but you have a friend who is a fervent believer and is spending large amounts of money going to psychics (see Photo 9.1). You and your friend decide to design a study to test if individuals who advertise as psychics can, in fact, predict the future to determine if data can be found to support your friend's argument. (Remember that supporting your argument would be more difficult and require multiple studies because you can only provide evidence against the null hypothesis of no ability in a single research study. You cannot provide evidence in a study for the null hypothesis using the hypothesis-testing procedure.) There are many ways you could design such a study, but in this chapter, let's consider a design where you use a simple card prediction task with a sample of psychics. In your study, you recruit a sample of 50 psychics to perform this task. Each psychic participant is asked to perform 100 trials in which a researcher selects a card at random from a deck of 52 playing cards; the psychic's task is to predict the suit (i.e., hearts, clubs, spades, or diamonds; see Photo 9.2) of the card selected. Thus, if the participants are guessing, their average accuracy rate should be about 25 correct trials out of the 100 total trials (or 25%). The guess rate tells us the population mean μ (i.e., $\mu = 25\%$) for people with no ESP, but it does not tell us the population σ, so we cannot use the one-sample z test we discussed in Chapters 7 and 8 because we cannot calculate the standard error ($\sigma_{\bar{x}}$) needed for the denominator of the z score calculation. However, as mentioned in Chapter 8, we can estimate it using the sample standard

Photo 9.1 Research question: Can psychics really predict the future?

©iStock/logoff

Photo 9.2 Your study includes a card prediction task in which psychics are asked to predict the suit of a card chosen at random from a deck of cards.

©iStock/Rob_Heber

❧

Estimated standard error: an estimate of sampling error that is determined from the standard deviation of the distribution of sample means using the sample standard deviation to represent the population standard deviation

---

deviation to calculate an estimated standard error and then use a one-sample *t* test instead to look for evidence against the null hypothesis.

Before we consider the *t* test, let's briefly review the process of hypothesis testing with this example. Using hypothesis testing, we can look for evidence in our sample data that counters the null hypothesis that the population of psychics has no ESP (i.e., this population has an accuracy rate in the card prediction task equal to or lower than 25%). We will do this,

as we did with the *z* test, by comparing our sample mean with the distribution of sample means for the general population of non-psychics, which has a mean equal to the population μ of 25%. If we find that our sample mean is an extreme score in this distribution, there is a good chance that a distribution of sample means exists for psychics with a different population μ (e.g., a μ that is higher than our guessing rate of 25%). Figure 9.1 illustrates this comparison for these distributions. Calculating an inferential statistic (for our example, a *t* score) will provide the location of our sample mean in the population distribution of sample means for the null hypothesis (i.e., the general population of non-psychics). This is shown in the distribution on the left in Figure 9.1. However, if the statistical value is an extreme score in this distribution, there is a good chance that it comes from a different distribution—one for a population of psychics, shown on the right in Figure 9.1. Remember that these are hypothetical distributions because we cannot test the entire population of individuals, psychics or non-psychics. Thus, we are proposing that the distribution on the right exists only if we find an extreme enough score in our test to suggest it does not belong in the distribution on the left (the population of people

Figure 9.1   Hypothetical Distributions for the Null and Alternative Hypotheses

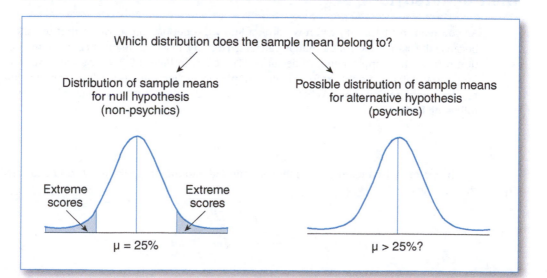

Which distribution does the sample mean belong to?

Distribution of sample means for null hypothesis (non-psychics)

Possible distribution of sample means for alternative hypothesis (psychics)

Extreme scores

Extreme scores

μ = 25%

μ > 25%?

with no ESP). The *p* value for our inferential statistic indicates the probability of getting our *t* score in the distribution of sample means shown on the left for the null hypothesis. We did this in Chapter 8 with *z* scores by looking at the distribution of sample means after a *z* score transformation and then finding the *p* value for our *z* score in the new distribution. A comparison of the *p* value to our alpha level helps us make the decision to reject the null hypothesis (i.e., our sample mean likely belongs to the distribution on the right in Figure 9.1) or to retain the null hypothesis (i.e., our sample mean could belong to the distribution on the left; we do not have evidence supporting the existence of the distribution on the right). This comparison will tell us whether our sample mean is in the critical region(s) or not for null hypothesis distribution (the shaded potion of the distribution on the left labeled *extreme scores*). In the next section, we will look at the *t* score distribution a bit more to better understand why a one-sample *t* test is the appropriate test for our study before we work through the hypothesis-testing steps to make a decision for our psychic study.

Stop and Think

9.1   For our psychic study, write out the alternative and null hypotheses. Is this a one-tailed or two-tailed test?

9.2   In order to use a one-sample *z* test in our psychic study, what else would we need to know?

9.3   Can you identify any sources of bias in the psychic study that might influence the results? How could we control for these biases in the study?

THE *t* DISTRIBUTION

As you read in Chapter 8, when we do not know the population σ, we cannot use the *z* test because the standard error cannot be calculated exactly. Instead, we must estimate the population σ from the sample standard deviation. The chart in Figure 9.2 shows the portion of the inferential statistics flowchart for the one-sample *t* test when the σ is not known (see Figure 7.8 for the complete flowchart). What we will use instead is the estimated standard error with the following formula:

$$s_{\bar{X}} = \frac{s}{\sqrt{n}}$$

The estimated standard error is then substituted into the original *z* test formula to calculate the statistic *t*:

$$t = \frac{(\bar{X} - \mu)}{\dfrac{s}{\sqrt{n}}}$$

Figure 9.2   Portion of the Statistical Test Decision Flowchart for a One-Sample *t* Test

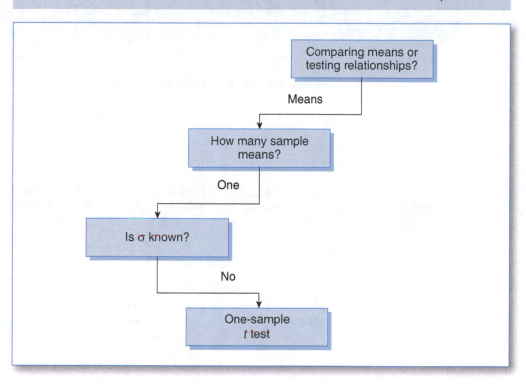

The statistic *t* distribution differs slightly from the statistic *z* distribution. As also described in Chapter 8, the central limit theorem states that the distribution of sample means will approach a normal distribution with a very large sample size. Thus, the larger the sample size, the closer *t* is to the value of *z*. Figure 9.3 illustrates this using degrees of freedom ($df = n - 1$) as the indication of sample size. The larger the *df*, the closer the distribution of *t* scores is to a normal distribution. For very large *df*, the *t* distribution will be the same as the *z* distribution. However, it will be slightly different from normal anytime the *df* are less than infinity, so it's best to use the *t* test when we must estimate the population σ with the sample *s*. As you can see in Figure 9.3, the variability of the distribution increases with a smaller sample size. As I have discussed previously, this is what we expect because a smaller sample size makes it less likely that we are close to the population σ. Thus, the critical region(s) associated with our alpha level will change with the degrees of freedom. The *t* score that is the boundary of the critical region(s) will be higher as the sample size decreases. In other words, as the sample size increases, we will find that a smaller difference between the sample and population means results in a *t* score that falls in the critical region(s) for our sample.

In using *t* as an inferential statistic, we follow the same procedure covered in Chapter 8 for the *z* test: We will calculate the *t* score for our sample and then consider where that *t* score falls

Figure 9.3   The Shape of the *t* Score Distribution Will Change as the Sample Size (Measured in Degrees of Freedom) Changes—It Becomes More Normal With Large *df*

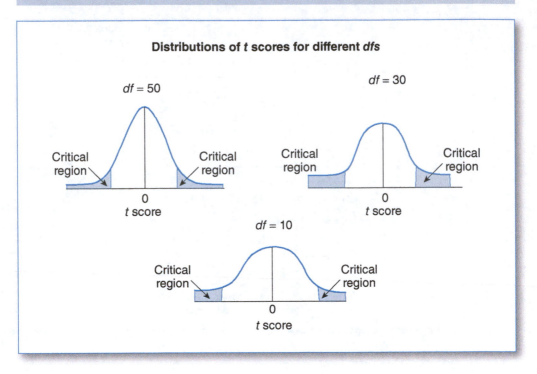

in the distribution of *t* scores for the distribution of sample means when the null hypothesis is true. We will find the critical region(s) that denote the most extreme scores in the distribution. However, because the *t* distribution is a slightly different shape from the normal distribution, the *p* values will be different, and we must now use the *t* Table instead of the Unit Normal Table. You will find a *t* Distribution Table in Appendix C of this text. As we begin to use the *t* Table in the next section to conduct a one-sample *t* test, you will see that the table has a different structure from the Unit Normal Table. Instead of looking up a *p* value in the table, we will be looking up the *t* score(s) that borders the critical region(s) and comparing it to our calculated *t* score for our sample.

ONE-SAMPLE *t* TEST

Now that we understand the *t* distribution a bit more and how it differs from the normal distribution of *z* scores, let's use the one-sample *t* test to conduct a hypothesis test for our psychic study.

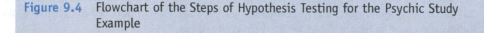

Figure 9.4   Flowchart of the Steps of Hypothesis Testing for the Psychic Study Example

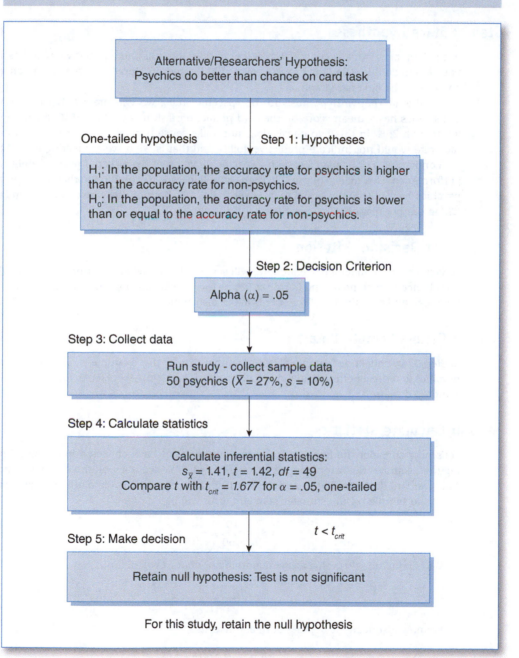

Alternative/Researchers' Hypothesis:
Psychics do better than chance on card task

One-tailed hypothesis   Step 1: Hypotheses

H_1: In the population, the accuracy rate for psychics is higher than the accuracy rate for non-psychics.
H_0: In the population, the accuracy rate for psychics is lower than or equal to the accuracy rate for non-psychics.

Step 2: Decision Criterion

Alpha (α) = .05

Step 3: Collect data

Run study - collect sample data
50 psychics ($\overline{X}$ = 27%, *s* = 10%)

Step 4: Calculate statistics

Calculate inferential statistics:
$s_{\overline{X}}$ = 1.41, *t* = 1.42, *df* = 49
Compare *t* with t_{crit} = 1.677 for α = .05, one-tailed

Step 5: Make decision $t < t_{crit}$

Retain null hypothesis: Test is not significant

For this study, retain the null hypothesis

We will go through each of the steps of hypothesis testing to review the steps and see how they differ for the one-sample *t* test as compared with the *z* test we conducted in Chapter 8. You can follow the chart in Figure 9.4 as we go through the steps.

Step 1: State Hypotheses

In the Stop and Think section, 9.1 asks you to state the null and alternative hypotheses. Were you able to do this using the process covered in Chapter 8? Hopefully so; you can check your answers in the next paragraph.

For the alternative hypothesis for our psychic study, we will predict that the population of psychics has a mean score on the card prediction task higher than 25%. Including scores lower than 25% in this hypothesis does not make sense because a lower-than-chance accuracy rate would not indicate predictive ability and that is what we are testing here. Thus, we are conducting a one-tailed test with a specific direction of the effect of psychic ability on task performance. This means our null hypothesis will include the prediction that the population of psychics has an accuracy equal to *or* lower than 25%. Both of these results would indicate no ESP in our population.

Step 2: Set Decision Criterion

As is typical for behavioral research, we will set our alpha level at 0.05 (remember that this sets our chance of making a Type I error at 5% or less). Thus, our one critical region will be above the mean and contain 5% of the scores in the distribution.

Step 3: Collect Sample Data

In Step 3, we collect our sample data. Remember that for this example, our sample contains 50 psychics to represent the population of all psychics. See Figure 9.4, Step 3, for sample mean and standard deviation.

Step 4: Calculate Statistics

Let's now consider the hypothetical data that we might have collected in our psychic study. Figure 9.4 shows the sample mean we obtained of 27% accuracy on the card prediction task. The standard deviation in the sample was 10%. Now we can calculate our estimated standard error and sample *t*. Our estimated standard error will be

$$s_{\bar{x}} = \frac{10}{\sqrt{50}} = \frac{10}{7.07} = 1.41$$

We can include this value as the denominator of our *t* calculation:

$$t = \frac{(27-25)}{1.41} = 1.42$$

We now just need the degrees of freedom term:

$$df = n - 1 = 50 - 1 = 49$$

With these values, we can use the *t* Table in Appendix C to look up the critical *t* value (t_{crit}) for a one-tailed test, *df* = 49, and α = 0.05. A portion of the table appears in Table 9.1. You must first choose the correct column based on your alpha level and whether you are conducting a one- or two-tailed test. Then you can find the correct row for your degrees of freedom. Looking at Table 9.1, you can see in the highlighted portion that our t_{crit} is 1.677 for our one-tailed test. Figure 9.5 shows where this t_{crit} value falls relative to our sample *t* score. Notice that it does not fall in the critical region.

Table 9.1 A Section of the *t* Distribution Table

One-tailed	.05	.025	.01
Two-tailed	.10	.05	.02
df			
35	1.690	2.030	2.438
36	1.688	2.028	2.435
37	1.687	2.026	2.431
38	1.686	2.024	2.429
39	1.685	2.023	2.426
40	1.684	2.021	2.423
41	1.683	2.020	2.421
42	1.682	2.018	2.419
43	1.681	2.017	2.416
44	1.680	2.015	2.414
45	1.679	2.014	2.412
46	1.679	2.013	2.410
47	1.678	2.012	2.408
48	1.678	2.011	2.407
49	1.677	2.010	2.405
50	1.677	2.009	2.404

NOTE: The entire table is shown in Appendix C, but not all degrees of freedom rows are shown in this appendix.

Figure 9.5   Distribution of t Scores for $df = 49$

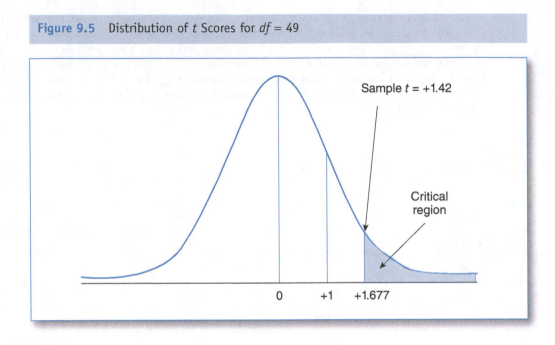

Sample $t = +1.42$

Critical
region

0   +1   +1.677

Step 5: Make a Decision

When we use the t Table to conduct a t test, we must make a decision to reject or retain the null hypothesis by comparing our sample t score with the t_{crit} value from the table. The table does not provide exact p values as the Unit Normal Table does. However, if we use a software package (such as SPSS) to conduct our test, we can determine an exact p value to compare with α as we did in Chapter 8 (I will discuss using SPSS for this test in the next section). However, our completion of the t test by hand in this section using the t Table requires a comparison of our calculated t score and the t_{crit} from the table to determine if our t score falls in the critical region as shown in Figure 9.5. Note that when df equal infinity, the t_{crit} is the same as the z_{crit} that border the critical region(s) in the z distribution.

Figure 9.4 shows this comparison in Step 5 and the corresponding decision to retain the null hypothesis because our sample t score does not exceed the t_{crit} value from the table. This means that our sample t score does not fall in the critical region of the most extreme scores in the distribution (as shown in Figure 9.5). Thus, it is still fairly likely that the sample mean came from the distribution of sample means for the null hypothesis. Our test does not support the alternative hypothesis that psychics have the ability to predict the suit of a card drawn from the deck at random, but it also does not provide evidence for the null hypothesis. We can say that the test is not significant because it failed to provide evidence against the null hypothesis. The best thing to do in this case would be to continue testing our hypothesis with additional samples and possibly some additional tasks to further test the null hypothesis.

Stop and Think

9.4   Suppose 36 participants complete an experiment where ads are presented subliminally during a task (e.g., Coke ads are flashed at very fast rates during movie ads).
Participants are then given a recognition test for images of the ads, where two images
are presented and participants must choose which of the two was presented earlier. If
participants are able to process the subliminal ads when they are first presented, then
their performance should be above chance (50%). This is what the researcher predicts.
However, if the ads were not processed and the participants are only guessing, then
their performance should be similar to chance.

a.   State the alternative and null hypotheses for this study.

b.   The sample mean for this study was 67% with a standard deviation of 12%.
Calculate the sample *t* score for this study.

c.   What decision should the researcher make about the null hypothesis in this
study? (You can use Table 9.1 to find the t_{crit}.) What can the researcher conclude
about their prediction from this decision?

9.5   Without looking at the table, for which sample size will there be a higher t_{crit}: $n = 30$
or $n = 50$? Explain your answer.

USING SPSS TO CONDUCT A ONE-SAMPLE *t* TEST

As mentioned in the previous section, statistical software packages will calculate the estimated
standard error and sample *t* score for us. Most software packages also provide the exact *p* value
that corresponds to the sample *t* score, allowing researchers to compare the *p* value with their
alpha level to make their decision. In this section, we will consider the process of using SPSS to
conduct a one-sample *t* test.

Consider the example in Stop and Think 9.4. Suppose that this study only had 10 participants with the mean recognition accuracy rates shown in Table 9.2 (we will assume that the
scores in the population are normally distributed so that we can use a *t* test even though our
sample size is small). How would these data look if we entered them into the data window in
SPSS? Figure 9.6 shows the data window for these data. To conduct the one-sample *t* test for
these data, choose Compare Means from the Analyze menu at the top. Select the One-Sample
t Test option in the menu of tests. The window that opens will allow you to click the data column (labeled *accuracy* in Figure 9.6) into the Test Variable box on the right to indicate that this
column contains the dependent variable to be analyzed. You also need to indicate the known
mean for comparison in the Test Value box by typing it in. For this example, the test value is 50
(for the chance value of 50 %). When you click the OK button, the analysis begins automatically,
and the output will appear in the Output Window.

Table 9.2 Data for 10 Participants for the Subliminal Ad Example Study (See Stop and Think 9.4 for Details)

Participant 1	56
Participant 2	60
Participant 3	49
Participant 4	35
Participant 5	51
Participant 6	65
Participant 7	70
Participant 8	44
Participant 9	58
Participant 10	47

Figure 9.6 View of Data Window in SPSS With Subliminal Ad Study Data

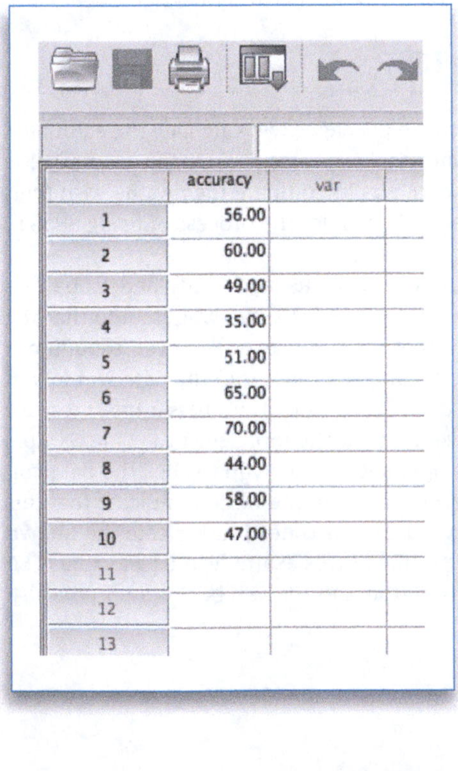

A view of the output window can be seen in Figure 9.7. The output from the test contains several important values. The sample mean can be seen in the first box along with the standard deviation and estimated standard error. These are the standard descriptive statistics included in the output for a t test. The t test values are included in the second box in the output. The t value (1.064 for this example), the df, and the p value listed in the Sig. (for significance) column are shown in this box. Thus, unlike our hand calculation of the t score in the previous section, with SPSS, we can compare p to α as we did in Chapter 8. The default test in SPSS is a two-tailed test, but you can convert the value to a one-tailed test by dividing the p value in half if the means differ in the predicted direction (remember that the one-tailed test has a critical region at one end of the t distribution that is twice the size of the critical region for a two-tailed test—thus, the one-tailed test has a p value that is half the p value for the two-tailed test).

The p value in the output for this example is 0.315. If there was an effect of the ads, we expected the mean recognition score to be higher than 50%. In other words, a one-tailed test is warranted. Thus, we must divide the given p value in half to obtain a $p = 0.1575$ for this one-tailed t test. As this value is *not* equal to or lower than our alpha of 0.05 (our chosen alpha level for this example), the null hypothesis cannot be rejected and must be retained. In other words, there is no evidence that

Figure 9.7   Output Window from the One-Sample *t* Test for the Subliminal Ad Study

➜ **T-Test**

One-Sample Statistics

	N	Mean	Std. Deviation	Std. Error Mean
accuracy	10	53.5000	10.40566	3.29056

One-Sample Test

	Test Value = 50					
					95% Confidence Interval of the Difference	
	t	df	Sig. (2–tailed)	Mean Difference	Lower	Upper
accuracy	1.064	9	.315	3.50000	−3.9438	10.9438

participants in this experiment remembered the subliminal ads because their performance was not better than what is expected by chance.

If you were asked to report the outcome of this test in APA style, you might include a statement such as "The mean recognition score for subliminal ads ($M = 53.50$) was not significantly higher than the chance value of 50%, $t(9) = 1.06$, $p = 0.16$, one-tailed." The statistical values (rounded here to two significant digits) are given as support for a statement about the results of the study. If a two-tailed hypothesis had been made for this study, then the result would be reported as "not significantly different" instead of "not significantly higher" because we would expect a difference in either direction for a two-tailed hypothesis.

Summary of Steps

- Type the data into a column in the data window.
- Choose Compare Means from the Analyze menu at the top.
- Choose One-Sample *t* Test from the list of tests.
- In the Variable window, click your data column into the Test Variable box.
- Enter your known population mean (μ) into the Test Value box.
- Click OK; your statistics will appear in the Output window as shown in Figure 9.7.
- Compare the *p* value from the Sig. column to your alpha level.

Stop and Think

9.6   Use the following data to conduct a one-sample *t* test (with α = 0.05) to determine if the score on a standardized test (for scores that are normally distributed) with a known population mean of 100 is influenced by a new instructional method:

95, 105, 110, 90, 120, 110, 100, 95, 105, 125, 80, 100, 120, 115, 115, 120, 120, 105

9.7   Use the output shown in Figure 9.8 for a new data set to decide which decision is appropriate for a two-tailed test with an alpha level of 0.05: to reject or retain the null hypothesis.

Figure 9.8   SPSS Output for Stop and Think 9.7

➡ T–Test

One–Sample Statistics

	N	Mean	Std. Deviation	Std. Error Mean
Rating	20	5.0500	2.08945	.46721

One–Sample Test

	Test Value = 4					
					95% Confidence Interval of the Difference	
	t	df	Sig. (2–tailed)	Mean Difference	Lower	Upper
Rating	2.247	19	.037	1.05000	.0721	2.0279

TEST ASSUMPTIONS

Each of the inferential tests that we will discuss in Part IV of this text will have some assumptions that must be met in order to use the test. I will present these assumptions for each new statistic at the ends of the chapters that introduce that statistic. In this chapter, I will list the assumptions for the *t* statistic that our study must meet so that we can use a *t* test.

There are two assumptions that a researcher must know to be true in order to use a *t* test:

1.   The population the sample is drawn from must be a normal distribution. This assumption is necessary in order to ensure that the values in the *t* Table are accurate. However, when

the sample size n is larger than 30 and the sample was selected at random from the population, violating this assumption does not change the critical t values enough to change the outcome of the hypothesis test because the distribution will be normal. Thus, this assumption is not very important if your sample size is large enough. However, if you use a small sample size in your study and you analyze the data with a t test, this will be an important assumption to verify for your population.

2. The scores in your sample must be independent observations. This means that the scores cannot be related in some systematic way to each other. If, for example, the data of one subject affects the data you collect for another subject, then the scores in your data are no longer independent. Thus, your sample must be chosen such that the scores do not affect each other. An extreme example of how this assumption could be violated in our psychic study would be if we tested more than one psychic at the same time in different rooms. If the rooms were not soundproof, the participants might be able to hear each other's responses and change their response based on what they heard the other person say. If we set up our study this way (a very bad idea), then our observations would no longer be independent because the responses of one participant depend on the responses of other participants.

It is important to be aware of these assumptions whenever you choose a t test to analyze your data.

Calculation Summary

Estimated standard error: Sample standard deviation divided by the square root of the sample size

One-sample t test: Sample mean minus the population mean, divided by the estimated standard error

CHAPTER SUMMARY

9.1 How does the distribution of t scores differ from the distribution of z scores?

Unlike the distribution of z scores, the shape of the distribution of t scores changes as sample size increases. The larger the sample size, the closer the t value will be to the z score for that sample. This is due to the use of estimated standard error (from the sample standard deviation) instead of the standard error calculated from a known population σ.

9.2 How can we use the t Table to make a hypothesis-testing decision?

As with Unit Normal Table, we can use the t Table to figure out if our sample mean is in the critical region(s) of the distribution of sample means when the null hypothesis is true. However, instead of obtaining a p value from the table, the t Table provides the t_{crit} value that borders the critical region(s). We must then compare the t_{crit} with our sample t score in order to make a decision about the null hypothesis.

9.3   How do standard error and estimated standard error differ?

Estimated standard error is used when we do not know the population σ. In this case, we estimate σ with the sample s and calculate the estimated standard error as our measure of the sampling error in our calculation of t.

9.4   How can we conduct a one-sample t test using statistical software?

When we use statistical software such as SPSS to conduct a one-sample t test, the output provides the exact p value for our sample t score. We can then compare the p with our α to make a decision about the null hypothesis.

THINKING ABOUT RESEARCH

A summary of a research study in psychology is given below. As you read the summary, think about the following questions:

1. State the alternative and null hypotheses for the population of 5-month-olds for this study.

2. What is the likely alpha level chosen for this study? What is the comparison population μ?

3. The standard deviation in the proportion of time spent looking at the face who sang the unfamiliar song was 0.18. Using this sample s and the sample size, calculate the estimated standard error used in the t tests in this study.

4. Is this sample size sufficient to determine that a t test can be used even if the researchers do not know that the population scores are normally distributed? Why or why not?

5. Why was it important to test whether the infants looked longer at the person who sang the familiar song in the testing session before they actually heard them sing the song?

Mehr, S. A., Song, L. A., & Spelke, E. S. (2016). For 5-month-old infants, melodies are social. *Psychological Science, 27,* 486–501.

Note: Experiment 1 of this study is summarized here.

Purpose of the Study. These researchers were interested in examining the social value of songs sung to young children. To study the social aspect of melodies, 5-month-old children were sung one of two songs (each with a different melody). The researchers then tested whether they selectively attended to an unfamiliar person singing the song their parents had sung to them. They predicted that infants would look longer at the unfamiliar person who sang the familiar song showing social affiliation to the person singing the song they knew. Because infants typically prefer to look at novel things, looking longer at the person singing the familiar song indicates good support for a preference for the familiar song in a social setting (looking at faces is a sign of social affiliation in infants).

Method of the Study. Participants included 32 infants with ranging in age between 5.06 and 6.11 months old. At the first study session, parents of the infants were taught one of the two songs selected at random. Songs were of similar length and rhythm but differed in melody. Lyrics were the same for the two songs. They were also given music and lyrics to take home and a website to use to practice the song at home. One parent of the child sang the learned song to the infant at home as often as they wished for a period of 1 to 2 weeks. At the second study session, the infants were given a selective attention test where they viewed two unfamiliar smiling faces for baseline looking measurement, each of those people singing the two songs (one of which had been sung to the infant by their parent), and then the same smiling faces again. Looking time at each face was recorded during baseline viewing and during the post-song viewing.

Results of the Study. Analyses involved comparison of the proportion of time the infant looked at the face of the person who sang the familiar song to chance. At baseline before the song was sung, the infants did not look at the person who would sing the familiar song more than chance ($M = 0.521$, $t(31) = 0.67$, $p = 0.51$). However, at final viewing after the song had been sung, the infants looked more at the face that had sung the familiar song than is expected by chance ($M = 0.593$, $t(31) = 2.96$, $p = 0.006$).

Conclusions of the Study. Because infants looked at the face that had sung the familiar song longer than expected by chance (but did not do so at baseline viewing before the song had been sung), the researchers concluded that melodies sung to young children contribute to social affiliation in terms of face viewing.

TEST YOURSELF

1. When we do not know the population σ, we use the _____ to calculate estimate standard error.

   a. population mean

   b. sample mean

   c. sample standard deviation

   d. sampling error

2. With a sample size of 25, our degrees of freedom would be _____.

   a. 26

   b. 25

   c. 24

   d. 20

3. In the calculation of a *t* score, the estimated standard error is an estimate of _____.

   a. the population mean

   b. the population standard deviation

   c. the difference between the sample mean and the population mean

4. When we calculate an inferential statistic looking at mean differences, the numerator is the _____ and the denominator is the _____.

   a. actual mean difference, mean difference expected by chance due to sampling

   b. mean difference expected by chance due to sampling, actual mean difference

c. population mean, sample mean

d. sample mean, population mean

5. For a sample of 36 participants and sample standard deviation of 3, the estimated standard error would be _____.

a   0.08

b. 0.50

c. 1.0

d. 3.0

6. The shape of the t distribution will be normal whenever the population is normal.

a. True

b. False

7. An assumption of the t test is that the scores must be independent observations.

a. True

b. False

8. The t Table provides the p value for each t score to allow the researcher to compare p with α.

a. True

b. False

9. A researcher wants to know if using videos to illustrate concepts in class improves exam scores. He uses the videos before the first exam in his course and collects exam scores from the 62 students in his class. On average, they score 78%, with a standard deviation of 5%. Use this description to answer the questions below.

a. What else does the researcher need to know in order to use a one-sample t test to test his hypothesis?

b. What is the null hypothesis for this study?

c. What t_{crit} should the researcher use in this study if his $\alpha = 0.05$?

10. Your instructor tells you that his exam scores always show a 75% average score. But he thinks the class you're in seems to be grasping the material better than his previous classes. You decide to test this. The reported mean on the exam for your class is 80% with a 10% standard deviation. There are 49 people in your class. Assuming $\alpha = 0.05$, is he right about your class understanding better than previous classes (using the exam score as a measure of this)?

Chapter 10

Related/Paired Samples *t* Test

As you read the chapter, consider the following questions:

10.1   How can we compare data from two different situations for the same participants?

10.2   What is the difference between a within-subjects design and a matched pairs design?

10.3   How are difference scores used in a *t* test?

10.4   How does our hypothesis-testing procedure differ for a one-sample *t* test and a related/paired samples *t* test?

Let's consider once again the psychic study example introduced in Chapter 9. Recall that you are testing the hypothesis that the population of psychics has extrasensory perception (ESP) and can predict the suit of a randomly drawn playing card at a rate higher than chance (i.e., 25%). In Chapter 9, we looked at a study testing this hypothesis in which a sample of psychics was tested with the card prediction task. No evidence was found in that study to reject the null hypothesis, which states that the population of psychics can predict the card suit no better than chance (which is the rate expected in the population of people who are not psychics). Thus, we found no evidence for the hypothesis that psychics have ESP, but we also could not find evidence against this hypothesis in our hypothesis-testing procedure. Therefore, we need to continue testing the hypothesis.

Suppose, for example, that your friend (who believes that psychics have ESP) suggests that perhaps psychics need their normal fortune-telling environments (e.g., low lighting, candles, a crystal ball) in order to accurately predict the card suit (see Photo 10.1). To test this idea, you decide to do another study with a sample of psychics tested both in a fortune-telling environment and in the lab environment you used in the previous study. In this new study, a new sample of 50 psychics will each perform the card prediction task in both the fortune-telling environment and in the lab environment. They will complete 100 trials of the task in each environment and their accuracy rate will be measured for each environment. This study is considered a within-subjects design because all the psychic participants will complete the same

Photo 10.1   Research question: Does psychics' ESP depend on the environment they are in?

©iStock/kzenon

task in two different environments. This type of design was first discussed in Chapter 1 of this text and is different from the design we used in our first psychic study in Chapter 9. In this new study, we are no longer comparing a single sample with a known population mean. Instead, we are collecting data twice (once in the original environment and once in the fortune-telling environment) from a single sample to see if there is a difference between their average scores in the two environments. This will provide another test of the hypothesis that they have ESP—in this case, we expect a difference between the environments because the hypothesis is that they have ESP only in the fortune-telling environment.

SAMPLES WITH RELATED/PAIRED DATA

In this chapter, we will consider how to test hypotheses with a single sample under different conditions. For our new psychic study, we will compare data on the card prediction tasks for two environments: a lab environment and a fortune-telling environment for this one sample. This will be done using a within-subjects design. In this design, each participant in the study will give you two accuracy rates, one in the lab room and one in the fortune-telling room. Other common within-subjects designs include comparisons of data before and after some event or treatment has occurred. In this way, we can determine if the scores on a measure have changed from before and after some treatment of interest (e.g., a new teaching method). This is known as a pretest–posttest design because you are comparing scores for a sample from before the treatment (the pretest) to after the treatment (the posttest).

Another way to examine related/paired data is using a matched design. In a matched design, participants are paired across the treatment conditions on some variable of interest. For example, suppose an instructor wants to compare the use of online quizzes to help students learn the material in her course. To test this hypothesis, she might decide to compare final exam scores in two sections of her course,

---

❧

Pretest–Posttest design: a type of research design (often a quasi-experiment) in which behavior is measured both before and after a treatment or condition is implemented

Matched design: a between-subjects experiment that involves sets of participants matched on a specific characteristic, with each member of the set randomly assigned to a different level of the independent variable

---

one that is given the online quizzes and one that is not given the quizzes. However, she might be concerned that there are more students in one section who already know more of the material than the students in the other section. To control for this source of bias across the sections, she could use a matched design in which students are matched in pairs across the two sections based on their preexisting knowledge of the course material before they start the course. This can be accomplished by giving a test to all the students at the start of the semester and matching the students into pairs who have the same or similar scores on the test, with one member of each pair in each section. Figure 10.1 shows how this can be done. Matched designs can also be done with

Figure 10.1   A Matched Pairs Design Comparing Two Sections' Final Exam Scores, With One Section Given Online Quizzes and the Other Section Not Given the Quizzes

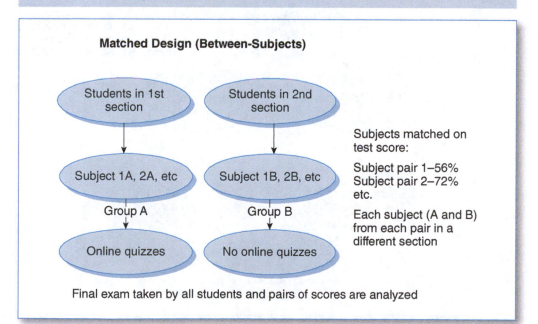

twins to match genetics and/or upbringing in a study or couples to examine differences across members of the couple while matching the dynamics of the relationship within each couple.

In a related/paired samples *t* test, we compare scores that are related in some way (i.e., the same subjects or pairs of subjects matched on some characteristic), conducting the hypothesis in a very similar way to the one-sample *t* test case covered in the previous chapter. In the case of related samples, we will use the difference scores between the pairs of scores for each match as our dependent variable and compare the difference score mean with the difference expected if there is no difference: $\mu = 0$ (or with a specific difference that is expected in the population). In other words, we combine the two sets of scores into a single score (i.e., the difference score) so that we have a single sample mean to compare with a population mean. Our new test conducted this way is the related/paired samples *t* test (both labels are given because *related* and *paired* labels are used frequently).

Let's consider our new psychic study to see how this is done. Imagine that we have conducted our study. Our new sample of 50 psychics has participated in the study in which each psychic has completed the card prediction task in a lab room and in a room set up as a fortune-telling environment (see Photo 10.1). Which room they use first is decided randomly such that half of the psychics complete the task in the lab room first and half of them complete the task in the fortune-telling room first. This is done to ensure that room order does not affect the results. Figure 10.2 shows the design of this study. You can see in this figure that each participant has

Figure 10.2   Design of the Within-Subjects Psychic Study

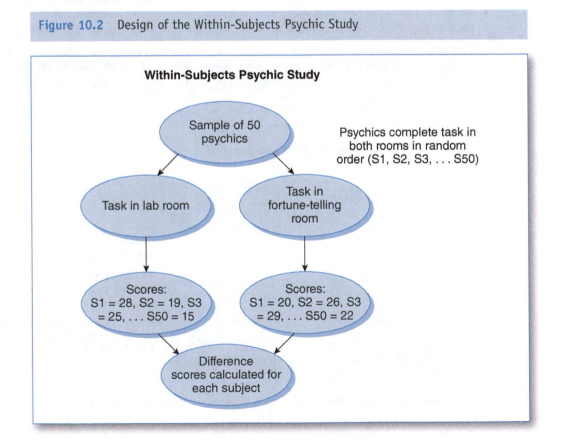

an accuracy score for each room. However, in order to test our hypothesis about whether there is a difference in accuracy across the room types, we need to calculate the difference scores between the rooms for each participant.

To calculate our difference scores, we simply need to subtract the score for each psychic while in the fortune-telling room from their score while in lab room. In other words, the difference score will equal $X_{\text{fortune-telling}} - X_{\text{lab}}$. We will need to calculate this difference score (D) for each participant. Thus, from Figure 10.2, for S1 = (20 − 28) = −8, S2 = (26 − 19) = 7, S3 = (29 − 25) = 4, . . . S50 = (22 − 15) = 7. We can then calculate the mean of the difference scores, $\overline{D}$ by adding up all the difference scores and dividing by the total number of subjects, as we have done in calculating the mean for any set of scores. In the next section, we will work through all of the hypothesis-testing steps for our related samples *t* test and consider a new formula for *t*.

Stop and Think

10.1 For the online quizzes study shown in Figure 10.1, is this an experiment? Why or why not? What about our new psychic study shown in Figure 10.2: Is this an experiment? What are the differences between the designs of these studies?

10.2 What are the alternative and null hypotheses for our new psychic study? Be sure to state these hypotheses in terms of populations of difference scores.

CALCULATING A RELATED/PAIRED SAMPLES *t* TEST

Let's continue with our new within-subjects psychic study to work through our hypothesis-testing process and see how the process will change for our new *t* test.

Step 1: State Hypotheses

Were you able to state the hypotheses for the study in Stop and Think 10.2? If so, they should match the hypotheses listed here:

H_1: *In the population, the mean difference score should be greater than zero.*

H_0: *In the population, the mean difference score should be less than or equal to zero.*

Why did we compare our sample mean for difference scores to zero? We compare the sample mean to zero because if there is no effect of room type on prediction accuracy, then we expect no difference between the scores the participants provide in the two rooms. Thus, on average, the difference scores will be zero. Why did we include *less than . . . zero* as part of the null hypothesis? We include *less than . . . zero* in the null hypothesis because a negative difference score would indicate higher accuracy in the lab room than in the fortune-telling room. This is not what we expect for our psychics. We specifically predicted higher accuracy for the fortune-telling room as our researcher's hypothesis; thus, our alternative hypothesis is one-tailed with a *greater than zero* predicted direction. To understand what the positive and negative difference scores tell us about our prediction, we must pay attention to the order in which we do our subtraction when calculating the difference scores. In our psychic study, we calculated difference scores as $X_{\text{fortune-telling}} - X_{\text{lab}}$. This means we expect a positive difference score mean if our hypothesis is correct. However, it is also possible that we would be expecting a negative difference if we expected the lab setting to show higher accuracy in the task and we considered this mean difference in our study. Thus, it is important to consider which condition we expect will be higher in our study and set up our mean comparison to reflect the difference score (positive or negative) that we expect in our hypothesis.

Step 2: Set Decision Criterion

Once again, we will set our alpha level at 0.05. Thus, our one critical region will contain positive mean difference scores and contain 5% of the scores in the distribution.

Step 3: Collect Sample Data

In Step 3, we collect our sample data. Our sample contains 50 psychics that represent the population of all psychics. Each of the psychics in our sample will provide two accuracy scores: one for the lab room and one for the fortune-telling room. However, our test relies on an analysis of the difference scores so our difference scores will be our dependent variable of interest in this study, calculated as $X_{\text{fortune-telling}} - X_{\text{lab}}$.

Step 4: Calculate Statistics

Once we have the difference score data from our sample, we are ready to calculate the statistics for our sample. We first need to calculate the sample mean for the difference scores, $\bar{D}$. We will also need to calculate the standard deviation for our difference scores, s_D, in order to calculate the estimated standard error, which will serve as the estimate of sampling error in our t calculation. Figure 10.3 shows the portion of the inferential statistics flowchart for the paired samples t test. Let's assume that our descriptive statistics for the psychic sample are $\bar{D} = 1.0$ and $s_D = 2.9$. With these values and our sample size, n, we are ready to calculate the estimated standard error:

$$s_{\bar{D}} = \frac{s_D}{\sqrt{n}} = \frac{2.9}{\sqrt{50}} = \frac{2.9}{7.07} = .41$$

We can then insert the $s_{\bar{D}}$ value into our t formula:

$$t = \frac{\bar{D} - \mu_{\bar{D}}}{s_{\bar{D}}} = \frac{1 - 0}{.41} = 2.44$$

Now, we can use the t Distribution Table in Appendix C to find our t_{crit} value. But we'll need the df in order to find the correct value for our sample size:

$$df = n - 1 = 50 - 1 = 49$$

Because our alpha and df are the same as in our psychic study from Chapter 9 and we are again conducting a one-tailed test, our t_{crit} will be the same ($t_{crit} = 1.677$). Thus, our critical region

Figure 10.3   Portion of the Statistical Test Decision Flowchart for a Paired Samples *t* Test

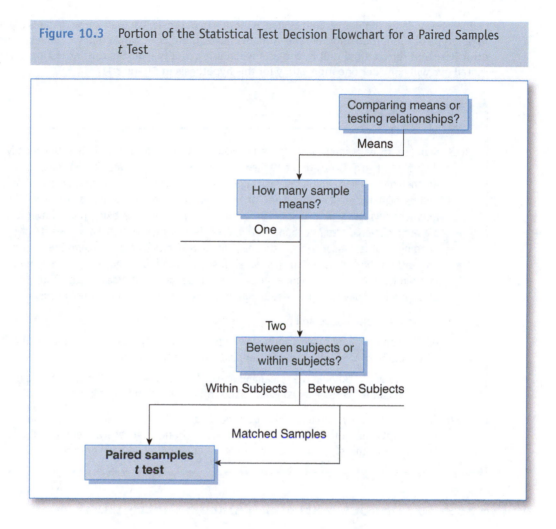

is the same as the one shown in Figure 9.5. However, our sample *t* value is higher here and falls in a different place in our *t* distribution. Let's see how this changes our decision.

Step 5: Make a Decision

Remember that with a hand-calculated *t* test, we must compare our sample *t* score with the t_{crit} value from the table to decide if we have evidence against our null hypothesis. If our sample *t* score falls in the critical region, we can reject the null hypothesis. For this study, our sample *t* is greater than the t_{crit} and because our alternative hypothesis predicts a positive *t* score (which is what we have from our sample), we have enough evidence here to reject the null hypothesis and conclude that accuracy is higher for our psychics in the fortune-telling room than the lab room. Our study provides evidence that the room does have an effect on psychics' accuracy rates. However, we will still need more testing of our hypothesis that their accuracy is higher than chance, because we did not yet find evidence for this hypothesis. We only know that it is higher in one type of room than another type. And, of course, there is a chance that we made a Type I error here and rejected the null hypothesis when it is actually true. So, further testing is warranted (we will consider one more study for this hypothesis in Chapter 11).

Stop and Think

10.3 Suppose 36 participants complete an experiment where ads are presented subliminally during a task (e.g., Coke ads are flashed at very fast rates during movie ads). Participants are then given a recognition test for images in the ads, in which two images are presented and participants must choose which one of the two was presented earlier. However, the researcher wants to know if standard ads (e.g., a glass of Coke being poured over ice) are remembered differently than emotional ads (e.g., a person drinking a Coke is tightly hugging another person). To test this, each of the 36 participants completes the recognition task for both types of ads (i.e., when first presented, both types of ads are shown in a random order and recognition trials are included for both types of ads). Thus, each participant will have a separate recognition score for standard and emotional ads.

a. State the alternative and null hypotheses for this study.

b. The sample mean for the difference scores in this study was 15% with a standard deviation of 5%. Calculate the sample t score for this study.

c. What decision should the researcher make about the null hypothesis in this study? What can the researcher conclude about their prediction from this decision?

10.4 Suppose the study described in 10.3 was conducted with two separate samples of participants—one that received standard ads and one that received emotional ads. Describe how this study might be conducted with a matched pairs design.

USING SPSS TO CONDUCT A RELATED/PAIRED SAMPLES t TEST

Like the one-sample t test, SPSS will also calculate a paired/related samples t test for you, providing the exact p value for your sample t score. Consider the example study described in Stop and Think 10.3. This is a within-subjects design comparing recognition performance for two types of subliminal ads, standard and emotional. Suppose you conducted this study with 10 participants. If you had done so, you might have obtained the data shown in Figure 10.4. Notice how the data are organized in this window: There is a row for each subject in the study and separate columns for the recognition scores for the two types of ads. This is how you would enter data for a within-subjects or matched design into SPSS. Because the scores come from either the same subjects or pair of subjects, each score from that subject/pair goes in the same row with separate columns for scores from each condition.

To run the test, choose the Paired Samples t test in the Compare Means portion of the Analyze menu. To compare the two types of ads, click the Standard column to add it as Variable 1 and then the Emotional column as Variable 2. Then, click the arrow to add them as a Paired Variable.

When you click OK, the test runs, and the output appears in the Output Window.

The output indicates descriptive statistics in the first box and the test statistic and *p* value in the third box labeled Paired Samples Test (see Figure 10.5). For this study, the *t* value is −2.624 with a *p* value of 0.028. In this case, the *p* value is lower than the alpha level of 0.05. Therefore, the null hypothesis (that there is no difference between the ad types) can be rejected and the alternative hypothesis (that there is a difference between the ad types) is supported. The means indicate which ad type was remembered better: In this study, the emotional ads ($M = 66.3$) were remembered better than the standard ads ($M = 53.5$), $t(9) = -2.62$, $p = 0.03$. The second box of the output provides a test of the relationship between the two sets of scores (see Chapter 15 for more information about tests for relationships).

Figure 10.4   SPSS Data Window for the Subliminal Ad Study with 10 Participants

	Standard	Emotional	va
1	56.00	71.00	
2	60.00	59.00	
3	49.00	66.00	
4	35.00	78.00	
5	51.00	49.00	
6	65.00	82.00	
7	70.00	77.00	
8	44.00	52.00	
9	58.00	51.00	
10	47.00	78.00	
11			
12			
13			

Summary of Steps

- Type the data for each condition in separate columns in the data window, with one row per subject or matched pair of subjects.
- Choose Compare Means in the Analyze menu.
- Choose Paired Samples *t* test from the list of tests.
- Click on each column in the window to add them as Variable 1 and Variable 2.
- After the two conditions are indicated as the variables, click the arrow to add them as a Paired Variable.
- Click OK to run the test and look for the *p* value in the Sig column under Paired Samples Test in the Output window (see Figure 10.5) to compare with your alpha level.

Figure 10.5 SPSS Output for the Paired Samples *t* Test on the Ad Study Data

t **Test**

Paired Samples Statistics

		Mean	N	Std. Deviation	Std. Error Mean
Pair 1	Standard Ads	53.5000	10	10.40566	3.29056
	Emotional Ads	66.3000	10	12.68464	4.01123

Paired Samples Correlations

		N	Correlation	Sig.
Pair 1	Standard Ads and Emotional Ads	10	.118	.745

Paired Samples Test

		Paired Differences							
					95% Confidence Interval of the Difference				
		Mean	Std. Deviation	Std. Error Mean	Lower	Upper	t	df	Sig. (two-tailed)
Pair 1	Standard Ads and Emotional Ads	−12.800	15.42581	4.87807	−23.835	−1.7650	−2.624	9	.028

Stop and Think

10.5 You are trying to decide whether you should purchase paper copies of the textbooks required for your courses next semester or purchase the online copies of the texts that are much cheaper. You are concerned that with the online texts, staring at the computer screen may be too distracting because you also receive texts and instant/chat messages on your computer. To help you make this decision, you look at the research done on paper versus computer text reading. You find a study that had participants read two passages about two different topics. Each participant read both passages, one as a paper copy and one on the computer screen. After a distractor task lasting 30 minutes, the participants were tested then for their comprehension of the passages with a multiple choice test containing 10 questions about each passage. Their scores were then input into SPSS and a paired samples *t* test was conducted. Use the SPSS output in Figure 10.6 to answer the questions below.

a. What is the sample *t* score for the difference scores?

b. What is the *p* value for the sample *t* score?

c. Assuming the researchers used an $\alpha = 0.05$, what does this test tell you about comprehension of paper versus computer text? Does this help you decide which types of texts you should buy? Why or why not?

TEST ASSUMPTIONS

The assumptions that must be satisfied to use the related/paired samples *t* test are similar to those of the one-sample *t* test:

1. The population of difference scores must be a normal distribution. Recall that this assumption is needed to ensure the accuracy of the t_{crit} values in the *t* Table. However, as was the case with the one-sample *t* test, violating this assumption will not change the outcome of the test for sample sizes greater than 30 (i.e., $df = 30$ or higher).

2. The scores from different participants or pairs of participants must be independent. This means that across the subjects (or across the pairs of subjects for matched designs), the scores cannot depend on the scores of the other participants (or pairs). However, because scores will be related for the same or pairs of subjects by definition, this assumption does not apply to scores within subjects or pairs of subjects.

Calculation Summary

Estimated standard error: Sample difference scores standard deviation divided by the square root of the sample size

Figure 10.6   SPSS Output for the Paired Samples *t* Test Run for the Study Described in Stop and Think 10.5

Paired Samples Statistics

		Mean	N	Std. Deviation	Std, Error Mean
Pair 1	Paper Text	6.3000	10	1.41814	.44845
	Computer Text	5.8000	10	1.87380	.59255

Paired Samples Correlations

		N	Correlation	Sig.
Pair 1	Paper Text and Computer Text	10	.109	.765

Paired Samples Test

	Paired Differences							
	Mean	Std. Deviation	Std. Error Mean	95% Confidence Interval of the Difference		t	df	Sig. (two-tailed)
				Lower	Upper			
Pair 1 Paper Text Computer Text	.50000	2.22361	.70317	−1.09068	2.09068	.711	9	.495

Related/paired samples *t* test: Sample mean of the difference scores minus the population mean for difference scores, divided by the estimated standard error

CHAPTER SUMMARY

10.1 How can we compare data from two different situations for the same participants?

This is done with within-subjects designs. Because the scores across treatment conditions are necessarily related (as they are from the same subjects), we need to use the related/paired samples *t* test to test hypotheses about the difference predicted across treatment conditions.

10.2 What is the difference between a within-subjects design and a matched pairs design?

In a within-subjects design, all the subjects provide more than one score, with one mean score per treatment condition. In a matched pairs design, subjects are paired based on some characteristic on which they are similar, and then one subject in each pair receives a different treatment condition. However, the data from matched designs are analyzed in the same way as for within-subjects designs.

10.3 How are difference scores used in a *t* test?

In the related/paired samples *t* test, the difference scores for each subject/pair are calculated to be used as the data to be analyzed. The sample mean of the difference scores is then used to calculate a sample *t* score in the test.

10.4 How does our hypothesis-testing process differ for a one-sample *t* test and a related/paired samples *t* test?

The process is very similar for these two tests. However, for a related/paired samples *t* test, the data analyzed will be the difference scores, and the null hypothesis predicts a difference score of zero (for a two-tailed test).

THINKING ABOUT RESEARCH

A summary of a research study in psychology is given below. As you read the summary, think about the following questions:

1. Is this study an experiment? Explain your answer.

2. Does the study appear to be a within-subjects or between-subjects design? What part of the Method indicates this?

3. What are the null and alternative hypotheses for these studies?

4. The *p* values for liking ratings in the comparison of shared and unshared experiences were 0.01 for Study 1 and 0.025 for Study 2. With a chosen $\alpha = 0.05$, what did the researchers learn about the null hypothesis in each study?

5. Why did the researchers test both pleasant and unpleasant shared experiences in their study?

Boothby, E. J., Clark, M. S., & Bargh, J. A. (2014). Shared experiences are amplified. *Psychological Science, 25*, 2209–2216.

Purpose of the Study. The researchers conducted two studies to examine the social effect on one's subjective experiences based on past studies showing that shared experiences are psychologically stronger than unshared experiences. In their studies, they had subjects participate in both pleasant (Study 1) and unpleasant (Study 2) experiences. They predicted that when another person present was sharing the experience, the ratings of the experience would be stronger than when the other person present was engaged in a different activity.

Figure 10.7 Mean Liking of Chocolate in Studies 1 and 2

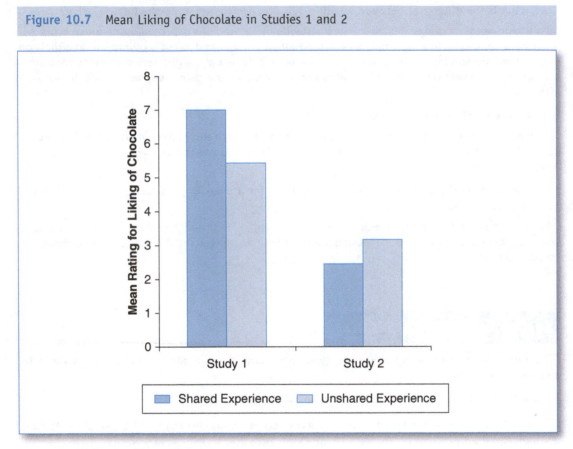

SOURCE: Results from Boothby et al.'s (2014) study.

Method of the Study. In both studies, participants (*n* = 23 in Study 1 and *n* = 22 in Study 2) completed both the shared experience and unshared experience conditions in a random order. In both studies, subjects and a research confederate were asked to complete some tasks based on a card draw. Subjects tasted the same chocolate in both conditions but were led to believe that the chocolate was different in the two tasks. In Study 1, the chocolate was pleasant-tasting (pleasant experience), and in Study 2, the chocolate was bitter-tasting (unpleasant experience). In the shared condition, the confederate tasted the same chocolate as the subject. In the unshared experience, the confederate appeared to be tasting a different chocolate. The subjects were not allowed to communicate during the tasks. After tasting the chocolate, the subjects completed a survey about their rating of the chocolate (e.g., "How much do you like the chocolate? How flavorful is the chocolate?" etc.) and a survey about their impressions of the confederate. For both surveys, responses were made by checking a box on a 0 to 10 scale, with higher numbers indicating higher ratings.

Results of the Study. In both studies, ratings for the chocolate were stronger (higher for pleasant and lower for unpleasant) in the shared experience conditions. Figure 10.7 shows the ratings for liking of chocolate for both studies based on the social condition.

Conclusions of the Study. The results of the study showed that shared experiences are more intense than unshared experiences, even when one does not communicate with someone else. This effect was present for both pleasant and unpleasant experiences, showing that the sharing of an experience does not simply make it more pleasurable but makes it stronger overall.

TEST YOURSELF

1. In the related/paired samples *t* test, the difference scores typically predicted by the null hypothesis _____.

   a. equal 0

   b. equal 1

   c. equal − 1

   d. depends on the alternative hypothesis

2. For a sample size of _____, we do not need to be worried about violating the assumption of a normal distribution for the population.

   a. 10

   b. 25

   c. 30

   d. 31 or higher

3. The dependent variable for a within-subjects design is _____.

   a. accuracy

   b. speed

   c. difference scores across conditions

   d. difference scores across participants

4. A matched design might involve _____.

   a. couples

   b. twins

   c. the same participants completing all the conditions

   d. both (a) and (b)

5. The estimated standard error in a related/paired samples *t* test is based on the standard deviation of the difference scores.

   a. True

   b. False

6. The *df* for a matched pairs design is based on the total number of participants instead of the number of pairs.

   a. True

   b. False

7. An assumption of the related/paired samples t test is that all scores across conditions are independent.

   a. True

   b. False

8. A researcher wants to know if using videos to illustrate concepts in class improves exam scores. He uses the videos after the first exam in his course and then collects exam scores from the 62 students in his class for the second exam. He wants to compare scores on the first exam and the second exam to see if the scores increased after he started using the videos. On average, the difference in scores between the first exam and the second exam was 5%, with a standard deviation of 8%. Use this description to answer the questions below.

   a. What is the alternative hypothesis for this study?

   b. What is the null hypothesis for this study?

   c. What t_{crit} should the researcher use in this study if his $\alpha = 0.05$?

   d. Do the videos seem to help? Explain your answer.

9. A group of students is tested on their driving ability in a research study that was done to investigate the effect of cell phone use on driving performance. A sample of 25 students drives a test course in a driving simulator to measure their driving accuracy (based on how often they deviate from the course, miss a red light, etc.). Then, all 25 students are tested on the driving course again while holding a conversation on their cell phone with a researcher. The mean difference score in driving accuracy shows that, on average, accuracy decreases by 25% while talking on the cell phone, with a standard deviation of 15%. Does cell phone use cause a significant decrease in driving performance?

Chapter 11

Independent Samples *t* Test

As you read the chapter, consider the following questions:

11.1 How can we compare two different populations in a research study?

11.2 With two samples in a study, how do we calculate estimated standard error?

11.3 How do we calculate a *t* score for two samples?

11.4 What is the pooled variance and how does it help us handle unequal sample sizes in our hypothesis test?

In the last chapter, we considered a study where we found evidence for a difference in psychics' prediction abilities in lab and fortune-telling environments. However, we are still lacking evidence for our original prediction from Chapter 9 that psychics do have ESP that allows them to predict the suit of a randomly drawn card in our card prediction task. In Chapter 9, we tested this hypothesis with a single sample of psychics who performed our card prediction task, but our sample did not show an accuracy rate significantly greater than the chance guessing rate of 25%. Thus, we still need to conduct further tests of our hypothesis, because a nonsignificant result provides evidence neither for nor against the alternative hypothesis. In this chapter, we will consider a more common design used to test hypotheses in behavioral research, in which two samples are compared for two possible populations that differ on the factor of interest in the study.

In the new study to test our hypothesis, we will test both self-proclaimed psychics in our card prediction task and a sample of non-psychics. The sample of psychics will represent the population of psychics, and the sample of non-psychics will represent the population of non-psychics. We will compare the mean accuracy rates for the two samples to test the hypothesis that the two populations (psychics and non-psychics) have different population means for card suit prediction accuracy. Figure 11.1 illustrates the design of this study. Our null and alternative hypotheses will be stated as comparisons of the population means for these two populations

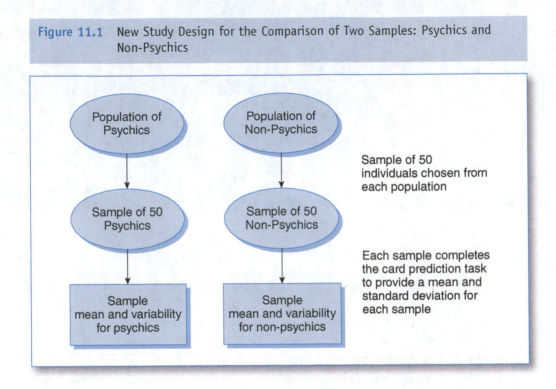

Figure 11.1 New Study Design for the Comparison of Two Samples: Psychics and Non-Psychics

with the sample means and sample variability used to calculate our sample *t* score. With two samples to compare, we will use the independent samples *t* test to complete our hypothesis-testing process for this new study.

INDEPENDENT SAMPLES

Our new study design is a between-subjects design because it involves the comparison of two separate and independent samples. The samples may be drawn from different populations, as in our new psychic study, or come from the same population but be exposed to different treatment conditions.

Here is another example: Suppose you wanted to know whether rereading one's notes from lecture or taking quizzes is a better study technique for exams (a two-tailed test would be used here because there is no prediction about which one is better). To answer this question, you might conduct a study in which you recruit a sample from the population of students at your school to participate in the study. The students in the sample might then be randomly assigned to one of two conditions: (1) a condition in which they read a paragraph of text about a topic and then reread the paragraph before a multiple choice test about the topic or (2) a condition in which they read the paragraph of text and then attempt to recall the main ideas from the paragraph before taking the topic test. In this study, the group of students who rereads the paragraph represents the population of students who use this study technique, and the group

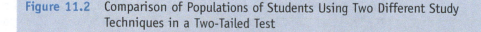

Figure 11.2   Comparison of Populations of Students Using Two Different Study Techniques in a Two-Tailed Test

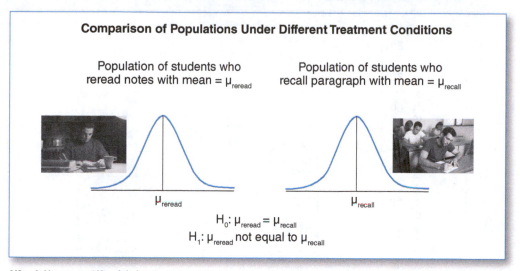

of students who recalls the ideas from the paragraph represents the population of students who use this study technique (see Figure 11.2). The mean and variability for the multiple choice test scores for each sample can then be calculated to compare them using an independent samples *t* test. The top part of the *t* score calculation will contain the mean difference observed between the samples, and the bottom part of the *t* score calculation will contain the mean difference expected by chance due to sampling error (i.e., these are different samples drawn from the population of students, so we wouldn't expect the two samples to always have the same mean test score even if they used the same study technique). The *t* test is then completed in the same way we have done in the previous two chapters: finding the t_{crit} value in the *t* Table and deciding if our sample *t* score is in the critical region(s) for the *t* distribution based on the distribution of sample means. If it is, we have evidence against the null hypothesis and can conclude that the populations in the different treatment conditions have different mean scores. If our sample *t* score is not in the critical region(s), we cannot conclude that the population means are different and must retain the null hypothesis.

Consider the mean data shown in Figure 11.3. These data show the mean memory score on a final memory test after two groups of participants used the two study techniques described here (rereading the paragraphs or recalling the main ideas from the paragraphs) before taking a delayed final memory test on the paragraph topic. These data came from a study conducted by Roediger and Karpicke (2006) in an experiment in which they waited two days (a realistic amount of time between the study time and the time of the test) before giving a final memory test after the participants studied the paragraph information using one of these two techniques (this study was described more fully in the Thinking About Research section of Chapter 3). These researchers directly compared these two conditions

Figure 11.3   Comparison of Mean Memory Scores for Two Study Techniques Tested by Roediger and Karpicke (2006) With a Two-Day Delay between Study and Final Test

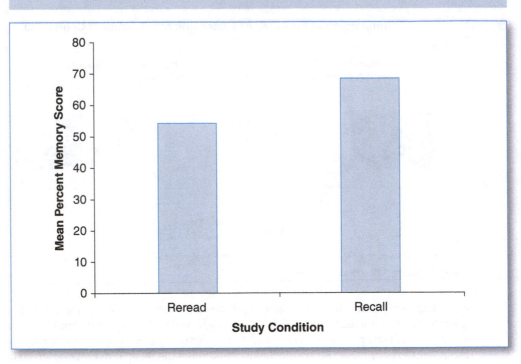

using an independent samples *t* test and found that the difference was significant, meaning that the *t* score for their sample was within the critical regions of the *t* distribution for an alpha level of 0.05.

Stop and Think

11.1 For our new psychic study with psychic and non-psychic samples, is this an experiment? Why or why not?

11.2 For the study technique example just described, is this an experiment? Why or why not?

Estimating Sampling Error for Two Samples

One important difference between the way we calculate the sample *t* score for a between-subjects design and the one-sample and related-samples designs is the way we estimate sampling error with the estimated standard error. Up to this point, we have calculated the estimated standard error with the standard deviation (from the one sample or the difference scores) divided by the square root of the sample size n. In formula form, this is

$$s_{\bar{X}} = \frac{s}{\sqrt{n}}$$

for one-sample designs and

$$s_{\bar{D}} = \frac{s_D}{\sqrt{n}}$$

for difference scores from the same sample of participants or a matched pair of participants. You could also write these formulas using the variance instead of the standard deviation (remember that the variance is the standard deviation squared):

$$s_{\bar{X}} = \sqrt{\frac{s^2}{n}} \text{ and } s_{\bar{D}} = \sqrt{\frac{s_D^2}{n}}$$

This works because taking the top part of this formula is the same (algebraically) as the top part of the first set of formulas we've been using (i.e., the square root of a squared number is the number itself). And how do we calculate the variance for a sample? If you review how we calculated the standard deviation in Chapter 5, you will find the formula

$$s = \sqrt{\frac{SS}{n-1}}$$

where SS is the sum of squared deviations of the scores from the mean. The variance is the square of the standard deviation, so if we remove the square root symbol, our formula for the variance of a sample is

$$s^2 = \frac{SS}{n-1}$$

which is also the SS divided by the df (remember, $df = n-1$).

Why am I showing you all these different ways to write the same formula? Well, in order to calculate the estimated standard error for two samples, we'll need to use these terms (SS, s^2, df) in order to first calculate the pooled variance for the samples. This is a value that is the variance for two samples with the size of the sample considered in the calculation. This is important because in some cases the sample sizes will be different across groups (e.g., $n = 25$ for one group and $n = 28$ for the other group) and

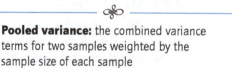

Pooled variance: the combined variance terms for two samples weighted by the sample size of each sample

we need to determine one standard error term for both groups. The pooled variance is denoted by s_p^2 and is used to calculate the estimated standard error, $s_{\bar{X}_1 - \bar{X}_2}$, for the bottom of our sample *t* score calculation. This will serve as the estimate of sampling error in our independent samples *t* test and is based on the variability from the two samples in the study. We will examine how to conduct the independent samples *t* test for our new psychic study in the next section.

CALCULATING THE INDEPENDENT SAMPLES t TEST

Let's go back now to our new psychic study and consider how we can compare mean accuracy scores on the card prediction task for our two samples. We can follow the same steps for hypothesis testing as we have done in previous chapters. The step that will change a bit is the calculation of statistics step (Step 4).

Step 1: State Hypotheses

What are our hypotheses for the new study? Remember that we will state these as differences between populations. Our prediction is that the psychics will have a higher accuracy score than the non-psychics, so we can state our alternative hypothesis as

H_1: *The population mean for psychics will be higher than the mean for the population of non-psychics or* $\mu_{psychics} > \mu_{non\text{-}psychics}$.

This means that our null hypothesis will state that the means are equal or that the non-psychics' mean will be higher:

H_0: *The population mean for psychics will be less than or equal to the mean for the population of non-psychics or* $\mu_{psychics} \leq \mu_{non\text{-}psychics}$.

Step 2: Set Decision Criterion

Once again, we will set our alpha level at 0.05. Thus, our one critical region will be above the mean difference score (i.e., $\mu_{psychics} - \mu_{non-psychics}$) of zero and contain 5% of the scores in the distribution.

Step 3: Collect Sample Data

In the current study, we are looking at two samples of data. Let's suppose that although we recruited 50 psychics and 50 non-psychics, only 45 of the psychics showed up (the other five had clients that day). Thus, our samples have different sizes, $n_{psychics} = 45$ and $n_{non\text{-}psychics} = 50$. For each sample, we will need to determine the mean accuracy score and the variance to determine the pooled variance in Step 4.

Step 4: Calculate Statistics

Now, let's calculate our descriptive and inferential statistics. Figure 11.4 shows the portion of the inferential statistics flowchart for the independent samples t test. Let's suppose the mean accuracy score for the psychics was 26%, and the mean accuracy score for the non-psychics was 25%. We also need to calculate the variance from the individual scores in each sample using the formula given earlier in the chapter that includes the SS and df values. Let's use the values: $SS_{psychics} = 550$, $SS_{non\text{-}psychics} = 350$ and $df_{psychics} = 45 - 1 = 44$, $df_{non\text{-}psychics} = 50 - 1 = 49$. We can now calculate the pooled variance using the following formula:

$$s_p^2 = \frac{SS_{psychics} + SS_{non\text{-}psychics}}{df_{psychics} + df_{non\text{-}psychics}}$$

Figure 11.4   Portion of the Statistical Test Decision Flowchart for an Independent Samples *t* Test

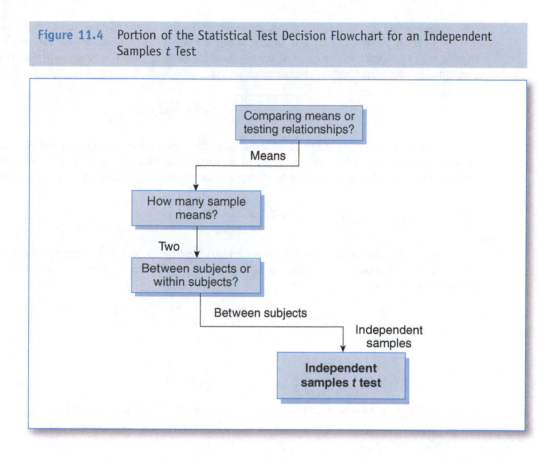

This formula will take into account the variability in each sample using the sum of squares (*SS*) and the sample size of each sample (using *df*). Remember that the variance for one sample is the *SS* divided by the *df*, so here we have a formula that combines these values for the two samples. So, for our study, we have

$$s_p^2 = \frac{550 + 350}{44 + 49} = \frac{900}{93} = 20.93$$

Thus, our pooled variance is 20.93. This is a variance term that combines the variability from our two samples. This value will be used to calculate the estimated standard error for our sample *t* score with the formula:

$$s_{\bar{X}_1 - \bar{X}_2} = \sqrt{\frac{s_p^2}{n_{psychics}} + \frac{s_p^2}{n_{non-psychics}}}$$

In other words, the estimated standard error is the square root of the sum of the pooled variance divided by each sample size. This is analogous to the estimated standard error from our single sample in which we had the standard deviation divided by the square root of n. Because we have a variance term, the top part is also under the square root, and because we have two samples, we need to add in the value separately for each sample based on its sample size. Thus, our estimated standard error for the current study is

$$s_{\bar{X}_1-\bar{X}_2} = \sqrt{\frac{20.93}{45}+\frac{20.93}{50}} = \sqrt{.47+.42} = .94$$

Our sample t score is also calculated using the values for each sample. The actual mean difference minus the expected mean difference is the top of the equation and the estimated standard error representing the mean difference expected by chance (i.e., sampling error) is the bottom of the equation:

$$t = \frac{\left(\bar{X}_1-\bar{X}_2\right)-\left(\mu_1-\mu_2\right)}{s_{\bar{X}_1-\bar{X}_2}}$$

The $\left(\mu_1-\mu_2\right)$ difference is the mean population difference expected under the null hypothesis, just as it was for our related/paired samples t test (typically, zero). We can now substitute in our sample statistics:

$$t = \frac{\left(\bar{X}_{psychics}-\bar{X}_{non-psychics}\right)-\left(\mu_{psychics}-\mu_{non-psychics}\right)}{s_{X_{psychics}-X_{non-psychics}}}$$

$$t = \frac{(26-25)-0}{.94} = \frac{1}{.94} = 1.06$$

We now have our sample t score and can move on to Step 5 to make a decision.

Step 5: Make a Decision

In Step 5, we need to compare our sample t score with the t_{crit} value from the t Distribution Table. We will need to know our alpha level (0.05), our total df: $df_{1+2} = df_1 + df_2 = [(45-1)+(50-1)] = 44+49 = 93$, and whether we have a one- or two-tailed test (one-tailed). Using this information, our t_{crit} from the table is $t_{crit} = 1.658$ (this is the more conservative value from the table for $df = 120$, the closest value to $df = 93$). Comparing our sample t score with this t_{crit}, we find that $t_{sample} < t_{crit}$. Thus, our sample t is not in the critical region and we cannot reject the null hypothesis. Although we still cannot use this as evidence for the null hypothesis, the results from this study provide one additional set of data that is inconsistent with our hypothesis that psychics have ESP. We are slowly building a case against the idea that psychics have ESP that helps them predict the suit of a card chosen from a deck of cards.

Stop and Think

11.3 Suppose 36 participants complete an experiment where ads are presented subliminally during a task (e.g., Coke ads are flashed at very fast rates during movie ads). Participants are then given a recognition test for images of the ads, where two images are presented and participants must choose which one of the two was presented earlier. Both men and women (18 of each gender) participate in the study and the researcher predicts that the recognition accuracy will differ across gender.

a. State the alternative and null hypotheses for this study.

b. The difference between the sample means in this study was 6%. The *SS* for the men was 250 and the *SS* for the women was 150. Calculate the sample *t* score for this study (remember to start with the pooled variance before you calculate the estimated standard error).

c. What decision should the researcher make about the null hypothesis in this study? What can the researcher conclude about their prediction from this decision?

11.4 Calculate the pooled variance for these two samples' scores:

Sample 1: 45, 59, 65, 26, 70, 52, 55

Sample 2: 81, 72, 69, 59, 75, 71, 62

USING SPSS TO CONDUCT AN INDEPENDENT SAMPLES *t* TEST

Data for the comparison of gender study described in Stop and Think 11.3 are shown in the SPSS Window in Figure 11.5. Notice that the data for all participants are typed into a single column. In the next column, code numbers indicate which sample the data belong to. The men were coded in Rows 1 through 10 with a *1*, and the women were coded in Rows 11 through 20 with a

Figure 11.5 Data for Stop and Think 11.3 Shown in the SPSS Data Window

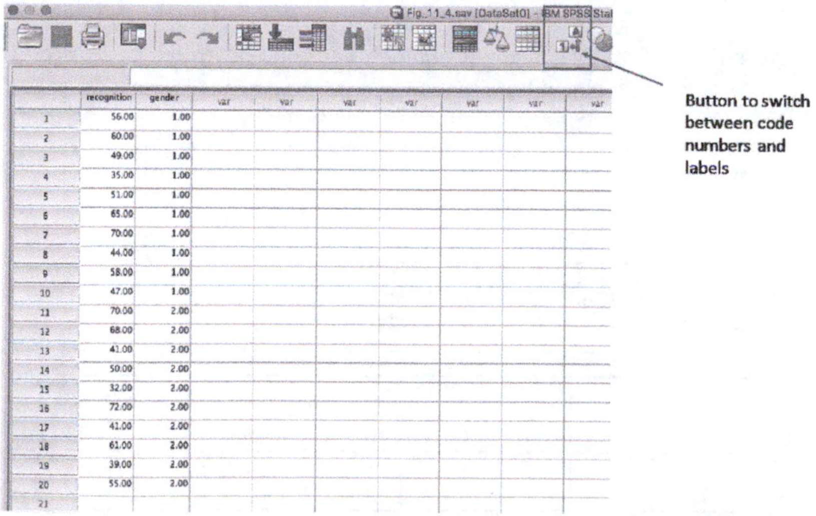

	recognition	gender
1	56.00	1.00
2	60.00	1.00
3	49.00	1.00
4	35.00	1.00
5	51.00	1.00
6	65.00	1.00
7	70.00	1.00
8	44.00	1.00
9	58.00	1.00
10	47.00	1.00
11	70.00	2.00
12	68.00	2.00
13	41.00	2.00
14	50.00	2.00
15	32.00	2.00
16	72.00	2.00
17	41.00	2.00
18	61.00	2.00
19	39.00	2.00
20	55.00	2.00
21		

Button to switch between code numbers and labels

2. In the Variable View, the codes were defined for these groups by indicating labels for each number in the Values column for this variable. A button appears in the menu at the top, allowing you to switch back and forth between the code numbers and code labels.

To conduct the independent samples *t* test for these data, go to the Compare Means tab in the Analyze menu and choose the Independent Samples *t* Test option. The test window allows you to click over the recognition score column as the Test Variable and the gender codes as the Grouping Variable. You must then choose Define Groups to indicate that the values in this column range from 1 to 2. When you click OK, the test automatically runs and the output appears in the Output Window (see Figure 11.6). The first box in the output provides descriptive statistics for each group. The second box contains the test statistic and *p* value. For this study, the *t* value is 0.107 and the *p* value (see the Sig. column) is 0.916. This is a two-tailed test (it is possible that either men or women could have higher recognition scores) so the *p* value given can be directly compared with alpha. In this analysis, the *p* value is greater than the alpha level of 0.05, so the null hypothesis cannot be rejected. Therefore, there is no evidence in these data that men and women differ in their recognition of subliminally presented ads.

Summary of Steps

- Type the data into a column in the data window.
- Add number codes for the groups in another column in the data window.
- Define codes in the Values column in the Variable View tab.
- Choose Compare Means from the Analyze menu.
- Choose Independent Samples *t* Test option from the list of tests.
- Click your data variable into the Test Variable box using the arrow.
- Click Define Groups to type in the range of codes used for your groups (e.g., 1 and 2).
- Click OK and view the *p* value in the Sig. column in the Output window to compare with your alpha level (see Figure 11.6).

Figure 11.6 Output Window for Data From Stop and Think 11.3 for an Independent Samples *t* Test

➔ **T–Test**

Group Statistics

	gender	N	Mean	Std. Deviation	Std. Error Mean
recognition	Men	10	53.5000	10.40566	3.29056
	Women	10	52.9000	14.44107	4.56667

Independent Samples Test

		Levene's Test for Equality of Variances		t-test for Equality of Means					95% Confidence Interval of the Difference	
		F	Sig.	t	df	Sig. (2-tailed)	Mean Difference	Std. Error Difference	Lower	Upper
recognition	Equal variances assumed	2.217	.154	.107	18	.916	.60000	5.62870	−11.22545	12.42545
	Equal variances not assumed			.107	16.361	.916	.60000	5.62870	−11.31092	12.51092

Stop and Think

11.5 For the following set of data from two independent samples, conduct an independent samples t test (by hand or using SPSS) to determine if the mean scores for each sample are significantly different.

Sample 1: 5, 7, 4, 7, 2, 6, 7, 3, 4, 5

Sample 2: 3, 4, 3, 4, 3, 3, 3, 4, 5, 4, 3

TEST ASSUMPTIONS

The assumptions that must be satisfied to use the independent samples t test are the same as those of the other t tests, but there is also a third assumption regarding the variability in the two populations:

1. The population of scores must be a normal distribution. This allows us to use the t Distribution Table to find our t_{crit} value.

2. The scores from different participants within each sample must be independent. Thus, the scores from the different individuals within each sample cannot be related in some way.

3. The populations that the samples represent must have equal variance. This means that the two populations being compared in the study must have the same variability. This assumption is known as homogeneity of variances. Meeting this assumption allows for good estimates of the sampling errors using the pooled variance term. However, an adjustment can be made (see next paragraph) if this assumption has been violated. You will see in later chapters that all tests (t tests and analyses of variance) that involve between-subjects variables include the homogeneity of variances assumption.

❧

Homogeneity of variances: assumption of independent samples t tests and analyses of variance (ANOVAs) that the variance in the scores in the populations is equal across groups

---

The new assumption regarding equal variance across the two populations being compared can be tested when SPSS is used to conduct the independent samples t test. Take another look at Figure 11.6. Notice that there are two rows of values for the t statistic for the independent samples test. The first row is labeled *equal variances assumed*, and the second row is labeled *equal variances not assumed*. These statements refer to the homogeneity of variances assumption of between-subjects tests (t tests and ANOVAs). If this assumption is violated, the t test may be inaccurate. Thus, Levene's test for this assumption is provided in the SPSS output (left side of the second box) for the test. If this test is significant (comparing p to the alpha level), then the statistical values need to be adjusted, and the second row of values in this box should be used. The two rows in this box are given to allow for both possibilities.

Calculation Summary

Pooled variance: The sum of the sum of squares of each sample divided by the sum of the degrees of freedom for each sample

Estimated standard error: The square root of the pooled variance divided by the first sample size plus the pooled variance divided by the second sample size

Independent samples *t* test: Difference between sample means minus the expected population mean difference for the null hypothesis, divided by the estimated standard error

CHAPTER SUMMARY

11.1 How can we compare two different populations in a research study?

This is done by drawing a sample from each population (separately for the two populations or two samples randomly assigned to different conditions to represent the populations for those conditions) and comparing the mean scores for the two samples using an independent samples *t* test.

11.2 With two samples in a study, how do we calculate estimated standard error?

With two samples in a study, we must first determine the pooled variance based on the sum of squares and degrees of freedom for each sample and then use the pooled variance and the two sample sizes to calculate the estimated standard error. This allows us to estimate the sampling error for each sample in a single value.

11.3 How do we calculate a *t* score for two samples?

The independent samples *t* test is similar to the other *t* tests in that the sample *t* is a ratio of the mean difference observed between the samples and the mean difference expected by chance from the estimated standard deviation.

11.4 What is the pooled variance and how does it help us handle unequal sample sizes in our hypothesis test?

The pooled variance is the average variance across the two samples. It is weighted according to the sample sizes so unequal sample sizes can be used in a study with the independent samples *t* test.

THINKING ABOUT RESEARCH

A summary of a research study in psychology is given below. As you read the summary, think about the following questions:

1. Is this study an experiment? Explain your answer.

2. What part of the design of this study tells you that an independent samples *t* test is an appropriate test to use?

3. What are the null and alternative hypotheses for these experiments?

4. If the mean difference between younger and older adults had not been significant in Experiment 2, do you think the researchers' conclusions for the study overall would have changed? Why or why not?

5. Suppose the researchers had created pairs of younger and older adults (one of each age group per pair) based on a pretest score before they conducted the study. With this design, which *t* test would be the appropriate test to use to test their hypotheses?

Worthy, D. A., Gorlick, M. A., Pacheco, J. L., Schnyer, D. M., & Maddox, W. T. (2011). With age comes wisdom: Decision making in younger and older adults. *Psychological Science, 22,* 1375–1380.

Purpose of the Study. To compare decision making in different age groups, the researchers recruited samples of younger and older adults to complete tasks where rewards were either dependent on their previous choices or independent of their previous choices. According to the authors, most previous studies had examined younger and older adult decision making in response-independent tasks, finding that younger adults outperform older adults. However, the authors argue that many decisions in life depend on previous choices (e.g., the type of career one has chosen affects one's retirement options, the type of student one is in high school affects one's college options) and that these types of decisions may involve different processes. Thus, the researchers predicted that the younger adult advantage in decision making may not hold for response-dependent tasks.

Method of the Study. The current study involved two experiments. In Experiment 1, younger and older adults performed a decision-making task where the rewards (points) for their responses (choosing one of four decks of cards shown on the screen) were independent of their previous choices. In this task, the rewards were always higher for one type of deck than the others. In Experiment 2, samples of younger and older adults performed the same decision-making task, but the rewards in Experiment 2 depended on their responses on previous trials. In each experiment, the participants completed 100 trials of the decision-making task. The number of reward points each participant earned in the task was measured as their performance on the task.

Results of the Study. In Experiment 1 (the response-independent task), younger adults showed the performance advantage found in previous studies. However, in Experiment 2, older adults earned more points on average than the younger adults with the response-dependent task. Both of these differences were significant. Figure 11.7 shows the comparison of younger and older adults' performance in the two experiments.

Conclusions of the Study. The results of the study showed that the difference in younger and older adults' decision-making performance depends on the type of task being performed: Younger adults performed better with the response-independent task, but older adults performed better with the response-dependent task. The researchers concluded from these results that younger and older adults approach decision-making tasks in different ways.

Figure 11.7 Data From the Experiments Conducted by Worthy et al. (2011)

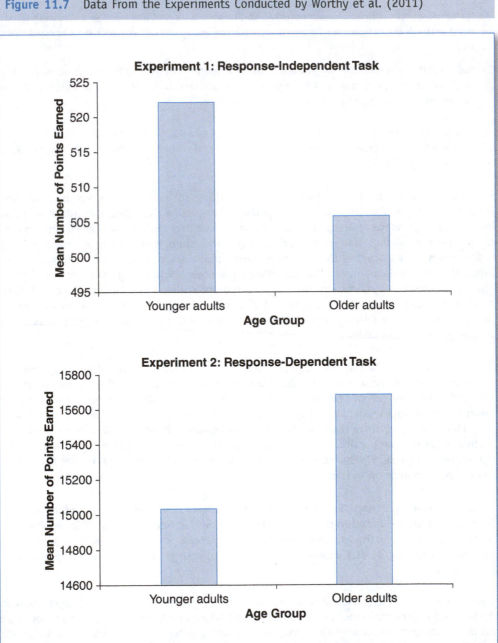

TEST YOURSELF

1. The pooled variance is _____.
   a. the estimated standard in an independent samples *t* test
   b. the combined variance for two independent samples
   c. the variance in the populations the samples were drawn from in a study

2. The variance of a sample depends on _____ and _____.
   a. the mean of the sample; the sample degrees of freedom
   b. the mean of the sample; the sum of squares for the sample
   c. the sum of squares for the sample; the sample degrees of freedom

3. With an independent samples *t* test, a researcher can draw conclusions about _____.
   a. a comparison of two population means
   b. a comparison of two population variances
   c. the importance of sample size to the sampling error in a test

4. Levene's test in SPSS will help a researcher know if the assumption of _____ for the independent samples *t* test holds for their study.
   a. a normal population of scores
   b. the homogeneity of variances
   c. the independent observations

5. The homogeneity of variances assumption states that the variance in the two samples must be equal.
   a. True
   b. False

6. A between-subjects study with results showing no significant mean difference between conditions supports the null hypothesis that no difference exists between the populations the samples represent.
   a. True
   b. False

7. Like other *t* tests, the independent samples *t* test assumes that the scores between participants are independent.
   a. True
   b. False

8. Suppose you conducted a study to test the hypothesis that social pressure affects memory accuracy. You set up a study in which participants view a video of a person robbing a convenience

store. Then, half of the participants watch a video of other participants discussing the crime. In reality, the participants in the video are part of the experiment, and some of the details of the crime that are discussed are inaccurate. The actual participants are told that they should consider other people's perspectives on the crime because it is difficult for any one person to accurately remember all the details. The other half of the participants do not view the video discussion of the crime but are also told that it is difficult for any one person to accurately remember all the details of the crime. Thirty minutes after viewing the original crime video, all participants are given a recognition memory test about details of the crime. For this study, answer the following questions:

a. What are the alternative and null hypotheses for this study?

b. Suppose that 10 participants participated in each group in the study. For the recognition accuracy data provided below, conduct an independent samples *t* test to analyze these data.

   • Video Discussion Group: 67, 80, 69, 72, 75, 79, 66, 71, 69, 79

   • No Video Discussion Group: 78, 65, 79, 84, 88, 79, 89, 90, 85, 87

c. From the test result you obtained, what can be concluded about the null hypothesis you stated?

Figure 11.8   Statistical Test Decision Flowchart for Comparing Two Means

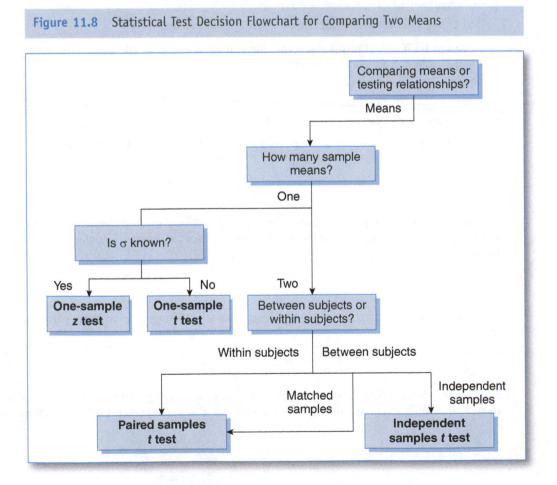

9.   For each description below, indicate which *t* test would be most appropriate for analyzing the data. The test decision flowchart in Figure 11.8 can help you decide which *t* test to use.

a.   A researcher matches two groups of participants on their average grade point average (GPA). The groups are compared on their memory scores after studying a list of words. Group 1 sleeps for eight hours after studying the words, and Group 2 stays awake for eight hours after studying the words.

b.   Participants are randomly assigned to either a treatment group or a control group. The groups' answers on a depression questionnaire are then compared.

c.   An ACT practice class compares the mean scores on the test for students who took the class with the known mean of 18 on the test for all students who took the test that year.

d.   Participants are tested on time to complete a Sudoku puzzle both with and without caffeine. Each participant completes one puzzle in each condition (with caffeine and without).

Chapter 12

One-Way Analysis of Variance (ANOVA)

As you read the chapter, consider the following questions:

12.1 How do we test hypotheses about populations for three or more groups?

12.2 Why does ANOVA use variance instead of mean differences in its calculation?

12.3 What is an *F* ratio and how is it calculated?

12.4 How do between-groups and within-groups variance terms differ?

12.5 How do we use the *F* Table to conduct a one-way ANOVA?

In the last three chapters, we examined *t* tests that allow us to compare two means: a sample mean with the population mean (one-sample *t* test), two means from the same sample under two different conditions (paired/related samples *t* test), and two means from different samples (paired/related samples *t* test for matched samples and independent samples *t* test for independent samples). But what if there are more than two conditions or samples that we want to compare in our study? It would be inefficient to make this comparison in multiple studies if we can compare three or more conditions/samples all at once in a single study. But if we compare three or more groups in our study, how do we calculate an inferential statistic based on mean differences? This is when analysis of variance (ANOVA) can help us.

Let's consider a new example. Text publishers are often trying to figure out in which format they should release a text that will help students the most in learning course material. Is a traditional paper text the best type of text for students to use or is an electronic text preferable? And if an electronic text is better, should it be interactive to allow students to take quizzes and complete activities on specific concepts as they go, or should an electronic text be set up as a paper text (but in electronic form) with the activities at the ends of the chapters? Can we answer these questions with a single study? Yes, we can. To answer these questions, our study would have a single independent variable of *text format* with three conditions: paper text, standard electronic text, and interactive electronic text. Figure 12.1

Figure 12.1 Study Comparing Effect of Text Formats on Student Satisfaction

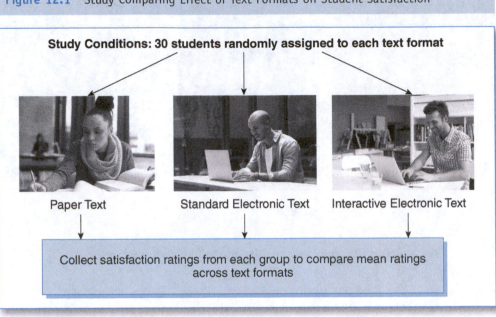

Study Conditions: 30 students randomly assigned to each text format

Paper Text Standard Electronic Text Interactive Electronic Text

Collect satisfaction ratings from each group to compare mean ratings across text formats

©iStock/Ridofranz, ©iStock/BartekSzewczyk, ©iStock/jacoblund

illustrates this design. To compare these three text formats, we could conduct a study with 90 students in which 30 students are randomly assigned a format to use in a course. We might ask students to rate their satisfaction with the text at the end of the course on a 1 to 10 scale and then compare the ratings across text formats to determine which format received the highest rating.

To compare the sample means for our text format study, we will use an ANOVA with the hypothesis-testing procedure. ANOVA is an inferential test that examines mean differences as a variance term instead of looking at the mean difference between two sample means. Because it uses variance terms, ANOVA allows us to compare more than two means at once in a ratio value that represents the mean differences observed in the samples over the mean differences expected due to sampling error. As we go through this chapter, you will see how the variance terms are calculated to create the statistic known as an F value that can be compared with the distribution of F values, as we did with the t distribution.

MORE THAN TWO INDEPENDENT SAMPLES

Our example study shown in Figure 12.1 uses a design that includes three sample means from different groups of participants. Studies that compare more than two samples or conditions within a single study are common in psychology. If you begin reading journal articles in psychology, you will notice that ANOVA is a common inferential test used by researchers to test their hypotheses. Although ANOVA can be used with both between-subjects and within-subjects designs, we will focus in this chapter on between-subjects designs with one independent variable

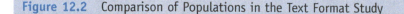

Figure 12.2 Comparison of Populations in the Text Format Study

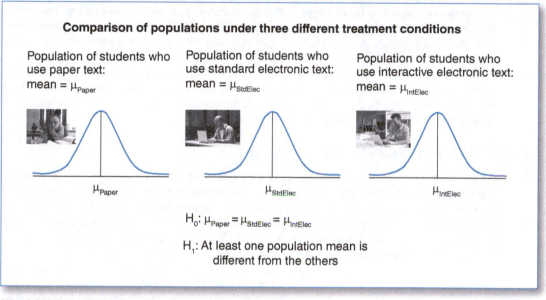

that has three or more levels. Between-subjects designs with more than one independent variable and within-subjects designs are discussed in Chapters 13 and 14, respectively.

Between-Subjects Designs With Three or More Groups

When we compare scores across three or more groups, we are using a between-subjects design, in which the individuals in the sample either come from different populations (e.g., children, young adults, and older adults; different ethnic groups; etc.) or where the individuals in a sample are randomly assigned to different conditions within the study. The goal in both cases is for the groups created in the study to represent the population that group comes from—the different populations they are drawn from or the population under those conditions. Figure 12.2 illustrates this comparison for our example study looking at text formats. The groups in the text format conditions represent the population of students using each format. Thus, we will make hypotheses comparing these three grouped populations in our hypothesis-testing procedure.

Hypotheses With Three or More Groups

To state our hypotheses for a study with three or more groups, we will need to consider all the groups in stating both the null and alternative hypotheses. Our null hypothesis will always predict that all the population means are equal to each other. However, there are many possibilities for our alternative hypothesis. For example, we could predict that just one population mean is greater (or less) than the others but that the rest are equal to one another. Or we could predict that all the population means are different from one another. Or we could simply predict that at least one of the population means will be different from the others. This is the alternative hypothesis we will make for our text format study (see Figure 12.2) because we do not know which text format might be the most preferred format. The number of ways the alternative hypothesis can be stated for a design with more than two samples will depend on how many samples we are comparing in our study. We no longer have a choice between one- and two-tailed tests when we compare three or more sample means. In fact, you will see later in this chapter that the *F* distribution only has one tail because it can never be a negative value. Therefore, you should state your alternative hypothesis according to the design of your study and how you expect the different sample means to be ordered in comparing the groups. But regardless of how we state our hypotheses, we should always make predictions about the *population* means (not the sample means) that our groups represent in our study.

Using Variance Instead of Mean Differences

In fact, the reason that our *F* value will always be a positive value is that we use variance terms in the *F* ratio instead of sample mean differences in our calculations. As mentioned earlier, with three or more means to compare, we cannot simply use the difference between sample means in the top portion of our *F* ratio. We would have multiple mean differences (e.g., the difference between the first and second groups, the difference between the second and third groups, etc.) to consider with three or more groups to compare. To get around this issue, we will use a variance term in our *F* ratio to represent the mean differences. Remember that the variance is simply the standard deviation squared. So in looking at mean differences, we will be looking at the sum of the squared differences between each sample mean and the overall mean (called the *grand mean*) for all of the groups in our study. This is called the between-groups variance. It is calculated from the average squared difference between the sample mean and the overall mean for all the groups in our study. The between-groups variance term makes up the top (numerator) of the *F* ratio because it tells us how much our sample means differ from the average of all the sample means.

❧

Between-groups variance: the average squared difference between the sample means and the overall (grand) mean

---

❧

Within-groups variance: the average squared difference between the scores in each group and the group mean

---

The bottom (denominator) of the *F* ratio is still an estimate of sampling error—how much of a mean difference we expect by chance. This is called the within-groups variance because it is based on the average difference between the scores within each group and the group mean. This is similar to what we calculated in the pooled variance term for the independent samples *t* test, but for an ANOVA, we have to calculate this term for all of our groups and then add the terms together. It is also sometimes called the *error term* in the *F* ratio because it is our estimate of sampling error. Thus, the *F* ratio is

$$F = \frac{between\ groups\ variance}{within\ groups\ variance}$$

Just as in our *t* score calculation, the *F* value is a ratio of the treatment (i.e., independent variable) effect plus error over the estimate of error:

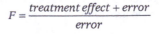

$$F = \frac{treatment\ effect + error}{error}$$

The *F* value then represents the average mean difference across groups due to the treatment with sampling error divided out. Later in this chapter, we will examine how we calculate these variance terms from our data.

The between- and within-groups variance terms divide the total variance in the data in two (not equally, though). The total variance in the data can be determined from the sum of the squared differences of each individual score from the overall (grand) mean, regardless of which group the score came from. When we calculate between- and within-groups variance, we are adding together two parts of the total variance such that the between- and within-groups variances added together equal the total variance in the data.

The between- and within-groups variance terms separate the total variance into two parts, one that shows us the differences due to the treatment and the error (between groups) and one that shows us the differences due to sampling error (within groups).

The *F* Distribution

The *F* distribution is similar to the distribution of *t* scores, except that because we are using variance terms that are squared, *F* can never be less than zero. In fact, the *F* ratio can never equal zero, unless there is no variability in the data (i.e., everyone has the same score in the data set) and this will never happen in real data collected from a sample. You should also consider that the *F* ratio will equal 1.0 if there is no effect of the treatment/independent variable, because in this case, you will have a ratio of error divided by error. Thus, the closer the *F* value gets to 1.0, the less of an effect there is of the independent variable in the data.

Because of these characteristics of the ratio, the shape of the *F* distribution is positively skewed with a tail of extreme values at the positive end. Figure 12.3 shows the

Figure 12.3   The *F* Distribution

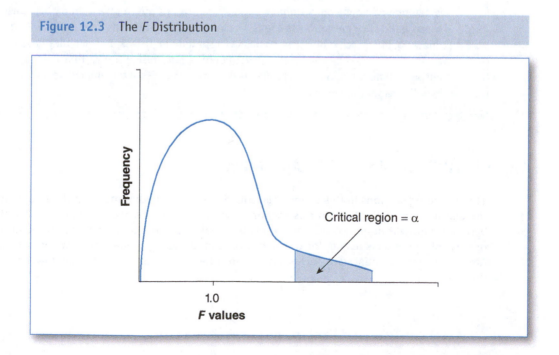

F distribution shape with the critical region indicated in the tail. However, the exact shape of the distribution will depend on the sample size and the number of groups in our study represented by degrees of freedom (df) terms in the between- and within-groups variance. Therefore, for an ANOVA, we will have two df terms: $df_{between}$ and df_{within}. The between-groups df is one less than the number of groups in the study, because this term is the average of mean differences for the groups (i.e., the sample size in this term is the number of groups). The within-groups df is one less than the number of subjects in each group times the number of groups, because this term comes from the average of the differences between the scores in each group and the group means (i.e., the sample size in this term is the sum of the dfs for each group).

Stop and Think

12.1 Thinking about what you know about how to calculate the variance and the description of the between and within groups variance terms in this last section, how do you think we will calculate these terms in our F ratio? (Hint: Review the formula for the pooled variance from Chapter 11 and think about which difference scores will contribute to each term.)

12.2 A researcher is interested in differences in spatial abilities that might exist between individuals with different hand dominance because she suspects that left-handed individuals have superior spatial abilities, as suggested by results from past studies. She designs a study to compare spatial abilities for three groups: right hand dominant, left hand dominant, and ambidextrous (i.e., neither hand is dominant). Hand dominance is determined from a questionnaire given at the start of the study asking participants which hand they prefer to use (right, left, or either) for different tasks (e.g., writing, throwing, etc.). Each group then completes a spatial ability task in which they have to navigate a dot on the computer screen through a maze using a map that they study ahead of time. Time to complete the maze is measured. State the alternative and null hypotheses for this study.

CALCULATING THE F SCORE IN AN ANOVA

The preceding sections in this chapter described the concepts that make up the F ratio and the distribution of F values. In this section, I will focus on how we actually calculate the between- and within-groups variance terms that make up the ratio as we work through the process of hypothesis testing for our text format study using a one-way between-subjects ANOVA as our inferential statistics test (see Figure 12.4 for the portion of the test flowchart for this test).

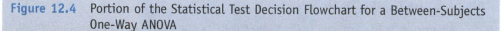

Figure 12.4   Portion of the Statistical Test Decision Flowchart for a Between-Subjects One-Way ANOVA

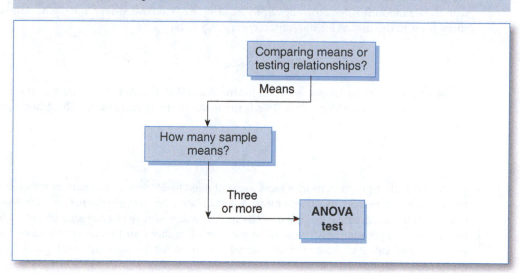

Step 1: State Hypotheses

As described previously, the null hypothesis for a one-way ANOVA will always predict that the population means across groups are equal. Consistent with this, our null hypothesis for the text format study is

H_0: *The population means for students using paper, standard electronic, and interactive electronic texts are equal* or H_0: $\mu_{Paper} = \mu_{StdElec} = \mu_{IntElec}$.

The alternative hypothesis could be stated in several ways (examples were given earlier in the chapter), but for this example, we'll assume that we do not have a specific prediction about which text format is preferred. Thus, our alternative hypothesis is

H_1: *At least one population mean is different from the rest for the text format populations.*

When you state the alternative hypothesis, carefully consider what prediction you can reasonably make for the population means for all the groups in your study.

Step 2: Set Decision Criterion

As we have done in previous chapters, we will set our alpha level at 0.05. This will give us one critical region in the F distribution (see Figure 12.3) that contains 5% of the F scores in the distribution.

Step 3: Collect Sample Data

We are now ready to consider the sample data for our study. Let's assume that we ran this study with three randomly selected groups from the sample of students we recruited. The data for this study showed the means for the satisfaction ratings to be

$$\bar{X}_{Paper} = 4.17, \bar{X}_{StdElec} = 5.33, \bar{X}_{IntElec} = 7.83$$

We will also need to know the overall mean, also called the *grand mean*, in order to calculate the between-groups variance term. This is the mean of the group means. The grand mean for our data is

$$\bar{X}_{Total} = 5.78$$

For the within-groups variance term, we will need to determine the sum of squared deviations of each score from its sample mean. We calculated the sum of squares for each sample in Chapter 11 when we calculated the pooled variance, and you have already seen several examples in previous chapters of how to calculate the sum of squares, so this term should be familiar. Here, we have calculated the sum of squared deviations for the scores in each group from the group mean. For our data, we have

$$SS_{Paper} = 53, SS_{StdElec} = 75, SS_{IntElec} = 75$$

Also recall that we have $n = 30$ per group in our study. We will use the n when we calculate our variance terms in the next step.

Step 4: Calculate Statistics

Now, we can begin to calculate our sample F value using the between- and within-groups variance terms. As described earlier in this chapter, the F value is a ratio of the between- and within-groups variance terms:

$$F = \frac{Between\,Group\,Variance}{Within\,Groups\,Variance}$$

where the between-groups variance is based on the effect of the treatment + error and the within-groups variance is based on the sampling error estimate from our data. Recall that the general formula for the variance is $\frac{SS}{df}$. Thus, for the between-groups variance term, we use the formula

$$Between\,Group\,Variance\,(also\,called\,Mean\,Square\,Between) = \frac{SS_{Between}}{df_{Between}}$$

and for our within-groups variance term, we use the formula

$$Within\,Group\,Variance\,(also\,called\,Mean\,Square\,Within) = \frac{SS_{Within}}{df_{Within}}$$

Note that the variance terms are also known as mean square (*MS*) terms because they represent the average (i.e., mean) sum of squared deviations for that term.

Let's break each of these formulas into the parts we will calculate separately. For the $SS_{Between}$ term, we will consider the group means' squared deviations from the grand mean:

$$SS_{Between} = n\Sigma\left(\bar{X}_{Group} - \bar{X}_{Total}\right)^2$$

This formula shows the sum of the differences between each group mean ($\bar{X}_{Group}$) and the grand mean ($\bar{X}_{Total}$) times the number of scores per group (*n*). We can use the sample means we determined in Step 3 to calculate the $SS_{Between}$:

$$SS_{Between} = 30\left[\left(4.17-5.78\right)^2 + \left(5.33-5.78\right)^2 + \left(7.83-5.78\right)^2\right]$$
$$= 30\left(2.59+.20+4.20\right) = 30\left(6.99\right) = 209.7$$

We will also need the $df_{Between}$ term that is one less than the number of groups (a) to complete the between-groups variance calculation:

$$df_{Between} = a - 1 = 3 - 1 = 2$$

Thus, the between-groups variance ($MS_{Between}$) is

$$MS_{Between} = \frac{SS_{Between}}{df_{Between}} = \frac{209.7}{2} = 104.9$$

This will be the top (numerator) of our *F* ratio.

Next, we need to calculate the MS_{Within} term to determine the bottom (denominator) of our *F* ratio. We'll begin with the SS_{Within} term. The formula for the within *SS* term is

$$SS_{Within} = \Sigma\left(X - \bar{X}_{Group}\right)^2$$

This is the sum of squared deviations of each score from its group mean. This is the same as

$$SS_{Within} = \Sigma\left(SS_{Group}\right)$$

or the sum of the sum of squares for each group. Each SS_{Group} term was given in Step 3:

$$SS_{Within} = \left(53 + 75 + 75\right) = 203$$

We also need the df_{Within} term, which is the number of groups (*a*) times *n* minus 1 (the same as adding together the *df*s for each group). For our study, we have

$$df_{Within} = a\left(n-1\right) = 3\left(30-1\right) = 87$$

So our MS_{Within} term is

$$MS_{Within} = \frac{SS_{Within}}{df_{Within}} = \frac{203}{87} = 2.33$$

Now, we can calculate our F ratio:

$$F = \frac{Between\ Group\ Variance}{Within\ Groups\ Variance} = \frac{MS_{Between}}{MS_{Within}} = \frac{104.9}{2.33} = 45.02$$

With this value, we can move on to Step 5, where we will determine the F_{crit} and make a decision about the null hypothesis.

Step 5: Make a Decision

As described in an earlier section of this chapter, the shape of the F distribution depends on both the $df_{Between}$ and df_{Within}. In addition to our alpha level (determined in Step 2), we need to use the df terms to find the F_{crit} value to compare with the F value we calculated from our data. Table 12.1 shows a portion of the F Distribution Table provided in Appendix D. Because the standard alpha level used in behavioral research is 0.05 in most cases, the table provides F_{crit} values for this alpha level. The columns represent the different values of the $df_{Between}$ term and the rows represent the different values of df_{Within}. Table 12.1 shows the portion of the table for df_{Within} in the range of 60 to 100. The closest value for df_{Within} without going over is 80 so that's the row we'll use to find our F_{crit}. Moving over to the column for df_{Within} = 2, we see that F_{crit} = 3.11. This value is highlighted in Table 12.1.

Table 12.1   Portion of the F Distribution Table for Alpha Level = 0.05

df_{Within} → $df_{Between}$ ↓	1	2	3
60	4.00	3.15	2.76
65	3.99	3.14	2.75
70	3.98	3.13	2.74
80	3.96	3.11	2.72
100	3.94	3.09	2.70

❧

Main effect: test of the differences between all means for an independent variable

Post hoc tests: additional significance tests conducted to determine which means are significantly different for a main effect

Compared with the F_{crit} = 3.11, is our calculated F value in the critical region for the F distribution? Yes, it is: 45.02 is larger than 3.11. Figure 12.5 shows this distribution and the critical region. Thus, we have enough evidence to reject the null hypothesis and conclude that there is at least one difference across the population means for the different text formats. But which ones are different? Our one-way ANOVA cannot tell us this. It only tells us about the main effect—the overall effect of our independent variable. In other words, a main effect will indicate that a difference exists across the conditions but not which conditions are significantly different. Instead, we will need to conduct post hoc tests to determine which means are significantly different from one another.

Figure 12.5   *F* Distribution and Critical Region for Text Format Study ($df_{Between} = 2$, $df_{Within} = 80$)

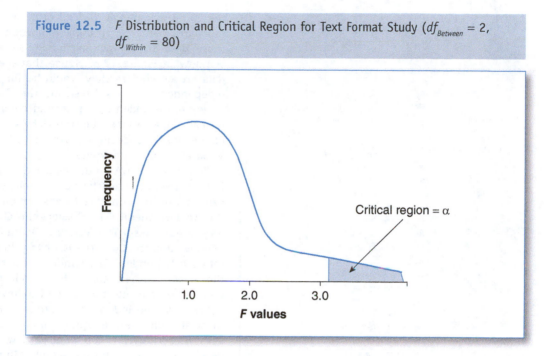

Post hoc tests are *t* tests that compare pairs of sample means to determine where a difference found in an ANOVA is across the conditions. In most cases, we will want to use a post hoc test that controls for the increase in alpha that will occur each time we conduct a paired *t* test on the same set of data. Because each additional test is done with the same set of data, the chance of making at least one Type I error increases with each test. In other words, with each test we run on our data set, we increase the Type I error rate, so we must correct for this increase. In fact, this is one of the reasons to use an ANOVA for studies with three or more conditions, instead of multiple *t* tests: An ANOVA does not increase the Type I error rates across the tests.

The most common post hoc test used to correct for this increase in Type I error (and also the post hoc test that controls for the increase in Type I error most conservatively) is a Bonferroni test, where our chosen alpha level is divided by the number of tests we are doing. If we want to compare each of the three means in our text format study with each other, we would need three extra *t* tests, so our alpha level for these tests would be $\frac{.05}{3} = .017$. However, conducting a post hoc test is *only* appropriate if the overall effect (the main effect) is significant. *Do not con-duct post hoc tests for nonsignificant main effects.* In addition, post hoc tests are only needed for main effects with three or more levels to compare. With only two levels of an independent variable, a significant main effect indicates that the means for those two levels are different. We will consider post hoc tests further in the next section.

USING SPSS TO CONDUCT A ONE-WAY BETWEEN-SUBJECTS ANOVA

Let's now look at how we can conduct the one-way ANOVA for our text format study using SPSS. Our data come from the satisfaction ratings on a 1 to 10 scale that were collected from

	Ratings	Format	var	var
1	6.00	Paper Text		
2	7.00	Standard Electronic Text		
3	8.00	Interactive Electronic Text		
4	8.00	Interactive Electronic Text		
5	9.00	Interactive Electronic Text		
6	4.00	Standard Electronic Text		
7	5.00	Interactive Electronic Text		
8	6.00	Paper Text		
9	4.00	Standard Electronic Text		
10	7.00	Interactive Electronic Text		
11	7.00	Paper Text		
12	5.00	Standard Electronic Text		
13	9.00	Interactive Electronic Text		
14	6.00	Paper Text		
15	9.00	Interactive Electronic Text		
16	7.00	Standard Electronic Text		
17	5.00	Paper Text		
18	6.00	Interactive Electronic Text		
19	6.00	Standard Electronic Text		
20	3.00	Paper Text		
21	7.00	Interactive Electronic Text		
22	3.00	Paper Text		
23	6.00	Standard Electronic Text		
24	7.00	Standard Electronic Text		
25	5.00	Standard Electronic Text		

the 90 participants at the end of the study (30 participants per group). A portion of these data are shown in the SPSS Data Window in Figure 12.6. Notice that these data are entered as they would be for an independent samples t test, but there are three groups coded in the second column instead of two groups. The group labels were entered for the code numbers in the Variable View tab for the data window.

To run an ANOVA on the satisfaction ratings data with the text format variable, you can choose the Compare Means option in the Analyze menu. Then, select the One-Way ANOVA test. The Variable Definition window appears. Click the Ratings column into the Dependent List window to define the dependent variable. Then click the Format column into the Factor window to define it as the independent variable. You must also choose the Options button and select Descriptives if you want to view the descriptive statistics for the samples. In the Options window, you will also see a box you can check to conduct the test for homogeneity of variances (see Test Assumptions section).

The Output window contains a box with descriptive statistics (if you chose that option) and a box with the F statistic and p value (see Figure 12.7). The between-groups row of the statistics box shows the between-groups variance terms (SS, df, and Mean Square). This row also contains the calculated F and p values. The within-groups row contains the values for the within-groups variance (i.e., error) term. For our text format data, we have an F value of 45.12 and a p value less than 0.001 (the value is low enough that the rounded p is shown as 0.000, but remember that p can never equal zero, so you should report this this value as $p < 0.001$). The test is significant because the p value (less than 0.001) is lower than our alpha level of 0.05. In other words, we can reject the null hypothesis that there is no difference between the condition means. This result might be reported as "The effect of text format on satisfaction ratings was significant, $F(2,87) = 45.12$, $p < 0.001$." However, this test does not tell us which conditions are different from one other. To learn which means are significantly different from the others, we need to conduct post hoc tests.

Summary of Steps

- Type the data into each data window. Add codes for condition in a separate column.
- Choose Compare Means from the Analyze menu.
- Choose the One-Way ANOVA test from the options.
- Click the data column into the Dependent List box.
- Click the codes column into the Factor box.
- Click the Options button and choose Descriptive if you would like the means and variability statistics printed into the Output (you can also choose Homogeneity of Variance Test under Options to check this assumption).

NOTE: A one-way ANOVA can also be run using the General Linear Model function from the Univariate options in the Analyze menu; this method will be discussed in Chapter 13.

Figure 12.7   SPSS Output for the Text Format Study Data

→ **Oneway**

Descriptives

Satisfaction Ratings

	N	Mean	Std. Deviation	Std. Error	95% Confidence Interval for Mean Lower Bound	95% Confidence Interval for Mean Upper Bound	Minimum	Maximum
Paper Text	30	4.1667	1.84177	.29974	3.5536	4.7797	1.00	8.00
Standard Electronic Text	30	5.3333	1.62594	.29685	4.7262	5.9405	1.00	8.00
Interactive Electronic Text	30	7.8333	1.28877	.23530	7.3521	8.3146	5.00	10.00
Total	90	5.7778	2.15562	.22722	5.3263	6.2293	1.00	10.00

ANOVA

Satisfaction Ratings

	Sum of Squares	df	Mean Square	F	Sig.
Between Groups	210.556	2	105.278	45.119	.000
Within Groups	203.000	87	2.333		
Total	413.556	89			

Post Hoc Tests

The post hoc button allows you to run post hoc tests along with the ANOVA. These tests are useful if the main effect of your independent variable is significant (as it is for our example here), indicating a difference between at least two of the groups. Selecting the post hoc button brings up a list of different post hoc tests. These tests vary according to how conservatively they control for Type I errors across the set of post hoc tests. SPSS provides options for the three most common post hoc tests used in psychological studies, which are the least significant difference (LSD), Bonferroni, and Tukey tests. The LSD test does not provide any correction for Type I errors across tests. The Bonferroni test provides the strongest control for Type I errors across tests. The Tukey test falls somewhere between these two tests in control for Type I errors. For our example, we will use the Bonferroni test that was described in the section on calculating the ANOVA by hand. Click on the Bonferroni box to conduct this test. Then click Continue and OK to begin the ANOVA.

The post hoc tests indicate which pairs of means are significantly different from one another. These tests are shown in the Post Hoc Tests box in the SPSS Output window (see Figure 12.8). The Bonferroni test chosen for this example is listed above the box. The box shows p values (in the Sig. column) lower than 0.05 for all the comparisons. If we examine the means shown in the first box of Figure 12.7, we find that the Interactive Electronic text was the most preferred format, followed by the Standard Electronic format and then the Paper format as the least preferred, with significant differences for each of these differences.

Figure 12.8 SPSS Output for the Text Format Study Data With Bonferroni Post Hoc Tests

Post Hoc Tests

Multiple Comparisons

Dependent Variable: Satisfaction Ratings
Bonferroni

(I) Text Format	(J) Text Format	Mean Difference (I–J)	Std. Error	Sig.	95% Confidence Interval	
					Lower Bound	Upper Bound
Paper Text	Standard Electronic Text	−1.16667*	.39441	.012	−2.1295	−.2039
	Interactive Electronic Text	−3.66667*	.39441	.000	−4.6295	−2.7039
Standard Electronic Text	Paper Text	1.16667*	.39441	.012	.2039	2.1295
	Interactive Electronic Text	−2.50000*	.39441	.000	−3.4628	−1.5372
Interactive Electronic Text	Paper Text	3.66667*	.39441	.000	2.7039	4.6295
	Standard Electronic Text	2.50000*	.39441	.000	1.5372	3.4628

*The mean difference is significant at the 0.05 level.

Although all the differences were significant in this example, you may conduct tests in which only some of the differences are significant. In these cases, you can conclude that there is a significant mean difference between the conditions where the p value given is lower than your alpha level, but you cannot conclude that there is a difference if the p value is higher than the alpha level. In those cases, you must retain the null hypothesis that there is no difference between groups until further testing can be done.

Stop and Think

12.3 Use the terms below to calculate the F ratio and determine if the main effect is significant:

$$SS_{Between} = 150, \, df_{Between} = 3, \, SS_{Within} = 900, \, df_{Within} = 57$$

12.4 Based on what you know about the component parts of the F ratio, approximately what value should F equal if there is no treatment (i.e., independent variable) effect on the data? Explain why.

12.5 What is the purpose of a post hoc test? What does it tell us? Explain why we do not need a post hoc test if there are only two groups in our study.

TEST ASSUMPTIONS

The test assumptions for a one-way between-subjects ANOVA are the same as those for the independent samples t test because the test is doing the same thing as a t test, but with additional groups. Thus, the assumptions include the following:

1. The population of scores must be a normal distribution. As you have seen in previous chapters, this is a standard assumption for inferential tests that compare means.

2. The scores from different participants within each sample must be independent. Thus, the scores from the different individuals within each sample cannot be related.

3. The populations that the samples represent must have equal variance. In other words, the assumption of homogeneity of variances must hold. This assumption was introduced in Chapter 11 along with Levene's test for this assumption in SPSS.

Calculation Summary

Between-groups sum of squares: The sum of the sum of squared deviations for each group mean from the grand mean times the group sample size

Within-groups sum of squares: The sum of the sum of squared deviations for each score from its group mean

Between-groups degrees of freedom: The number of groups minus one

Within-groups degrees of freedom: The sample size minus one times the number of groups *or* the sum of the degrees of freedom (sample size minus one) for all the groups

Between-groups mean squares: The between-groups sum of squares divided by the between-groups degrees of freedom

Within-groups mean squares: The within-groups sum of squares divided by the within-groups degrees of freedom

F ratio: The between-groups mean square divided by the within-groups mean square

CHAPTER SUMMARY

12.1 How do we test hypotheses about populations for three or more groups?

We can test hypotheses about populations for three or more groups in a similar way as with two groups. We can represent each population (different types of individuals or the same individuals under different conditions) with a different group in our study and then compare the sample means on our dependent variable using a one-way between-subjects ANOVA. The ANOVA will tell us if there is a difference among the means, and post hoc tests can tell us which means are significantly different if the ANOVA is significant.

12.2 Why does ANOVA use variance instead of mean differences in its calculation?

We cannot use mean differences when we have more than two groups because there would be more than one mean difference to consider. Thus, ANOVA uses variance terms based on the sum of squared differences between the sample means and the overall (grand) mean to give us a value in the numerator of our statistic representing the effect of the treatment plus error.

12.3 What is an *F* ratio and how is it calculated?

The *F* ratio represents the treatment plus error over error. It is calculated from the between-groups mean variance (the sum of squared differences between the groups divided by degrees of freedom) over the within-groups mean variance (the sum of squared differences within the groups divided by the degrees of freedom).

12.4 How do between-groups and within-groups variance terms differ?

The between-groups variance term is based on how much the groups differ from each other, whereas the within-groups variance term is based on how much the scores differ from each other within each group.

12.5 How do we use the *F* Table to conduct a one-way ANOVA?

We use the *F* Table the same way we used the *t* Table to find a critical value that tells us where the critical region is in the *F* distribution. However, the F_{crit} is based on both degrees of freedom terms: $df_{Between}$ and df_{Within}.

THINKING ABOUT RESEARCH

A summary of a research study in psychology is given below. As you read the summary, think about the following questions:

1. Is this study an experiment? Explain your answer.

2. Explain why an ANOVA is needed for this study instead of a *t* test.

3. What factor would have been included in the ANOVA analysis for comparison of the switch–stay scores?

4. How do we know that the one-way ANOVA was significant in this study?

5. Explain why these researchers used post hoc tests as part of their analyses.

> Haun, D. B. M., Rekers, Y., & Tomasello, M. (2014). Children conform to the behavior of peers; other great apes stick with what they know. *Psychological Science, 25,* 2160–2167.
>
> Note: Study 1 from this article is described below.

Purpose of the Study. The study examined social learning behaviors in order to compare human social learning to social learning in nonhuman primates. Past studies (e.g., Laland & Galef, 2009) have shown that, similar to humans, many different animal species show evidence of social groups with behavioral differences. In addition, both humans and animals have shown evidence of social learning. In the current study, the researchers were interested in examining whether nonhuman primates show the same level of conformity to peer behavior that humans show. Study 1 was conducted to examine how often human children, chimpanzees, and orangutans change their current problem-solving strategy after watching peers perform a different strategy for the problem. Study 2 was conducted to examine whether the presence and number of peers during the strategy test phase would influence the children's strategy-switching behavior.

Method of the Study. In this study, 18 children, 12 chimpanzees, and 12 orangutans participated. Participants completed a task of dropping balls into one of three slots in boxes presented to them on a display (see Figure 12.9 for a diagram of the task). One of the boxes dispensed a reward (chocolate for children, peanuts for animals) when a ball was dropped into its top slot. Participants completed the task until they received the reward on eight of 10 consecutive trials. They then watched three familiar peers (one at a time) perform the task for two trials each using a different box than the one the participant had used in the initial phase. Peers were rewarded on both of their trials. Participants were then tested on the task again while the peers watched. They performed three trials in the test phase. Each of the three trials was recorded as a *stay* response (they used their same box from the initial phase), a *switch* response (they used the box they had seen their peers use), or an *other* response (they used a different box from both the initial phase and their peers).

Figure 12.9   Task Performed by Participants in the Haun et al. (2014) Study

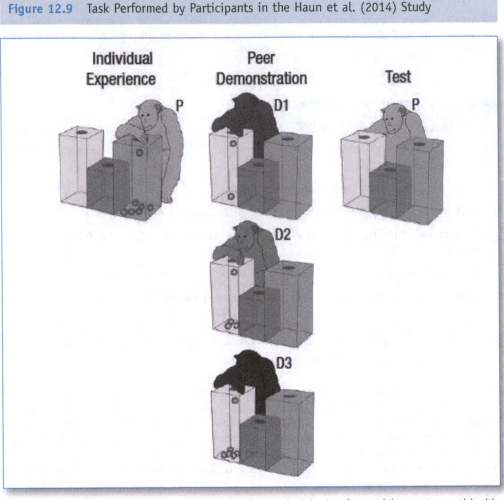

SOURCE: Haun, Rekers, & Tomasello (2014). Children conform to the behavior of peers; Other great apes stick with what they know. *Psychological Science, 25,* 2160–2167.

NOTE: P = Participant, D = Demonstration (D1, D2, and D3).

Results of the Study. A switch–stay score was calculated for each participant for the three trials they performed in the test phase. Positive scores indicate more *switch* responses, and negative scores indicate more *stay* responses. Figure 12.10 illustrates the results for the three participant groups. The graph shows that, on average, children switched their responses to those shown by their peers, whereas animals stayed with their original responses, showing less influence of the peer demonstrations.

Conclusions of the Study. From the results of the study, the researchers concluded that humans are more willing to adjust their behavior to match peers' behavior than are nonhuman primates. From their studies, the researchers concluded that nonhuman primates are not influenced socially by peers' behavior as much as humans are.

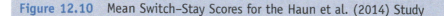

Figure 12.10   Mean Switch–Stay Scores for the Haun et al. (2014) Study

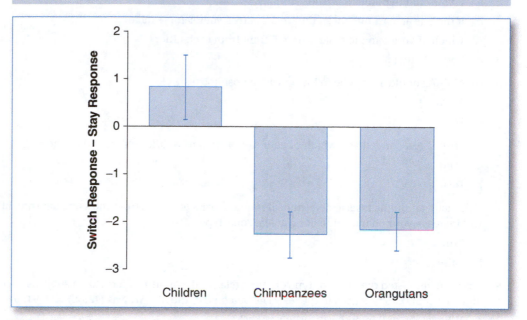

SOURCE: Haun, Rekers, & Tomasello (2014). Children conform to the behavior of peers; Other great apes stick with what they know. *Psychological Science, 25,* 2160–2167.

TEST YOURSELF

1. Instead of the estimated standard error, the *F* ratio uses the _____ as the estimate of sampling error in its calculation.

   a.   pooled variance

   b.   between-groups variance

   c.   within-groups variance

2. With more than two groups in a study, the appropriate statistical test to use is a _____.

   a.   one-way between-subjects ANOVA

   b.   one-way within-subjects ANOVA

   c.   independent samples *t* test

   d.   multi-sample *t* test

3. To find F_{crit} in the *F* Table, you need to know _____.

   a. $df_{Between}$

   b. df_{Within}

   c.   your alpha level

   d.   all of the above

4. An ANOVA can tell you _____.

   a. if your null hypothesis is true

   b. if there is at least one mean difference across your sample means

   c. which of your sample means are different from each other

   d. both (b) and (c)

5. An ANOVA should always be followed with a post hoc test.

   a. True

   b. False

6. A post hoc test can tell you which of your sample means is different from the others.

   a. True

   b. False

7. Conducting multiple tests to determine if multiple pairs of means from the same data are different will increase your chance of making at least one Type I error.

   a. True

   b. False

8. A researcher tested the effect of type of music (classical, country, and rock) on subjects' mood. An alpha level of 0.05 was used in the test. The outcome of the ANOVA was $F(2,65) = 16.91, p < 0.001$.

   a. What is the null hypothesis for this study?

   b. Is there evidence to reject the null hypothesis? How do you know?

   c. What can the researcher conclude from the outcome of this test?

9. Using the sample data below, conduct an ANOVA to determine if there is a significant main effect:

   Group 1: 74, 62, 59, 78, 65, 90, 45, 51, 67, 71

   Group 2: 88, 90, 54, 79, 85, 78, 92, 74, 89, 77

   Group 3: 72, 86, 93, 91, 80, 79, 84, 75, 78, 92

10. Explain why the mean of the F distribution for the null hypothesis is 1.0.

Chapter 13

Two-Way Analysis of Variance (ANOVA)

As you read the chapter, consider the following questions:

13.1 Can we examine more than one causal factor in a single study?

13.2 How do levels of a factor and conditions differ in a factorial design?

13.3 What is the difference between a main effect and an interaction?

13.4 How do we calculate an F ratio for an interaction?

13.5 What does a significant interaction tell us about our data?

In Chapter 12, we considered a study with three test format groups to compare all at once. Although this type of factor (one with more than two groups) is common in behavioral research studies, it is even more common to examine multiple causal factors in a single study. This allows a researcher to gain more information about factors that influence the behaviors of interest in one study. For example, suppose we think that not only does the text format affect student satisfaction ratings with the text but that the subject topic of the text matters as well. It is possible that satisfaction ratings are lower for chemistry texts than for psychology texts in addition to the lower ratings we saw in the last chapter for paper texts than electronic text formats. It is also possible that the difference in satisfaction between the text formats *depends* on the subject topic, such that for psychology texts, the interactive electronic format is best but for chemistry texts, it is not the best.

We can test all these possible effects in one study with two main factors: text format (with paper text, standard electronic text, and interactive electronic text) and subject topic (with a psychology text and a chemistry text). Figure 13.1 illustrates the design of this study. Different participants would be randomly assigned to each of the different conditions in the study. This means that to have the same number of participants in each condition in the study as when we only had the text format factor, we need to double the total sample size to 180 so that 60 participants can be assigned to each text format, with 30 of those participants assigned to each

Figure 13.1   Study Design With Two Factors: Text Format and Subject Topic

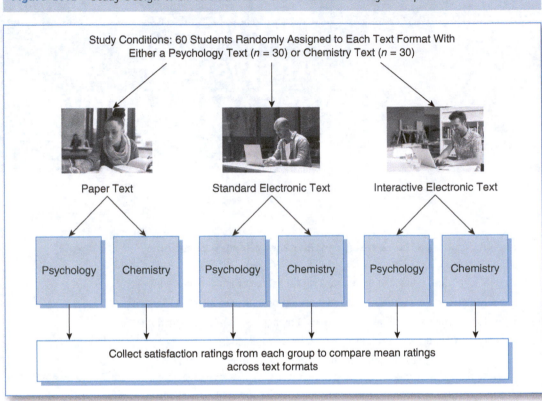

©iStock/Ridofranz, ©iStock/BartekSzewczyk, ©iStock/jacoblund

of the subject topics in each text format (possibly dependent on which courses the participants are currently enrolled in). We can then compare satisfaction ratings for the three text formats and the two topic subjects and then determine if the difference across text formats (if any is found) depends on which topic subject the participants are studying. In the next section, we will discuss the different parts of multifactor studies and what we can learn about behavior in these studies.

FACTORIAL DESIGNS

—— ❧ ——

Factorial design: an experiment or quasi-experiment that includes more than one independent variable

In previous chapters, most of the examples we have looked at have been studies with one independent variable. However, many studies in psychology involve more than one independent variable as a way to gain information about multiple causal factors in one study. These studies have a factorial design. Factorial designs are studies that examine more than one independent variable to determine the separate and combined effects of the independent variables on the dependent variable. In fact, this is the primary advantage of a factorial design: You can examine multiple factors at once *and* their combined effects on the data. This design provides more information to the researcher all at once with only one sample. Because of the benefits of this design, many experiments conducted by psychologists are factorial designs.

Testing the combined effects of the independent variables is the unique feature of factorial designs. Without including multiple independent variables in a single experiment, we would not be able to detect the different effects a factor might have on behavior in different situations. For example, if we only compare satisfaction ratings for the three text formats for psychology texts, as we did in the last chapter, we might miss a different effect of text format on other subject topics, such as chemistry. In the single-factor experiment described in Chapter 12, we concluded that the interactive electronic format was most preferred by students. But what if students prefer a paper text or a standard electronic text when they are studying a different topic? Our single factor study would lead us to believe that the interactive electronic text was best when, in fact, it is only best for one subject topic. By including the subject topic as a second independent variable in our factorial experiment, we are able to determine whether, overall, the interactive electronic text format is best for both subject topics or if a different text format is preferred when the subject topic changes. When the effect of one independent variable (e.g., text format) *depends* on the levels of another independent variable (e.g., subject topic), this is called an interaction effect.

❧

Interaction effect: tests the effect of one independent variable at each level of another independent variable in an ANOVA

In factorial designs, the comparison of the mean scores for the levels of the independent variable is the test of the main effect of that independent variable. This is no different than the comparison of the overall test formats we made in the previous chapter. The levels of the independent variable are the different conditions that are part of the independent variable. The different types of texts we are comparing in our example study are the levels of the independent variable of text format. The main effects provide a test of the effect of each independent variable on the dependent variable. When we have more than one independent variable in a study, we can test the separate effect of each independent variable on the dependent variable by looking at the main effect for each of the independent variables. An analysis of variance (ANOVA) will provide a test for each main effect in our design.

❧

Levels of the independent variable: different situations or conditions that participants experience in an experiment because of the manipulation of the independent variable

---

The other type of effect tested in a factorial ANOVA is an interaction effect. The interaction effect compares the effect of one independent variable across the levels of another independent variable to determine how the independent variables *interact* to affect the dependent variable. A test for an interaction effect compares the differences between the levels of one independent variable across the levels of another independent variable. This will determine if the effects of one independent variable *depend* on the level of the other independent variable. Thus, we can make separate hypotheses in a factorial experiment about each main effect and the interaction of the factors in our hypothesis-testing procedure.

To make the concept of an interaction more concrete, consider a simple factorial design with two independent variables that investigates the effect of outdoor temperature on mood. Participants are asked to complete a simple puzzle task either inside a lab with windows or outside the lab on a patio next to the lab building. The temperature outside on the day of testing is recorded as either in the 75 to 80 degree range or in the 90 to 95 degree range (the study is only run on days with these temperature ranges) with participants randomly assigned to task setting. At the end of the testing session, participants are asked to rate on a 1 to 10 scale how much they enjoyed doing the task. In this type of study, we might find an interaction: Participants enjoy the task more in the outdoor setting than the lab setting with the 75 to 80 degree weather but enjoy the task more in the lab setting (with air conditioning) than the outdoor setting with the 90 to 95 degree weather. In other words, which setting the participant prefers for the task *depends* on what the weather is outside.

The factorial design in Figure 13.2 shows this type of 2 × 2 design in general terms. This design contains two independent variables (IVs): IVA (e.g., task setting) and IVB (e.g., weather outside), each with two levels. The columns indicate levels of IVA, and the rows indicate levels of IVB. The cells/boxes indicate the conditions (e.g., lab setting with 75–80 degree weather) in the study created by combining the levels of the two independent variables. To determine the overall means for a level of an independent variable (i.e., the means compared in a main effect), the researcher averages the means for the cells in the columns and the rows. Main effects are determined by comparing the level means for each independent variable (i.e., comparing means for the columns for the main effect of IVA and comparing means for the rows for the main effect of IVB). To examine the interaction effect, the researcher must consider the differences between rows or columns. For example, one way to look at an interaction effect would be to consider the

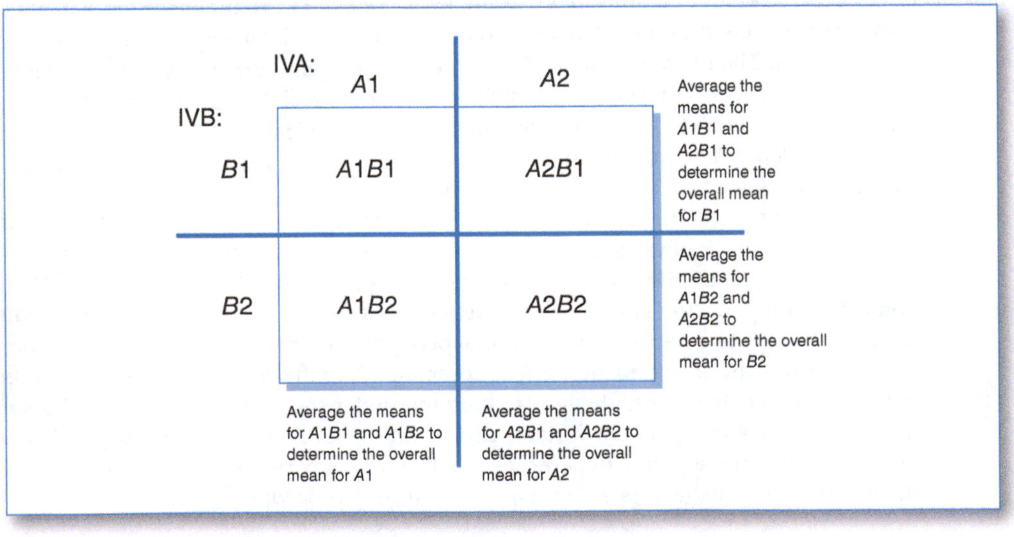

Figure 13.2 Diagram of a General Factorial Design With Two Independent Variables (IV), Each With Two Levels

difference between A1B1 (e.g., lab setting with 75–80 degree weather) and A2B1 (e.g., outdoor setting with 75–80 degree weather) and compare it with the difference between A1B2 (e.g., lab setting with 90–95 degree weather) and A2B2 (e.g., outdoor setting with 90–95 degree weather). If those differences are not the same, then there is an interaction effect. In other words, the effect of IVA depends on whether you are looking at the B1 level or the B2 level of IVB.

It may take some time to understand interactions, so let's consider another example to further illustrate the concept. When our dog, Daphne, became a member of our family, she did not like to be left in the house without us. Whenever we went out, even for short periods of time, she would have accidents on the rug and engage in destructive chewing behaviors. She ruined a few small items of furniture and more than a few pairs of my husband's shoes. In an attempt to improve her behavior, we researched the issue and found several suggested treatments for this sort of behavior. We bought her a toy that held treats, accessed by chewing, that we could give her while we were away from home. We also gave her some objects that we had used recently and smelled like us (e.g., an old T-shirt) to help her feel that we were nearby. Because we did not know which of these would best improve her behavior, we decided to try these treatments one at a time, five times each to make sure that the treatments were tested under different conditions (different days of the week, different times of day, etc.). After each trip away from home, when one of these treatments was applied, we counted the number of bad behaviors there was evidence of in the house.

However, we also thought that the length of time we were away might have an effect on her behavior, so we also tried these treatments for different lengths of trips: five trials of each treatment for short trips of two hours or less and five trials of each treatment for longer trips in which we were gone for a larger portion of the day at work (five hours or more). Figure 13.3 illustrates the design of this experiment. This factorial experiment with two independent variables allowed us to not only learn whether the worn clothing or the chew toy worked best overall but also whether one of these treatments worked best for short trips and the other treatment worked best for long trips. In other words, our factorial design answered the

Figure 13.3 Design of the Factorial Experiment With Daphne

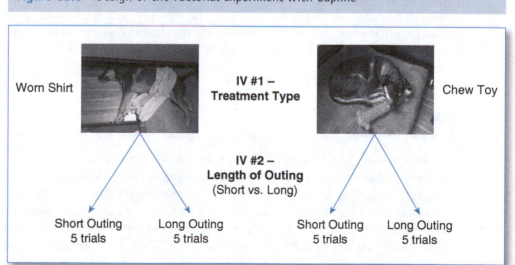

Worn Shirt

IV #1 –
Treatment Type

Chew Toy

IV #2 –
Length of Outing
(Short vs. Long)

Short Outing
5 trials

Long Outing
5 trials

Short Outing
5 trials

Long Outing
5 trials

Figure 13.4 Results From the Factorial Experiment With Daphne

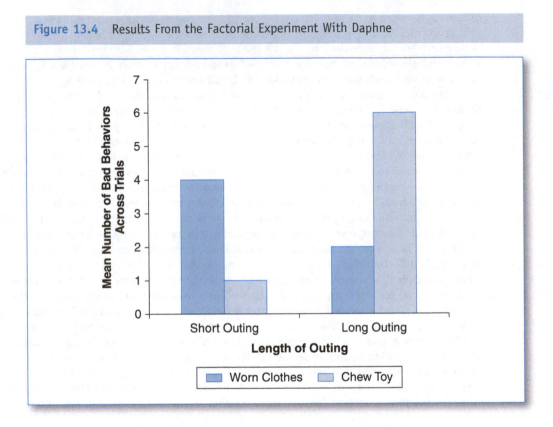

question "Does the effect of treatment type depend on the length of trip we take away from home?" Figure 13.4 shows an outcome of our experiment with Daphne. In this case, our hypothesis that different treatments are effective for different trip lengths was supported. The graph shows that when we leave for short outings, the chew toy is better at reducing her bad behaviors, but when we are gone all day for long trips, the worn clothing is better at reducing her bad behaviors.

Stop and Think

Suppose that you work for a company that makes ice cream. Your boss has tasked you with finding out if two proposed changes affect ice cream sales by conducting an experiment to test the effects of these changes on consumer preferences. One proposal is to add more chocolate chips to the chocolate chip flavor of the ice cream (i.e., compare current amount of chips to 30% more chips). The other proposal is to use real vanilla in all the ice cream flavors (currently, the company uses artificial vanilla flavoring, so you need to compare chocolate chip ice cream with real and artificial vanilla). Both changes would cost the company money, so they want you to determine if either change increases consumer preference for the ice cream to decide if these changes are worthwhile. You collect ratings of the ice cream in each condition from a group of 400 consumers, each of whom rates one type of ice cream on a scale of 1 to 7 for desire to purchase.

13.1 What are the independent and dependent variables in this study?

13.2 Describe the main effects that would be tested in this study—which levels would be compared in each main effect test?

13.3 Describe one way that the independent variables in this study might interact to affect the dependent variable.

CALCULATING A TWO-WAY ANOVA

Let's look again at our factorial text format by subject topic experiment shown in Figure 13.1. To conduct our hypothesis test, we will need to calculate an F ratio for each main effect and for the interaction. The main effects are similar to the one-way between-subjects ANOVA we calculated in Chapter 12, but our within-groups variance term will be a bit different because we now have to consider the deviations within all of our conditions (six conditions in our 3×2 design). The F ratio for the interaction will be our new term, but it will use the same within-groups variance term as the main effects, so we only need to calculate one within-groups variance term that will be used in the denominator of all three F ratios. Let's begin with Step 1 of our process.

Step 1: State Hypotheses

In Step 1, we need to state hypotheses for our two main effects (for text format and for subject topic) and for the interaction. We will use the data from the one-way design in Chapter 12 to predict that the interactive electronic text will receive the highest satisfaction ratings as our alternative hypothesis for the text format main effect. Let's assume that there might be a difference in satisfaction between our psychology and chemistry texts, but that no specific direction is predicted. Finally, we will predict that there will be interaction between these two factors, such that the difference across the text formats is different for psychology and chemistry texts. Therefore, our hypotheses for this study are:

Main Effect of Text Format

H_0: *The population means for students using paper, standard electronic, and interactive electronic texts are equal.*

H_1: *The population mean for the interactive electronic format is higher than the rest of the population means for text format.*

Main Effect of Subject Topic

H_0: *The population means for psychology and chemistry texts are equal.*

H_1: *The population means for psychology and chemistry texts are not equal.*

Interaction between Text Format and Subject Topic

H_0: *There is no interaction effect in the population for text format and subject topic.*

H_1: *There is an interaction effect in the population for text format and subject topic.*

Step 2: Set Decision Criterion

Our alpha level will be set at 0.05.

Step 3: Collect Sample Data

Let's look at the descriptive statistics we will need in order to calculate the between- and within-groups variance terms for our F ratios. The condition means are shown in Figure 13.5. We will also need the means for each level of our independent variables, which can be calculated by averaging across the condition means for each level. These are shown at the ends of the rows and columns in Figure 13.5 and are called marginal means. The marginal means will be used to calculate between-groups variance terms in Step 4 for our main effects. The grand mean

--- ✂ ---

Marginal means: the means for each level of an independent variable in a factorial design

---

$\bar{X}_{Grand}$ is also shown in Figure 13.5 and can be calculated by averaging either set of marginal means or the six condition means. With the descriptive statistics shown in Figure 13.5, we are ready to move on to Step 4 and calculate our F ratios.

Step 4: Calculate Statistics

To conduct our ANOVA, we have three separate F ratios to calculate: one for the main effect of text format, one for the main effect of subject topic, and one for the interaction between these two factors. Each of the F ratios will use the same within-groups error in the denominator, but the between-groups terms in the numerator will differ. Let's begin with the between-groups terms.

Main Effects Between-Groups Variance Terms

For the main effect of text format, the between-groups variance term will be very similar to the one we calculated in Chapter 12. However, we have to collapse across two levels of our other factor, subject topic, so we need to add those levels (b) to our calculation. The between-groups SS term is

$$SS_{Text\ Format} = n(b)\Sigma\left(\bar{X}_A - \bar{X}_{Grand}\right)^2$$

Figure 13.5	Descriptive Statistics for Step 3 of Hypothesis Testing for the Format by Subject Topic Study

| IVB – Subject Topic | IVA – Text Formats | | | Marginal Means |
	Paper	Standard Electronic	Interactive Electronic	
Psychology	Mean = 5.4	Mean = 6.2	Mean = 8.8	Mean = 6.8
Chemistry	Mean = 5.2	Mean = 7.2	Mean = 6.4	Mean = 6.3
Marginal Means	Mean = 5.3	Mean = 6.7	Mean = 7.6	Grand Mean = 6.53

where $\bar{X}_A$ is the marginal mean for each level of text format and b is the number of levels of IVB (in this case, subject topic). Thus, the between-groups SS for text format is

$$SS_{Text\ Format} = 30(2)\left[(5.3-6.53)^2 + (6.7-6.53)^2 + (7.6-6.53)^2\right] =$$
$$60[1.5129 + .029 + 1.145] = 60[2.6869] = 161.2$$

We next need to determine the $df_{TextFormat}$, which is $df = a - 1 = 3 - 1 = 2$. With these two terms, we can calculate the between-groups variance for text format:

$$MS_{Text\ Format} = \frac{161.2}{2} = 80.6$$

The main effect for subject topic will be calculated in the same way, collapsing across the levels of text format:

$$SS_{Subject\ Topic} = n(a)\Sigma\left(\bar{X}_B - \bar{X}_{Grand}\right)^2 =$$

$$SS_{Subject\ Topic} = 30(3)\left[(6.8-6.53)^2 + (6.3-6.53)^2\right] = 90[.073 + .053] = 11.34$$

with $df_{SubjectTopic} = b - 1 = 2 - 1 = 1$. Thus, $MS_{SubjectTopic} = 11.34$.

Interaction Between-Groups Variance Term

The between-groups variance term for the interaction will involve the condition means, the marginal means for both factors, and the grand mean. The interaction SS is based on the deviation of the condition mean from the grand mean. However, this also contains the difference between the marginal means and the grand mean that we used in the terms in the previous section, so we need to subtract these differences out. With some algebra, our SS for the interaction becomes

$$SS_{Interaction} = n\Sigma\left(\bar{X}_{AB} - \bar{X}_A - \bar{X}_B + \bar{X}_{Grand}\right)^2$$

Thus, our SS for the interaction is

$$SS_{Interaction} = 30\begin{bmatrix}(5.4-5.3-6.8+6.53)^2 + (6.2-6.7-6.8+6.53)^2 + (8.8-7.6-6.8+6.53)^2 \\ +(5.2-5.3-6.3+6.53)^2 + (7.2-6.7-6.3+6.53)^2 + (6.4-7.6-6.3+6.53)^2\end{bmatrix}$$

$$= 30[.029+.59+.86+.017+.53+.94] = 30[2.966] = 88.98$$

The $df_{Interaction} = (a-1)(b-1) = 2(1) = 2$, so the between-groups variance term is

$$MS_{Interaction} = \frac{88.98}{2} = 44.49$$

Within-Groups Variance Term

The within-groups variance (i.e., error term) will be the same for all three effects (the two main effects and the interaction), so we only need to calculate it once. As in the one-way ANOVA, it is based on the deviations between each score and its group mean. The within-groups SS term for the factorial design is calculated with the formula

$$SS_{Within} = \Sigma\left(X - \bar{X}_{AB}\right)^2$$

This means that you need to calculate the sum of the squared differences between each score and its condition mean. Remember that the SS is the sum of squared deviations of each score from its condition mean: $SS = \Sigma(X - \bar{X}_{AB})^2$. The $\bar{X}_{AB}$ means for this calculation are shown in Figure 13.5. Suppose that the first score in the paper text/psychology condition is a rating of 5; its deviation from the group mean is $(5 - 5.4) = -0.4$, and that squared is 0.16. You would do this for all 180 scores and add them together to calculate the within-groups SS term. Imagine that we did this for our data set and got $SS_{Within} = 1000$. We can now calculate the df_{Within} term to find the within-groups variance:

$$df_{Within} = a(b)(n-1)$$

Thus, the $df_{Within} = 3(2)(30-1) = 174$ and the within-groups variance is

$$MS_{Within} = \frac{1000}{174} = 5.75$$

Now we are ready to calculate our F ratios for each effect.

F Ratios

With the values we have calculated for the between-groups variance terms and the within-groups error term, we can calculate our three F ratios for the ANOVA. For the main effect of text format, the F ratio is

$$F_{TextFormat} = \frac{80.6}{5.75} = 14.02$$

For the main effect of subject topic, the F ratio is

$$F_{SubjectTopic} = \frac{11.34}{5.75} = 1.97$$

For the interaction effect of text format × subject topic, the F ratio is

$$F_{Interaction} = \frac{44.49}{5.75} = 7.74$$

In Step 5, we will find the F_{crit} for each of these effects based on the df terms used in the calculation of the F ratios.

Step 5: Make a Decision

It is time to go back to our F Table to find the F_{crit} values for each of our F ratios to determine if our calculated values fall in the critical region for the F distribution. For the main effect of text format, we need $F_{crit}(2,174)$, where 2 is the $df_{Between}$ value and 174 is the df_{Within} value. If we use the table in Appendix D to find the F_{crit} in the column with 2 df and the row with 120 df, we find $F_{crit}(2,120) = 3.92$ (the highest df_{Within} value in the table is 120, so we can use that value from the table). Our calculated F value is 14.02, which is higher than 3.92, so the main effect of text format is significant, meaning there is a difference between at least two of the mean ratings for the formats. We would need to conduct a post hoc test to determine which levels of text format are different from the others.

Our next effect to test is the main effect of subject topic. We need $F_{crit}(1,174)$ for this effect. From the table in Appendix D, we find $F_{crit}(1,120) = 3.92$ (we can continue to use $df_{Within} = 120$ as the closest value to our error df). Our calculated F ratio for the main effect of subject topic was 1.97, so this effect is not significant (1.97 is lower than 3.92). This tells us that we have no evidence for an overall difference in satisfaction based on subject topic.

Finally, we can examine the interaction effect between the two factors. A significant interaction will tell us that the effect of text format on satisfaction ratings depends on which subject topic the text covers. The F_{crit} will be the same as that for the main effect of text format because the degrees of freedom for the interaction are the same. Thus, $F_{crit}(2,120) = 3.92$. Once again, our calculated F of 7.74 is higher than the critical value, so the interaction is significant. To fully describe the interaction effect, we should conduct follow-up tests called *simple effects*, but for now, let's just look at a graph of the condition means to see what the interaction looks like.

Figure 13.6　Mean Satisfaction Ratings for the Text Format by Subject Topic Study Showing the Interaction Between the Two Factors

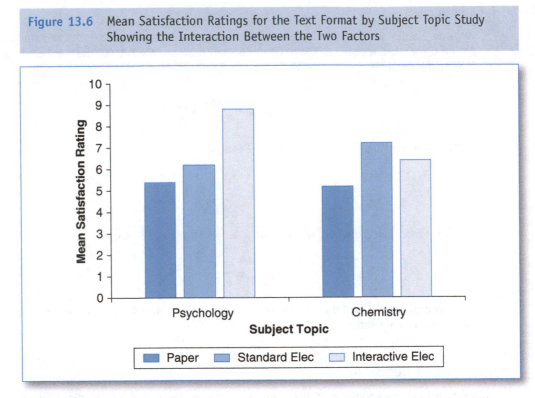

Figure 13.6 shows the condition means for each text format grouped by subject topic. What we can see in this graph is that the most preferred text format differs for the two subject topics: For the psychology text, students prefer the interactive electronic text, but for the chemistry text, they prefer the standard electronic text. This is how the text format preference *depends* on the subject topic: A different format is rated highest across the subject topics. Because the interaction showed a different ordering of satisfaction for the text formats for the two subject topics, the main effect of text format becomes less important in our analysis. The overall differences across the text formats are no longer meaningful because the main effect pattern doesn't apply to both the psychology and chemistry texts in the same way. In the next section, we will examine interactions further to see some different ways an interaction can occur within our data.

Stop and Think

13.4　For each description below, indicate which type of effect is being tested (main effect or interaction):

　　a.　Three groups of subjects are exposed to three different types of stories to compare the effect of type of story on reading speed.

　　b.　Researchers examine whether the effect of note-taking method (by hand or on a computer) on test score depends on the type of class a student is taking.

c. A study tested the effects of both room color and presence/absence of plants on recovery time in a hospital. The individual effects of room color and presence/absence of plants were tested.

13.5 A study was conducted to compare effects of gender and mood on spatial abilities. Men and women participated in a study in which half of the participants of each gender were placed in a positive mood (by watching an uplifting film clip) and half of each gender were placed in a negative mood (by watching a sad film clip). Immediately after watching the film clips, the participants were asked to navigate through a maze to reach the exit point. The amount of time to navigate the maze (in seconds) was measured and is listed below for each participant by condition. Use these data to test the main effects of the gender and mood variables and the interaction between these variables.

Male/Positive Mood: 56, 36, 75, 23, 55, 70, 82, 41, 88, 52, 60, 49

Female/Positive Mood: 57, 82, 43, 59, 66, 79, 88, 71, 75, 70, 80, 69

Male/Negative Mood: 90, 102, 69, 82, 79, 95, 103, 110, 84, 90, 99, 105

Female/Negative Mood: 110, 94, 85, 66, 79, 120, 93, 97, 82, 80, 104, 95

UNDERSTANDING INTERACTIONS

Interactions between independent variables can reveal interesting effects of the variables beyond what is seen in the main effects of each variable. Let's go back to our experiment with Daphne to figure out which treatment helps Daphne feel less anxious when she's home alone. The results of the study shown in Figure 13.4 illustrate an interaction between the type of treatment and the length of outing. In these data, the effect of the treatment *depends* on the length of time we are gone: The chew toy is best for short outings and the worn clothing is best for long outings. But there are other ways that the effect of the treatment type could interact with outing length. For example, we could find in this study that the worn clothing is the best treatment overall, but that its effect is smaller with short outings than with long outings. This interaction is shown in Figure 13.7 as Interaction A. Or we could find that there is no difference between the treatments for short outings but a large difference (with the worn clothing showing fewer bad behaviors than the chew toy) for long outings. This interaction is shown in Figure 13.7 as Interaction B. In other words, there are multiple ways that an interaction can occur between two factors in our data.

Another example may help further illustrate the concept of an interaction. Go back and reread the ice cream study described in Stop and Think 13.1 through 13.3 in this chapter. In this study, you have two independent variables: chocolate chip ice cream with (1) type of vanilla (artificial or real) and (2) amount of chips (current amount or 30% more chips). Figure 13.8

Figure 13.7 Different Types of Interactions From the Study With Daphne

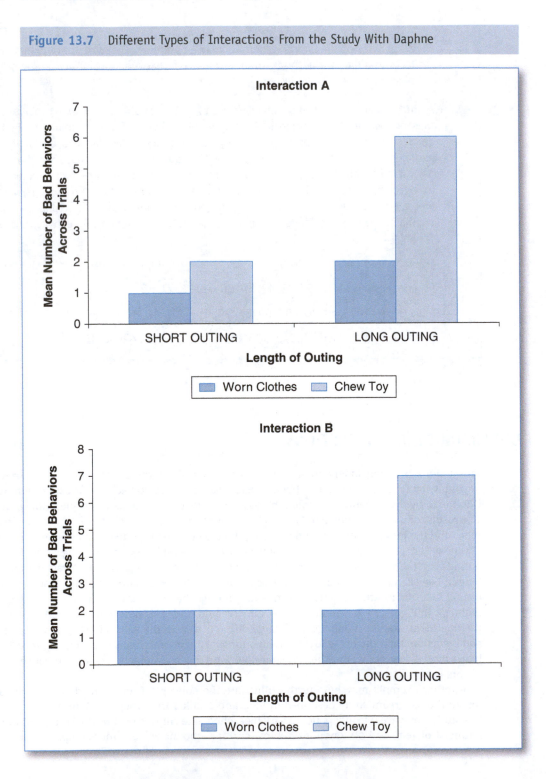

Figure 13.8   Diagram of the Ice Cream Experiment Design

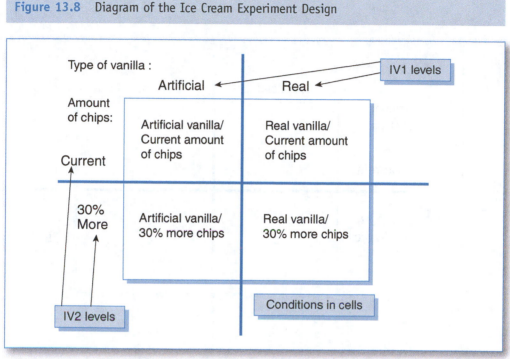

NOTE: IV stands for independent variable.

illustrates this design. You collect ratings of the ice cream from a group of 400 consumers, each of whom rates one type of ice cream on a scale of 1 to 7 for desire to purchase.

Figure 13.9 includes hypothetical mean ratings for each ice cream condition. Marginal means are also included for each level of the two independent variables. Looking at the marginal means, it appears as if the two independent variables each independently affected the participants' ratings. For type of vanilla, the real vanilla received a mean rating of 4.5, whereas the artificial vanilla received a rating of only 3. The amount of chips variable shows similar results: Participants gave higher ratings to the ice cream with 30% more chips ($M = 4.5$, where M is the mean) than with the current level of chips ($M = 3.0$). Thus, if you just looked at the main effects, you might be tempted to recommend that your company implement both the proposals for their ice cream.

However, looking at the condition means indicates something different. All the condition means show a rating of 3.0 for the ice cream, except in the real vanilla/30% more chips condition, where the mean rating was much higher than the other conditions ($M = 6.0$). In other words, the two variables interacted in such a way that this single condition seemed to result in the most preferred type of ice cream. Changing from artificial to real vanilla did not affect the ratings if the amount of chips stayed the same. Likewise, adding 30% more chips did not affect ratings if artificial vanilla was used. Only the combination of real vanilla and 30% more chips resulted in high ratings for the ice cream. This description of the interaction of the two independent variables provides the clearest picture of the results. Based on the interaction shown

Figure 13.9   Hypothetical Means for the Ice Cream Experiment

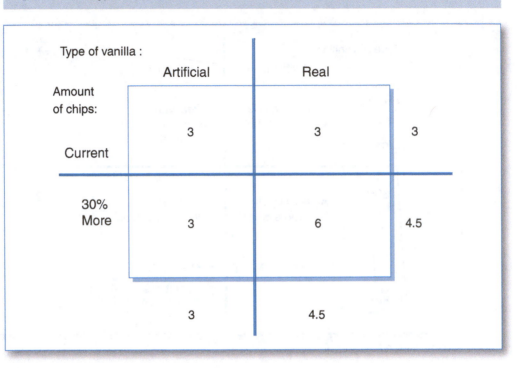

in the conditions means, your recommendation should be to only implement both proposals together for the chocolate chip ice cream (at least, until more flavors can be tested to determine how these factors affect other flavors). This example illustrates the importance of interactions in factorial designs.

Stop and Think

13.6 Imagine that the results of the ice cream experiment had been different. Suppose instead that ratings for the ice cream were higher whenever more chocolate chips were used, regardless of whether real or artificial vanilla was used. Would this represent an interaction? Why or why not?

13.7 Now imagine that the results from the ice cream experiment showed that ratings were higher when real vanilla was used regardless of the proportion of chocolate chips. Would this represent an interaction? Why or why not?

USING SPSS TO CALCULATE TWO-WAY BETWEEN-SUBJECTS ANOVAS

With more than one factor in our design, we'll need to begin using the General Linear Model function in the Analyze menu in SPSS to conduct a factorial ANOVA. Consider a factorial experiment where memory is compared for different types of items. In this experiment, two

Table 13.1 Data From a 2 × 2 (Study Format × Test Format) Memory Experiment

Participant No.	Picture Study/ Picture Test	Participant No.	Picture Study/ Word Test
1	92	11	68
2	88	12	50
3	87	12	54
4	78	14	80
5	95	15	85
6	90	16	78
7	71	17	92
8	89	18	74
9	93	19	79
10	89	20	77
	Word Study/Picture Test		**Word Study/Word Test**
21	56	31	88
22	62	32	90
23	59	33	67
24	70	34	79
25	65	35	85
26	67	36	78
27	45	37	90
28	51	38	74
29	67	39	89
30	71	40	77

factors are manipulated: the type of item studied (either pictures or words) and the type of test a participant receives for studied items (recognition of items formatted as words or pictures). In this study, we will consider whether memory performance differs for studied pictures and words (i.e., the main effect of study format) or differs for tests with pictures and words (i.e., the main effect of test format) and whether format match (picture or word) across study and test is better than when the format mismatches (i.e., the interaction of these factors). Percentage correct recognition data are presented in Table 13.1.

Recall from the examples we have already discussed for between-subjects designs that the data should all be entered into one column in the data window in SPSS because each score is from a different participant. However, you will need two additional columns to code the levels of the factors, one for the study format and one for the test format. Remember to label the columns with the variable names and to insert value labels for the codes.

To run the two-way between-subjects ANOVA, choose the Univariate test option in the General Linear Model portion of the Analyze menu. A definition window appears for you to click over the dependent and independent (Fixed Factor box) variables. You do not need to select any post hoc tests for the main effects in this design because there are only two levels of each independent variable, but you can choose them in Options tab if you have a design where one or more independent variables contains three or more levels. But in our 2×2 example, an examination of the means will indicate which level results in higher recognition for any significant main effects. If you select the factors in the Descriptives window, these means will appear in the output. Click OK to begin the analysis.

The output is similar to that shown in Figure 12.7; however, three tests of interest appear in the Tests of Between-Subjects Effects box (see Figure 13.10). The two main effects are indicated in the rows with the variable labels (*Study* and *Test*). The main effect of study format was significant, $F(1,36) = 8.91$, $p = 0.005$; however, the main effect of test format was not significant, $F(1,36) = 1.32$, $p = 0.257$. The means in the Descriptive Statistics box indicate that studied pictures ($M = 80.45$) were better remembered than studied words ($M = 71.50$), regardless of test format. This is a common finding in memory studies (Paivio, 2007). However, the interaction between study format and test format was also significant, $F(1,36) = 31.96$, $p < 0.001$. Note that the p value in the output for the interaction is listed as 0.000. Remember than p can never equal zero. The convention used in reporting such values is to indicate that

Summary of Steps

- Type the data into one column of the data window; add a column of codes for levels of each independent variable.
- Choose General Linear Model from the Analyze menu.
- Choose Univariate from the choices.
- In the definition window, click the data column over for the Dependent Variable and the columns of codes over to the Fixed Factor box.
- Under Options, choose Descriptive Statistics for means and variability and click Continue.

- Under Post Hoc, click the data variable over and check the box of the post hoc test you wish to run and click Continue (only appropriate if the independent variable has three or more levels and the main effect is significant).
- Click OK to run the ANOVA; results for each test appear in the Output window.

Figure 13.10 SPSS Output for the 2 × 2 Memory Study

Univariate Analysis of Variance

Between-Subjects Factors

		Value Label	N
Study format	1.00	Picture	20
	2.00	Word	20
Test format	1.00	Picture	20
	2.00	Word	20

Descriptive Statistics

Dependent Variable: Recognition Score

Study Format	Test Format	Mean	Std. Deviation	N
Picture	Picture	87.2000	7.29992	10
	Word	73.7000	13.08986	10
	Total	80.4500	12.42440	20
Word	Picture	61.3000	8.52513	10
	Word	81.7000	7.88881	10
	Total	71.5000	13.16894	20
Total	Picture	74.2500	15.36871	20
	Word	77.7000	11.29089	20
	Total	75.9750	13.42498	40

(Continued)

Figure 13.10   (Continued)

Tests of Between-Subjects Effects

Dependent Variable: Recognition Score

Source	Type III Sum of Squares	df	Mean Square	F	Sig.
Corrected model	3793.075[a]	3	1264.358	14.066	.000
Intercept	230888.025	1	230888.025	2568.673	.000
Study	801.025	1	801.025	8.912	.005
Test	119.025	1	119.025	1.324	.257
Study *test	2873.025	1	2873.025	31.963	.000
Error	3235.900	36	89.886		
Total	327917.000	40			
Corrected Total	7028.975	39			

a. r^2 = .540 (Adjusted r^2 = .501).

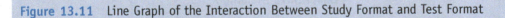

Figure 13.11   Line Graph of the Interaction Between Study Format and Test Format

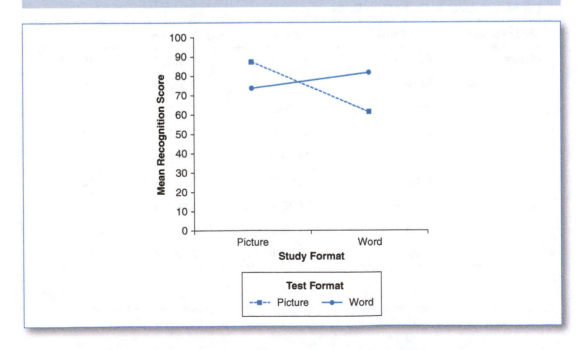

the p value was less than 0.001. The graph in Figure 13.11 illustrates this interaction. From the graph, we can see that the match in study and test format did affect recognition scores such that a match in format from study to test resulted in higher scores than the mismatch conditions.

TEST ASSUMPTIONS

The test assumptions for the two-way between-subjects ANOVA are the same as those for the one-way between-subjects ANOVA.

1. The population of scores must be a normal distribution. As you have seen in previous chapters, this is a standard assumption for inferential tests.

2. The scores from different participants within each sample must be independent. Thus, the scores from the different individuals within each sample cannot be related.

3. The populations that the samples represent must have equal variance. In other words, the assumption of homogeneity of variances must hold. Levene's test can be run to test for this assumption in SPSS using the Options tab.

Calculation Summary

<u>Interaction of between-groups sum of squares</u>: The sum of the sum of squared values for each group mean minus the two marginal means for that group plus the grand mean times the group sample size

<u>Within-groups sum of squares</u>: The sum of the sum of squared deviations for each score from its group mean

<u>Interaction of between-groups degrees of freedom</u>: The df for one factor times the df for the other factor

<u>Within-groups degrees of freedom</u>: The sample size minus one times the number of levels of each factor

CHAPTER SUMMARY

13.1 Can we examine more than one causal factor in a single study?

Yes, a factorial design includes multiple factors in a single study. The main effects of each factor can be tested, along with the interaction between factors.

13.2 How do levels of a factor and conditions differ in a factorial design?

In a factorial design, the levels of a factor are the different situations compared for that factor, whereas the conditions in the study are the situations encountered by the participants that come from combining the levels of the factors.

13.3 What is the difference between a main effect and an interaction?

Main effects test differences between the overall levels of a factorial (through the marginal means) and the interaction tests whether differences across the conditions for one level differ from the condition differences for the other level(s). In other words, the interaction tests whether the effect of one factor *depends* on the level of the other factor.

13.4 How do we calculate an *F* ratio for an interaction?

The *F* ratio for an interaction is based on the sum of squared deviations of the scores in each group from their condition mean (between-groups variance term) divided by the error (within-groups variance term).

13.5 What does a significant interaction tell us about our data?

A significant interaction tells us that the effect of one factor *depends* on the level of the other factor. An interaction can occur in a number of ways, including opposite effects at each level, a smaller effect at one level than the other, or an effect at one level and no effect at the other level.

THINKING ABOUT RESEARCH

A summary of a research study in psychology is given below. As you read the summary, think about the following questions:

1. What are the independent variables (IVs) in this experiment? Identify the levels of each IV.

2. What are the dependent variables? (Hint: Look at Figure 13.14.)

3. Describe the tests that the factorial ANOVAs for this study would conduct.

4. From what you see in Figure 13.14, did the results indicate an interaction effect between the IVs? If so, describe the interaction.

5. Does the graph in Figure 13.14 show main effects of either IV for either dependent variable? Why or why not?

> Bub, D. N., Masson, M. E. J., & Lin, T. (2013). Features of planned hand actions influence identification of graspable objects. *Psychological Science, 24,* 1269–1276.

Purpose of the Study. These researchers investigated how action plans (e.g., moving your hand and arm to pick up an object) influence object identification. One might think that object identification would affect action plans (e.g., you would plan your movements differently to pick up a mug versus a frying pan). However, these researchers suggested that the causal relationship can also go the other way, that the action plan can influence how well you identify an object. After familiarization trials, they gave subjects an action plan for their hand and then asked them to identify an object that could be held in the hand as quickly and accurately as possible. They hypothesized that when the action plan matched the way the object would be held, subjects would be faster at naming the objects.

Method of the Study. There were 20 undergraduate students in the experiment. The subjects first received familiarization trials with the action plans. They were shown pictures of hands and asked to mimic the hand posture (see Figure 13.12 for hand pictures). Subjects then received familiarization trials with the objects. Each object (see Figure 13.12 for pictures of the objects) was presented with its name, and the subject read the name out loud. Then the critical trials were presented. On

Figure 13.12   Stimuli Used in Bub et al.'s (2013) Experiment

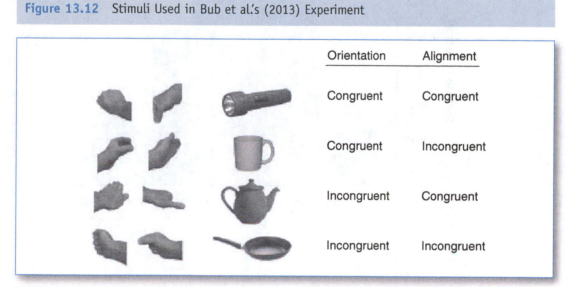

	Orientation	Alignment
	Congruent	Congruent
	Congruent	Incongruent
	Incongruent	Congruent
	Incongruent	Incongruent

SOURCE: Bub, Masson, & Lin (2013). Features of planned hand actions influence identification of graspable objects. *Psychological Science, 24*, 1269–1276.

Figure 13.13   Trial Sequence Used in Bub et al.'s (2013) Experiment

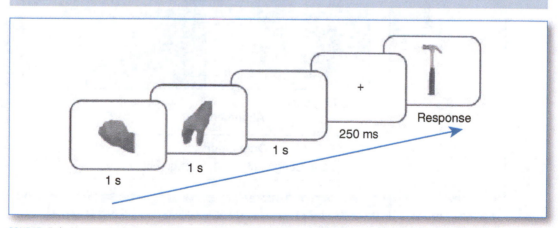

SOURCE: Bub, Masson, & Lin (2013). Features of planned hand actions influence identification of graspable objects. *Psychological Science, 24*, 1269–1276.

Figure 13.14 Results From Bub et al.'s (2013) Experiment

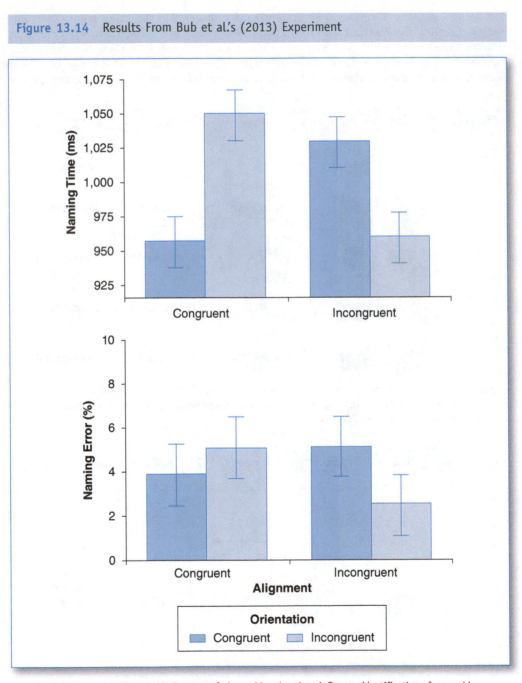

SOURCE: Bub, Masson, & Lin (2013). Features of planned hand actions influence identification of graspable objects. *Psychological Science, 24*, 1269–1276.

each trial, a hand action plan in two hand pictures was shown to the subjects one at a time (see Figure 13.13 for the sequence of events in a trial). Then, after a 250-millisecond fixation cross was shown, the object appeared and subjects were to name the object as quickly as possible. Their response was recorded by the computer's microphone with their naming time for each trial. Thus, trials were either congruent or incongruent in terms of the hand orientation (vertical or horizontal) for picking up the objects and the hand alignment (left hand or right hand) for picking up the objects.

Results of the Study. Figure 13.14 presents the results for naming time and naming errors according to the congruency of the orientation and alignment of the action plans shown before the pictures. These results show that naming time was fastest when both features (i.e., orientation and alignment) either matched or did not match the object shown for picking it up. Thus, if only one feature matched and the other feature did not, subjects were slower to name the object than when both features matched or both did not match.

Conclusions of the Study. The results of the study showed that action plans affected object identification as the author predicted. Having one motor feature in mind that can be used to pick up the object and one motor feature that cannot be used to pick up the object interfered with naming of the objects.

TEST YOURSELF

1. The benefit of a factorial design that is not present in a single factor study is that you can _____.

    a. test main effects
    b. examine effects of multiple factors in one ANOVA
    c. examine combined effect of multiple factors on the dependent measure
    d. both (b) and (c)

2. An interaction tells you that _____.

    a. there is an overall effect of your independent variable
    b. that the effect of one independent variable depends on the level of the other independent variable
    c. that neither of your independent variables affects your dependent variable
    d. none of the above

3. In a factorial design, levels of an independent variable are _____.

    a. compared with marginal means
    b. the same as the conditions
    c. cannot be defined

4. A researcher investigated the effects of color of a website background on consumer behavior. Three website colors were tested: blue, red, and yellow. In addition, the type of product being purchased was compared: The websites either contained sports equipment or books. The amount each individual purchased on the website they saw was measured. Overall, yellow websites resulted in larger purchase amounts than the other colors, but the color effect was only present for books. No color effect was present for sports equipment sites. According to this description, which of the following were significant in the ANOVA?

   a. The main effect of website color

   b. The main effect of type of product

   c. The interaction between website color and type of product

   d. Both (a) and (b)

   e. Both (a) and (c)

5. In a factorial experiment, an interaction between the independent variables will always be present.

   a. True

   b. False

6. For a factorial design, you only need to conduct one ANOVA to test all the effects.

   a. True

   b. False

7. If you find a significant interaction in your factorial design, then the main effects must also be significant.

   a. True

   b. False

8. A researcher conducted a study to investigate the effects of smiling on helping behavior. Participants completed a survey that they thought was the purpose of the study, but in reality, the experiment took place after they completed the survey. At the end of the survey session, half of the subjects were thanked with a smile and half were thanked without a smile. Whether the subject received a smile or not was randomly determined. The gender of the person giving the smile also varied by participant: Some subjects received the smile from a female researcher and some subjects received the smile from a male researcher. The subjects then passed a confederate in the hallway on their way out of the lab who had just dropped a large stack of books. The number of subjects who helped the confederate pick up his books was measured. The results showed that the subjects who were thanked by a male researcher showed similar helping behaviors across smile and no-smile conditions. However, subjects who were thanked by a female researcher showed more helping behaviors when they received a smile than when they did not.

   a. What are the independent variables in this experiment? Identify how each independent variable was manipulated (i.e., between subjects or within subjects).

b. Explain why you think the researcher decided to compare gender of the confederate in this study.

c. From the description of the results, was an interaction present? Explain your answer.

9. For the SPSS output in Figure 13.15, write a results section in APA style. (Hint: Some examples of presenting results in APA style were provided in Chapters 11 and 12.)

Figure 13.15   SPSS Output for a Factorial Design

➡ **Univariate Analysis of Variance**

Between–Subjects Factors

		Value Label	N
Instruction_Type	1.00	Live Lecture	6
	2.00	Online Lectures	6
Item_Type	1.00	Multiple Choice	6
	2.00	Short Answer	6

Descriptive Statistics

Dependent Variable: Test_Score

Instruction_Type	Item_Type	Mean	Std. Deviation	N
Live Lecture	Multiple Choice	5.3333	.57735	3
	Short Answer	10.6667	1.15470	3
	Total	8.0000	3.03315	6
Online Lectures	Multiple Choice	4.6667	.57735	3
	Short Answer	21.6667	2.88675	3
	Total	13.1667	9.49561	6
Total	Multiple Choice	5.0000	.63246	6
	Short Answer	16.1667	6.33772	6
	Total	10.5833	7.24203	12

Tests of Between–Subjects Effects

Dependent Variable: Test_Score

Source	Type III Sum of Squares	df	Mean Square	F	Sig.
Corrected Model	556.250ᵃ	3	185.417	71.774	.000
Intercept	1344.083	1	1344.083	520.290	.000
Instruction_Type	80.083	1	80.083	31.000	.001
Item_Type	374.083	1	374.083	144.806	.000
Instruction_Type * Item_Type	102.083	1	102.083	39.516	.000
Error	20.667	8	2.583		
Total	1921.000	12			
Corrected Total	576.917	11			

a. R Squared = .964 (Adjusted R Squared = .951)

Chapter 14

One-Way Within-Subjects Analysis of Variance (ANOVA)

As you read the chapter, consider the following questions:

14.1 How do within-subjects designs differ from between-subjects designs?

14.2 What are the advantages of using a within-subjects design? What are the disadvantages?

14.3 How does the calculation of the variance terms in an ANOVA change for within-subjects designs?

14.4 Are there new assumptions to consider for an ANOVA with a within-subjects design?

Remember the example presented in Chapter 13 about my dog, Daphne (see Photo 14.1)? In that chapter, I described an experiment we conducted to determine how to reduce separation anxiety in Daphne when we left her home alone. We varied the type of treatment (worn clothing and a chew toy) and the length of time we were gone (short outings and long outings) and measured the number of bad behaviors we found when we returned home after each combination of these factors (i.e., worn clothing for a short outing, worn clothing for a long outing, etc.). This design was shown in Figure 13.3. One thing that was different about this experiment, though (compared to the types of experiments I had described previously), was that Daphne experienced *all* the conditions in the experiment (she was the only subject tested). This means the experiment was conducted with a within-subjects design.

WITHIN-SUBJECTS DESIGNS

The difference between within-subjects and between-subjects designs is about how the independent variable is manipulated. In between-subjects designs, each participant in the study only experiences one condition in the study. In within-subjects designs, each participant in the study experiences all of the conditions in the study. In Chapters 10 and 11, we looked at two different

Photo 14.1   Chapter 13 described a study with our dog, Daphne, in which she experienced several treatments to try to reduce her separation anxiety.

t tests that are used for these types of designs when two means are being compared—the paired/related samples *t* test for within-subjects designs and the independent samples *t* test for between-subjects designs. For our study with Daphne, though, we are comparing more than two means in a within-subjects design. With more than two means to compare, we cannot use a *t* test to test our hypotheses. Instead, we will use an ANOVA as we did for the designs described in Chapters 12 and 13. However, we will need to calculate the *F* ratio in a different way to account for the measurement of the dependent variable from the same participants in all the conditions.

One advantage of the within-subjects design is the reduction of error in the data. Because participants are being compared with themselves (under different conditions), there are no between-group differences that contribute to the variability in the data (see Figure 14.1). There is only one group of individuals who contribute data under multiple conditions in the study. Because of this, the error term (i.e., within-groups variance) in our *F* ratio for this design will be lower than the error term that would be calculated for the same data if it were a between-subjects designs. This allows us a better chance of detecting an effect that exists (i.e., more power). I discussed power in Chapter 8, when the basics of hypothesis testing were introduced along with the types of errors that can be made in our tests. The chance of a Type II error is 1-power, so when we increase power, we reduce our chance of a Type II error (where we do not detect an effect that exists).

Figure 14.1   Within-Subjects Designs Reduce the Error Term in an ANOVA by Removing Between-Group Differences From the Data

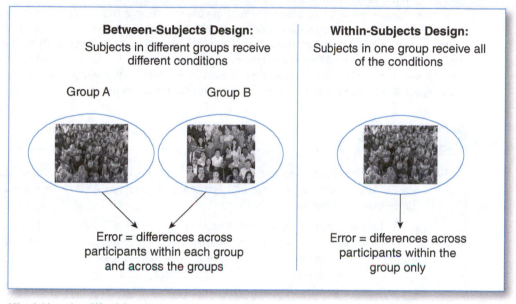

©iStock/skynesher, ©iStock/Rawpixel

Another advantage of a within-subjects design is the lower burden on the researcher to recruit participants for the study. Because the participants provide data in all conditions of the study, fewer individuals are needed in the sample. This is especially useful when sampling from smaller populations (e.g., rare clinical populations) or when a population is difficult to sample from (e.g., you have no incentive to offer participants). However, this advantage can become a disadvantage if the study procedure is long or difficult. Some participants may choose to drop out of the study (either explicitly withdrawing or indirectly withdrawing by failing to complete the task as instructed), reducing the sample size and possibly biasing the sample. The people who choose not to complete the study may be different in important ways from the people who choose to complete it, introducing a self-selection bias between our sample and the whole population.

Another issue to overcome in within-subjects designs is possible bias from the order of the conditions the participants experience. It is possible that the order in which they experience the conditions in the study will affect the behaviors/responses the participants make, biasing the data collected. Thus, order effects are a concern in a within-subjects study. This issue can be handled within the design by randomly assigning participants to different orders of the conditions to reduce this bias, a process known as counterbalancing. Counterbalancing allows the researcher to collect data in a within-subjects

Counterbalancing: a control used in within-subjects experiments where equal numbers of participants are randomly assigned to different orders of the conditions

design using different orders of conditions. Order effects can then be tested by including the order of conditions as a factor in the data analyses. Thus, there are both advantages and disadvantages to using within-subjects designs compared to the between-subjects designs we have discussed in the previous chapters.

In this chapter, we will consider some within-subjects designs that compare more than two means. The one-way within-subjects design involves one independent variable with three or more levels. We will go through the calculation of the *F* ratio for this design both by hand and using SPSS. However, the differences between the between-subjects and within-subjects ANOVA calculations also apply to two-way designs; I will briefly discuss two-way designs at the end of the chapter so you can see how to generalize these differences to more complex designs.

Stop and Think

14.1 For each study below, indicate whether it is a between-subjects or within-subjects design. Also indicate which type of inferential test (*t* test or ANOVA) is the correct choice for testing the hypothesis.

   a. A statistics instructor is interested in the best type of quiz to use to prepare students in her course. She randomly assigns students in her course to one of three groups: no study quiz, a multiple choice study quiz, or a short answer study quiz. She then compares the exam scores for the three groups.

   b. A statistics instructor is interested in the best type of quiz to use to prepare students in her course. She provides no quiz for the first exam, a multiple choice quiz for the second exam, and a short answer quiz for the third exam. She then compares the scores on the three exams for her class.

   c. A neuropsychologist is treating several Alzheimer's disease patients in a clinic. He wants to determine the best time of day to discuss treatment issues with his patients, but he notices that mental state seems to vary with time of day. Thus, he designs a study to determine which time of day his patients seem to have the most cognitive awareness: morning or afternoon. He tests each patient at both times of day and compares scores on a cognitive screening scale for morning and afternoon.

14.2 For the study above, explain why this study is not a true experiment. How can this study be redesigned to make it an experiment?

14.3 Explain how counterbalancing could be used in the studies described in (b) and (c) in 14.1.

CALCULATING A WITHIN-SUBJECTS ANOVA

Our hypothesis-testing steps will be very similar to those used with between-subjects ANOVAs. The main difference will be in the calculation of the *F* ratio in Step 4. I will describe those differences in that step.

Figure 14.2   Design of a Within-Subjects Study Looking at the Effects of Different Types of Distractions on Driving Performance

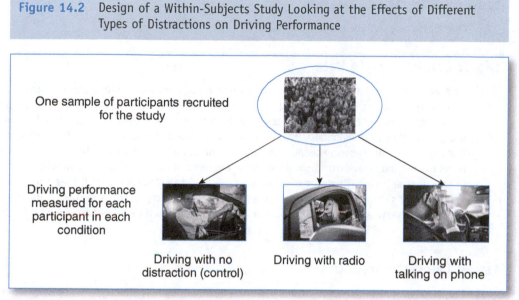

One sample of participants recruited for the study

Driving performance measured for each participant in each condition

Driving with no distraction (control)

Driving with radio

Driving with talking on phone

©iStock/skynesher, ©iStock/Geber86, ©iStock/Minerva Studio, ©iStock/Halfpoint

To go through the hypothesis-testing steps, let's consider a within-subjects study that examines the effects of different distractions on driving performance. Recall that we considered some different types of studies looking at distracted driving in Chapter 1. Here, we will consider a hypothetical experiment of this type that compares driving performance in terms of how quickly people can press a brake when an object suddenly appears in their path. Three conditions will be considered in this experiment: (1) driving while listening to the radio where the general topics of the songs played will need to be later recalled, (2) driving while listening to a phone conversation where the general topics of the conversation will need to be later recalled, and (3) driving with no extra task (the control condition). Because driving ability can differ from person to person, the study is conducted as a within-subjects design so that a participant's driving performance can be compared under each of the three conditions being tested. Figure 14.2 illustrates this design. This design will remove error in the data that occurs from the variability in driving performance that might exist between groups if the conditions were compared for different participants.

Step 1: State Hypotheses

In Step 1, we will state our hypothesis for the effect of driving condition—that driving with a distraction, most especially listening to a phone conversation, decreases driving performance relative to driving with no distraction. Thus, our hypotheses for the main effect in this study are

H_0: *The population means for people driving with and without distraction are equal:* $\mu_{control} = \mu_{radio} = \mu_{phone}$.

H_1: *The population means for people driving under different distraction conditions will be ordered as follows in terms of driving performance:* $\mu_{control} > \mu_{radio} > \mu_{phone}$.

Step 2: Set Decision Criterion

Our alpha level will be set at 0.05.

Step 3: Collect Sample Data

To make our calculations simple for this example, we'll only consider a sample size of $n = 5$ in this study. However, note that a larger sample size would be needed (at least 20 participants) if we were to conduct this study to test our hypothesis. As in our one-way between-subjects design, we'll need to calculate the condition means from the subjects' data for each condition. But for the within-subjects design, we will also need means for each subject across the conditions to calculate our error term (how these are used to calculate our F ratio will be described in the next section). Thus, for each subject, we will calculate an overall mean that collapses each subject's data across the conditions in the study. The condition and subject means for our driving study are shown in Table 14.1. In the next step, we'll use these means to calculate the F ratios.

Step 4: Calculate Statistics

For the F ratio, the between-groups variance term will be calculated the same way it was for a between-subjects design: with the sum of squared differences between the condition means and grand mean, multiplied by the number of subjects (n). However, the within-groups variance term will be quite different—it is the sum of squares interaction term for the interaction between the

Table 14.1 Data for Our Hypothetical Driving While Distracted Study—Values Represent Reaction Time for Braking When an Obstacle Appears

Subject #	A_1—No Distraction	A_2—Driving With Radio	A_3—Driving With Phone	Subject Marginal Means
1	800	1200	1900	$\bar{X}_{S1} = 1300$
2	800	1300	1400	$\bar{X}_{S2} = 1167$
3	900	1500	1600	$\bar{X}_{S3} = 1333$
4	500	1800	1200	$\bar{X}_{S4} = 1167$
5	1300	1500	2200	$\bar{X}_{S5} = 1667$
Marginal Means	$\bar{X}_{A1} = 860$	$\bar{X}_{A2} = 1460$	$\bar{X}_{A3} = 1660$	$\bar{X}_{Grand} = 1327$

subjects and the conditions, SS_{SXA}. Recall that an interaction tells us if the differences across the levels of one factor are the same or different for each level of the other factor (i.e., does the effect of one factor *depend* on the level of the other factor?). Here, one of our factors is the subjects, where each subject is a different level. We expect the subjects as a group to differ across the conditions if the independent variable has an effect. But when the subjects show differences from one another that are not the same across the conditions (i.e., an interaction between the subjects and the conditions), this represents the error we get from subject to subject in our study. This interaction means that the subject-to-subject differences *depend* on the condition. Therefore, we will use the interaction term as the error term because the interaction between the subjects and the conditions will give us an estimate of the error that exists in our data based on differences from subject to subject across the conditions of the study. We will examine the formulas for these terms next.

Between-Groups Variance Term

For the between groups variance term, we will use this formula:

$$SS_{Driving\ Condition} = n\Sigma\left(\bar{X}_A - \bar{X}_{Grand}\right)^2$$

where $\bar{X}_A$ is the marginal mean for each condition in our study and n is the number of subjects in our sample (for within-subjects designs, N and n are the same value). Thus, the between groups SS for driving condition is

$$SS_{DrivingCondition} = (5)\left[(860-1327)^2 + (1460-1327)^2 + (1660-1327)^2\right] =$$
$$5[218089+17689+110889] = 5[346667] = 1733335$$

We also need the $df_{DrivingCondition}$, which is $df = a-1 = 3-1 = 2$. With these two terms, we can calculate the between groups variance for driving condition:

$$MS_{DrivingCondition} = \frac{1733335}{2} = 866667.5$$

Within-Groups Variance Term

As indicated at the beginning of this section, the error term for a within-subjects ANOVA is based on the interaction between the subjects and the independent variable. Recall that the general formula presented in Chapter 13 for an interaction is

$$SS_{Interaction} = n\Sigma\left(\bar{X}_{AB} - \bar{X}_A - \bar{X}_B + \bar{X}_{Grand}\right)^2$$

Here the *A* term is our independent variable, but the *B* term is the subjects. Using this general formula, the SS for the subjects × driving condition interaction is

$$SS_{Subjects \times DrivingCondition} = 5\left[\begin{array}{l}(800-860-1300+1327)^2 + (800-860-1167+1327)^2 \\ +\ldots+(2200-1660-1667+1327)^2\end{array}\right]$$
$$5[1089+10000+1156+\ldots+90000+40000] = 5[664335] = 3321675$$

Although each value in the calculation is not shown above (only the first few and last values), this formula is calculated for each individual score (i.e., 15 scores for our example data set in

Table 14.1). You can verify this by completing the formula for all 15 scores shown in the table. The $df_{Interaction} = (a-1)(b-1) = 2(5) = 10$, making the within-groups variance term

$$MS_{Subjects \times DrivingCondition} = \frac{3321675}{10} = 332167.5$$

F Ratio

With the values we have calculated for the between-groups variance terms and the within-groups error term, we can calculate the F ratio for the ANOVA. For the main effect of driving condition (the only effect we will test in our one-way design), the F ratio is

$$F_{TextFormat} = \frac{866667.5}{332167.5} = 2.61$$

In Step 5, we will find the F_{crit} for this effect using the df terms included in its calculation.

Step 5: Make a Decision

In this step, we are looking for the F_{crit} value to determine if our calculated F ratio falls in the critical region for the F distribution. For the main effect of driving condition, we need $F_{crit}(2,10)$, where 2 is the $df_{Between}$ value and 10 is the df_{Within} value. If we use the Table in Appendix D to find the F_{crit} in the column with 2 df and the row with 10 df, we find $F_{crit}(2,10) = 4.10$. Our calculated F value of 2.61 for the main effect of driving condition is lower than the F_{crit}, meaning that our test is not significant—there is not enough of a mean difference between the three driving conditions to conclude that driving condition had an effect on driving performance. In this case, we must retain (hold on to) our null hypothesis until we can conduct further tests of this hypothesis. One possible reason for this result might be our low sample size; a replication of our study with a larger N would be a good next step in our investigation of the effects of distracted driving.

Stop and Think

14.4 You are conducting a study to determine the best study technique to prepare for multiple choice exams. Your friends agree to participate in your study. Across the course of the semester, each of your friends agrees to use each of the study techniques you're interested in to prepare for one of their multiple choice exams: rereading their notes, taking the multiple choice quizzes that come with their textbooks, and working with a study partner to quiz each other. You compare exam scores (a percentage out of 100) for exams in which your friends used each of the three study techniques. Explain how you could use counterbalancing to control for order effects in this study.

14.5 You have conducted the study described above and found the data shown below by condition. Conduct the within-subjects ANOVA to determine if you found an effect of study technique in your study.

Reread Notes: 67, 89, 78, 75, 77, 80

Multiple Choice Quizzes: 95, 95, 85, 100, 87, 86

Quiz With Study Partner: 75, 77, 80, 66, 85, 90

14.6 Regardless of what you found in 14.5, imagine that your ANOVA was significant. What is another possible explanation of this result (other than that study technique had an effect on exam scores)?

USING SPSS TO CALCULATE ONE-WAY WITHIN-SUBJECTS ANOVAS

In this section, we will look at how to conduct the one-way within-subjects ANOVA using SPSS. In SPSS, within-subjects designs are referred to as *repeated measures*, so keep this in mind as you work through the example in this section. To illustrate the analysis in SPSS, we will go back to the SPSS example we covered in Chapter 12 for the one-way between-subjects design. This will allow us to compare how the ANOVA differs for the same data for between- and within-subjects designs. Recall that this example is for a study comparing satisfaction ratings for three different text format conditions with 30 participants per group. In our revised example here, let's assume the participants were the same individuals in each group. Thus, each participant rated each text format (perhaps for different chapters of the text). These data are shown in Figure 14.3 for the SPSS data window and correspond to the data analyzed (for a between-subjects design) in Chapter 12.

For within-subjects designs, two things change in SPSS from the between-subjects examples described in earlier chapters: (1) The data appear in separate columns for each condition in the data window (remember that each participant or set of matched participants has data in a single row), and (2) we use the Repeated Measures test in the General Linear Model option of the Analyze menu. Each of the text format conditions is listed in a different column in the

Figure 14.3   SPSS Data Window for the Text Format Study Data

	Paper	Standard	Interactive	var	var
1	6.00	7.00	8.00		
2	6.00	4.00	8.00		
3	6.00	4.00	9.00		
4	7.00	5.00	5.00		
5	6.00	7.00	7.00		
6	5.00	6.00	9.00		
7	3.00	6.00	9.00		
8	3.00	7.00	6.00		
9	3.00	5.00	7.00		
10	5.00	6.00	5.00		
11	1.00	4.00	9.00		
12	8.00	2.00	10.00		
13	4.00	8.00	7.00		
14	2.00	7.00	7.00		
15	3.00	6.00	5.00		
16	3.00	5.00	8.00		
17	3.00	5.00	8.00		
18	3.00	5.00	8.00		
19	2.00	5.00	9.00		
20	4.00	6.00	9.00		
21	5.00	6.00	8.00		

Figure 14.4 SPSS Output for the Text Format Study Data

→ General Linear Model

Within-Subjects Factors

Measure: MEASURE_1

Textcond	Dependent Variable
1	Paper
2	Standard
3	Interactive

Descriptive Statistics

	Mean	Std. Deviation	N
Paper Text	4.1667	1.64177	30
Standard Electronic Text	5.3333	1.62594	30
Interactive Electronic Text	7.8333	1.28877	30

Tests of Within-Subjects Effects

Measure: MEASURE_1

Source		Type III Sum of Squares	df	Mean Square	F	Sig.
Textcond	Sphericity Assumed	210.556	2	105.278	37.979	.000
	Greenhouse-Geisser	210.556	1.912	110.128	37.979	.000
	Huynh-Feldt	210.556	2.000	105.278	37.979	.000
	Lower-bound	210.556	1.000	210.556	37.979	.000
Error(Textcond)	Sphericity Assumed	160.778	58	2.772		
	Greenhouse-Geisser	160.778	55.446	2.900		
	Huynh-Feldt	160.778	58.000	2.772		
	Lower-bound	160.778	29.000	5.544		

Textcond

Estimates

Measure: MEASURE_1

Textcond	Mean	Std. Error	95% Confidence Interval	
			Lower Bound	Upper Bound
1	4.167	.300	3.554	4.780
2	5.333	.297	4.726	5.940
3	7.833	.235	7.352	8.315

Pairwise Comparisons

Measure: MEASURE_1

(I) Textcond	(J) Textcond	Mean Difference (I-J)	Std. Error	Sig.[b]	95% Confidence Interval for Difference[b]	
					Lower Bound	Upper Bound
1	2	-1.167	.470	.057	-2.361	.028
	3	-3.667*	.391	.000	-4.659	-2.674
2	1	1.167	.470	.057	-.028	2.361
	3	-2.500*	.425	.000	-3.581	-1.419
3	1	3.667*	.391	.000	2.674	4.659
	2	2.500*	.425	.000	1.419	3.581

Based on estimated marginal means

*. The mean difference is significant at the

b. Adjustment for multiple comparisons: Bonferroni.

Multivariate Tests

	Value	F	Hypothesis df	Error df	Sig.
Pillai's trace	.769	46.518[a]	2.000	28.000	.000
Wilks' lambda	.231	46.518[a]	2.000	28.000	.000
Hotelling's trace	3.323	46.518[a]	2.000	28.000	.000
Roy's largest root	3.323	46.518[a]	2.000	28.000	.000

Each F tests the multivariate effect of Textcond. These tests are based on the linearly independent pairwise comparisons among the estimated marginal means.

a. Exact statistic

data window in SPSS, with the column labeled by condition (see Figure 14.3). In addition, the within-subjects ANOVA is run by choosing the Repeated Measures test in the General Linear Model portion of the Analyze menu. This test is used to conduct an ANOVA for any design comparing three or more means that contains a within-subjects variable. The first window that appears for this test is the within-subjects variable definition window. In the top space, name the variable (e.g., Textcond) and then indicate the number of conditions for this variable (e.g., 3) by typing the number into the Number of Levels space and adding this variable to the list. Then, click Define to choose the columns for each level on the right side of the next window that appears. If your design also contains a between-subjects variable, you can define that variable here as well as in the Between-Subjects factor box. To run post hoc tests for this design (in the case that the main effect of text condition is significant in the ANOVA), you must choose the Options button (the Post Hoc button is used only for between-subjects variables), click over the text condition variable into the Display Means box, and then check the Compare Main Effects box. You can then choose a post hoc test from the drop-down bar. You may also wish to choose the Display Descriptive Statistics option in this window. Click Continue and OK to run the test.

The output (see Figure 14.4) is more complex for the repeated measures test than for the other tests we have seen. However, the output still contains the information needed to determine if the tests are significant. Figure 14.4 shows the portions of the output needed to interpret the results for this example. To evaluate the main effect of the text condition, look for the Tests of Within-Subjects Effects box. The first column of this box shows the F and p values. For this example, the $F = 37.979$ and $p < 0.001$. Therefore, we can reject the null hypothesis that there is no difference in condition means because the main effect of text condition is significant.

The post hoc tests are shown in the box of the output labeled Pairwise Comparisons. The conditions are indicated by code value, with p values listed in the Sig. column. The post hoc tests indicate that ratings for the paper text condition are lower than ratings for the interactive electronic text and that the standard electronic text had lower ratings than the interactive electronic text; both $p < 0.001$.

If you compare the sum of squares terms across the two analyses for the same data analyzed as a between-subjects design in Chapter 12, you will see that the between-groups terms (labeled as Textcond for the within-subjects effects in Figure 14.4) are the same, but the within groups/error sum of squares is lower for the within-subjects design than the between-subjects design. However, because we had fewer overall subjects in the within-subjects design than the between-subjects design, the error df is higher in the between-subjects design, giving us a lower F value.

Summary of Steps

- Enter the data into each data window, with one column for each condition.
- Choose the General Linear Model from the Analyze menu.
- Choose Repeated Measures from the list of tests.
- Define conditions of within-subjects variables by typing in a name for the variable and the number of levels of this variable; click Add.
- Click Define and then choose the columns from the left for the conditions of the Within-Subjects Variable.
- If there are any between-subjects variables in the design, click those columns into the Between-Subjects Factor box.

(Continued)

(Continued)
- To display means and choose post hoc tests, click the Option tab.
- For means, click the Descriptive Statistics box.
- For post hoc tests, move the within-subjects variable label over to the Display Means For: box—then click the Compare main effects box and choose the post hoc you want to run form the dropdown menu under Confidence interval adjustment.
- Click Continue and OK to run the analyses (see Figure 14.4 for example output).

TEST ASSUMPTIONS

The first two test assumptions for the within-subjects ANOVA are the same as those for the between-subjects ANOVA:

1. The population of difference scores must be a normal distribution.

2. The scores from different participants within each sample must be independent.

❦

Sphericity assumption: the assumption of the repeated measures (within-subjects) ANOVA that pairs of scores in the population have equal variance

However, the third assumption for the within-subjects ANOVA is a new assumption known as the sphericity assumption. This assumption is that pairs of scores in the population for the same individuals have similar variability. The new assumption is stated as

3. Sphericity: In the population of scores, the differences between pairs of scores from the same individuals are equal.

SPSS provides a test of the sphericity assumption for repeated measures (i.e., within-subjects) ANOVAs. This test for the example data analyzed in the previous section is shown in Figure 14.5. If the sphericity test is significant, the F statistic needs to be adjusted to retain accuracy of the test. To make these adjustments, the Tests of Within-Subjects Effects box (shown in Figure 14.4) contains a few different corrections below the Sphericity Assumed row. The sphericity assumed values are used if the sphericity test is not significant. However, if the sphericity test is significant, a correction is used because violations of this assumption can increase the chance of a Type I error (Keppel & Wickens, 2004). A common correction used in psychological research is the Greenhouse–Geisser correction. A full discussion of the correction techniques is provided in Howell's (2013) statistics text (as well as other more advanced statistics texts).

Figure 14.5   SPSS Output for the Sphericity Test

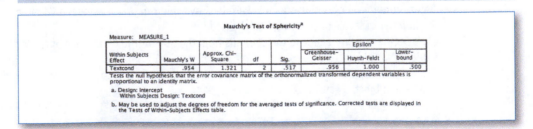

Mauchly's Test of Sphericity[a]

Measure: MEASURE_1

Within Subjects Effect	Mauchly's W	Approx. Chi-Square	df	Sig.	Epsilon[b] Greenhouse–Geisser	Huynh–Feldt	Lower-bound
Textcond	.954	1.321	2	.517	.956	1.000	.500

Tests the null hypothesis that the error covariance matrix of the orthonormalized transformed dependent variables is proportional to an identity matrix.

a. Design: Intercept
   Within Subjects Design: Textcond

b. May be used to adjust the degrees of freedom for the averaged tests of significance. Corrected tests are displayed in the Tests of Within–Subjects Effects table.

MORE COMPLEX WITHIN-SUBJECTS DESIGNS

The analyses conducted in this chapter were done for within-subjects designs with a single independent variable. However, the analyses can also be done in a similar fashion for factorial within-subjects designs. As in between-subjects designs, the ANOVA would test the main effects for each independent variable and the interaction between the variables. As in the one-way designs considered in this chapter, the between-groups variance terms of the F ratios would be calculated the same way they are in between-subjects designs. But the within-groups variance terms will include the interaction with the subjects factor, as you saw in the calculations conducted in this chapter. Any test that involves a within-subjects factor (main effects and interactions) will use the error term calculated in this chapter. However, the calculation of the error term becomes more complicated as each independent variable is added to the design—SPSS and other software packages are helpful in conducting these analyses.

Calculation Summary

Within-subjects error term: The interaction between subjects and the independent variable

CHAPTER SUMMARY

14.1 How do within-subjects designs differ from between-subjects designs?

The primary difference between between-subjects and within-subjects designs is that in within-subjects design, data are collected from each participant in all the conditions of the study, instead of only one condition as in between-subjects designs.

14.2 What are the advantages of using a within-subjects design? What are the disadvantages?

The advantages of within-subjects designs (relative to between-subjects designs) is that there is less error (due to a lack of between group differences across different groups of participants) and fewer participants are needed in the study to collect the same amount of data. The disadvantages are that there may be order effects from the order of the conditions the participants receive (which can be controlled with counterbalancing) and that the participants' procedure will be longer in the study, which could result in loss of subjects across the procedure and/or fatigue effects.

14.3 How does the calculation of the variance terms in an ANOVA change for within-subjects designs?

The between-groups variance term is calculated the same way in both types of designs. However, the within-groups error term is calculated differently. For within-subjects designs, the error term is calculated from the interaction between subjects and the independent variable.

14.4 Are there new assumptions to consider for an ANOVA with a within-subjects design?

Yes, the within-subjects ANOVA has a sphericity assumption to satisfy that states that pairs of scores from the same participants in the population must have equal variance. SPSS provides a test of the sphericity assumption and some corrections if the test is significant.

THINKING ABOUT RESEARCH

A summary of a research study in psychology is given below. As you read the summary, think about the following questions:

1. Identify the primary independent variable in this experiment that provided a test of the researchers' hypothesis. What are the levels of this variable?

2. The independent variable in this study was manipulated within-subjects, but counterbalancing was not used in the procedure. Explain why counterbalancing was not needed in this study.

3. Why do you think the researchers used a within-subjects design in this study? What source of bias might have been present in the data if they had used a between-subjects design?

4. The main effect of the primary independent variable was significant for alpha level = 0.05. The ANOVA showed an $F(1,53) = 44.90$ for this effect. What F_{crit} value would this need to be compared with to determine if the main effect was significant?

5. The main effect F value given above had a $df_{error} = 53$. Why do you think this df value was used in the analysis? (Hint: Look at Figure 14.6 and think about how the analysis was conducted.)

Nairne, J. S., VanArsdall, J. E., Pandeirada, J. N. S., Cogdill, M., & LeBreton, J. M. (2013). Adaptive memory: The mnemonic value of animacy. *Psychological Science, 24*, 2099–2105.

Note: Study 2 from this article is described here.

Purpose of the Study. The researchers conducted an experiment to investigate whether living things have a memory advantage over nonliving things. Their research was motivated by an evolutionary perspective on the development of memory in that being able to distinguish between living and nonliving things is essential for survival. In their study, they tested the hypothesis that subjects would recall more words of living objects than nonliving objects.

Method of the Study. Undergraduate students ($N = 54$) were asked to remember 24 words presented to them in random order. Twelve of the words represented living things, and 12 of the words represented nonliving things. The word sets were matched on several other characteristics (e.g., familiarity, how well an image can be brought to mind by the word, number of letters in the word, etc.). After studying the words, subjects completed a short task to categorize presented numbers as odd or even. Subjects were then asked to recall the words in any order for four minutes. This entire procedure was repeated a total of three times (i.e., they studied and recalled the words three times).

Results of the Study. The results showed that subjects recalled more of the words for living objects than nonliving objects. Figure 14.6 presents the recall results from this experiment.

Conclusions of the Study. The researchers concluded that the living objects hold a memorial advantage such that memory is attuned to this characteristic of objects. They suggest that this conclusion is consistent with an evolutionary perspective on the development of memory.

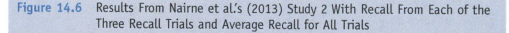

Figure 14.6   Results From Nairne et al.'s (2013) Study 2 With Recall From Each of the Three Recall Trials and Average Recall for All Trials

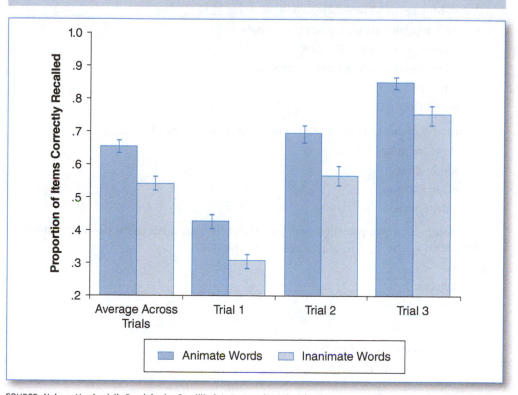

SOURCE: Nairne, VanArsdall, Pandeirada, Cogdill, & LeBreton (2013). Adaptive memory: The mnemonic value of animacy. *Psychological Science, 24,* 2099–2105.

TEST YOURSELF

1. In a within-subjects ANOVA, the error term is calculated from the interaction between the independent variable and the _____.

    a. other independent variables in the study

    b. between-groups variance term

    c. subjects as a factor

    d. none of the above

2. An advantage of a within-subjects design is _____.

    a. fewer participants are needed in the study

    b. there is less error in the data

    c. that counterbalancing is not needed

    d. both (a) and (b)

    e. both (b) and (c)

3. A disadvantage of within-subjects designs is that _____.

    a. more participants are needed in the study

    b. there is more error in the data

    c. order effects can be present in the data

    d. both (a) and (b)

    e. both (b) and (c)

4. Counterbalancing is a procedural technique that helps control for _____.

    a. between-groups error

    b. within-groups error

    c. subject fatigue

    d. order effects

5. The assumption that pairs of scores from the same individuals in the population have equal variance is called the _____ assumption.

    a. Levene's

    b. sphericity

    c. independence

    d. pairs

6. In within-subjects analyses, $N = n$.

    a. True

    b. False

7. With the same number of participants, a between-subjects design should result in less error than a comparable within-subjects design.

    a. True

    b. False

8. In within-subjects designs, order effects can be tested by including order as a factor in the analysis.

    a. True

    b. False

9. Suppose you conducted a study to test the hypothesis that social pressure affects memory accuracy. You set up a study in which all of the participants view three different videos of a person robbing a convenience store (order of the videos is counterbalanced across participants). After one crime video, participants watch other participants discussing the crime. After another crime video, the participants read a summary of the crime written by another participant. In reality, these other participants are part of the experiment, and some of the details of the crime that are discussed or written are inaccurate. The actual participants are told that they should consider other people's perspectives on the crime because it is difficult for any one person to accurately

remember all the details. After the third crime video, the participants do not view the discussion or read a summary of the crime (i.e., the control condition) but are also told that it is difficult for any one person to accurately remember all the details of the crime. Thirty minutes after viewing the crime videos, all participants are given a recognition memory test about details of the crimes. For this study, answer the following questions:

a. What is the correct statistical test that should be used to analyze the data?

b. What is the null hypothesis that will be tested?

c. Suppose that 10 participants participated in the study. For the recognition accuracy data provided below, use SPSS to conduct the correct statistical test to analyze these data:

   • Video Discussion Watched: 67, 80, 69, 72, 75, 79, 66, 71, 69, 79

   • Video Summary Read: 80, 75, 65, 77, 60, 69, 73, 79, 71, 80

   • No Video Discussion/Summary Control: 78, 65, 79, 84, 88, 79, 89, 90, 85, 87

d. From the SPSS output you obtained, what can be concluded about the null hypothesis you stated?

e. Why should the researchers consider whether the order of the video conditions had an effect on recognition accuracy in this study?

Chapter 15

Correlation Tests and Simple Linear Regression

As you read the chapter, consider the following questions:

15.1 How do hypothesis tests differ across experiments and correlational studies?

15.2 What can you learn from testing relationships between measures?

15.3 What can you learn from conducting a regression analysis?

15.4 What does it mean to find the best-fit line for a set of data?

15.5 How much causal information can be gained from correlation and regression hypothesis tests?

In the chapters in this section of the text, I have described different types of hypothesis tests that are appropriate for experiments and quasi-experiments in which a researcher is comparing measures for different groups of participants or for the same participants under different conditions. In this chapter, we will consider how to test hypotheses for the other type of research study discussed in Chapter 1: correlational studies. Recall that in correlational studies, the goal is to examine the relationship between two (or more) measures of behavior to determine whether the measures change together or whether one can predict the other. For example, colleges and universities use test scores from high school students (e.g., the SAT or ACT) to predict how well those students will perform in college to decide who to admit. This prediction can be made because test scores and college grade point average were found to be related in studies looking at the relationship between these measures. I do something similar when I am recruiting students to serve as teaching assistants for my courses: I assume that the scores on exams in my course are related to how much knowledge a student has of the material in the course (an important quality in a teaching assistant) and ask students who have earned high exam scores to be teaching assistants. Correlational studies can test whether these relationships exist and examine what kind of relationship (positive/negative, predictive) is present.

CORRELATION VERSUS CAUSATION

Correlational studies can help us test hypotheses about relationships between measured variables and whether the value for one measure can predict a value on another measure. However, we must be cautious about the conclusions we make from data collected in correlational studies. Experiments are designed to minimize other possible explanations for the results of the study besides the causal factor(s) tested in the study. In correlational studies, we cannot control for these other explanations as well as we can in experiments; thus, we cannot draw causal conclusions in correlational studies as well as we can in experiments. Correlational studies are designed to test if a relationship exists and, if so, what type of relationship. They can also tell us how we can predict one measure from another if a relationship exists. If we find evidence that a relationship exists, we must be careful not conclude one factor *caused* another to change, as we do when we conduct experiments. Causation from one factor to another may not exist or may be in a different direction than we think it is. This sort of error is easy to make from research results presented in the media. If we hear that a study showed a link between drinking a lot of coffee and certain types of cancers, we might be tempted to conclude that drinking a lot of coffee can cause cancer. However, there are other types of relationships that could exist to produce the relationship reported in the study. It's possible that people who are developing cancer already drink a lot of coffee because it eases their symptoms. This would mean that the causal relationship is in the opposite direction to what we first concluded: Developing cancer

Figure 15.1   Some Possible Relationships Between Drinking Coffee and Developing Cancer

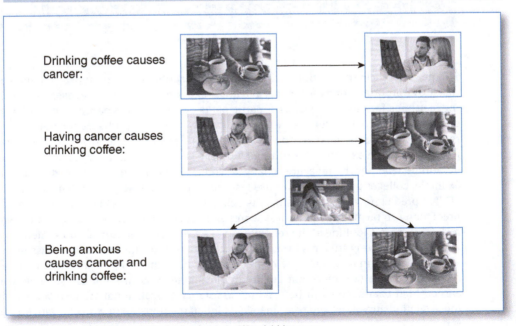

©iStock/KatarzynaBialasiewicz, ©iStock/elenaleonova, ©iStock/shironosov

causes one to drink a lot of coffee, not the other way around. It could also be that something else causes both things to happen. Perhaps people who are generally anxious drink a lot of coffee and are also more likely to develop certain types of cancer (e.g., due to chronic inflammation). In this case, it is the high level of anxiety that causes both the drinking of a lot of coffee and cancer, meaning that these factors are not directly related in a causal way. Instead, they are both related to a third factor that causes both of them. Figure 15.1 illustrates these different types of relationships, showing that correlations do not always mean causation.

Statistical Relationships

In Chapter 7, we first examined a flowchart for statistical test decisions in inferential tests (Figure 7.8). In the past several chapters, we focused on tests that compared means in the left portion of this chart. In this chapter, we are focusing on tests for relationships in the right portion of the chart. Figure 15.2 shows the right portion from Figure 7.8 for tests designed to examine relationships between variables. This section of the chart is separated according to the type of scale the data

Figure 15.2 Portion of the Statistical Test Decision Flowchart for Testing Relationships

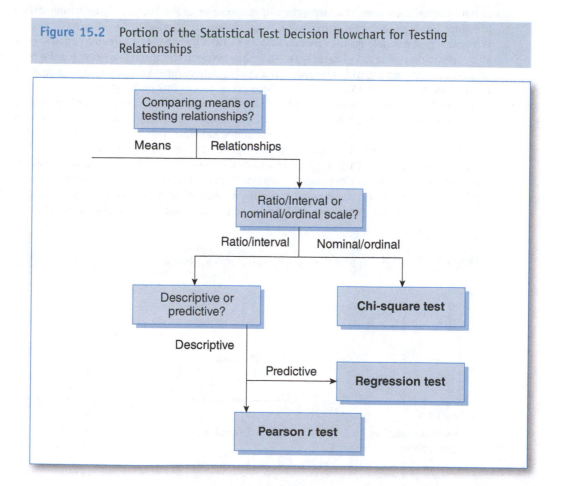

for a study are measured on: ratio/interval or nominal/ordinal. This chapter will examine tests used for ratio/interval data. Chapter 16 will examine a common test that can be used for nominal/ordinal data.

Recall that ratio/interval data involve numerical responses or measures that are equally spaced on the scale. In many cases, these scales are also continuous scales of measurement in which the units of measure can be divided into smaller and smaller units (e.g., distance can be in yards or meters and then divided into feet, and further divided into inches or centimeters, etc.). The *t* tests and ANOVAs used for comparing means are also appropriate for ratio/interval data, as discussed in the previous chapters in this section of the text, but when testing relationships with interval/ratio data, a common inferential test used is the Pearson *r* test. You will see this test listed in the chart in Figure 15.2 if you follow the decision tree down through the ratio/interval data to the descriptive branch. The Pearson *r* is a value between −1.0 and +1.0 that indicates the size and direction of a relationship between two numerical measures. The larger the numerical value of the Pearson *r*, the stronger the relationship. The sign of the Pearson *r* value indicates the direction of the relationship, where +1.0 is the strongest possible positive relationship and −1.0 is the strongest possible negative relationship. A Pearson *r* of zero indicates no relationship between the variables. Note that the relationship we are considering with a Pearson *r* is a linear relationship—you can imagine a straight line running through Figure 15.2 that comes close to the data points in this graph.

Pearson *r* test: a significance test used to determine whether a linear relationship exists between two variables measured on interval or ratio scales

Figure 15.3 presents example graphs of three different relationships. A graph of data points that can show the relationship between two variables is presented with one measure on the *x*-axis and the other measure on the y-axis and is called a *scatterplot*. Scatterplots were first introduced in Chapter 6. The scatterplots in Figure 15.3 show relationships with the Pearson *r*s of −1.0, 0, and +1.0. Each scatterplot shows a different possible relationship between two measures. The first is a perfect negative relationship. It shows that each data point (a data point represents the scores on the two measures for an individual in the sample) follows a straight line descending down from the top left of the graph. The middle graph shows no relationship.

Figure 15.3   Three Types of Relationships Between Measures

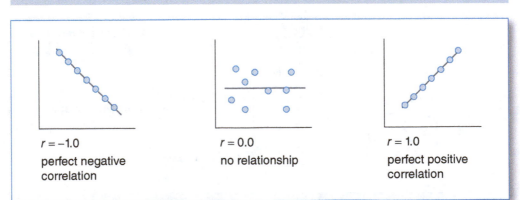

$r = -1.0$
perfect negative correlation

$r = 0.0$
no relationship

$r = 1.0$
perfect positive correlation

The data points do not cluster in any systematic way; they are spread across the whole graph. The last graph shows a perfect positive relationship. It is similar to the first graph, but the straight line ascends from the bottom left to the top right. Most data sets, however, will look like something in-between these graphs, either on the positive or negative side of $r = 0$.

Stop and Think

15.1 You read in a news article on the web about a study that found that older adults who exercise regularly are less likely to develop dementia (i.e., a decline in cognitive abilities) as they age. Describe three different types of causal relationships that could be present in this study's results. (Hint: Use Figure 15.1 as a model for the three types of causal relationships possible.)

15.2 For the scatterplot shown below, choose the most likely Pearson r value that describes the relationship in the graph:

  a $r = +0.85$

  b. $r = 0$

  c. $r = -0.80$

  d. $r = -0.15$

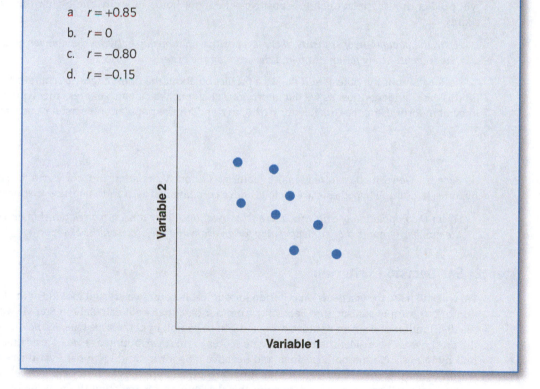

HYPOTHESIS TESTING WITH PEARSON r

Like the previous inferential statistics we have discussed, we can use Pearson r correlations to test hypotheses about relationships. We can complete our hypothesis-testing steps for hypotheses about relationships just as we did for hypotheses about mean differences. But for a correlational study, we will predict a relationship (and perhaps its direction) for our alternative hypothesis and no relationship (and possibly one in the opposite direction from the alternative hypothesis) for our null hypothesis. The data collected in our study will involve two measured variables collected from a group of individuals. A Pearson r test will be the inferential statistic calculated in Step 4, and it is based on a ratio of how much our two measured variables of interest change together versus how much they change in total. In other words, a Pearson r is a ratio of two different variability measures calculated from the two dependent variables in our data.

Let's begin our hypothesis testing with a hypothetical study looking at the relationship between the number of hours that students study for a final exam and their final exam scores.

Step 1: State Hypotheses

In Step 1, we will state our hypotheses for the relationship between hours of study and final exam scores. Our alternative hypothesis for this relationship will be one-tailed, because we will predict that the relationship is positive—the more hours of study, the higher the exam score:

H$_1$: *In the population of students, there is a positive relationship between the number of hours that students study for an exam and the score on the exam.*

Notice that our hypothesis still makes a prediction about the population we're interested in (in this case, students), just as we did in previous chapters. We can also express the hypothesis in symbol form using the Greek letter ρ (rho) to stand for the population Pearson r correlation value:

$\rho_{students} > 0$

Because we've made a directional hypothesis (a positive relationship) for our alternative hypothesis, our null hypothesis will include both a correlation of zero and a negative relationship:

H$_0$: *In the population of students, there is no relationship or a negative relationship between the number of hours that students study for an exam and the score on the exam or* $\rho_{students} \leq 0$.

Step 2: Set Decision Criterion

We will still need to set a decision criterion for our test because we are still looking at the location of our sample statistic (the Pearson r from our data that we'll calculate in Step 4) within the distribution of Pearson r values expected when the null hypothesis is true. As we did with the t test, we will consider the most extreme scores in this distribution as evidence against the null hypothesis (within both positive and negative tails for a nondirectional hypothesis and within either the positive or negative tail for a directional hypothesis). If our alpha level is set at 0.05, this will create critical regions in this distribution for rejecting the null hypothesis. However, unlike the distribution of sample means, the distribution of r values will stop at values of +1.0 on the high end and −1.0 on the low end because r cannot be a value beyond +1.0 or −1.0. Thus, the shape will be a bit different but will still depend on the sample size in our study. We will still use a table of critical values (see Appendix E) to compare with our calculated Pearson r in Step 5.

Remember that the logic of our hypothesis test is to consider the probability of obtaining the data in our study if the null hypothesis is true (i.e., there is no relationship between the variables). That is what we are measuring with the p value that comes from the test. A Pearson r test will provide the same kind of p value that our previous tests provided, giving us the probability of obtaining our data when the null hypothesis is true. If this p value is low enough (i.e., at our chosen alpha level or lower), we will use that as evidence against the null hypothesis.

Step 3: Collect Sample Data

To make the calculations for this example easier to understand, let's consider a sample size of only $n = 5$ for this study. It would certainly be better to test our hypothesis with a larger sample size, but for our hand calculations, we will look at five data points. The measures for the number of hours studied and exam score variables from our five study participants are as follows:

	Number of Hours Studied	Final Exam Score
Subject #1	6	96
Subject #2	1	72
Subject #3	5	88
Subject #4	3	72
Subject #5	3	78

To calculate the Pearson r statistic in Step 4, we will need to know some of the descriptive statistics for this data set. Specifically, we will need the means for each variable so that we can calculate the sum of squared deviations for the variables and a new measure known as the **sum of products**. The sum of products is the product (i.e., multiplication) of the deviations from the mean for each measure, summed across all the participants in the study. We will calculate these values in Step 4, but for now, we just need the means for the two measures:

---- ⚜ ----

Sum of products: The sum of the products of the squared deviations from the mean of the scores for each variable

---

$$M_{HoursStudied} = 3.6 \text{ hours}; \; M_{ExamScore} = 81.2$$

Figure 15.4 shows a scatterplot of these data. In this figure, the data points are closely clustered together and slope up toward the top right of the graph, indicating a strong positive relationship between the variables.

Step 4: Calculate Statistics

As with the other inferential statistics, the Pearson r value is a ratio of variance terms. It is the calculation of the sum of products (SP) divided by the square root of the product of the individual sums of squares for each variable (SS_x and SS_y). In other words,

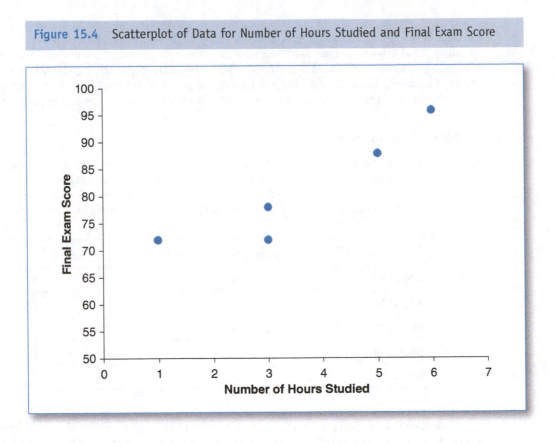

Figure 15.4 Scatterplot of Data for Number of Hours Studied and Final Exam Score

$$r = \frac{SP}{\sqrt{SS_X SS_Y}}$$

where *SP* is the sum of products, SS_x is the sum of squared deviations for one of the dependent variables (the one that appears on the *x*-axis of a scatterplot), and SS_y is the sum of squared deviations for the other dependent variable (the one that appears on the *y*-axis of a scatterplot). If we are interested in predicting one variable from the other (e.g., predicting the final exam score using the number of hours studied score), then the variable that predicts is our *X* variable (also called the *predictor variable*) and the one being predicted is our *Y* variable (also called the *response variable*).

Now, let's begin our calculations using the data and means presented in Step 3. We will start with the SS_x and SS_y terms because these are values we have calculated in past chapters and should be familiar to you. SS_x is the sum of squared deviations for our *X* variable: number of hours studied.

$$SS_X = \left[(6-3.6)^2 + (1-3.6)^2 + (5-3.6)^2 + (3-3.6)^2 + (3-3.6)^2\right]$$
$$= [5.76 + 6.76 + 1.96 + .36 + .36] = 15.2$$

and

$$SS_Y = \left[(96-81.2)^2 + (72-81.2)^2 + (88-81.2)^2 + (72-81.2)^2 + (78-81.2)^2\right]$$
$$= [219.04 + 84.64 + 46.24 + 84.64 + 10.24] = 444.8$$

These terms will make up the denominator of the Pearson r value. Now we just need our sum of products term. We will also use the deviations from the mean for SP, but we will multiply these for each subject across the variables, instead of squaring them as we did in the sum of squares.

$$SP = \left[\begin{matrix}(6-3.6)(96-81.2) + (1-3.6)(72-81.2) + (5-3.6)(88-81.2) + \\ (3-3.6)(72-81.2) + (3-3.6)(78-81.2)\end{matrix}\right]$$
$$= \left[(2.4)(14.8) + (-2.6)(-9.2) + (1.4)(6.8) + (-.6)(-9.2) + (-.6)(-3.2)\right]$$
$$= [35.53 + 23.92 + 9.52 + 5.52 + 1.92] = +76.41$$

Notice that the SP term is positive in this case. If you examine the details of the calculation above, you may notice that if the individual terms can also be negative (they are products, not squares). Because we are calculating products for SP, it can be a negative value. Thus, the SP term will determine whether the Pearson r is a positive value, representing a positive relationship, or a negative value, representing a negative relationship.

Now we are ready to calculate the Pearson r using our SP, SS_X, and SS_Y values.

$$r = \frac{SP}{\sqrt{SS_X SS_Y}} = \frac{+76.41}{\sqrt{(15.2)(444.8)}} = \frac{+76.41}{\sqrt{6760.96}} = \frac{+76.41}{82.22} = +.93$$

The Pearson $r = +0.93$ indicates a rather strong positive relationship between number of hours studied and final exam score. But we still need to complete Step 5 to decide if we have evidence against the null hypothesis that the relationship between these variables is negative or does not exist in the population of students. The last value we need to calculate in Step 4 to assist us in Step 5 is the degrees of freedom. For a Pearson r correlation, $df = n - 2$. This is because we use up one degree of freedom for each variable in the calculation its mean. For this calculation, remember that n refers to the number of subjects per group. We only have one group of subjects in this study, with each dependent variable measured once from each subject. Thus, $N = n = 5$ so $df = 5 - 2 = 3$. Now we are ready for Step 5, in which we will make the decision to reject or retain the null hypothesis.

Step 5: Make a Decision

To complete our test, we need to find the Pearson r critical value for our one-tailed test with $\alpha = 0.05$. Appendix E contains the critical values for a Pearson r with separate columns for different alpha levels and whether we are conducting a one- or two-tailed test. Rows in this appendix indicate critical values based on degrees of freedom. With a one-tailed test and $\alpha = 0.05$, we will look in the first column of the appendix. The row for $df = 3$ shows a critical r value of ± 0.805. Our calculated r of $+0.93$ is higher than this critical value, indicating that our calculated r is in the critical region. Thus, we can reject the null hypothesis and conclude that there is a positive relationship between number of hours studied and final exam score, as we predicted.

USING SPSS TO CONDUCT A PEARSON *r* TEST

We can also use SPSS to conduct a Pearson *r* hypothesis test. Let's consider a new example in this section. Suppose we were interested in the relationship between age and memory ability. To measure this relationship, we give a sample of participants a task to mail a postcard back to us in exactly five days. We measure the age in years for each participant and then measure the number of days late that the postcard was mailed based on the postmark on the postcards we receive (with a score of zero days late if the card is mailed on time). These data are shown in Table 15.1. To conduct a Pearson *r* test using SPSS, we will enter the age and memory data into the data window as they appear in Table 15.1. Thus, the data window should contain two columns of data: age in years and number of days the postcard was late for each participant.

Table 15.1   Data for Age/Memory Example

Participant No.	Age	Number of Days
1	81	1
2	77	0
3	69	0
4	73	2
5	89	0
6	67	1
7	65	1
8	70	0
9	78	2
10	75	0
11	21	3
12	18	10
13	19	8
14	24	7
15	20	5
16	21	8
17	22	7
18	18	6
19	19	7
20	20	9

To run the Pearson r test, choose the Bivariate test in the Correlate option of the Analyze menu. Click the two variables into the Variables box. The Pearson r test box should be clicked. You can also choose to conduct either a two-tailed test (either a positive or negative relationship is predicted) or a one-tailed test if the prediction is for a specific type (positive or negative) of relationship. Two-tailed tests are the default, so you will need to click the other box to change to a one-tailed test in those cases. We will conduct a two-tailed test for these data to consider both a positive and a negative relationship that might exist between age and this memory ability, so no change is needed for this example. Click OK to run the test. The Correlations box in the output (see Figure 15.5) indicates the Pearson r value (the sign indicates the direction of relationship) in the first row and the p value in the second row. For our example, the variables are significantly related (negatively) with $r = -0.90$ and $p < 0.001$. In other words, in this study as age increased, the number of days it took participants to remember to mail the card decreased. Thus, the older the participant was, the closer they remembered to mail the postcard to the date requested.

Summary of Steps

- Enter the data in the data window with each measure in a separate column.
- Choose the Correlate option from the Analyze menu.
- Select the Bivariate test from the test choices.
- Click each of your measured variables over to the Variables box (you can click more than two variables at once if you have more than two to analyze).
- Click the Pearson test box to select this test.
- The default is a two-tailed test, so if you have a one-tailed test, click that option in the window.
- Click OK to run the test; the Pearson r and associated p value will appear in the Output Window (see Figure 15.5).

Figure 15.5 SPSS Output for a Pearson r Test

➡ **Correlations**

Correlations

		Age in Years	Number of Days Late
Age in Years	Pearson Correlation	1	-.900[**]
	Sig. (2–tailed)		.000
	N	20	20
Number of Days Late	Pearson Correlation	-.900[**]	1
	Sig. (2–tailed)	.000	
	N	20	20

[**]. Correlation is significant at the 0.01 level (2–tailed).

Stop and Think

15.3 For a correlational study looking at the relationship between mood score and outside high temperature recorded on a particular day, we find $r(58) = -0.75$, $p = 0.002$. With this test result, what can we conclude about the relationship between mood and weather temperature? Looking at the statistics reported, from how many subjects was mood measured in this study?

15.4 For the data presented below, conduct a Pearson r test to determine if a significant relationship exists between the variables. If there is a significant relationship, indicate if the relationship is positive or negative.

Student's Grade Point Average: 3.56, 2.79, 3.01, 3.95, 4.00, 2.90, 3.35, 3.67, 3.77, 3.30, 2.75, 3.04

Number of Hours Spent Playing Video Games per Week: 12, 25, 45, 15, 20, 50, 16, 25, 40, 15, 40, 20

REGRESSION ANALYSES

If your goal is to predict a score on one variable from the score on another, regression will help you do that (see Figure 15.2 for predictive relationships). Regression analyses will provide the equation for the line that best fits the data. If you consider the data presented in the scatterplot in Figure 15.4, you can imagine a straight line passing through these data points that is as close as possible to all the data points in the graph. A regression analysis will give us the equation for that line.

We will use some of the same calculations we conducted for our Pearson r calculation to find the equation for the best-fit line to our data. Our equation is based on the equation of a line, which is $Y = X(slope) + intercept$, where Y is a score on the Y variable, X is a score on the X variable, $slope$ is the amount of slant of the line (steeper slant = higher slope value), and the $intercept$ is the value of Y where the line crosses the y-axis. This equation is often expressed as $Y = Xb + a$, such that a is the intercept and b is the slope. Because the X and Y values are the scores on the variables we measured, we do not need to calculate these values for our equation, but we do need to calculate values for a and b using our data to find the equation. The values for both a and b will depend on the strength and direction of the linear relationship between the two measured variables. As an example of how to calculate these values, we will go back to the example looking at number of hours studied and final exam score.

Slope

The first part of the equation we will calculate is the slope. This calculation is based on the ratio of the sum of products term and sum of squared deviations for the X variable (our predictor variable). Thus, the slope for the best-fit line equation to predict final exam score from the number of hours studied is

$$b = \frac{SP}{SS_X} = \frac{+76.41}{15.2} = 5.03$$

Note that if the *SP* term is positive, the slope will be positive and the line will slant up to the right, but if the *SP* term is negative, the slope will be negative and the line will slant down to the right.

Intercept

Now that we have calculated the slope value, we can use it and the means of the *X* and *Y* variables to calculate the intercept where the line will cross the *y*-axis. We will use the equation

$$a = \bar{Y} - b\bar{X} = 81.2 - (5.03)(3.6) = 81.2 - 18.11 = 63.09$$

This means the line equation for the best-fit line to our data is

$$Y = 5.03X + 63.09$$

This line will pass through the means for the *X* and *Y* variables on our scatterplot and show the line that best describes the linear relationship between number of hours studied and final exam score (see Figure 15.6).

Figure 15.6 Scatterplot of Number of Hours Studied and Final Exam Score Data With Best-Fit Line

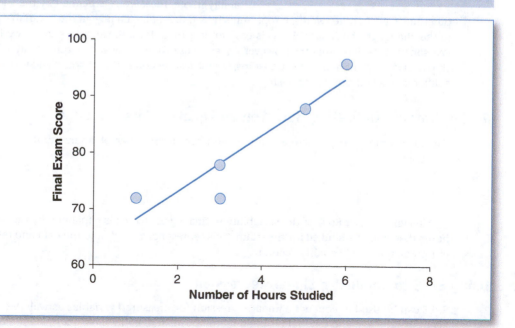

To show you how this is useful, suppose you wanted to use this equation to predict our exam based on how many hours you planned to study for the exam. You want to do well on the exam, but you need time to study for two other exams that same week, so you want to make sure your planned study time in optimal. Your plan is to study for six hours for the exam; what score do you expect to receive with this amount of study? We can calculate a predicted score using the equation we found: $Y = 5.03X + 63.09$. To make the prediction, you need to enter in the hours you plan to study as X in the equation (this is the predictor variable):

$$Y = 5.03(6) + 63.09 = 30.18 + 63.09 = 93.27$$

Using this equation, you can predict you will get about 93% on the exam, so six hours of study should be enough for you to get an A.

R^2 Fit Statistic

We have the equation for the best-fit line that we can use to predict the value of our Y variable (the response variable) from a value of our X variable (the predictor variable). But how accurate will our prediction be? This depends on how well the best-fit line fits (gets close to) the data points. If the line gets very close to the data points, our prediction will be good, but if the data points are spread out across the graph and our line does not get very close to all of them, then our prediction may not be very accurate. Thus, when we conduct a linear regression, it is important to look at an accuracy measure of how well the best-fit line fits the data so we will know how accurate our predictions will be. A fit statistic can help us determine the accuracy of our best-fit line. For linear regression, we can use R^2 as the fit statistic. R^2 is a measure of how much of the variability in one measure is explained by the value of the other measure. In other words, it represents how much of the change in the Y variable is related to the change in the X variable. R^2 is easy to determine for a linear regression if we know the Pearson r value—it is simply r^2. However, R^2 can be used as a fit statistic for other kinds of relationships as well (e.g., nonlinear relationships; see the last section in this chapter) and is calculated in a different way for those relationships.

❧

R^2: fit statistic indicating how well an equation fits the data

R^2: Fit Statistic Indicating How Well an Equation Fits the Data

For our example for predicting exam score from the number of hours studied using linear regression,

$$R^2 = (.93)^2 = .86$$

This tells us that 86% of the variability in final exam scores is explained by the number of hours that students studied for the exam. This represents a good fit to the data and tells us that our predictions will be fairly accurate.

Using SPSS to Conduct a Linear Regression

SPSS can be used to conduct a linear regression for measured variables as well. We will once again use the age and days late in mailing the postcard data in Table 15.1 as our example. To determine the best-fit line for these data using SPSS, we will use the Regression option in the Analyze menu. We will choose the Linear option from Regression and then define our X and Y variables by clicking them over to the boxes. In this example, we want use age to predict the number of days late the postcard was mailed, so age will be the X or independent variable (predictor variable) and number of days late will be the Y or dependent variable (response variable) for this analysis. We can click these variables into the boxes and then click OK to run the analysis.

Several sets of boxes appear in the Output Window for our linear regression (see Figure 15.7) so we will need to find the pieces we need to build our linear equation. Remember that our line equation is $Y = Xb + a$, so we need to find the slope (b) and the intercept (a) in the output. Both values are listed in the last box under B for Unstandardized Coefficients. The slope is listed in the line with the variable Age in Years (-0.113) and the intercept is listed in the row labeled Constant (9.209). With these values, we can state our best-fit line equation as

$$Y = -.113X + 9.209$$

This equation will allow us to predict the number of days late for the postcard mailing using the subject's age in years. However, we do not yet know how accurate our prediction will be—we need to also look at the R^2 value to know how much of the variability in days late is explained by the subject's age. We can find the R^2 value in the Model Summary box at the top of the Output under R Square: 0.811. This value is quite high, so our prediction will be fairly accurate, although R^2 values of 0.90 and higher are generally preferred to ensure good accuracy in our predictions.

Figure 15.7   SPSS Output for Linear Regression

Model Summary

Model	R	R Square	Adjusted R Square	Std. Error of the Estimate
1	.900[a]	.811	.800	1.59066

a. Predictors: (Constant), Age in Years

ANOVA[a]

Model		Sum of Squares	df	Mean Square	F	Sig.
1	Regression	195.006	1	195.006	77.071	.000[b]
	Residual	45.544	18	2.530		
	Total	240.550	19			

a. Dependent Variable: Number of Days Late
b. Predictors: (Constant), Age in Years

Coefficients[a]

Model		Unstandardized Coefficients B	Std. Error	Standardized Coefficients Beta	t	Sig.
1	(Constant)	9.209	.707		13.035	.000
	Age in Years	-.113	.013	-.900	-8.779	.000

a. Dependent Variable: Number of Days Late

Summary of Steps

- Enter the data in the data window with each measured variable in a separate column.
- Choose the Regression option in the Analyze menu.
- Select the Linear type of relationship from the list.
- Click your predictor (X) variable into the Independent variable box.
- Click your response (Y) variable into the Dependent variable box.
- Click OK to run the analysis.
- Find the intercept labeled Constant and the slope labeled with the predictor variable in the Coefficients table of the Output Window; the R^2 will appear in the Model Summary table.

NONLINEAR RELATIONSHIPS

The analyses presented in this chapter examine linear relationships between measured variables. However, relationships between variables can exist that are not functionally linear. For example, suppose that in our study looking at the relationship between number of hours studied and final exam score, we had also measured the students' anxiety level with a 1 to 10 rating scale just before they took their final exam (higher ratings indicate more anxiety). With this additional variable of anxiety score, we can examine the relationship between anxiety level and final exam score to see if there is a relationship. Our data might look something like this:

	Anxiety Rating	Final Exam Score
Subject #1	5	96
Subject #2	1	72
Subject #3	7	88
Subject #4	10	72
Subject #5	2	78

You might notice in looking at these values that anxiety rating is not consistently increasing or decreasing with final score. Instead, it might look like there is no relationship. But let's look at a scatterplot of these data points shown in Figure 15.8. These data points look more like an inverted U shape than a straight line. Thus, a quadratic equation is likely a better fit to these data than a linear equation. In this case, a nonlinear regression would be better to conduct than a linear regression to examine the possibility of a nonlinear relationship. Looking at a scatterplot of your data is a good idea before deciding what kind of equation you want to fit to your data if you do not have a theoretical prediction about the form of the relationship before you start

Figure 15.8 Scatterplot of Anxiety Ratings and Final Exam Score Data

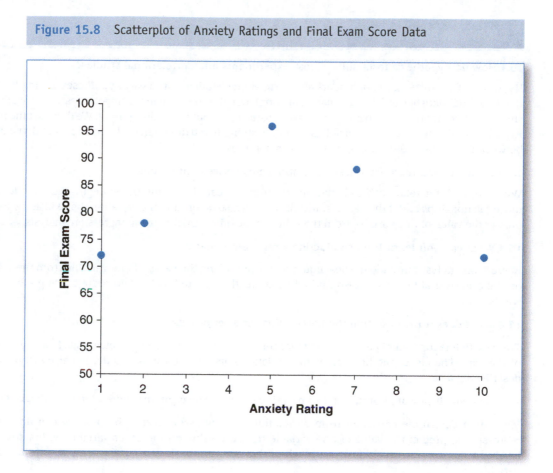

your study. However, this is only a starting place: You should not draw conclusions about the relationship or how well a function fits your data without first conducting a regression analysis and examining a fit statistic.

Calculation Summary

Sum of products: The sum of the products of the squared deviations from the mean of the scores for each variable

Pearson r: The sum of products divided by the square root of the product of the sum of squares of the X variable and the sum of squares of the Y variable

Slope: The sum of products divided by the sum of squares for the X variable

Intercept: The mean of the Y variable minus the slope times the mean of the X variable

CHAPTER SUMMARY

15.1 How do hypothesis tests differ across experiments and correlational studies?

Hypothesis tests differ for experiments and correlational studies in the way hypotheses are made and the inferential statistics that are calculated. In correlational studies, we make hypotheses about relationships and whether they are positive or negative instead of about mean differences. We then test the null hypothesis using tests designed to tell us about the strength and direction of the relationship that exists between two measured variables, such as a Pearson r test.

15.2 What can you learn from testing relationships between measures?

When we look for relationships between measures, we can determine the strength and direction of those relationships and if they are significant. We can also determine the equation that will allow us to predict the value of one variable from the value on the other variable using regression analysis.

15.3 What can you learn from conducting a regression analysis?

Regression analyses provide the best equation for predicting the value of one variable from the value on the other variable. We can also find a fit statistic that can tell us how accurate those predictions will be.

15.4 What does it mean to find the best-fit line for a set of data?

The best-fit line for a set of data is the line that comes the closest to the most data points in a scatterplot of the data. The closer the line comes to the data points overall, the better the linear equation will describe the data.

15.5 How much causal information can be gained from correlation and regression hypothesis tests?

We cannot determine causation from correlation and regression tests. The best we can do is use regression to predict the value of one variable from the value on the other variable with a specific level of accuracy. However, this does not tell us that one variable is *causing* the value the of the other variable.

THINKING ABOUT RESEARCH

A summary of a research study in psychology is given below. As you read the summary, think about the following questions:

1. Identify the dependent variables in this study that provided a test of the researchers' hypothesis.

2. What are the advantages and disadvantages of conducting this study as a correlational study instead of an experiment?

3. Based on the scatterplot and the Pearson r shown in Figure 15.9, is the relationship between the measures positive or negative? How do you know?

4. Using the reported sample size, an alpha level of 0.05, and Appendix E, determine if the Pearson r value shown in Figure 15.9 is significant or not.

5. Both of the measures in this study were based on self-reports from the participants. What are the disadvantages of using self-report measures in research?

Inzlicht, M., McKay, L., & Aronson, J. (2006). How being the target of prejudice affects self-control. *Psychological Science, 17,* 262–269.

Note: Study 1 from this article is described here.

Purpose of the Study. This study was designed to examine the relationship between stigma and one's sense of their own self-control. In Study 1, the researchers examined the correlation between one's sensitivity to race-based prejudice and self-reported self-regulation abilities in Black college students. They predicted that higher sensitivity to prejudice would be related to lower self-regulation ability.

Method of the Study. Black university students ($N = 38$) completed two surveys to measure sensitivity to race-based stigma and self-regulation abilities. The stigma sensitivity measure contained 12 scenarios describing situations with a negative outcome. Participants read each scenario and imagined themselves in the situation. They then rated how concerned they were and how likely it was that the outcome was

Figure 15.9   Scatterplot From the Inzlicht et al. (2006) Study

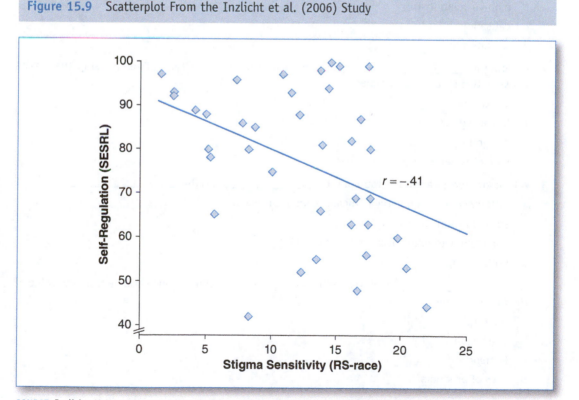

SOURCE: Inzlicht, McKay, & Aronson (2006). Stigma as ego depletion; How being the target of prejudice affects self-control. *Psychological Science, 17,* 262–269.

due to their race. The self-regulation measure contained 11 items for participants to rate concerning the confidence they had in their abilities (e.g., motivating themselves to do schoolwork, studying when there were other things to do, etc.).

Results of the Study. Figure 15.9 shows a scatterplot of the stigma sensitivity and self-regulation scores with the calculated Pearson *r* score.

Conclusions of the Study. The researchers concluded that Black college students who are more sensitive to race-based stigma also reported lower self-regulation abilities. Follow-up studies in this article also showed that students who had the race-based stigma activated showed reduced self-control in cognitive and motor control tasks.

TEST YOURSELF

1. In correlational studies, _____ is not as well-tested as it is in experiments.

    a. a relationship

    b. a linear relationship

    c. causation

    d. a scatterplot

2. Creating a _____ is a good way to view the type of relationship that exists between two measured variables.

    a. scatterplot

    b. linear regression

    c. bar graph

    d. sum of squares

3. A Pearson *r* correlation is a ratio of the _____ and the _____.

    a. difference between variable means, sum of products

    b. sum of products, scatterplot

    c. change in variables together, total variability

    d. both (a) and (c)

4. A _____ analysis can help you predict the value of one variable from the value of the other variable.

    a. scatterplot

    b. regression

    c. Pearson *r*

    d. sum of products

5. Which of the following is an appropriate null hypothesis for a Pearson r test?

   a. The means of the two variables do not differ in the population.

   b. There is no relationship between the two variables in the population.

   c. There is a negative relationship between the two variables in the sample.

   d. Both (b) and (c).

6. In a linear regression, the X variable is the _____ variable, and the Y variable is the _____ variable.

   a. predictor, dependent

   b. dependent, predictor

7. Finding a significant relationship between two variables in a correlational study tells you that one of the variables caused the change in the other variable, even though you do not know which variable was the causal factor.

   a. True

   b. False

8. A Pearson r of +0.85 indicates a strong, positive relationship between the dependent variables.

   a. True

   b. False

9. A linear regression can determine the best-fit line to the data.

   a. True

   b. False

10. Regression analyses can only determine if a relationship between variables is linear.

    a. True

    b. False

11. For the data below, determine if there is a significant correlation between the variables.

    Number of Books in One's Office: 155, 67, 25, 3, 80, 75, 15, 200, 67, 85, 55, 30

    Extraversion Score: 57, 97, 89, 40, 36, 98, 68, 75, 80, 43, 55, 85

12. A study reported $r(98) = 0.32$. Is this a significant correlation? How do you know?

Chapter 16

Chi-Square Tests

As you read the chapter, consider the following questions:

16.1 What is the difference between a parametric and a nonparametric test?

16.2 What does it mean that a nonparametric test is less powerful than a parametric test?

16.3 How can we test relationships across categorical variables?

16.4 What is the expected frequency?

16.5 What does a chi-square test tell us about relationships between categorical variables?

Figure 16.1 once again shows the portion of the Statistical Test Decision Flowchart (first seen in Figure 7.8) for testing relationships. In Chapter 15, we discussed the tests designed for descriptive and predictive relationships between variables measured on ratio and interval scales of measurement. In this chapter, we will examine a common test used for relationships between categorical variables measured on nominal and ordinal scales: a chi-square test.

Imagine that we are interested in whether class standing and grade in a class are related. This could be helpful in knowing which year it is best to take a specific required course. If, for example, juniors and seniors get higher grades than freshmen and sophomores, perhaps it is best to take the class in one's later years in college. But in this case, class standing and grade (i.e., A, B, C, D, F) are not continuous variables measured in numbers. Instead, they are ordinal variables with categorical levels. Thus, the Pearson r and linear regression tests we discussed in Chapter 15 will not be the best tests to examine the relationship we want to know about. A quick look at Figure 16.1 shows that a chi-square test is one we can use to test relationships between these variables.

❧

Chi-square (χ^2) test: a significance test used to determine whether a relationship exists between two variables measured on nominal and ordinal scales

---

Figure 16.1 Portion of the Statistical Test Decision Flowchart for Testing Relationships

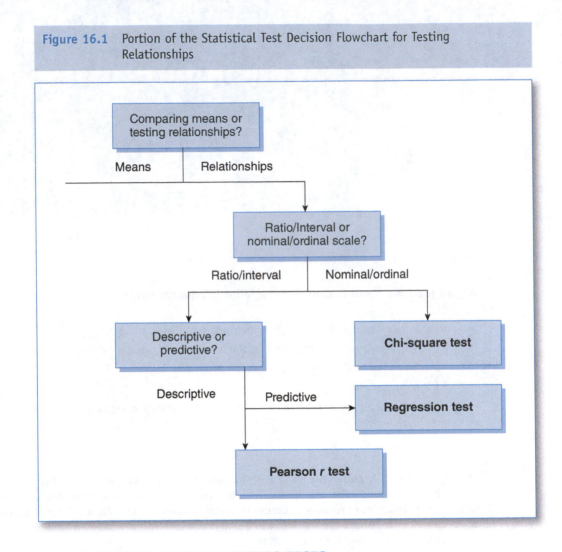

PARAMETRIC VERSUS NONPARAMETRIC TESTS

Nonparametric test: an inferential statistics test that can be used to test hypotheses about categorical variables

Parametric test: an inferential statistics test that can be used to test hypotheses about continuous variables

The chi-square test is what is known as a nonparametric test to set it apart from the tests used for continuous variables (called parametric tests). Parametric tests are the tests we have discussed in this text so far that involve calculations on numerical data. If data are not in numerical form but instead involve categories, these calculations cannot be computed (primarily because the distributions will not be normal in shape, as required by the assumptions for these tests). Thus, for categorical variables, we need a different kind of test—a nonparametric test. For nonparametric tests, the data are typically in the form of frequencies for different categories on a variable, such as how many students in the class were juniors and how many students earned an *A* grade. They are useful when we want to test hypotheses about categorical variables. However, they are not as powerful as parametric tests, so they should only be used when necessary. Recall that *power* is the ability to detect an effect or relationship when one exists in the population. In other words, when the power of a test is reduced, we are less likely to obtain a significant relationship, even if the relationship exists. This means our Type II error (the chance of retaining the null hypothesis when it is false) is higher for nonparametric tests. Therefore, we may need to conduct several tests to detect a relationship that exists for categorical variables.

Stop and Think

16.1 For each set of variables below, indicate if a parametric or a nonparametric test is more appropriate to examine the relationship between the variables:

- Percentage grade on final exam and number of hours of sleep the night before the exam

- Students' expected letter grade in a course and the actual grade in the course

- Preference rank of five different campus activities (e.g., 1st, 2nd, 3rd, etc.) and major in college

- Score on a depression questionnaire (out of 100) and course satisfaction ratings (on a scale of 1 to 5)

16.2 Explain why we cannot calculate the mean and standard deviation for scores on a categorical variable.

OBSERVED VERSUS EXPECTED FREQUENCIES

The chi-square test will examine the relationship between categorical variables in terms of what frequencies are expected if there is no relationship between the variables (i.e., the null hypothesis). These expected frequencies are then compared to the frequencies observed in the data collected from the sample in our study to determine if the expected and observed frequencies differ significantly. If they do, then the null hypothesis is rejected and you can conclude that a relationship exists between the variables.

Let's consider the expected frequencies for the class standing and grade example. Table 16.1 shows the cells for each possible combination of these two variables. We will fill in each cell with the frequency we would expect if there is no relationship between class standing and grade in the class. To calculate the expected frequencies ($f_{Expected}$), we first need to examine the data collected. Suppose there are 200 people in the course and we obtain their class standing and course grades from the Registrar's Office on campus (with identifying information removed, of course). The data in the form of observed frequencies ($f_{Observed}$) are shown in the

Table 16.1   Table of Cells for Class Standing and Grade in the Class

Grade/Class Standing	Freshman	Sophomore	Junior	Senior
A				
B				
C				
D				
F				

cells in Table 16.2. We will need the row and columns total frequencies for the calculations of expected frequencies; these totals are also shown in Table 16.2.

To calculate the expected frequencies, we will use the formula

$$f_{Expected} = \frac{f_{column} f_{row}}{n}$$

where f_{column} is the column total for that cell and f_{row} is the row total for that cell. With this formula, we can calculate the expected frequency for each cell in Table 16.1. For example, the $f_{Expected}$ for Freshman/A is

$$f_{Expected} = \frac{50(30)}{200} = \frac{1500}{200} = 7.5$$

Table 16.2   Table of Observed Frequencies for Class Standing and Grade in the Class in the Sample

Grade/Class Standing	Freshman	Sophomore	Junior	Senior	Row Totals
A	3	6	10	11	30
B	21	20	25	4	70
C	12	15	15	18	60
D	8	6	6	5	25
F	6	3	4	2	15
Column Totals	**50**	**50**	**60**	**40**	**200**

Table 16.3 Table of Expected Frequencies for Class Standing and Grade in the Class if There Is No Relationship Between These Variables

Grade/Class Standing	Freshman	Sophomore	Junior	Senior
A	7.5	7.5	9	6
B	17.5	17.5	21	14
C	15	15	18	12
D	6.25	6.25	7.5	5
F	3.75	3.75	4.5	3

This $f_{Expected}$ will be placed in the first cell of the expected frequency table (see Table 16.3). Using this formula, we can calculate the rest of the $f_{Expected}$ values to complete Table 16.3. Note that the expected frequencies for the Freshman and Sophomore columns are identical because the column totals for these columns are the same. We will use the observed and expected frequencies to calculate the chi-square statistic in Step 4 of our hypothesis test in the next section.

CALCULATING A CHI-SQUARE BY HAND

Even though the chi-square test is a nonparametric test, we can still conduct a hypothesis test using this statistic. The five steps of hypothesis testing will still apply. However, we will not consider a population parameter (e.g., μ, ρ) in our hypotheses because there are no parameters to estimate from our sample (e.g., sample means) in a nonparametric test. Instead, the hypotheses will simply be stated in terms of whether a relationship exists between the variables or not.

Step 1: State Hypotheses

As I mentioned in the previous section, the null hypothesis will predict no relationship between the variables. The alternative hypothesis will predict a relationship. If we find a significant difference between the expected and observed frequencies (calculated using the chi-square statistic), we can reject the null hypothesis. Thus, our null hypothesis is

H_0: *In the population of students, there is no relationship between class standing and the letter grade in the course.*

Our alternative hypothesis is

H_1: *In the population of students, there is a relationship between class standing and the letter grade in the course.*

Step 2: Set Decision Criterion

Like the other inferential statistics, the chi-square statistic has a distribution of values when the null hypothesis is true with a different shape based on the degrees of freedom. It cannot be negative; therefore, there is only a tail of extreme values on the positive end of the distribution, as with the F statistic. The critical region will be located in this positive tail bounded by the critical chi-square value determined by the degrees of freedom in our study. The size of this region is still based on the chosen alpha level. As with our previous tests, we will choose an alpha level of 0.05, setting the size of the critical region at 5% of the chi-square distribution.

Step 3: Collect Sample Data

We have already completed Step 3 for our example in the previous section (looking at expected versus observed frequencies). Our observed frequencies (i.e., our data) are shown in Table 16.2 and our calculated expected frequencies are shown in Table 16.3. We will use these frequencies to calculate our chi-square statistic in Step 4.

Step 4: Calculate Statistics

The chi-square statistic is calculated from the sum of the squared differences between the observed and expected frequencies divided by the expected frequencies. In other words, it uses the squared deviations between the frequencies divided by the frequency expected by chance when the null hypothesis is true. This is very similar to the ratios we calculated in our parametric tests, so it is based on the same logic as those tests. The formula is

$$\chi^2 = \Sigma \frac{\left(f_{Observed} - f_{Expected}\right)^2}{f_{Expected}}$$

From Tables 16.2 and 16.3, we can insert the frequencies for each cell.

$$\chi^2 = \Sigma \frac{\left(f_{Observed} - f_{Expected}\right)^2}{f_{Expected}}$$

$$= \left[\frac{(3-7.5)^2}{7.5}\right] + \left[\frac{(21-17.5)^2}{17.5}\right] + \left[\frac{(12-15)^2}{15}\right] + \left[\frac{(8-6.25)^2}{6.25}\right]$$

$$+ \left[\frac{(6-3.75)^2}{3.75}\right] + \left[\frac{(6-7.5)^2}{7.5}\right] + \left[\frac{(20-17.5)^2}{17.5}\right] + \left[\frac{(15-15)^2}{15}\right]$$

$$+ \left[\frac{(6-6.25)^2}{6.25}\right] + \left[\frac{(3-3.75)^2}{3.75}\right] + \left[\frac{(10-9)^2}{9}\right] + \left[\frac{(25-21)^2}{21}\right] + \left[\frac{(15-18)^2}{18}\right]$$

$$+ \left[\frac{(6-7.5)^2}{7.5}\right] + \left[\frac{(4-4.5)^2}{4.5}\right] + \left[\frac{(11-6)^2}{6}\right] + \left[\frac{(4-14)^2}{14}\right] + \left[\frac{(18-12)^2}{12}\right]$$

$$+ \left[\frac{(5-5)^2}{5}\right] + \left[\frac{(2-3)^2}{3}\right]$$

$$= 2.7 + .7 + .6 + .49 + 1.35 + .3 + .36 + 0 + .01 + .15 + .11 + .76 + .5 + .3$$

$$+ .06 + 4.17 + 7.14 + 3 + 0 + .33 = 23.03$$

We also need to calculate degrees of freedom to find the $\chi^2_{critical}$ value in Step 5. The degrees of freedom for a chi-square test depend on the number of columns and rows:

$$df = (\#Columns - 1)(\#Rows - 1) = (4-1)(5-1) = 3(4) = 12$$

With $df = 12$ and our $\alpha = 0.05$, we can move on to Step 5 to find the critical value and make a decision.

Step 5: Make a Decision

To complete our chi-square test, we need to find the $\chi^2_{critical}$ for 12 degrees of freedom and alpha level of 0.05. We will compare our calculated χ^2 to the $\chi^2_{critical}$. Appendix F contains the chi-square critical values. In this case, $\chi^2_{critical} = 21.03$, and our calculated $\chi^2 = 23.03$ [for APA style, include the df and N as well: $\chi^2(1, N = 200) = 23.03$]. This means our calculated χ^2 is in the critical region (our calculated value is larger), and we can reject the null hypothesis. For this example, we can conclude that class standing and grade in the class are related. If we look back at Tables 16.2 and 16.3, we can examine where the observed and expected frequencies differ to determine the characteristics of the relationship: More As were earned by seniors and fewer were earned by freshmen and sophomores than expected if there is no relationship between class standing and grade. This tells us that students taking the class as a senior tended to earn As more often than students who were freshmen and sophomores. But remember, this is a correlation and does not tell us that class standing has a causal relationship to grade earned. Other characteristics of the students may have cause them to take the class later in their college careers and earn higher grades.

CALCULATING A CHI-SQUARE USING SPSS

Like the other tests conducted in previous chapters, SPSS can calculate a chi-square test for you. Because the data are category frequencies, you need to enter those categories in as your data in the data window to run the test. If you have two variables to compare, each row will contain two category labels, one for each variable. Consider the example included in Chapter 15 that examined the variables of age and days late returning a postcard. Suppose that instead of continuous variables of age in years, we simply grouped the participants into two groups: younger and older adults. We could also consider accuracy of returning the postcard as a categorical variable—either they mailed the postcard on time or they did not (see Table 16.4). With these categorical variables, we can use a chi-square test to examine the relationship.

The data window in SPSS would be organized by variable columns with these categories. Table 16.4 shows the categorical data for this example. To run the chi-square analysis, choose the Crosstabs option in the Descriptive Statistics portion of the Analyze menu. Click one variable into the Row box and the other variable into the Column box. Choose the statistics tab to click the chi-square test from the list. Click Continue and then OK to begin the analysis.

Table 16.4 Categorical Data for Chi-Square Analysis With Age and Postcard Mailing Accuracy Variables

Participant 1	Older	Yes	Participant 11	Younger	No
Participant 2	Older	Yes	Participant 12	Younger	No
Participant 3	Older	No	Participant 13	Younger	Yes
Participant 4	Older	Yes	Participant 14	Younger	Yes
Participant 5	Older	Yes	Participant 15	Younger	No
Participant 6	Older	No	Participant 16	Younger	No
Participant 7	Older	Yes	Participant 17	Younger	No
Participant 8	Older	Yes	Participant 18	Younger	Yes
Participant 9	Older	Yes	Participant 19	Younger	No
Participant 10	Older	Yes	Participant 20	Younger	Yes

The Output Window from the test is shown in Figure 16.2. The second box in the output shows the observed frequencies from the data. The χ^2 value is shown in the box labeled Chi-Square Tests. The chi-square value of 3.333 is shown in the first row with its p value of 0.068. For this example, the relationship is not significant because the p value is larger than our alpha level of 0.05. In other words, the accuracy of returning the postcard on time did not depend on the age group of the participant when these variables were categorical.

Recall from Chapter 15 that the Pearson r correlation we conducted on these data was significant. In that case, we used continuous variables of age in years and number of days late and found that these variables were significantly related. This comparison across the tests illustrates the issue of power with nonparametric tests. With the categorical variables and nonparametric test used in this chapter, the power to detect a relationship is lower than the example in Chapter 15, and we failed to find a significant relationship. This illustrates how the use of continuous variables and a parametric test is a more powerful way to test hypotheses about populations.

Summary of Steps

- Enter the categorical data in separate columns in data window—be sure to define the values in the Variable View tab.
- Choose Descriptive Statistics from the Analyze menu.
- Select Crosstabs from the Descriptive Statistics options.
- Click one variable in the Row box and the other variable into the Column box.
- Click the Statistics tab and check the Chi-Square box in the window.
- Click OK to run the test; the test and p values will appear in the Output window (see Figure 16.2).

Figure 16.2   SPSS Output From the Chi-Square Analysis

Crosstabs

Case Processing Summary

		Cases				
		Valid		Missing		Total	
		N	Percentage	N	Percentage	N	Percentage
Age* Response		20	100.0%	0	.0%	20	100.0%

Age* Response Crosstabulation

Count

		Response		
		Yes	No	Total
Age	Older	8	2	10
	Younger	4	6	10
Total		12	8	20

Chi-square Tests

	Value	df	Asymp. Sig. (2-sided)	Exact Sig. (2-sided)	Exact Sig. (1-sided)
Pearson chi-square	3.333[a]	1	.068		
Continuity correction[b]	1.875	1	.171		
Likelihood ratio	3.452	1	.063		
Fisher's exact test				.170	.085
N of valid cases	20				

a. 2 cells (50.0%) have expected count less than 5. The minimum expected count is 4.00
b. Computed only for a 2x2 table

Stop and Think

16.3 Using the row and column frequencies given, calculate the expected frequencies for each cell in the table below.

Smoking Status/ Gender	Men	Women	Row Totals
Smoker			30
Nonsmoker			170
Column Totals	100	100	200

16.4 For the observed frequencies in the table below, conduct a chi-square test to determine if there is a relationship between the variables.

Sleep/Exam Outcome	Slept	Did Not Sleep
Pass	40	20
Fail	5	10

Calculation Summary

Expected frequency: The frequency total for the column times the frequency total for the row divided by the sample size

Chi-square: The sum of the squared differences between the observed and expected frequencies divided by the expected frequencies

CHAPTER SUMMARY

16.1 **What is the difference between a parametric and a nonparametric test?**

A parametric test is used with continuous variables and a nonparametric test is used with categorical variables. Nonparametric tests are needed when sample statistics cannot be calculated to estimate population parameters. They are less powerful than a parametric test.

16.2 **What does it mean that a nonparametric test is less powerful than a parametric test?**

Nonparametric tests are less powerful than parametric tests, which means that they are less able to detect relationships between variables that exist in the population. In other words, a Type II error is more likely with a nonparametric test than with a parametric test.

16.3 How can we test relationships across categorical variables?

Nonparametric tests can be used to test relationships across categorical variables. For example, a chi-square test compares the observed category frequencies on the variables with the expected category frequencies on the variables when the null hypothesis is true.

16.4 What is the expected frequency?

The expected frequency is the number of participants expected in a cell category when there is no relationship between the variables (i.e., the null hypothesis is true).

16.5 What does a chi-square test tell us about relationships between categorical variables?

A chi-square test can tell us if there is evidence to reject the null hypothesis (that there is no relationship between two categorical variables). In other words, we can find evidence that there is a relationship between the variables.

THINKING ABOUT RESEARCH

A summary of a research study in psychology is given below. As you read the summary, think about the following questions:

1. What were the variables included in this study? Were these variables categorical or continuous? How do you know?

2. Why was the chi-square test appropriate to test the researchers' hypothesis? Include all possible reasons for the use of this test.

3. Based on the results given in the description below, was the chi-square test significant? How do you know? Using the information given for the study, what is the appropriate $\chi^2_{critical}$ for this study?

4. Based on the information presented in the Results section below, what type of relationship was present for the variables you described earlier? Describe this relationship in your own words.

Converse, B. A., Risen, J. L., & Carter, T. J. (2012). Investing in karma: When wanting promotes helping. *Psychological Science, 23,* 923–930.

Note: Experiment 1a from this article is described here.

Purpose of the Study. The researchers conducted an experiment to investigate whether desiring an outcome that someone has no control over (e.g., getting a job you applied for) is related to helping behavior (e.g., donating to a charity). Desiring an outcome was expected to relate to subsequent helping behavior.

Method of the Study. Undergraduate students ($N = 95$) were asked to participate for $3 compensation. Participants were assigned to either a wanting or routine condition using instructions for an essay they were to write. Those in the wanting condition were asked to write about a current event from their lives in which they wanted a specific outcome that was important to them. Those in the routine condition were asked to write about one of their daily routines. After being compensated for the study, an experimenter asked if the participant would be willing to sign up to work on a boring task for monetary compensation that would be donated to a local food bank. The researchers recorded how many participants agreed to do the task for charity.

Results of the Study. A chi-square test was conducted to examine the relationship between assigned essay condition (wanting or routine) and the number of participants who said yes and no to completing the boring task for charity. The calculated χ^2 was 4.90 and p value was 0.027. Overall, 94% from the wanting condition and 78% from the routine condition agreed to complete the boring task.

Conclusions of the Study. The researchers concluded that the essay condition assigned to the participants in the experiment was related to their helping behavior.

TEST YOURSELF

1. Parametric tests are used with _____ variables; nonparametric tests are used with _____ variables.

   a. nominal, ordinal

   b. ratio, interval

   c. nominal and ordinal, interval and ratio

   d. interval and ratio, nominal and ordinal

2. The chi-square test is a(n) _____ test.

   a. inferential

   b. parametric

   c. nonparametric

   d. both (a) and (b)

   e. both (a) and (c)

3. The chi-square statistic is based on _____.

   a. expected frequencies divided by the degrees of freedom

   b. the difference between the observed and expected frequencies

   c. the difference between the means of the two variables

4. Expected frequencies are the frequencies we would expect if _____.

   a. the null hypothesis is true

   b. the null hypothesis is false

   c. the alternative hypothesis is true

   d. both (b) and (c)

5. If we want to determine if there is a relationship between grade point average (on a 4-point scale) and ACT score, it would be best to use a chi-square test.

   a. True

   b. False

6. We cannot calculate the expected frequencies until we collect the categorical data from our sample.

   a. True

   b. False

7. The chi-square hypothesis test does not rely on a critical region of a distribution.

   a. True

   b. False

8. When conducting a chi-square test using SPSS, the data must be entered into the data window as categories for the variables.

   a. True

   b. False

9. The chi-square test can be conducted as a one-tailed or two-tailed test.

   a. True

   b. False

10. Using the row and column frequencies given, calculate the expected frequencies for each cell in the table below.

Voting Status/ Supports Candidate	Voted	Did Not Vote	Row Totals
Yes			300
No			200
Column Totals	200	300	500

11. For the observed frequencies in the table below, conduct a chi-square test to determine if there is a relationship between the variables.

Class Section/Grade Outcome	Live Class	Online Class
Pass	50	130
Fail	10	20

Appendix A

Answers to Stop and Think Questions

CHAPTER 1

1.1. Answers may vary.

The *New York Times* is running a graphic on its website that gives the probability of who will win the November presidential election. It changes daily (or more often). Yesterday, it gave an 88% chance to Hillary Clinton and 12% chance to Donald Trump. Such a graphic makes me think the election is essentially wrapped up.

1.2. Answers may vary.

We would need more detail about the population polled. What were the ages of the participants? The exercise habits? Diets?

1.3. Answers may vary.

Yes, I would be in favor of a nationwide increase. Based on the statistics, the implementation of higher legal smoking age cut down on purchases by people under 18 years old. The health benefits would be worth it.

1.4.

   a. Independent: Presence of a cell phone

      Dependent: Time studying on task

   b. Independent: List of words meant to be recalled later

      Dependent: Ability to decide if strings of letters are words

1.5.

   a. Quasi-experiment

   b. Experiment

1.6.

 a. Between Subjects

 b. Within Subjects

1.7.

 a. Experimental. You could set up a study in which energy drinks are the independent variable.

 b. Experimental. The level of anxiety would be the independent variable in a two-group study. Anxiety could be determined through self-report or some other way.

 c. Correlational. Because you can't realistically impose the consumption of red meat over a lifetime, a comparison of dietary data and medical files is more appropriate.

 d. Correlational. You're looking for a relationship between two types of scores and salary, not a cause.

1.8. Researchers could have designed a study in which they regulated distracting events (as the independent variable) in order to measure the students' self-regulation. The stigma sensitivity of the African American students would have been recorded before the administration of the stimuli. But an experiment of that kind would be unethical. A correlational study is more appropriate.

1.9.

 a. Validity

 b. Reliability

1.10. Answers may vary.

Take a study that seeks to determine how much water college students consume on Tuesdays. The poll is given four times a year on a Tuesday. The measure is unreliable because, if the students live in a location with drastically different seasons, the amount of water consumed may vary considerably. That is, more water is likely to be consumed on the Tuesday in summer than the Tuesday in winter. The internal validity, then, is low. The day of the week may not contribute to the amount of water consumed. Other factors may be at work.

CHAPTER 2

2.1.

 a. Population: Schoolchildren ages 9 and 10

 Sample: Students in a fifth-grade class at a particular elementary school

 b. Population: Likely meant to be adults, possibly specifically college students

 Sample: College students recruited from a specific subject pool

 c. Population: Retirees

 Sample: Retirees at a particular retirement center

   d. Population: People who have had a TBI

     Sample: Patients recovering from TBI at a local hospital who agree to participate

2.2.

   a. Interval

   b. Ratio

   c. Interval

   d. Ratio

2.3. Descriptive. They give a visual that helps describe the gathered data. They have not yet been used to test the researcher's hypothesis.

2.4. A study can be designed to more directly observe behavior, for instance, by bringing subjects into the controlled environment of a lab. Doing so would increase internal validity but possibly at the sacrifice of external validity.

2.5. Symmetrical. The scores on either side of the middle score are nearly a mirror image.

2.6. Skewed. There are more scores on the high end, particularly in the B range.

2.7. Seven received an A, 12 received a D or F.

CHAPTER 3

3.1. Thirty-six outcomes. Value of 7. Probability: 1/6.

3.2. Answers will vary, but the most common scores should be near the middle of the range (i.e., 5 to 7).

3.3. Answers will vary, but the distribution is more likely to be symmetrical because the middle scores are most common and the low and high scores should be equally but less common.

Generally speaking, if they roll enough, the distribution should be symmetrical.

3.4.

   a. The population is college students at that particular school. A stratified random sample was used to make sure the proportion of men and women was that of the entire school.

   b. The population is adults, but a volunteer sample of psychology students is used.

3.5. Answers will vary.

I would probably narrow the scope to adults in the United States. I would then set salary requirements for each group ("people with more money" and "people with less money"). Either through census data or a survey, I would create equal-sized pools of people to poll. I would use a cluster sample to make sure there are the same amount of people in each group.

CHAPTER 4

4.1. Symmetrical

4.2.

- 55.6
- 60.2

The mean for the second set is nearly five points higher. The second set has an outlier at 96, which gives the distribution a positive skew.

4.3. Median: 4

Mode: 4

The median and mode scores are the same, so both are representative of the distribution.

Median: 87

Mode: 87

The median and mode scores are the same, so both are representative of the distribution.

(In both sets of numbers, the median and mode are the same.)

4.4. One or two outliers will tilt the mean toward that end, whether high or low. A median score gives a more accurate figure to associate with the average for a particular distribution of scores.

4.5. Median is best for a measure of speed because it is typically a skewed distribution.

Time of day is a categorical variable here, so the mode is the best measure to use.

Mean is likely to be used for rating scales, but if the distribution is skewed, the median can be used or if the distribution is bimodal (e.g., mostly *1*s and *5*s), the mode can be used.

4.6. Because the last value is opened-ended, calculating a mean is not accurate (a value of 4 could mean 4 siblings, 5 siblings, 6 siblings, and so on). The mode would be best here, or you can use the median to show where the midpoint of the distribution is.

CHAPTER 5

5.1. Answers may vary.

The second set looks like it has more variability because there are a couple *1*s and *7*s in the set, whereas the first list does not have any of those extremes.

5.2. 3 and 6.

Yes, the second set of numbers has a wider range.

5.3. Answers may vary.

The standard deviation gives you an average variance of the data points—how far away from the mean they tend to be. A range merely gives you an idea of lowest and highest boundaries for where a data point might fall. The standard deviation is best used when the mean is your measure of central tendency.

5.4. 1.55, 3.01

Answers will vary. The range is narrower in the first set (4), so the standard deviation of those nine data points is small. The range of the second set is 8, so we have more variability and the standard deviation is greater.

5.5. 1.64, 3.28

The standard deviations will be a little larger because we're using degrees of freedom to correct for fewer scores than we would have with a whole population. We're dividing by a number that is smaller than N.

CHAPTER 6

6.1.

   a. Continuous

   b. Continuous

   c. Categorical

   d. Categorical

6.2.

   • A bar graph would give a visual breakdown of the different majors, which is a categorical variable. It would likely be too many categories for a pie chart.

   • A line graph, because the variable (amount of time) is a continuous variable

   • A line graph, because the variable (mean performance on a task—likely percentage correct) is a continuous variable

6.3.

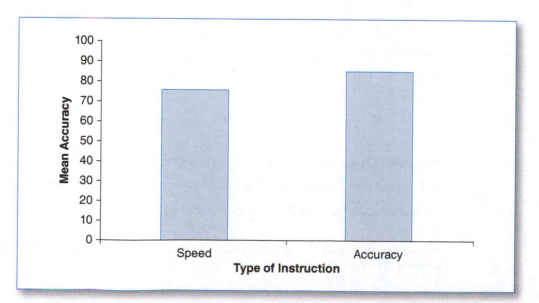

6.4. (c)

6.5. (d)

CHAPTER 7

7.1. Jeff ($z = -0.89$) is heavier than Rafiki ($z = -4.25$).

7.2. Answers will vary.

7.3. It is to the left of (less than) the mean by 1.5 standard deviations.

7.4.

   a. 11%
   b. 79%
   c. 98%

7.5. Proportion in *Body* refers to the percentage of scores at or above the z score. Proportion in *Tail* refers to the percentage of scores below the z score, or what remains of the distribution.

7.6. The probability is 0.006 or about 1%.

CHAPTER 8

8.1. $z = 1.64$

You can reject the null hypothesis. The probability that null hypothesis is true is very low.

8.2. Yes

8.3.

- One-tailed
- One-tailed
- Two-tailed
- Two-tailed

8.4.

- Alternative: Aspirin decreases the chance of heart attacks in the population.

  Null: Aspirin increases or has no effect on the chance of heart attacks in the population.

- Alternative: Quizzing oneself, rather than rereading notes, increases test scores in the population.

  Null: Quizzing oneself, rather than rereading notes, decreases or has no effect on test scores in the population.

- Alternative: Time constraints will increase or decrease your accuracy in completing a puzzle in the population.

  Null: Time constraints will have not affect your accuracy in completing a puzzle in the population.

- Alternative: The amount of sleep one gets affects depression in the population.

  Null: The amount of sleep one gets does not affect depression in the population.

8.5. $p = 0.01$

We can reject the null hypothesis and accept the alternative hypothesis.

8.6.

- Alternative: The task of preparing a 5-minute speech increases anxiety among the population of college students.

  Null: The task of preparing a 5-minute speech decreases or does not affect anxiety among the population of college students.

This is a one-tailed test.

- $z = 11.27$

There's a less than 0.00003 chance that the null hypothesis is true.

- Since the p value is less than alpha, we can reject the null hypothesis. The results suggest that preparing for a speech increases anxiety.

8.7.

- Type II
- Correct decision
- Type I

CHAPTER 9

9.1. Alternative: The population of psychics will perform better than the population of non-psychics (higher than 25% correct) when predicting the suit of individual playing cards.

Null: The population of psychics will perform the same (25% correct) or worse than the population of non-psychics when predicting the suit of individual playing cards.

This is a one-tailed test.

9.2. The population standard deviation

9.3. Answers will vary, but some common biases for this type of study might be experimenter bias (experimenters could inadvertently indicate correct answers) and possible marks on the cards that could help participants pick the correct answer, so using a computer to present stimuli and collect responses would be best.

9.4.

    a. Alternative: Those in the population shown subliminal Coke ads will choose the Coke image more than 50% of the time.

        Null: Those in the population shown subliminal Coke ads will choose the Coke image 50% of the time or at a lower rate.

    b. $t = 8.5$

    c. $t_{crit} = 1.69$

Our t score falls into the critical region, so we can reject the null hypothesis. The results support the idea that people process subliminal ads.

9.5. $n = 30$

The smaller the sample size, the greater the variability of the distribution. It's harder to tell how close we are to the population standard deviation. So the t_{crit} score will be larger, necessitating a smaller critical area in which to hit in order to reject the null hypothesis.

9.6. $t = 2.04$

Given that it's a two-tailed experiment, the t score (2.04) does not fall in the critical area ($t_{crit} = 2.11$). We must retain the null hypothesis. The new method doesn't have a significant effect on test scores.

9.7. We can reject the null hypothesis because the t score (2.25) falls in the critical area ($t_{crit} = 2.09$).

CHAPTER 10

10.1. Both the online quizzes and psychic studies are experiments. They both compare behavior between two groups in which participants are randomly assigned to groups. That is, the independent variable is not subject to their choice. The difference is that the online quizzes study uses a between-subjects design (each subject is assigned to one group) while the psychic study is a within-subjects design (each subject partakes in both groups to find a difference score).

10.2.

Alternative: In the population, the mean difference score should be greater than zero.

Null: In the population, the mean difference score should be less than or equal to zero.

10.3.

    a. Alternative: In the population, the mean difference score should be greater than or less than zero.

        Null: In the population, the mean difference score should be zero.

   b. $t = 18.07$

   c. The null hypothesis can be rejected. The t score falls into the critical area. There appears to be a difference in recognition between standard and emotional ads.

10.4. Group A would receive standard ads and Group B would receive emotional ads. Pairs of subjects between groups would be assigned. Ideally, you would pair subjects based on recognition accuracy. You could give all subjects an initial trial with a different (non-Coke) subliminal ad. Based on their recognition abilities, pair one subject in Group A with one subject in Group B. After running the Coke ad trials, you would find difference scores by comparing Subject 1A to Subject 1B, Subject 2A to Subject 2B, and so on. You could then find a mean for difference scores.

10.5.

   a. 0.711

   b. 0.495

   c. The p value is greater than α, so we must retain the null. There is not enough evidence to suggest there's a difference between paper or computer text. The results do not help you decide which types of textbooks to buy because comprehension appears approximately the same between texts.

CHAPTER 11

11.1. It is a quasi-experiment. One group is made up of self-proclaimed psychics and the other group is made up of non-psychics. Because the independent variable (psychic/non-psychic) is already a characteristic of the subjects, it cannot be randomly assigned (which would make it a true experiment). Otherwise, behavior between two conditions is being measured and compared.

11.2. Yes, it is an experiment because subjects are randomly assigned to one of two groups—the reread group or the recall group.

11.3.

   a. Alternative: The population mean for men will be different than the population mean for women.

      Null: The population mean for men will be the same as the population mean for women.

   b. $t = 5.25$

   c. The t score falls in the critical region, so the null hypothesis can be rejected. The results suggest that men and women recognize subliminal ads at a different rate.

11.4. $s_p^2 = 133.64$

11.5. $SS_1 = 28$ $SS_2 = 4.73$

$X_1 = 5$ $X_2 = 3.55$

$$s_p^2 = 1.72$$

$$s_{\bar{X}_1 - \bar{X}_2} = 0.57$$

$$t = 2.55$$

$$t_{crit} = 2.09$$

Our t score falls in the critical region, so we can reject the null hypothesis. The same mean scores are significantly different.

CHAPTER 12

12.1. Answers will vary.

We will combine the sum of squares of the groups and divide by the sum of degrees of freedom.

12.2. Alternative: The population mean time is less for left-handed individuals than right-handed or ambidextrous individuals.

Null: The population mean time is equal between left-handed, right-handed, and ambidextrous individuals.

12.3. There is a significant main effect. The F ratio (3.17) is greater than the critical score (2.79).

12.4. F would equal 1. That would indicate the ratio of between-groups and within-groups variance is balanced.

12.5. Answers will vary.

A post hoc test can help tell us if there is a significant difference between groups. Our hypothesis might state that one group sees a significant difference, but it might not identify which group. We don't need a post hoc test in a study with two groups because we can perform a two-tailed test if we don't hypothesize a specific direction for a difference between groups.

CHAPTER 13

13.1.

Independent variables:

- Amount of chocolate chips (normal or 30% more)
- Presence of real vanilla (real vanilla or artificial vanilla)

Dependent variable:

- Ratings on desire to buy ice cream

13.2. The ratings between ice cream with the normal amount of chocolate chips and 30% more chocolate chips.

The ratings between ice cream with artificial vanilla and ice cream with real vanilla

13.3. The addition of real vanilla could affect the ratings of the chocolate chip ice cream. Maybe additional chocolate chips on their own don't raise the rating, but the combination of additional chocolate chips and vanilla might.

13.4.

a. Main effect

b. Interaction

c. Main effect

13.5.

The main effect of gender was not significant ($F = 2.09$, $p = 0.155$).

The main effect of mood was significant ($F = 43.74$, $p < 0.001$).

The interaction between gender and mood was not significant ($F = 2.20$, $p = 0.145$).

13.6. No. It would represent a main effect. The increase in ratings is not contingent on the combination of variables, only that particular variable.

13.7. No. Again, it would represent a main effect because the increase would be dependent on that one variable.

CHAPTER 14

14.1.

a. Between-subjects, ANOVA

b. Within-subjects, ANOVA

c. Within-subjects, *t* test

14.2. It's not a true experiment because the grouping criteria could not be randomly assigned. The test would also need to be controlled. To make it an experiment, keep the three conditions but randomly assign participants to each condition. Then, give each group of participants the same test.

14.3. For the quiz study, the class would need to be divided into three groups so that a third of the participants get the no-quiz condition first, a third get the multiple choice condition first, and a third get the short answer condition first. Each group would be run in different order to eliminate sequencing bias. For the Alzheimer's study, test each participant only once a day—half in the morning and half in the afternoon. After that, test again, but at the alternate time of day.

14.4. Divide your friends into three groups. Tell one of the groups to try rereading notes for the first exam, quizzes for the second exam, and a study partner for the third exam. Have the second group start with the quizzes for the first exam. Have the third group start with the study partner for the first exam.

14.5. There is a significant effect on study technique.

$F = 5.310, p = 0.027$

14.6. The exam that showed the highest scores could simply have covered easier material.

CHAPTER 15

15.1. The regular exercise could be staving off dementia.

Sharper cognitive abilities (a lack of dementia) could lead to regular exercise.

A third variable (favorable climate, for instance) could be behind both the regular exercise and avoidance of dementia.

15.2. (c)

15.3. There is a significant negative correlation between mood and weather temperature.

There were 60 subjects in the study.

15.4. There is not a significant relationship, though there is a negative correlation.

CHAPTER 16

16.1.

- Parametric
- Nonparametric
- Nonparametric
- Parametric

16.2. Scores on a categorical variable do not have a true numerical value.

16.3.

Smoker/Men = 15

Smoker/Women = 15

Nonsmoker/Men = 85

Nonsmoker/Women = 85

16.4. The χ^2 figure falls into the critical region, so we can reject the null hypothesis. Results suggest that there is a relationship between the variables.

$\chi^2 = 5.56$

$df = 1$

$\chi^2_{crit} = 3.84$

Appendix B

Unit Normal Table (z Table)

A	B	C	A	B	C	A	B	C	A	B	C
z score	Body	Tail	z score	Body	Tail	z score	Body	Tail	z score	Body	Tail
0.00	0.5000	0.5000	0.22	0.5871	0.4129	0.44	0.6700	0.3300	0.66	0.7454	0.2546
0.01	0.5040	0.4960	0.23	0.5910	0.4090	0.45	0.6736	0.3264	0.67	0.7486	0.2514
0.02	0.5080	0.4920	0.24	0.5948	0.4052	0.46	0.6772	0.3228	0.68	0.7517	0.2483
0.03	0.5120	0.4880	0.25	0.5987	0.4013	0.47	0.6808	0.3192	0.69	0.7549	0.2451
0.04	0.5160	0.4840	0.26	0.6026	0.3974	0.48	0.6844	0.3156	0.70	0.7580	0.2420
0.05	0.5199	0.4801	0.27	0.6064	0.3936	0.49	0.6879	0.3121	0.71	0.7611	0.2389
0.06	0.5239	0.4761	0.28	0.6103	0.3897	0.50	0.6915	0.3085	0.72	0.7642	0.2358
0.07	0.5279	0.4721	0.29	0.6141	0.3859	0.51	0.6950	0.3050	0.73	0.7673	0.2327
0.08	0.5319	0.4681	0.30	0.6179	0.3821	0.52	0.6985	0.3015	0.74	0.7704	0.2296
0.09	0.5359	0.4641	0.31	0.6217	0.3783	0.53	0.7019	0.2981	0.75	0.7734	0.2266
0.10	0.5398	0.4602	0.32	0.6255	0.3745	0.54	0.7054	0.2946	0.76	0.7764	0.2236
0.11	0.5438	0.4562	0.33	0.6293	0.3707	0.55	0.7088	0.2912	0.77	0.7794	0.2206
0.12	0.5478	0.4522	0.34	0.6331	0.3669	0.56	0.7123	0.2877	0.78	0.7823	0.2177
0.13	0.5517	0.4483	0.35	0.6368	0.3632	0.57	0.7157	0.2843	0.79	0.7852	0.2148
0.14	0.5557	0.4443	0.36	0.6406	0.3594	0.58	0.7190	0.2810	0.80	0.7881	0.2119
0.15	0.5596	0.4404	0.37	0.6443	0.3557	0.59	0.7224	0.2776	0.81	0.7910	0.2090
0.16	0.5636	0.4364	0.38	0.6480	0.3520	0.60	0.7257	0.2743	0.82	0.7939	0.2061
0.17	0.5675	0.4325	0.39	0.6517	0.3483	0.61	0.7291	0.2709	0.83	0.7967	0.2033
0.18	0.5714	0.4286	0.40	0.6554	0.3446	0.62	0.7324	0.2676	0.84	0.7995	0.2005
0.19	0.5753	0.4247	0.41	0.6591	0.3409	0.63	0.7357	0.2643	0.85	0.8023	0.1977
0.20	0.5793	0.4207	0.42	0.6628	0.3372	0.64	0.7389	0.2611	0.86	0.8051	0.1949
0.21	0.5832	0.4168	0.43	0.6664	0.3336	0.65	0.7422	0.2578	0.87	0.8078	0.1922

(Continued)

(Continued)

A	B	C	A	B	C	A	B	C	A	B	C
z score	Body	Tail	z score	Body	Tail	z score	Body	Tail	z score	Body	Tail
0.88	0.8106	0.1894	1.22	0.8888	0.1112	1.56	0.9406	0.0594	1.90	0.9713	0.0287
0.89	0.8133	0.1867	1.23	0.8907	0.1093	1.57	0.9418	0.0582	1.91	0.9719	0.0281
0.90	0.8159	0.1841	1.24	0.8925	0.1075	1.58	0.9429	0.0571	1.92	0.9726	0.0274
0.91	0.8186	0.1814	1.25	0.8944	0.1056	1.59	0.9441	0.0559	1.93	0.9732	0.0268
0.92	0.8212	0.1788	1.26	0.8962	0.1038	1.60	0.9452	0.0548	1.94	0.9738	0.0262
0.93	0.8238	0.1762	1.27	0.8980	0.1020	1.61	0.9463	0.0537	1.95	0.9744	0.0256
0.94	0.8264	0.1736	1.28	0.8997	0.1003	1.62	0.9474	0.0526	1.96	0.9750	0.0250
0.95	0.8289	0.1711	1.29	0.9015	0.0985	1.63	0.9484	0.0516	1.97	0.9756	0.0244
0.96	0.8315	0.1685	1.30	0.9032	0.0968	1.64	0.9495	0.0505	1.98	0.9761	0.0239
0.97	0.8340	0.1660	1.31	0.9049	0.0951	1.65	0.9505	0.0495	1.99	0.9767	0.0233
0.98	0.8365	0.1635	1.32	0.9066	0.0934	1.66	0.9515	0.0485	2.00	0.9772	0.0228
0.99	0.8389	0.1611	1.33	0.9082	0.0918	1.67	0.9525	0.0475	2.01	0.9778	0.0222
1.00	0.8413	0.1587	1.34	0.9099	0.0901	1.68	0.9535	0.0465	2.02	0.9783	0.0217
1.01	0.8438	0.1562	1.35	0.9115	0.0885	1.69	0.9545	0.0455	2.03	0.9788	0.0212
1.02	0.8461	0.1539	1.36	0.9131	0.0869	1.70	0.9554	0.0446	2.04	0.9793	0.0207
1.03	0.8485	0.1515	1.37	0.9147	0.0853	1.71	0.9564	0.0436	2.05	0.9798	0.0202
1.04	0.8508	0.1492	1.38	0.9162	0.0838	1.72	0.9573	0.0427	2.06	0.9803	0.0197
1.05	0.8531	0.1469	1.39	0.9177	0.0823	1.73	0.9582	0.0418	2.07	0.9808	0.0192
1.06	0.8554	0.1446	1.40	0.9192	0.0808	1.74	0.9591	0.0409	2.08	0.9812	0.0188
1.07	0.8577	0.1423	1.41	0.9207	0.0793	1.75	0.9599	0.0401	2.09	0.9817	0.0183
1.08	0.8599	0.1401	1.42	0.9222	0.0778	1.76	0.9608	0.0392	2.10	0.9821	0.0179
1.09	0.8621	0.1379	1.43	0.9236	0.0764	1.77	0.9616	0.0384	2.11	0.9826	0.0174
1.10	0.8643	0.1357	1.44	0.9251	0.0749	1.78	0.9625	0.0375	2.12	0.9830	0.0170
1.11	0.8665	0.1335	1.45	0.9265	0.0735	1.79	0.9633	0.0367	2.13	0.9834	0.0166
1.12	0.8686	0.1314	1.46	0.9279	0.0721	1.80	0.9641	0.0359	2.14	0.9838	0.0162
1.13	0.8708	0.1292	1.47	0.9292	0.0708	1.81	0.9649	0.0351	2.15	0.9842	0.0158
1.14	0.8729	0.1271	1.48	0.9306	0.0694	1.82	0.9656	0.0344	2.16	0.9846	0.0154
1.15	0.8749	0.1251	1.49	0.9319	0.0681	1.83	0.9664	0.0336	2.17	0.9850	0.0150
1.16	0.8770	0.1230	1.50	0.9332	0.0668	1.84	0.9671	0.0329	2.18	0.9854	0.0146
1.17	0.8790	0.1210	1.51	0.9345	0.0655	1.85	0.9678	0.0322	2.19	0.9857	0.0143
1.18	0.8810	0.1190	1.52	0.9357	0.0643	1.86	0.9686	0.0314	2.20	0.9861	0.0139
1.19	0.8830	0.1170	1.53	0.9370	0.0630	1.87	0.9693	0.0307	2.21	0.9864	0.0136
1.20	0.8849	0.1151	1.54	0.9382	0.0618	1.88	0.9699	0.0301	2.22	0.9868	0.0132
1.21	0.8869	0.1131	1.55	0.9394	0.0606	1.89	0.9706	0.0294	2.23	0.9871	0.0129

A	B	C	A	B	C	A	B	C	A	B	C
z score	Body	Tail	z score	Body	Tail	z score	Body	Tail	z score	Body	Tail
2.24	0.9875	0.0125	2.56	0.9948	0.0052	2.88	0.9980	0.0020	3.20	0.9993	0.0007
2.25	0.9878	0.0122	2.57	0.9949	0.0051	2.89	0.9981	0.0019	3.21	0.9993	0.0007
2.26	0.9881	0.0119	2.58	0.9951	0.0049	2.90	0.9981	0.0019	3.22	0.9994	0.0006
2.27	0.9884	0.0116	2.59	0.9952	0.0048	2.91	0.9982	0.0018	3.23	0.9994	0.0006
2.28	0.9887	0.0113	2.60	0.9953	0.0047	2.92	0.9982	0.0018	3.24	0.9994	0.0006
2.29	0.9890	0.0110	2.61	0.9955	0.0045	2.93	0.9983	0.0017	3.25	0.9994	0.0006
2.30	0.9893	0.0107	2.62	0.9956	0.0044	2.94	0.9984	0.0016	3.26	0.9994	0.0006
2.31	0.9896	0.0104	2.63	0.9957	0.0043	2.95	0.9984	0.0016	3.27	0.9995	0.0005
2.32	0.9898	0.0102	2.64	0.9959	0.0041	2.96	0.9985	0.0015	3.28	0.9995	0.0005
2.33	0.9901	0.0099	2.65	0.9960	0.0040	2.97	0.9985	0.0015	3.29	0.9995	0.0005
2.34	0.9904	0.0096	2.66	0.9961	0.0039	2.98	0.9986	0.0014	3.30	0.9995	0.0005
2.35	0.9906	0.0094	2.67	0.9962	0.0038	2.99	0.9986	0.0014	3.31	0.9995	0.0005
2.36	0.9909	0.0091	2.68	0.9963	0.0037	3.00	0.9987	0.0013	3.32	0.9995	0.0005
2.37	0.9911	0.0089	2.69	0.9964	0.0036	3.01	0.9987	0.0013	3.33	0.9996	0.0004
2.38	0.9913	0.0087	2.70	0.9965	0.0035	3.02	0.9987	0.0013	3.34	0.9996	0.0004
2.39	0.9916	0.0084	2.71	0.9966	0.0034	3.03	0.9988	0.0012	3.35	0.9996	0.0004
2.40	0.9918	0.0082	2.72	0.9967	0.0033	3.04	0.9988	0.0012	3.36	0.9996	0.0004
2.41	0.9920	0.0080	2.73	0.9968	0.0032	3.05	0.9989	0.0011	3.37	0.9996	0.0004
2.42	0.9922	0.0078	2.74	0.9969	0.0031	3.06	0.9989	0.0011	3.38	0.9996	0.0004
2.43	0.9925	0.0075	2.75	0.9970	0.0030	3.07	0.9989	0.0011	3.39	0.9997	0.0003
2.44	0.9927	0.0073	2.76	0.9971	0.0029	3.08	0.9990	0.0010	3.40	0.9997	0.0003
2.45	0.9929	0.0071	2.77	0.9972	0.0028	3.09	0.9990	0.0010	3.41	0.9997	0.0003
2.46	0.9931	0.0069	2.78	0.9973	0.0027	3.10	0.9990	0.0010	3.42	0.9997	0.0003
2.47	0.9932	0.0068	2.79	0.9974	0.0026	3.11	0.9991	0.0009	3.43	0.9997	0.0003
2.48	0.9934	0.0066	2.80	0.9974	0.0026	3.12	0.9991	0.0009	3.44	0.9997	0.0003
2.49	0.9936	0.0064	2.81	0.9975	0.0025	3.13	0.9991	0.0009	3.45	0.9997	0.0003
2.50	0.9938	0.0062	2.82	0.9976	0.0024	3.14	0.9992	0.0008	3.46	0.9997	0.0003
2.51	0.9940	0.0060	2.83	0.9977	0.0023	3.15	0.9992	0.0008	3.47	0.9997	0.0003
2.52	0.9941	0.0059	2.84	0.9977	0.0023	3.16	0.9992	0.0008	3.48	0.9997	0.0003
2.53	0.9943	0.0057	2.85	0.9978	0.0022	3.17	0.9992	0.0008	3.49	0.9998	0.0002
2.54	0.9945	0.0055	2.86	0.9979	0.0021	3.18	0.9993	0.0007	3.50	0.9998	0.0002
2.55	0.9946	0.0054	2.87	0.9979	0.0021	3.19	0.9993	0.0007	3.51	0.9998	0.0002

Appendix C

t Distribution Table

TABLE C.1 The *t* Distribution

Table entries are values of *t* corresponding to proportions in one tail or in two tails combined.

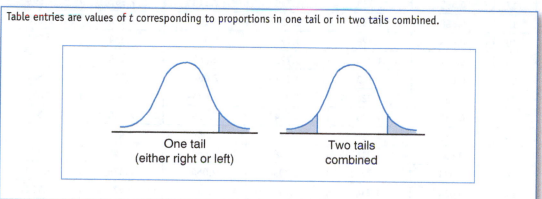

One tail
(either right or left)

Two tails
combined

	Proportion in One Tail					
	0.25	**0.10**	**0.05**	**0.025**	**0.01**	**0.005**
	Proportion in Two Tails Combined					
df	**0.50**	**0.20**	**0.10**	**0.05**	**0.02**	**0.01**
1	1.000	3.078	6.314	12.706	31.821	63.657
2	0.816	1.886	2.920	4.303	6.965	9.925
3	0.765	1.638	2.353	3.182	4.541	5.841
4	0.741	1.533	2.132	2.776	3.747	4.604
5	0.727	1.476	2.015	2.571	3.365	4.032
6	0.718	1.440	1.943	2.447	3.143	3.707
7	0.711	1.415	1.895	2.365	2.998	3.499
8	0.706	1.397	1.860	2.306	2.896	3.355
9	0.703	1.383	1.833	2.282	2.821	3.250

(Continued)

(Continued)

df	Proportion in One Tail					
	0.25	0.10	0.05	0.025	0.01	0.005
	Proportion in Two Tails Combined					
	0.50	0.20	0.10	0.05	0.02	0.01
10	0.700	1.372	1.812	2.228	2.764	3.169
11	0.697	1.363	1.796	2.201	2.718	3.106
12	0.695	1.356	1.782	2.179	2.681	3.055
13	0.694	1.350	1.771	2.160	2.650	3.012
14	0.692	1.345	1.761	2.145	2.624	2.977
15	0.691	1.341	1.753	2.131	2.602	2.947
16	0.690	1.337	1.746	2.120	2.583	2.921
17	0.689	1.333	1.740	2.110	2.567	2.898
18	0.688	1.330	1.734	2.101	2.552	2.878
19	0.688	1.328	1.729	2.093	2.539	2.861
20	0.687	1.325	1.725	2.086	2.528	2.845
21	0.686	1.323	1.721	2.080	2.518	2.831
22	0.686	1.321	1.717	2.074	2.508	2.819
23	0.685	1.319	1.714	2.069	2.500	2.807
24	0.685	1.318	1.711	2.064	2.492	2.797
25	0.684	1.316	1.708	2.060	2.485	2.787
26	0.684	1.315	1.706	2.056	2.479	2.779
27	0.684	1.314	1.703	2.052	2.473	2.771
28	0.683	1.313	1.701	2.048	2.467	2.763
29	0.683	1.311	1.699	2.045	2.462	2.756
30	0.683	1.310	1.697	2.042	2.457	2.750
40	0.681	1.303	1.684	2.021	2.423	2.704
60	0.679	1.296	1.671	2.000	2.390	2.660
120	0.677	1.289	1.658	1.980	2.358	2.617
∞	0.674	1.282	1.645	1.960	2.326	2.576

SOURCE: Fisher, R. A., & Yates, F. (1974). *Statistical Tables for Biological, Agricultural and Medical Research* (6th ed., Table III). London: Longman Group Ltd. (Previously published by Oliver and Boyd Ltd., Edinburgh.) Adapted and reprinted with permission of Addison Wesley Longman.

Appendix D

F Distribution Table

Critical Values for the F Distribution

Critical values at $\alpha = 0.05$ level of significance are given in lightface type.

Critical values at $\alpha = 0.01$ level of significance are given in boldface type.

Degrees of Freedom (df) Numerator													
		1	2	3	4	5	6	7	8	9	10	20	∞
	1	161 **4052**	200 **5000**	216 **5403**	225 **5625**	230 **5764**	234 **5859**	237 **5928**	239 **5928**	241 **6023**	242 **6056**	248 **6209**	254 **6366**
	2	18.51 **98.49**	19.00 **99.00**	19.16 **99.17**	19.25 **99.25**	19.30 **99.30**	19.33 **99.33**	19.36 **99.34**	19.37 **99.36**	19.38 **99.38**	19.39 **99.40**	19.44 **99.45**	19.5 **99.5**
	3	10.13 **34.12**	9.55 **30.92**	9.28 **29.46**	9.12 **28.71**	9.01 **28.24**	8.94 **27.91**	8.88 **27.67**	8.84 **27.49**	8.81 **27.34**	8.78 **27.23**	8.66 **26.69**	8.5 **26.1**
	4	7.71 **21.20**	6.94 **18.00**	6.59 **16.69**	6.39 **15.98**	6.26 **15.52**	6.16 **15.21**	6.09 **14.98**	6.04 **14.80**	6.00 **14.66**	5.96 **14.54**	5.80 **14.02**	5.6 **13.5**
Degrees of Freedom (df) Denominator	5	6.61 **16.26**	5.79 **13.27**	5.41 **12.06**	5.19 **11.39**	5.05 **10.97**	4.95 **10.67**	4.88 **10.45**	4.82 **10.27**	4.78 **10.15**	4.74 **10.05**	4.56 **9.55**	4.37 **9.02**
	6	5.99 **13.74**	5.14 **10.92**	4.76 **9.78**	4.53 **9.15**	4.39 **8.75**	4.28 **8.47**	4.21 **8.26**	4.15 **8.10**	4.10 **7.98**	4.06 **7.87**	3.87 **7.39**	3.67 **6.88**
	7	5.59 **13.74**	4.74 **9.55**	4.35 **8.45**	4.12 **7.85**	3.97 **7.46**	3.87 **7.19**	3.79 **7.00**	3.73 **6.84**	3.68 **6.71**	3.63 **6.62**	3.44 **6.15**	3.23 **5.65**
	8	5.32 **11.26**	4.46 **8.65**	4.07 **7.59**	3.84 **7.01**	3.69 **6.63**	3.58 **6.37**	3.50 **6.19**	3.44 **6.03**	3.39 **5.91**	3.34 **5.82**	3.15 **5.36**	2.93 **4.86**
	9	5.12 **10.56**	4.26 **8.02**	3.86 **6.99**	3.63 **6.42**	3.48 **6.06**	3.37 **5.80**	3.29 **5.62**	3.23 **5.47**	3.18 **5.35**	3.13 **5.26**	2.93 **4.80**	2.71 **4.31**

(Continued)

(Continued)

Degrees of Freedom (df) Numerator												
		1	2	3	4	5	6	7	8	9	10	20	∞
10	4.96	4.10	3.71	3.48	3.33	3.22	3.14	3.07	3.02	2.97	2.77	2.54
	10.04	**7.56**	**6.55**	**5.99**	**5.64**	**5.39**	**5.21**	**5.06**	**4.95**	**4.85**	**4.41**	**3.91**
11	4.84	3.98	3.59	3.36	3.20	3.09	3.01	2.95	2.90	2.86	2.65	2.40
	9.65	**7.20**	**6.22**	**5.67**	**5.32**	**5.07**	**4.88**	**4.74**	**4.63**	**4.54**	**4.10**	**3.60**
12	4.75	3.89	3.49	3.26	3.11	3.00	2.92	2.85	2.80	2.76	2.54	2.30
	9.33	**6.93**	**5.95**	**5.41**	**5.06**	**4.82**	**4.65**	**4.50**	**4.39**	**4.30**	**3.86**	**3.36**
13	4.67	3.80	3.41	3.18	3.02	2.92	2.84	2.77	2.72	2.67	2.46	2.21
	9.07	**6.70**	**5.74**	**5.20**	**4.86**	**4.62**	**4.44**	**4.30**	**4.19**	**4.10**	**3.67**	**3.17**
14	4.60	3.74	3.34	3.11	2.96	2.85	2.77	2.70	2.65	2.60	2.39	2.13
	8.86	**6.51**	**5.56**	**5.03**	**4.69**	**4.46**	**4.28**	**4.14**	**4.03**	**3.94**	**3.51**	**3.00**
15	4.54	3.68	3.29	3.06	2.90	2.79	2.70	2.64	2.59	2.55	2.33	2.07
	8.68	**6.36**	**5.42**	**4.89**	**4.56**	**4.32**	**4.14**	**4.00**	**3.89**	**3.80**	**3.36**	**2.87**
16	4.49	3.63	3.24	3.01	2.85	2.74	2.66	2.59	2.54	2.49	2.28	2.01
	8.53	**6.23**	**5.29**	**4.77**	**4.44**	**4.20**	**4.03**	**3.89**	**3.78**	**3.69**	**3.25**	**2.75**
17	4.45	3.59	3.20	2.96	2.81	2.70	2.62	2.55	2.50	2.45	2.23	1.96
	8.40	**6.11**	**5.18**	**4.67**	**4.34**	**4.10**	**3.93**	**3.79**	**3.68**	**3.59**	**3.16**	**2.65**
18	4.41	3.55	3.16	2.93	2.77	2.66	2.58	2.51	2.46	2.41	2.19	1.92
	8.28	**6.01**	**5.09**	**4.58**	**4.25**	**4.01**	**3.85**	**3.71**	**3.60**	**3.51**	**3.07**	**2.57**
19	4.38	3.52	3.13	2.90	2.74	2.63	2.55	2.48	2.43	2.38	2.15	1.88
	8.18	**5.93**	**5.01**	**4.50**	**4.17**	**3.94**	**3.77**	**3.63**	**3.52**	**3.43**	**3.00**	**2.49**
20	4.35	3.49	3.10	2.87	2.71	2.60	2.52	2.45	2.40	2.35	2.12	1.84
	8.10	**5.85**	**4.94**	**4.43**	**4.10**	**3.87**	**3.71**	**3.56**	**3.45**	**3.37**	**2.94**	**2.42**
21	4.32	3.47	3.07	2.84	2.68	2.57	2.49	2.42	2.37	2.32	2.09	1.81
	8.02	**5.78**	**4.87**	**4.37**	**4.04**	**3.81**	**3.65**	**3.51**	**3.40**	**3.31**	**2.88**	**2.36**
22	4.30	3.44	3.05	2.82	2.66	2.55	2.47	2.40	2.35	2.30	2.07	1.78
	7.94	**5.72**	**4.82**	**4.31**	**3.99**	**3.76**	**3.59**	**3.45**	**3.35**	**3.26**	**2.83**	**2.31**
23	4.28	3.42	3.03	2.80	2.64	2.53	2.45	2.38	2.32	2.28	2.04	1.76
	7.88	**5.66**	**4.76**	**4.26**	**3.94**	**3.71**	**3.54**	**3.41**	**3.30**	**3.21**	**2.78**	**2.26**
24	4.26	3.40	3.01	2.78	2.62	2.51	2.43	2.36	2.30	2.26	2.02	1.73
	7.82	**5.61**	**4.72**	**4.22**	**3.90**	**3.67**	**3.50**	**3.36**	**3.25**	**3.17**	**2.74**	**2.21**
25	4.24	3.38	2.99	2.76	2.60	2.49	2.41	2.34	2.28	2.24	2.00	1.71
	7.77	**5.57**	**4.68**	**4.18**	**3.86**	**3.63**	**3.46**	**3.32**	**3.21**	**3.13**	**2.70**	**2.17**
26	4.22	3.37	2.98	2.74	2.59	2.47	2.39	2.32	2.27	2.22	1.99	1.69
	7.72	**5.53**	**4.64**	**4.14**	**3.82**	**3.59**	**3.42**	**3.29**	**3.17**	**3.09**	**2.66**	**2.13**
27	4.21	3.35	2.96	2.73	2.57	2.46	2.37	2.30	2.25	2.20	1.97	1.67
	7.68	**5.49**	**4.60**	**4.11**	**3.79**	**3.56**	**3.39**	**3.26**	**3.14**	**3.06**	**2.63**	**2.10**
28	4.20	3.34	2.95	2.71	2.56	2.44	2.36	2.29	2.24	2.19	1.96	1.65
	7.64	**5.45**	**4.57**	**4.07**	**3.76**	**3.53**	**3.36**	**3.23**	**3.11**	**3.03**	**2.60**	**2.07**

Degrees of Freedom (df) Denominator

Degrees of Freedom (df) Numerator

Degrees of Freedom (df) Denominator

df	1	2	3	4	5	6	7	8	9	10	20	∞
29	4.18	3.33	2.93	2.70	2.54	2.43	2.35	2.28	2.22	2.18	1.94	1.63
	7.60	**5.42**	**4.54**	**4.04**	**3.73**	**3.50**	**3.33**	**3.20**	**3.08**	**3.00**	**2.57**	**2.04**
30	4.17	3.32	2.92	2.69	2.53	2.42	2.34	2.27	2.21	2.16	1.93	1.61
	7.56	**5.39**	**4.51**	**4.02**	**3.70**	**3.47**	**3.30**	**3.17**	**3.06**	**2.98**	**2.55**	**2.01**
31	4.16	3.30	2.91	2.68	2.52	2.41	2.32	2.25	2.20	2.15	1.92	1.60
	7.53	**5.36**	**4.48**	**3.99**	**3.67**	**3.45**	**3.28**	**3.15**	**3.04**	**2.96**	**2.53**	**1.89**
32	4.15	3.29	2.90	2.67	2.51	2.40	2.31	2.24	2.19	2.14	1.91	1.59
	7.50	**5.34**	**4.46**	**3.97**	**3.65**	**3.43**	**3.26**	**3.13**	**3.02**	**2.93**	**2.51**	**1.88**
33	4.14	3.28	2.89	2.66	2.50	2.39	2.30	2.23	2.18	2.13	1.90	1.58
	7.47	**5.31**	**4.44**	**3.95**	**3.63**	**3.41**	**3.24**	**3.11**	**3.00**	**2.91**	**2.49**	**1.87**
34	4.13	3.28	2.88	2.65	2.49	2.38	2.29	2.23	2.17	2.12	1.89	1.57
	7.44	**5.29**	**4.42**	**3.93**	**3.61**	**3.39**	**3.22**	**3.09**	**2.98**	**2.89**	**2.47**	**1.86**
35	4.12	3.27	2.87	2.64	2.49	2.37	2.29	2.22	2.16	2.11	1.88	1.56
	7.42	**5.27**	**4.40**	**3.91**	**3.59**	**3.37**	**3.20**	**3.07**	**2.96**	**2.88**	**2.45**	**1.85**
36	4.11	3.26	2.87	2.63	2.48	2.36	2.28	2.21	2.15	2.11	1.87	1.55
	7.40	**5.25**	**4.38**	**3.89**	**3.57**	**3.35**	**3.18**	**3.05**	**2.95**	**2.86**	**2.43**	**1.84**
37	4.11	3.25	2.86	2.63	2.47	2.36	2.27	2.20	2.14	2.10	1.86	1.54
	7.37	**5.23**	**4.36**	**3.87**	**3.56**	**3.33**	**3.17**	**3.04**	**2.93**	**2.84**	**2.42**	**1.83**
38	4.10	3.24	2.85	2.62	2.46	2.35	2.26	2.19	2.14	2.09	1.85	1.53
	7.35	**5.21**	**4.34**	**3.86**	**3.54**	**3.32**	**3.15**	**3.02**	**2.92**	**2.83**	**2.40**	**1.82**
39	4.09	3.24	2.85	2.61	2.46	2.34	2.26	2.19	2.13	2.08	1.84	1.52
	7.33	**5.19**	**4.33**	**3.84**	**3.53**	**3.30**	**3.14**	**3.01**	**2.90**	**2.81**	**2.39**	**1.81**
40	4.08	3.23	2.84	2.61	2.45	2.34	2.25	2.18	2.12	2.07	1.84	1.51
	7.31	**5.18**	**4.31**	**3.83**	**3.51**	**3.29**	**3.12**	**2.99**	**2.88**	**2.80**	**2.37**	**1.80**
42	4.07	3.22	2.83	2.59	2.44	2.32	2.24	2.17	2.11	2.06	1.82	1.50
	7.27	**5.15**	**4.29**	**3.80**	**3.49**	**3.26**	**3.10**	**2.96**	**2.86**	**2.77**	**2.35**	**1.78**
44	4.06	3.21	2.82	2.58	2.43	2.31	2.23	2.16	2.10	2.05	1.81	1.49
	7.24	**5.12**	**4.26**	**3.78**	**3.46**	**3.24**	**3.07**	**2.94**	**2.84**	**2.75**	**2.32**	**1.76**
60	4.00	3.15	2.76	2.53	2.37	2.25	2.17	2.10	2.04	1.99	1.75	1.39
	7.08	**4.98**	**4.13**	**3.65**	**3.34**	**3.12**	**2.95**	**2.82**	**2.72**	**2.63**	**2.20**	**1.60**
120	3.92	3.07	2.68	2.45	2.29	2.18	2.09	2.02	1.96	1.91	1.66	1.25
	6.85	**4.79**	**3.95**	**3.48**	**3.17**	**2.96**	**2.79**	**2.66**	**2.56**	**2.47**	**2.03**	**1.38**
∞	3.84	3.00	2.60	2.37	2.21	2.10	2.01	1.94	1.88	1.83	1.57	1.00
	6.63	**4.61**	**3.78**	**3.32**	**3.02**	**2.80**	**2.64**	**2.51**	**2.41**	**2.32**	**1.88**	**1.00**

Appendix E

Pearson *r* Critical Values Table

Critical Values for the Pearson *r* Correlation*

*To be significant, the sample correlation (*r*) must be greater than or equal to the critical value in the table.

	Level of Significance for One-Tailed Test			
	0.05	0.025	0.01	0.005
	Level of Significance for Two-Tailed Test			
$df = n - 2$	0.10	0.05	0.02	0.01
1	0.988	0.997	0.9995	0.99999
2	0.900	0.950	0.980	0.990
3	0.805	0.878	0.934	0.959
4	0.729	0.811	0.882	0.917
5	0.669	0.754	0.833	0.874
6	0.622	0.707	0.789	0.834
7	0.582	0.666	0.750	0.798
8	0.549	0.632	0.716	0.765
9	0.521	0.602	0.685	0.735
10	0.497	0.576	0.658	0.708
11	0.476	0.553	0.634	0.684
12	0.458	0.532	0.612	0.661
13	0.441	0.514	0.592	0.641

(Continued)

(Continued)

	Level of Significance for One-Tailed Test			
	0.05	0.025	0.01	0.005
	Level of Significance for Two-Tailed Test			
$df = n - 2$	0.10	0.05	0.02	0.01
14	0.426	0.497	0.574	0.623
15	0.412	0.482	0.558	0.606
16	0.400	0.468	0.542	0.590
17	0.389	0.456	0.528	0.575
18	0.378	0.444	0.516	0.561
19	0.369	0.433	0.503	0.549
20	0.360	0.423	0.492	0.537
21	0.352	0.413	0.482	0.526
22	0.344	0.404	0.472	0.515
23	0.337	0.396	0.462	0.505
24	0.330	0.388	0.453	0.496
25	0.323	0.381	0.445	0.487
26	0.317	0.374	0.437	0.479
27	0.311	0.367	0.430	0.471
28	0.306	0.361	0.423	0.463
29	0.301	0.355	0.416	0.456
30	0.296	0.349	0.409	0.449
35	0.275	0.325	0.381	0.418
40	0.257	0.304	0.358	0.393
45	0.243	0.288	0.338	0.372
50	0.231	0.273	0.322	0.354
60	0.211	0.250	0.295	0.325
70	0.195	0.232	0.274	0.302
80	0.183	0.217	0.256	0.283
90	0.173	0.205	0.242	0.267
100	0.164	0.195	0.230	0.254

SOURCE: Fisher, R. A. & Yates, F. (1974). *Statistical Tables for Biological, Agricultural and Medical Research* (6th ed., Table VI). London: Longman Group Ltd. (Previously published by Oliver and Boyd Ltd., Edinburgh.) Adapted and reprinted with permission of Addison Wesley Longman.

Appendix F

Chi-Square Critical Values Table

Critical Values of Chi-Square (χ^2)

df	Level of Significance	
	.05	.01
1	3.84	6.64
2	5.99	9.21
3	7.81	11.34
4	9.49	13.28
5	11.07	15.09
6	12.59	16.81
7	14.07	18.48
8	15.51	20.09
9	16.92	21.67
10	18.31	23.21
11	19.68	24.72
12	21.03	26.22
13	22.36	27.69
14	23.68	29.14
15	25.00	30.58
16	26.30	32.00
17	27.59	33.41
18	28.87	34.80

(Continued)

(Continued)

	Level of Significance	
df	*.05*	*.01*
19	30.14	36.19
20	31.41	37.47
21	32.67	38.93
22	33.92	40.29
23	35.17	41.64
24	36.42	42.98
25	37.65	44.31
26	38.88	45.64
27	40.11	46.96
28	41.34	48.28
29	42.56	49.59
30	43.77	50.89
40	55.76	63.69
50	67.50	76.15
60	79.08	88.38
70	90.53	100.42

SOURCE: Fisher, R. A., & Yates, F. (1974). *Statistical Tables for Biological, Agricultural and Medical Research* (6th ed., Table IV). London: Longman Group Ltd. (previously published by Oliver and Boyd Ltd., Edinburgh.) Reprinted with permission of Addison Wesley Longman Ltd.

Glossary

alpha level: the probability level used by researchers to indicate the cutoff probability level (highest value) that allows them to reject the null hypothesis

bar graphs: graphs of data for categorical variables where the bar height represents the size of the value (e.g., mean)

between-groups variance: the average squared difference between the sample means and the overall (grand) mean

between-subjects variable: changing situations across different groups of subjects in a research study

categorical variables: measures with responses as categories that cannot be divided into smaller units

central limit theorem: a mathematical description of the shape of the distribution of sample means that states that for a population with mean μ and standard deviation σ, the distribution of sample means for sample size n will have a mean equal to μ, standard deviation equal to the standard error, and a shape approaching a normal distribution as n becomes very large

central tendency: representation of a typical score in a distribution

chi-square (χ^2) test: a significance test used to determine whether a relationship exists between two variables measured on nominal and ordinal scales

cluster sample: sample chosen randomly from clusters identified in the population

confidence interval: a range of values that the population mean likely falls into with a specific level of certainty

construct validity: the degree to which a measure is an accurate measure of the behavior of interest

continuous variables: measures with number scores that can be divided into smaller units

convenience/purposive sample: a sample chosen such that the probability of an individual being chosen cannot be determined

correlational study: a type of research design that examines the relationships between different measures of behavior

counterbalancing: a control used in within-subjects experiments where equal numbers of participants are randomly assigned to different orders of the conditions

critical region: the most extreme portion of a distribution of statistical values for the null hypothesis determined by the decision criterion (i.e., alpha level—typically 5%)

degrees of freedom: the number of scores that can vary in the calculation of a statistic

dependent variable: the behavior of interest that is observed in a research study

descriptive statistics: statistics that help researchers summarize or describe data

discrete variables: measures with whole number scores that cannot be subdivided into smaller units

distribution: a set of scores

distribution of sample means: the distribution of all possible sample means for all possible samples of a particular size from a population

estimated standard error: an estimate of sampling error that is determined from the standard deviation of the distribution of sample means using the sample standard deviation to represent the population standard deviation

experiment: a type of research design that involves the comparison of behavior observed in different situations

external validity: the degree to which the results of a study apply to individuals and realistic behaviors outside the study

factorial design: an experiment or quasi-experiment that includes more than one independent variable

frequency: how often a response or score occurs within a data set

frequency distribution: a graph or table of a distribution showing the frequency of each score in the distribution

homogeneity of variances: assumption of independent samples t tests and analyses of variance (ANOVAs) that the variance in the scores in the populations is equal across groups

independent variable: a variable in an experiment that changes across or within subjects to allow comparison of behavior in those different situations

inferential statistics: statistics that help researchers test hypotheses

interaction effect: tests the effect of one independent variable at each level of another independent variable in an ANOVA

internal consistency: a form of reliability that tests relationships between scores on different items of a survey

internal validity: the degree to which a research study provides causal information about behavior

interquartile range: the difference between the scores that mark the middle 50 % of a distribution

inter-rater reliability: a measure of the degree to which different observers measure behaviors in similar ways

interval scale: a scale of data measurement that involves numerical responses that are equally spaced, but the scores are not ratios of each other

levels of the independent variable: different situations or conditions that participants experience in an experiment because of the manipulation of the independent variable

line graphs: graphs of data for continuous variables in which each value is graphed as a point and the points are connected to show differences between scores (e.g., means)

main effect: test of the differences between all means for an independent variable

marginal means: the means for each level of an independent variable in a factorial design

matched design: a between-subjects experiment that involves sets of participants matched on a specific characteristic, with each member of the set randomly assigned to a different level of the independent variable

mean: the average score for a set of data

median: the middle score in a distribution, such that half of the scores are above and half are below that value

mode: the most common score in a distribution

negative relationship: a relationship between measures characterized by an increase in one measure that occurs with a decrease in the other measure

nominal scale: a scale of data measurement that involves non-ordered categorical responses

nonparametric test: an inferential statistics test that can be used to test hypotheses about categorical variables

normal distribution: a symmetrical distribution in which the percentage of scores in each portion of the distribution is known

null hypothesis: the hypothesis that an effect or relationship does not exist (or exists in the opposite direction of the alternative hypothesis) in the population

one-tailed hypothesis: only one direction of an effect or relationship is predicted in the alternative hypothesis of the test

operational definition: the way a behavior is defined in a research study to allow for its measurement

ordinal scale: a scale of data measurement that involves ordered categorical responses

outlier: an extreme high or low score in a distribution

_p_ value: probability value associated with an inferential test that indicates the likelihood of obtaining the data in a study when the null hypothesis is true

parametric test: an inferential statistics test that can be used to test hypotheses about continuous variables

Pearson _r_ test: a significance test used to determine whether a linear relationship exists between two variables measured on interval or ratio scales

pie charts: graphs of categorical variables where proportions are represented as a portion of the pie

pooled variance: the combined variance terms for two samples weighted by the sample size of each sample

population: a group of individuals a researcher seeks to learn about from a research study

positive relationship: a relationship between variables characterized by an increase in one variable that occurs with an increase in the other variable

post hoc tests: additional significance tests conducted to determine which means are significantly different for a main effect

power: the ability of a hypothesis test to detect an effect or relationship when one exists (equal to 1 minus the probability of a Type II error)

pretest–posttest design: a type of research design (often a quasi-experiment) in which behavior is measured both before and after a treatment or condition is implemented

probability sample: a sample chosen such that individuals are chosen with a specific probability

quasi-experiment: a type of research design that involves the comparison of behavior observed in different situations, but where subjects are not randomly assigned to the different situations

quota sample: a sample chosen from the population such that available individuals are chosen with equivalent proportions of individuals for a specific characteristic in the population and sample

R^2: fit statistic indicating how well an equation fits the data

range: the difference between the highest and lowest scores in a distribution

ratio scale: a scale of data measurement that involves numerical responses in which scores are ratios of each other

sample: the group of individuals chosen from the population to represent it in a research study

sampling error: the difference between the observations in a population and the observations in the sample representing that population in a study

scatterplot: a graph showing the relationship between two dependent variables for a group of individuals

scientific/alternative hypothesis: the hypothesis that an effect or relationship exists (or exists in a specific direction) in the population

significant test: the *p* value is less than or equal to the alpha level in an inferential test, and the null hypothesis can be rejected

simple random sample: sample chosen randomly from the population such that all individuals have an equal chance of being selected

skewed distribution: a distribution of scores where the shape of the distribution shows a clustering of scores at the low or high end of the scale

social desirability bias: bias created in survey responses from respondents' desire to be viewed more favorably by others

sphericity assumption: the assumption of the repeated measures (within-subjects) ANOVA that pairs of scores in the population have equal variance

standard deviation: a measure representing the average difference between the scores and the mean of a distribution

standard error: the estimate of sampling error that is determined from the standard deviation of the distribution of sample means

stratified random sample: a sample chosen from the population such that the proportion of individuals with a particular characteristic is equivalent in the population and sample

statistically significant: a statistical outcome indicating that the data from the individuals measured show that an effect or relationship exists

sum of products: the sum of the products of the squared deviations from the mean of the scores for each variable

symmetrical distribution: a distribution of scores where the shape of the distribution shows a mirror image on either side of the middle score

test–retest reliability: indicates that the scores on a survey will be similar when participants complete the survey more than once under similar circumstances

two-tailed hypothesis: both directions of an effect or relationship are considered in the alternative hypothesis of the test

Type I error: an error made in a hypothesis test when the researcher rejects the null hypothesis when it is actually true

Type II error: an error made in a hypothesis test when the researcher fails to reject the null hypothesis when it is actually false

Unit Normal Table: a table of the proportion of scores in a normal distribution for many different *z* score values

variables: attributes that can vary across individuals

variability: the spread of scores in a distribution

variance: the squared standard deviation of a distribution

volunteer sample: a sample chosen from the population such that available individuals are chosen based on who volunteers to participate

within-groups variance: the average squared difference between the scores in each group and the group mean

within-subjects variable: changing situations within a single group of subjects in a research study such that each subject experiences all the different situations being compared

z **score:** a standardized score that indicates the location of a score within a population distribution

References

ABC News/Washington Post/Pew Research. (2015). *Poll*. Retrieved December 18, 2015, from http://www.pollingreport.com/enviro.htm

American Psychological Association. (2009). *Publication manual of the American Psychological Association* (6th ed.). Washington, DC: Author.

Bakalar, N. (2015, June 17). To cut teen smoking, raise tobacco sales age. *New York Times*. Retrieved June 19, 2015, from http://well.blogs.nytimes.com/2015/06/17/to-cut-teen-smoking-raise-tobacco-sales-age/?ref=health

Boothby, E. J., Clark, M. S., & Bargh, J. A. (2014). Shared experiences are amplified. *Psychological Science, 25,* 2209–2216.

Brown-Iannuzzi, J. L., Lundberg, K. B., Kay, A. C., & Payne, B. K. (2015). Subjects status shapes political preferences. *Psychological Science, 26,* 15–26.

Bub, D. N., Masson, M. E. J., & Lin, T. (2013). Features of planned hand actions influence identification of graspable objects. *Psychological Science, 24,* 1269–1276.

Centers for Disease Control (CDC). (2015). *Distracted driving in the United States and Europe.* Retrieved June 19, 2015, from http://www.cdc.gov/features/dsdistracteddriving/index.html

Cohen, J. (1988). *Statistical power analysis* (2nd ed.). Hillsdale, NJ: Erlbaum.

Cohen, J. (1990). Things I have learned so far. *American Psychologist, 45*(12), 1304–1312.

Cohen, J. (1994). The earth is round ($p < .05$). *American Psychologist, 49,* 997–1003.

Converse, B. A., Risen, J. L., & Carter, T. J. (2012). Investing in karma: When wanting promotes helping. *Psychological Science, 23,* 923–930.

Drews, F. A., Hazdani, H., Godfrey, C. N., Cooper, J. M., & Strayer, D. L. (2009). Text messaging during simulated driving. *Human Factors, 51*(5), 762–770.

Duffy, K. A., & Chartrand, T. L. (2015). The extravert advantage: How and when extraverts build rapport with other people. *Psychological Science, 26,* 1795–1802.

Educational Testing Service. (2016). *2016–2017 Interpreting your GRE® scores.* Retrieved May 15, 2017, from https://www.ets.org/s/gre/pdr/gre_interpreting_scores.pdf

Francis, G. (2013). Replication, statistical consistency, and publication bias. *Journal of Mathematical Psychology, 57,* 153–169.

Greenwald, A. G. (1975). Consequences of prejudice against the null hypothesis. *Psychological Bulletin, 82,* 1–20.

Haun, D. B. M., Rekers, Y., & Tomasello, M. (2014). Children conform to the behavior of peers; other great apes stick with what they know. *Psychological Science, 25,* 2160–2167.

Howell, D. C. (2013). *Statistical methods for psychology* (8th ed.). Pacific Grove, CA: Wadsworth Publishing.

Inzlicht, M., McKay, L., & Aronson, J. (2006). Stigma as ego depletion: How being the target of prejudice affects self-control. *Psychological Science, 17,* 262–269.

Kane, J. (2012). Top 10 myths of heart health. *PBS Newshour*. Retrieved January 20, 2016, from http://www.pbs.org/newshour/rundown/the-top-10-myths-of-heart-health/

Keppel, G., & Wickens, T. D. (20004). *Design and analyses: A researcher's handbook* (4th ed.). Upper Saddle River, NJ: Pearson Education Inc.

Kolata, G. (2015). A sea change in treating heart attacks. *New York Times*. Retrieved June 19, 2015, from http://www.nytimes.com/2015/06/21/health/saving-heart-attack-victims-stat.html?rr

ef=collection%2Fsectioncollection%2Fscience&_r=0

Laland, K. N., & Galef, B. G. (2009). *The question of animal culture.* Cambridge, MA: Harvard University Press.

Lee, K., Talwar, V., McCarthy, A., Ross, I., Evans, A., & Arruda, C. (2014). Can classic moral stories promote honesty in children? *Psychological Science, 25,* 1630–1636.

Loftus, G. R. (1993). A picture is worth a thousand *p* values: On the irrelevance of hypothesis testing in the microcomputer age. *Behavior Research Methods, Instruments, & Computers, 25,* 250–256.

Macchi Cassia, V., Turati, C., & Simion, F. (2004). Can a nonspecific bias toward top-heavy patterns explain newborns' face preference? *Psychological Science, 15,* 379–383.

Mehr, S. A., Song, L. A., & Spelke, E. S. (2016). For 5-month-old infants, melodies are social. *Psychological Science, 27,* 486–501.

Metcalfe, J., Casal-Roscum, L., Radin, A., & Friedman, D. (2015). On teaching old dogs new tricks. *Psychological Science, 26,* 1833–1842.

Mueller, P. A., & Oppenheimer, D. M. (2014). The pen is mightier than the keyboard: Advantages of longhand over laptop notetaking. *Psychological Science, 25,* 1159–1168.

Nairne, J. S., VanArsdall, J. E., Pandeirada, J. N. S., Cogdill, M., & LeBreton, J. M. (2013). Adaptive memory: The mnemonic value of animacy. *Psychological Science, 24,* 2099–2105.

Oaklander, M. (2015). Here's what happens when you drink wine every night. *Time.* Retrieved January 20, 2016, from http://time.com/4070762/red-wine-resveratrol-diabetes/

Ogden, C. L., Fryar, C. D., Carroll, M. D., & Flegal, K. M. (2004). Mean body weight, height, and body mass index, United States 1960–2002. *Centers for Disease Control, 347,* 1–18.

Paivio, A. (2007). *Mind and its evolution: A dual coding theoretical approach.* Mahwah, NJ: Erlbaum.

Propper, R. E., Srickgold, R., Keeley, R., & Christman, S. D. (2007). Is television traumatic? Dreams, stress, and media exposure in the aftermath of September 11, 2001. *Psychological Science, 18,* 334–340.

Roediger, H. L., III, & Karpicke, J. D. (2006). Test-enhanced learning: Taking memory tests improves long-term retention. *Psychological Science, 17,* 249–255.

Sanders, M. A., Shirk, S. D., Burgin, C. J., & Martin, L. L. (2012). The gargle effect: Rinsing the mouth with glucose enhances self-control. *Psychological Science, 23,* 1470–1472.

Stephens, N. M., Townsend, S. S. M., Hamedani, M. G., Destin, M., & Manzo, V. (2015). A difference-education intervention equips first-generation college students to thrive in the face of stressful college situations. *Psychological Science, 26,* 1556–1566.

Van Allen J., Kuhl, E. S., Filigno, S. S., Clifford, L. M., Connor, J. M., & Stark, L. J. (2014). Changes in parent motivation predicts changes in body mass index z-score (zBMI) and dietary intake among preschools enrolled in a family-based obesity intervention. *Journal of Pediatric Psychology, 39,* 1028–1037.

von Hippel, W., Ronay, R., Baker, E., Kjelsaas, K., & Murphy, S. C. (2016). Quick thinkers are smooth talkers: Mental speed facilitates charisma. *Psychological Science, 27,* 119–122.

Wagman, J. B., Zimmerman, C., & Sorric, C. (2007). "Which feels heavier—a pound of lead or a pound of feathers?" A potential perceptual basis of a cognitive riddle. *Perception, 36,* 1709–1711.

Worthy, D. A., Gorlick, M. A., Pacheco, J. L., Schnyer, D. M., & Maddox, W. T. (2011). With age comes wisdom: Decision making in younger and older adults. *Psychological Science, 22,* 1375–1380.

Index

Note: In page references, f indicates figures and t indicates tables.